POST-WAR PROTECTION OF HUMAN RIGHTS
IN BOSNIA AND HERZEGOVINA

International Studies in Human Rights

VOLUME 53

The titles published in this series are listed at the end of this volume.

Post-War Protection Of Human Rights In Bosnia And Herzegovina

edited by

MICHAEL O'FLAHERTY

and

GREGORY GISVOLD

MARTINUS NIJHOFF PUBLISHERS
THE HAGUE / LONDON / BOSTON

A C.I.P Catalogue record for this book is available from the Library of Congress.

 ISBN 90-411-1020-8 1001419342

Published by Kluwer Law International,
P.O. Box 85889, 2508 CN The Hague, The Netherlands

Sold and distributed in North, Central and South America
by Kluwer Law International,
675 Massachusetts Avenue, Cambridge, MA 02139, USA

In all other countries, sold and distributed
by Kluwer Law International, Distribution Centre
P.O. Box 322, 3300 AH Dordrecht, The Netherlands

Printed on acid-free paper

Printed and bound in Great Britain by Arrowhead Books, Reading.

Table of Contents

Foreword

The Peace Agreement for Bosnia and Herzegovina, negotiated in Dayton and signed in Paris December 14 1995, is without doubt the most ambitious agreement of its sort in modern history, and perhaps in all of history. It sets out not only to end a war, but also to build a state out of the ruins of a conflict of extraordinary barbarity and brutality.

From the moment I began my work as High Representative for the implementation of the General Framework Agreement for Peace in Bosnia and Herzegovina, I recognised the central role that protection of human rights needed to play in our efforts. The embodiment of that belief was the Human Rights Coordination Centre established within my office in the early days of peace implementation.

The Human Rights Coordination Centre brings together representatives of all the major international peace-building partners to address human rights violations and to support building of enduring mechanisms for the promotion and protection of human rights in Bosnia and Herzegovina.

The Human Rights Coordination Centre is designed to help ensure effective implementation of the human rights provisions of the General Framework Agreement and to provide support and guidance in this regard to the parties to the agreement and to the many international organizations active in Bosnia and Herzegovina. This is no easy task, given the multiple references to human rights and the great complexity of a number of provisions. Recognition of the scale of the task prompted the editors to compile the present volume.

I applaud their endeavor and I offer my appreciation for their work, which was begun while they both were working within the Coordination Centre. Their efforts and those of the contributing authors will provide great assistance to all those concerned with building a durable and stable peace in Bosnia and Herzegovina.

That this volume concerns one of the most important and innovative peace agreements in recent history gives it significance well beyond the confines of Bosnia and Herzegovina. Never before have human rights been accorded so substantial and central a role. Never before have substantive human rights guarantees been supported by so elaborate a framework for their implementation.

Our history was by no means a history only of successes. Indeed, as a consequence of the ambitious nature of the agreement, the effort to turn it into reality was bound to be a long-term one, marked by successes as well as failures as events unfolded in the complex process of political change that was the essence of the implementation of the peace agreement.

Policy makers and peace-builders everywhere should closely study and monitor the peace agreement and its implementation in order to build on our achievements and learn from our mistakes. The papers which have been assembled here will greatly assist in this regard. It is my hope also that they will stimulate lively debate and critical reflection and, in so doing, will contribute to implementation of the human rights provisions of the Peace Agreement.

CARL BILDT

Introduction

The General Framework Agreement for Peace in Bosnia and Herzegovina[1], also known as the Dayton Agreement, is replete with unprecedented and highly elaborate provisions. Prominent among these are the arrangements for promotion and protection of human rights, which, together with human rights provisions in the 1994 Constitution of the Federation of Bosnia and Herzegovina, comprise one of the most complex regimes for the protection of human rights by law ever devised. This systemic complexity carries with it both the promise of potentially powerful tools for protection of human rights and liabilities in the form of considerable interpretive uncertainty and confusion. The Constitution of Bosnia and Herzegovina (contained in Annex 4 of the GFA) and the Constitution of the Federation of Bosnia and Herzegovina[2] each contain significant substantive human rights components. Both Entities – the Federation of Bosnia and Herzegovina and the Republika Srpska – are also bound by a range of human rights commitments by virtue of terms of the GFA and various Annexes other than Annex 4, notably Annexes 6 and 7.

The GFA and the various Constitutions incorporate into their respective domestic law a range of international human rights instruments. Many of these instruments had already been acceded to by Bosnia and Herzegovina and thus were, by virtue of the applicable domestic system, part of the legal order within the State. However, one instrument, the European Convention on Human Rights, to which Bosnia and Herzegovina is not a party is accorded a special status in domestic law. This status was accomplished in such a manner as to create uncertainty regarding its relationship to other international instruments. In addition, other international instruments, such as the UN General Assembly Declarations, which were never intended to

---

[1] General Framework Agreement for Peace in Bosnia and Herzegovina, *initialed* Dayton, Ohio, 21 November 1995, *signed* Paris, 14 December 1995, 35 ILM 75 (1996) [hereinafter "GFA"].

[2] Constitution of the Federation of Bosnia and Herzegovina, *signed* Vienna, 18 March 1994, 33 ILM 740 (1994) [hereinafter "Federation Constitution"].

impose legal obligations, are given binding effect in the Constitution of the Federation of Bosnia and Herzegovina. This complex interrelationship of substantive human rights laws was further complicated by the establishment and involvement of the International Criminal Tribunal for the Former Yugoslavia.

In addition to the interaction of differing, sometimes overlapping, and occasionally unusual substantive guarantees, the various domestic and international instruments establish or give jurisdiction to an array of monitoring and implementation procedures. The relationship between and amongst these procedures is not always obvious. At the domestic level, the relationship between the new Constitutional structures, the Federation Ombudsmen, the Human Rights Commission, and the Real Property Commission, remains to be clarified. The relative roles of these and all levels of the judiciary is also unclear. Confusion and misinterpretation regarding the exact interaction required between the International Criminal Tribunal and the national courts continue to confound the work of and relationships between these bodies. Also, uncertainty exists as to the mutual relationships of judiciary of each of the Entities and between them and the judicial machinery established under the Constitution of Bosnia and Herzegovina. Moreover, six international human rights treaty bodies have jurisdiction by reason of Bosnia and Herzegovina's accession to the respective instruments. The treaty bodies had been invited to participate in implementation of peace by virtue of innovative provisions of the GFA. The role to be played by treaty bodies under instruments listed in the GFA, but not ratified by Bosnia and Herzegovina, is unclear.

Side by side with the more formal or legal mechanisms stand an array of organizations in possession of international human rights monitoring and implementation mechanisms/mandates. These include the High Representative, the Organization for Security and Cooperation in Europe, the United Nations civilian police (International Police Task Force – IPTF), SFOR (formerly IFOR) and the United Nations Commission on Human Rights Special Rapporteur. Novel models have been elaborated and implemented in efforts to coordinate the efforts of these bodies, *inter-se*, and with the many other relevant organisations active in the region.

The papers in the present volume are intended as contributions to the process of interpreting and assessing both substantive and practical aspects of the human rights protection regime at work in Bosnia and Herzegovina. In so doing, it is hoped that they will be of use both to those hoping to negotiate the legal and quasi-legal maze, to the policy makers and others involved with implementation and reform of the system, as well as to scholars and researchers. The evaluation undertaken in various papers also contributes to determination of the extent of paradigmatic significance of the peace settlement in Bosnia and Herzegovina with regard to other complex emergency situations.

For the volume to play a useful role, it was essential that it be available during the period of development and initial implementation of the new human rights regime. Accordingly, contributors were asked to submit manuscripts within a very short period of time and every effort was made to accelerate the publication process. The price was incompleteness: tight timelines meant that some invited contributors were unable to submit manuscripts. It was not possible in some instances to find appropriate and available authors to comment on other topics. The editors, nevertheless, are of the view that the volume comprises a useful collection of papers which contribute substantially to an understanding of the range of issues, offer programmatic guidance, and lay the foundations for further reflection and debate.

Both the Foreword by the former High Representative, Carl Bildt, and the Afterword by the Ombudsperson for Bosnia and Herzegovina, Gret Haller, draw attention to the enormity of the human rights challenges confronted by the peace-builders of Bosnia and Herzegovina. In this context Bildt observes that one of his central tasks was that of promoting non-discriminatory and consistent respect for human rights obligations undertaken by the parties. Haller views the Bosnian situation from a more expansive perspective, reflecting on the manner in which any political system or entity based on notions of the nation-State can obstruct promotion and protection of human rights. An extension of her reasoning would suggest that we should be neither surprised by the deficiencies of the human rights regime in Bosnia and Herzegovina nor overly optimistic regarding possibilities for its reform.

Many of the grave problems for the human rights protection system which arise from the political context of the peace agreements are identified in the papers of Zoran Pajic and Nedo Milicevic. Both authors draw attention to the fundamental inconsistency between a Bosnia and Herzegovina re-ordered essentially on ethnic lines and the primacy of individual rights. Pajic observes, however, that the very imprecision of the GFA can be exploited for the promotion of human rights and that, " the new human rights protection system should be interpreted as an over-arching structure which could bridge and transcend the constitutional settlement by enforcing the principle of universality and non-discrimination". Milicevic is less confident regarding the capacity of the system to support the promotion of human rights. He also precisely identifies myriad problems of interpretation and procedure with regard to the functioning of national and Entity-based judicial, quasi-judicial and related institutions. Milicevic's list can usefully serve as the core content of a programme of clarification and reform which requires to be urgently put in place by those responsible for implementation of the system. It is obvious that this process will require the intimate and ongoing attention of the international community and especially of the High Representative.

One of the potentially great strengths of the GFA is the fact of and manner by which the European Convention on Human Rights is accorded a primary role in the new legal regime. The paper of Nico Mol explores the special status of the Convention and its substantive and procedural impact at all levels of the judicial system: described by him as, "a truly unique situation". Mol also explores the Convention's place in the activities of Bosnia and Herzegovina's national and Entity level mechanisms for the protection of human rights – in the court system, in the Entities and nationally, in the Federation Human Rights Court, the Human Rights Commission and elsewhere. A valuable feature of Mol's paper is its analysis of that jurisprudence and practice arising under the Convention which is most applicable to circumstances in Bosnia and Herzegovina.

The status and role in Bosnia and Herzegovina of the those international human rights instruments which originated in the "UN family", and particularly of their respective monitoring bodies is explored by Michael O'Flaherty. He surveys their involvement with the region over time, focusing on their activities during the period of the war in Bosnia and Herzegovina. O'Flaherty argues that while they had only a most limited role during periods of conflict that they can play a useful part in the current period of civil-society building. The paper concludes with the observation that, unlike other international initiatives, the treaty bodies will continue indefinitely to monitor the situation in Bosnia and Herzegovina and that action should be taken now so that they can do so in an efficient and effective manner.

In the shorter term, an array of *ad hoc* international initiatives will continue to play a central role in addressing issues of human rights. O'Flaherty undertakes a survey of these situating them with regard to each other and the judicial and quasi-judicial procedures. The paper makes clear the extent to which Bosnia and Herzegovina constitutes a testing ground for innovative models for the deployment of human rights support operations in post-conflict situations. One such is the Human Rights Coordination Centre, established by the High Representative, which offers a useful way to promote collaboration between the various organisations. The work of the various organisations and of the coordination structures is subjected by O'Flaherty to a close scrutiny which both acknowledges successes and identifies significant weaknesses, particularly with regard to the promotion and development of long-term sustainable human rights institutions within the country.

Among the most essential of the *ad hoc* international responses to the Bosnian situation and its aftermath have been those efforts regarding the tracing of missing persons, of whom there were some 20,000 at the end of 1996. Manfred Nowak, who from 1994 to 1997 was the UN Expert on the issue, identifies and situates the various initiatives. He concludes that a lack of the necessary political will has resulted in little being achieved. Another significant international initiative, the office of UN Special Rapporteur on the situation of human rights in former Yugoslavia, is not examined in the present volume. This omission, due in part to the inability of the invited contributor to submit a paper, is regrettable. It is to be hoped that other subsequent publications will do justice to the significant actions and achievements of the first Special Rapporteur, Tadeusz Mazowiecki, and his successor, Elisabeth Rehn.

A fundamental test for the new human rights protection regime will be its capacity to address the plight of refugees and internally displaced persons. Maria Stavropoulou undertakes an original assessment of the relevant provisions of international human rights and humanitarian law and explores the extent to which they are reflected or developed in the GFA. She notes that the GFA has addressed some of the "gray areas" of international law and she identifies the parameters of a right to return for Bosnia and Herzegovina's refugees and internally displaced persons. One of the most crucial issues relating to enjoyment and effective implementation of the right to return is respect for property rights. Elena Popovic's paper explores the content of the right, the primary obstacles to its enjoyment in each of the Entities and the manner in which it is addressed by GFA. She observes that the range of discriminatory war-time regulations on confiscation or re-allocation of housing, to the extent that they remain unrepealed, "represent a final act of ethnic cleansing".

It could be argued that the international community has devoted excessive attention to the issue of protecting property rights and that, in its strategies for return of displaced persons, it should have primarily, or at least equally, addressed issues of the right to shelter. The proper place and status of this and other economic, social and cultural rights is explored in the paper of Susanne Malmstrom. She draws attention to the importance of ensuring respect for these rights in the context of the establishment of a lasting peace. Malmstrom notes that the obligations undertaken by Bosnia and Herzegovina both require it to develop and implement systematic plans for social development and have a profound impact upon the content of such plans. In the present context of reconstruction and massive international intervention, the obligations and their programmatic implications require to be kept in mind as much by the donor community as by the various levels of Government in Bosnia and Herzegovina.

Programmatic response to the human rights needs of the people of Bosnia and Herzegovina, whether, economic, social, cultural, civil or political, requires that priority attention be paid to vulnerable groups. The success of the dramatic transformation underway in Bosnia and Herzegovina will in part be measured one day by the degree to which the rights of vulnerable groups are protected. The sufficiency of the GFA's structures to protect such groups is reviewed by Christine Chinkin, who explores in her paper the manner in which the rights of one such vulnerable group that suffered greatly during wartime, women, can be respected, protected and fulfilled.

Lasting peace in Bosnia and Herzegovina will only be achieved in the context of reconciliation based on justice. This is the context in which to situate the activities and ambitions of the International Criminal Tribunal. The paper of Drazen Petrovic comprises a critical review of the activities of the tribunal and of the manner in which issues of politics have been allowed to interfere with its work. He argues that, for the sake of former Yugoslavia and the entire evolving system of international accountability, the tribunal is an experiment which must not be allowed fail.

It can not, of course, be expected that a tribunal, even operating in an optimum fashion, can alone bring about reconciliation. Here, the paper of Gregory Gisvold takes up one of the more ambitious concepts contained in the GFA: that of a Commission of Inquiry, which is suggested in the side letters accompanying the GFA. It has been suggested that the Bosnian conflict will not be laid to rest without some manner of national reconciliation, that the examination and assessment of accountability though on a smaller and broader scale than envisioned in the work of the Tribunal will be necessary to prevent a re-initiation of the war. Gisvold suggests not a commission of inquiry, but a truth commission and examines arguments for and against such a body, as well as lessons which might be drawn from the experience of and scholarship on other nations' similar efforts to resolve lingering post-conflict issues.

Many people have participated in the assembling of this volume. The editors must, in the first place, thank the authors for so readily agreeing to contribute papers and for complying with tight deadlines. We regret both the haste and omissions necessary to bring this volume, in its present form, to fruition. Gratitude is also owed to the High Representative and his Office, without the support of which the project could not have been initiated. The Council of Europe graciously contributed to the editorial costs. The editors were aided in their editorial tasks by our indexer, Ms. Kari Bero, whose gracious response to the ever-shifting deadlines of this effort and professional guidance through the necessary but confusing nature of indexing alleviated many a worry. Further thanks go to our cite checker, Ms. Betsey Buckheit, who quickly and without complaint worked to assist our effort to standarize the authors' citations. On a personal note, the editors offer their heartfelt thanks to those in our respective lives who put up with us during a year of deadlines, trips, late nights, curtailed holidays required to produce this volume: our families, our loved ones, Jan and Paula, and our many friends and colleagues too numerous to mention (besides, you know who you are).

M.O'F and G.D.G.
September 1997

ZORAN PAJIC

1. An Overview of the Substantive Human Rights Regime after Dayton: A Critical Appraisal of the Constitution of Bosnia and Herzegovina

The General Framework Agreement for Peace in Bosnia and Herzegovina, which was initialled in Dayton on November 21 1995, and signed in Paris on December 14 of the same year[1], provided a comprehensive initial framework for ending the war, and indeed has already secured a peace in the country which has lasted more than a year. However, there are still very serious obstacles to a durable constitutional settlement and the establishment of the rule of law, both of which are crucial for the implementation of human rights provisions stipulated for in the Constitution of Bosnia and Herzegovina and in the Agreement on Human Rights, contained in Annexes 4 and 6 of the GFA respectively[2].

Before turning to assess those obstacles, the present author has specific concerns related to the foundations of the GFA and the current peace. High political prices have been paid for the brand of peace achieved in Dayton and two far-reaching precedents have been set. First, the GFA sends the wrong message to warlords worldwide by implicitly legitimising the gains of sectarian violence, which often amounted to commission of war crimes and crimes against humanity[3]. Second, it marginalizes the United Nations

---

[1] This agreement is usually referred to as "The Dayton Agreement" because it was entirely drafted in the course of negotiations held in the "Wright Patterson" Air Force Base in Dayton, Ohio, for 3 weeks in November 1995. General Framework Agreement for Peace in Bosnia and Herzegovina, *initialed* Dayton, Ohio, 21 November 1995, *signed* Paris, 14 December 1995, 35 ILM 75 (1996) [hereinafter "GFA" or "Dayton Agreement"].

[2] GFA, *supra*, contains the following annexes: 1-A) Military Aspects; 1-B) Regional Stabilization; 2) Inter-Entity Boundary; 3) Elections; 4) Constitution; 5) Arbitration; 6) Human Rights; 7) Refugees and Displaced Persons; 8) Commissions to Preserve National Monuments; 9) BiH Public Corporations; 10) Civilian Implementation; 11) International Police Task Force.

[3] This assertion could be elaborated at length, but two arguments seem relevant for this paper: a) inter-Entity boundaries follow, by and large, the frontline established during the war; b) the current "ethnic map" of Bosnia and Herzegovina accurately illustrates the policy of enforced expulsion and displacement of people, carried out on ethnic criteria.

M. O'Flaherty and G. Gisvold (eds.), Post-War Protection of Human Rights in Bosnia and Herzegovina, 1–12.
© 1998 *Kluwer Law International. Printed in Great Britain.*

in favour of NATO as the central mechanism for international conflict resolution[4].

At the same time, the GFA has implicitly put Bosnia and Herzegovina under the "protectorate" of the international community[5]. The present author is aware that this label is rather controversial, but it sounds more acceptable than "trusteeship"[6]. Leaving aside political sensitivities regarding the definition of the GFA's institutional structure in BiH, it is important to illustrate this argument about the protectorate. First and foremost, the Office of the High Representative (OHR) acts as the steering power on behalf of the international community and is based in Sarajevo. The OHR is instructed "to facilitate the Parties' own efforts and to mobilize and, as appropriate, coordinate the activities of the organizations and agencies involved in the civilian aspects of the peace settlement"[7]. The Constitutional Court of Bosnia and Herzegovina is composed of nine members, three of whom are foreign nationals appointed by the President of the European Court of Human Rights[8]. A non-BiH national appointed by the International Monetary Fund will be the Governor of the Central Bank[9]. The Human Rights Ombudsperson was appointed by the Organization for Security and Cooperation in Europe (OSCE). The Human Rights Chamber will have a majority of foreign members (8 out of 14) appointed by the Council of Europe[10]. Finally, the international military forces deployed in BiH is without precedent as far as manpower, heavy armour and mandate are concerned[11].

---

[4] *See* Security Council Resolution 1031 (15 December 1995), ("On implementation of the Peace Agreement for Bosnia and Herzegovina and Transfer of Authority from the UN Protection Force (UNPROFOR) to the Multinational Implementation Force (IFOR)"), ¶¶ 14 and 33; Security Council Resolution 1088 (12 December 1996), ("On Establishing ... a Multinational Stabilization Force (SFOR) as the Legal Successor to IFOR"), ¶ 18. On the IFOR mandate and on the role of NATO in the implementation of the Dayton Agreement, see GFA, *supra*, Annex 1-A, Art. I.

[5] Bosnia and Herzegovina [hereinafter "BiH"] is one of the states formerly a part of the Socialist Federal Republic of Yugoslavia (SFRY), which existed until 1992. Post-1992, other former constituents of the SFRY, Serbia and Montenegro now comprise the state known as the Federal Republic of Yugoslavia [hereinafter "FRY" or "Serbia"].

[6] However, it appears that the basic objectives of the trusteeship system, as they were formulated in the Charter of the United Nations in 1945, are not quite inappropriate for the situation in BiH after signing the Dayton Agreement. Article 76 of the U.N. Charter explains them as: furthering international peace and security; promoting the political, economic, social and educational advancement of the inhabitants ... ; encouraging respect for human rights and for fundamental freedoms for all without discrimination; facilitating the wishes of the peoples to be freely expressed; etc.

[7] On responsibilities of the High Representative , see GFA, *supra*, Annex 10.

[8] GFA, *supra*, Annex 4, (Constitution of Bosnia and Herzegovina), Art. IV, ¶ 1a. [hereinafter Constitution].

[9] *Id.*, Article VII, ¶. 2.

[10] GFA, *supra*, Annex 6, Articles IV and VII.

[11] *See*, "The Blue Helmets – A Review of United Nations Peace-keeping" (3rd ed. 1996, United Nations).

In this light, the respective implementation roles of the United Nations, OSCE, Council of Europe and other international organizations both in coordination with NATO and alone are much larger and more responsible than the politicians had presented to the general public. This kind of role was never fully acknowledged; "nation building", democratic elections, and the rule of law were expected to occur, by some miracle, within months in a country where the blood on the ground is still very fresh, where half of the population does not reside where it did in 1991[12], where hate is burning, and where an eventual new political thinking is overwhelmed by territorial-ethnic entrenchment. BiH is also a place where mercenaries, warlords, indicted war criminals and war profiteers are at large, active, and influential. Unless the civilian components of the GFA are fully implemented and greater arms reductions are carried out, the mere presence of SFOR will not be enough to prevent the parties from simply biding their time before resuming their fighting, rested, regrouped and rearmed.

It is not surprising that within such a gloomy picture, the Constitution of Bosnia and Herzegovina shines like the Phoenix "rising from the ashes", with its somehow "detached" provisions rather disconnected from reality but so much more challenging and inspired by the vision of reconciliation in an integrated BiH. The present author wishes to emphasize the utmost importance of the political environment for an efficient implementation of the GFA. In the five or six years since the process of transition started in Eastern and Central Europe, there has been a counter-productive tendency to separate human rights from the political, historical and, last but not least, psychological legacy of the recent history in those countries. Very often, unfounded optimism erupted after the first legislative changes were introduced, new constitutions adopted, multi-party elections held in countries where, as recently as the previous day, one (communist) party exercised all prerogatives of political and economic power for decades. One should not forget that the human rights ideal is not an "ivory tower" able to exist and glitter regardless of the immediate social surroundings and the existing political culture. Taken out of the current social context and general political settlement, the human rights provisions and institutional mechanisms contained in the GFA could face serious risks laying ahead. It is a long way and a very slow process to create a minimum human rights culture which is supportive of protection of individuals without discrimination.

This analysis should begin with brief comment on the Preamble to the Constitution. There is a strong emphasis here on some basic moral values, such as "human dignity, liberty, and equality", followed by a specific dedication to "peace, justice, tolerance and reconciliation". It is noticeable

---

[12] For the facts on refugees and displaced persons, see "UNHCR Information Notes", No. 6/7, June-July 1996, p. 4, and No. 8/9, August-September 1996, pp. 10-11. (UNHCR Office of the Special Envoy, Sarajevo).

that there is no reference to "general principles of international law" in the Preamble, although the purposes and principles of the Charter of the United Nations are reaffirmed[13]. However, the sovereignty, territorial integrity, and political independence of BiH is said to be in "accordance with international law". This language was probably included in order to dismiss any doubts about Bosnian statehood, which had been occasionally disputed in the last years. It is regrettable, though, that explicit reference to the "general principles" is missing from the Preamble, given the tendency and necessity to open domestic legal orders to international law, in principle[14]. This may be attributable to the strong American influence in drafting the GFA in that the outcome departs significantly from the constitutional tradition of the former Socialist Federal Republic of Yugoslavia, where primacy of "generally accepted rules of international law" and the principle of *pacta sunt servanda* stood prominently in previous constitutions[15].

At the same time, the Preamble reflects the recent tragic history of Bosnia and Herzegovina by emphasising the determination "to ensure full respect for international humanitarian law". This is followed by the reference to the Universal Declaration of Human Rights, the International Covenants on Civil and Political Rights, and on Economic, Social and Cultural Rights, and the Declaration on the Rights of Persons Belonging to National or Ethnic, Religious and Linguistic Minorities, "as well as other human rights instruments". Finally, the last paragraph of the Preamble illustrates certain structural confusion about the definition of the State and accepts a clumsy compromise between the requirement to guarantee "a pluralistic society" on one hand, and to protect the existing concept of a *de facto* "ethnic state" (or a few of them) within Bosnia and Herzegovina on the other. It says that "Bosniacs, Croats, and Serbs, as constituent peoples (along with Others), and citizens of Bosnia and Herzegovina hereby determine that the Constitution of Bosnia and Herzegovina is as follows".

Article II of the Constitution is entirely devoted to human rights. It has a special title, "Human Rights and Fundamental Freedoms", and is reminiscent of analogous declarations that could be found in some constitutions. Its paragraphs are a mixture of substantial rights and procedural rules, with explicit emphasis on the obligation of BiH, and all courts, agencies, governmental organs, and instrumentalities operated by or within the Entities to "apply and conform to the human rights and fundamental freedoms",

---

[13] GFA, *supra*, Annex 4, Preamble.

[14] *See*, E. Stein: "International Law in Internal Law: Toward Internationalization of Central-Eastern European Constitutions?", 88 AJIL 427 (1994); V.S. Vereshchetin: "New Constitutions and the Old Problem of Relationship between International Law and National Law", 7 EJIL 29 (1996).

[15] *See, e.g.*, The Constitution of the Socialist Federal Republic of Yugoslavia, of 1974. "SFRY shall strive ... for respect for generally accepted rules of international law" – Preamble, ¶ VII. "International treaties which have been promulgated shall be directly applied by the courts of law", *Id.*, Article 210.

which are understood to be those from the European Convention of Human Rights and its Protocols. This provision invites a debate on its effects regarding the eventual incorporation of the ECHR in a national legal system.

Paragraph 2 states explicitly that "[t]he rights and freedoms set forth in the European Convention for the Protection of Human Rights and Fundamental Freedoms and its Protocols shall apply directly in Bosnia and Herzegovina. These shall have priority over all other law". This is followed by a list of rights and freedoms picked from the ECHR. It is not quite clear if the same legal weight was accorded in the Constitution to the international human rights agreements referred to in the Paragraph 7 of this Article, and then listed in Annex I to the Constitution[16]. This paragraph refers mainly to the international human rights instruments adopted in the United Nations. Most of them had been well established in the legislative tradition of Bosnia and Herzegovina when it was part of the Socialist Federal Republic of Yugoslavia or have been accepted and incorporated in its law since independence was proclaimed in 1992. Paragraph 7 merely provides that BiH shall "remain or become party" to those international agreements, leaving the impression that this important positive legacy is ignored.

It can be argued that the European Convention has been "smuggled" into the legal order of BiH, which is not yet a member of the Council of Europe. It may be assumed that the GFA anticipates that BiH will satisfy the Council of Europe statutory principles, namely, respect for human rights and the rule of law. Nevertheless, Paragraph 2, of Article II, should be understood solely as the legal ground for appointing, by the Committee of Ministers of the Council of Europe, "specially qualified persons to sit on a court or other body responsible for the control of respect for human rights set up by this state within its internal legal system", as provided for in the Resolution (93)6 adopted by the Council of Europe Committee of Ministers on 9 March 1993. This has been fully implemented by establishing the Human Rights Commission for BiH in which non-BiH-national members constitute a majority. The place given to the ECHR in the jurisdiction of BiH is undoubtedly valuable for the human rights situation in that country, and, if properly used, could have far reaching results. But this value should be taken *cum grano salis*, for if the mechanism happens to

---

[16] Constitution, *supra*, Annex I (entitled "Additional Human Rights Agreements To Be Applied in Bosnia and Herzegovina", lists the following documents: 1948 Genocide Convention; 1949 Geneva Conventions and 1977 Protocols; 1951 Refugee Convention; 1957 Convention on the Nationality of Married Women; 1961 Convention on the Reduction of Statelessness; 1965 Racial Discrimination Convention; 1966 International Covenants on Human Rights and Optional Protocols; 1979 Convention on Discrimination Against Women; 1984 Torture Convention; 1987 European Torture Convention; 1989 Convention on the Rights of the Child; 1990 Convention on the Protection of Migrant Workers; 1992 European Charter for Regional and Minority Languages; and 1994 Framework Convention for the Protection of National Minorities).

fail, it may undermine the credibility of the ECHR protection system itself. The risk of lowering the established European standards of human rights · by trying to adapt them in haste to the "Bosnian case" is too great. This risk becomes apparent in particular when it is taken into account that during the war the judicial system in BiH and its entire state-structure had been devastated and are now back to *status nascendi*. The first serious surrender was made in this respect by European institutions when conditions previously proclaimed as necessary for the September 1996 elections in BiH ("fair, free and democratic elections") were largely disregarded for the sake of verification at any cost of the elections as this was seen as politically opportune at the time.

An elaborate non-discrimination clause can be found in Paragraph 4 of Article II, in which all internationally recognized grounds for discrimination were listed[17]. However familiar and appropriate this provision may sound, it will be shown later that the entire political structure of the country is based on quite the opposite principle – the principle of exclusive ethnic representation of the three "constituent peoples" only, at the expense of individual rights.

Paragraph 5 proclaims that "all refugees and displaced persons have the right freely to return to their homes of origin"[18]. Paragraph 5 and Annex 7 should be interpreted in the light of the general "freedom of movement throughout Bosnia and Herzegovina" guaranteed by the Constitution. The point is that there are at least three "constitutional rights" which are interconnected in this area. The "right to return" would be meaningless before "freedom of movement" was established because the refugees from BiH now residing in foreign countries are discouraged to return by the fact that even those who are already in BiH cannot move freely and safely throughout the country. Finally, the third right, the right of people "to remain" where they are (the so-called "freedom from harassment and expulsion") is not any less important in this respect. The call for return of refugees is at risk of becoming an empty "sound bite" unless the other two issues are dealt with effectively. After all, the Constitution cannot be more clear on this:

---

[17] "The enjoyment of the rights and freedoms provided for in this Article or in the international agreements listed in Annex I to this Constitution shall be secured to all persons in Bosnia and Herzegovina without discrimination on any ground such as sex, race, colour, language, religion, political or other opinion, national or social origin, association with a national minority, property, birth or other status".

[18] This may remain "wishful thinking" for the many years to come, but such provision is crucial for upholding two basic political goals of the peace settlement: reconciliation of the peoples in the region, and the reversal of ethnic cleansing. This issue is elaborated in detail in the "Agreement on Refugees and Displaced Persons", see GFA, *supra*, Annex 7.

"[t]here shall be freedom of movement throughout Bosnia and Herzegovina. Bosnia and Herzegovina and the Entities shall not impede full freedom of movement of persons, goods, services and capital throughout Bosnia and Herzegovina. Neither Entity shall establish controls at the boundary between Entities"[19].

Finally, Article II of the Constitution ends with a paragraph which represents a novelty in constitutional dealings with human rights. It compels "all competent authorities" in BiH to "cooperate with and provide unrestricted access to, *inter alia*, any international human rights monitoring mechanisms established for Bosnia and Herzegovina; the supervisory bodies established by any of the international agreements listed in Annex I to this Constitution; the International Tribunal for the Former Yugoslavia (and, in particular, to comply with orders issued pursuant to Article 29 of the Statute of the Tribunal); and any other organization authorized by the United Nations Security Council with a mandate concerning human rights or humanitarian law." This provision has enormous potential, provided it is used with commitment and credibility by the international community. Without this provision, the human rights section of the Constitution could be criticised as a mere catalogue of internationally recognised human rights and fundamental freedoms. Given the fact, already highlighted, that the GFA contains a number of elements reminiscent of the establishment of an international protectorate, this "human rights access clause" finally provides an opportunity for all concerned to "take human rights seriously". In other words, human rights provisions in the Constitution of Bosnia and Herzegovina represent an impressive achievement of incorporation of, in the first place, European standards in this field. All that is left is to take them seriously[20]!

The analysis of the GFA's "human rights regime" for BiH would be incomplete without a reference to the Annex 6 to the GFA. It should be read in conjunction with the Constitution because it designs procedural facilities and institutions for (international) "judicial review" of human rights cases. Unfortunately, the Commission on Human Rights does not appear to be *prima facie* "user-friendly". Even from an expert's view, it resembles an over-organized mechanism, consisting of the Office of the Ombudsperson and the Human Rights Chamber under one roof. It is not difficult to imagine these organs struggling against each other, competing over the same budget, and more or less similar cases. It is hoped that it will be possible to rationalise this system, to sharpen its role and relax its

---

[19] Constitution, Art. I, ¶ 4.

[20] Appeals for more "seriousness", or in other words against double standards and shallowness in dealing with human rights, can be heard also in the countries with much longer democratic tradition. *See*, Anthony Lester, "Taking Human Rights Seriously", *in* Robert Blackburn and James J. Busuttil (eds.), *Human Rights for the 21st Century* (1997), at 73-85.

procedural complexities to enable it to function as an international human rights court *in situ*.

The interpretation and further development of the Agreement on Human Rights will inevitably confront the actual political settlement, which is far from a human rights supportive environment. It is therefore necessary to indicate the most obvious problematic elements of that settlement and suggest how they can be overcome.

The GFA confirmed BiH as a state, but modified its internal structure in a very peculiar way. Article I, Paragraph 3, of the Constitution determines that "Bosnia and Herzegovina shall consist of the two Entities, the Federation of Bosnia and Herzegovina, and the Republika Srpska"[21]. Leaving aside the controversies about the definition of BiH as a state, what remains relevant for human rights debate is the assumption that both Entities are exclusively based on ethnic criteria and that this settlement is bound to determine the future of all people living under the jurisdiction of BiH. As was already observed, the Preamble of the Constitution defines Bosniacs[22], Bosnian Croats and Serbs as "constituent peoples" of BiH, while "Others" and "citizens" are mentioned only in passing.

The Preamble indicates that state sovereignty was taken from the citizens and transferred to three ethnic groups. But, even this rigorous concept does not apply throughout the country because, to be very precise, Bosniacs and Bosnian Croats are not constituent peoples in the entity of the Republika Srpska, in the same way as Bosnian Serbs are denied that status in the Federation[23]. It appears that all three peoples are constituent nations only at the level of the central state of BiH, which in reality hardly exists as

---

[21] On the eve of the proclamation of independence of the Republic of Bosnia and Herzegovina, in March 1992, the Bosnian Serbs proclaimed the "Republic of the Serbian People", which will be later renamed the "Serb Republic" ("Republika Srpska"). A year after their mutual armed conflict, Bosnian Croats and Bosnian Muslims accepted the Washington Agreement in March 1994 and established the federation of those two peoples, under the name of "Federation of Bosnia and Herzegovina". In international relations "Republika Srpska" was never granted any form of international recognition, save for internal negotiations and then mostly under the diplomatic cover of the Federal Republic of Yugoslavia. The Federation of Bosnia and Herzegovina, on the other hand, was implicitly accepted in international affairs as a substitute for the "Republic of Bosnia and Herzegovina", which under the latter name was internationally recognized and admitted in the United Nations in May 1992.

[22] "Bosniac" ("Bošnjak") is the new name introduced in the political vocabulary by the leading Muslim political party, SDA, in 1995. It can be questioned as unpractical and etymologically inconsistent because the name of the region (Bosnia) historically speaking has a much broader national base and this creates the risk of shrinking that foundation. Implicitly, this new name tends to eliminate the traditional label which used to embrace quite comfortably all inhabitants of that region – "Bosnian" ("Bosanac", in the local spelling), and was free of any national or political connotations.

[23] *Compare,* Article 1 of the Constitution of the Republika Srpska (from 1992, amended in 1994) *with* Article 1 of the Constitution of the Federation of Bosnia and Herzegovina (The Washington Agreement from 1994).

almost all state prerogatives, e.g. military, police and the administration of justice, are in the hands of the two entities, respectively.

In addition, a serious related, though separate, by-product of this principle has been largely ignored: namely, that all "Others" who do not belong to any of the three, constitutionally recognized ethnic groups, are left in limbo, wondering about their status in this clearly designed "ethnic" country. The principle of "constituent peoples" is reinforced in many operative paragraphs of the Constitution, where even a formal reference to "Others" or "citizens" cannot be found. The composition of all common institutions (the Parliamentary Assembly, the Presidency, the Council of Ministers, domestic judges of the Constitutional Court) is based on the "two entities – three nations" formula. Taking no chances, the Constitution's General Provisions dryly warns that "[o]fficials appointed to positions in the institutions of Bosnia and Herzegovina shall be generally representative of the peoples of Bosnia and Herzegovina"[24]. There is no doubt that the reference to "peoples" rather than "population" significantly narrows the general principle of representation to the three ethnicities only.

It is too easy to agree simply that the GFA was driven by compromise, forced to reflect the realities of the four-year long war, ethnic homogenization, and the then-current, ethnically defined nature of the map of the region. The diplomatic achievement of this compromise should not be underestimated, but its compatibility with the universal demand for the protection of individual human rights and freedoms remains to be tested. While it is true that the Constitution contains the listing of all relevant international human rights instruments, and strong non-discrimination clauses, it is also quite certain that, no matter what human rights guarantees are declared, their implementation will occur in an atmosphere of intensive ethnic exclusivity and distrust. It flows from this that members of any of the three distinctive ethnic groups will be protected by the carefully balanced compromise, but only on the basis of their collective (national) identity. But, this will leave no room for all those who do not "fit" into the group of either Bosniacs, Bosnian Croats or Bosnian Serbs, or those who simply would prefer to exercise their "right not to belong to a group".

The present author concludes that the human rights protection, as far as the present constitutional settlement is concerned, does not favour the protection of individuals in their own right. In fact, the concept of individual rights, which in general is deeply retarded in any formerly socialist country, has been all but obliterated in BiH. Preoccupation with the rights of ethnic groups reflects the transition from communist to nationalist collectivism, where the despotism of the "one and only" ruling party is replaced by the despotism of presupposed group (ethnic) interests. The GFA is a masterful diplomatic creation precisely because of its imprecision – allowing all sides to claim some kind of victory. But the document's

---

[24] Constitution, *supra*, Art. IX, ¶ 3.

fundamental contradictions – declaring a unified state while recognising two antagonised entities as constituent parts of the state; proclaiming democracy while entrenching apartheid structures and ethnic-based parties; re-affirming individual rights while legitimizing ethnic majoritarianism – raise serious concerns about which vision for Bosnia will prevail.

The present author suggests that the new human rights protection system, as it is designed in the Agreement on Human Rights in the GFA's Annex 6, could be used very well as a viable counter-balance against disintegrative tendencies. International human rights law upholds individual rights and freedoms, and the principle of universality is very much embodied in all of the instruments[25]. They should not be reinterpreted according to the current political settlement in the country and, in particular, must not surrender to ethnic criteria. This objective should be secured throughout the proceedings before the Human Rights Chamber and by the powers of the Ombudsperson. There is nothing in the Agreement on Human Rights to prevent all fourteen members of the Chamber from acting in their personal capacity. This can be already taken for granted as far as the eight non-BiH-national members are concerned. But in the case of those appointed by the Entities, it will require a lot of good will and professional courage to bring them to the level of unbiased and independent human rights lawyers with personal integrity. The role of the Council of Europe in the initial period of five years of office will be very demanding and complex in promoting the Commission on Human Rights as a focus of the new human rights system for BiH. Moreover, the credibility of the Commission will, to a great extent, determine the position and performance of other participants in this process. It might influence the domestic judiciary in a positive way, but only if the Commission first established itself as a fair, reliable and effective investigator and/or adjudicator.

---

[25] U.N. Charter, in its Preamble, states "to reaffirm faith in fundamental human rights, in the dignity and worth of the human person, in the equal rights of men and women and of nations large and small". Article 1, among purposes of the U.N., includes "respect for human rights and for fundamental freedoms for all without distinction as to race, sex, language, or religion". This formula is repeated in a few other provisions of the Charter, with the effect that "rights and freedoms for *all*" have become a symbol of international human rights protection. In the Preamble of the Universal Declaration of Human Rights (1948), the starting point is the "recognition of the inherent dignity and of the equal and inalienable rights of all members of the human family is the foundation of freedom, justice and peace in the world". In the Proclamation, it continues by encouraging "teaching and education to promote respect for these rights and freedoms ... to secure their universal and effective recognition and observance". The Vienna Declaration and Programme of Action, adopted at the World Conference on Human Rights in 1993, refers to the U.N. Charter and other U.N. instruments relating to human rights, and reiterates "the universal nature of these rights and freedoms is beyond question", and that "human rights and fundamental freedoms are the birthright of all human beings". *See* World Conference on Human Rights: Vienna Declaration and Programme of Action, UN Doc. A/CONF.157/23 (parts I & II) (1993), ¶ 5 [hereinafter "Vienna Programme for Action"].

Although human rights Non Governmental Organisations (NGOs) are not officially covered by the GFA, their input in the area of monitoring, dissemination and advocacy will be invaluable. Human rights education and promoting awareness of the dignity of a human being and of the government accountability in safeguarding lawful rights and freedoms are crucial segments of the process and traditionally fall under the mission of NGOs. NGOs could also concentrate on more practical work in order to help local lawyers to equip themselves with skills necessary to take up human rights cases, and encourage them to engage in *pro bono* advocacy, a widespread practice in the democratic world[26]. Pools of local lawyers should be established on this basis and major NGOs could seek proper funding to compensate for the expenses of such proceedings. There are signs already that true professionals among lawyers are willing to work and to represent clients throughout the country[27]. It can be assumed that certain "style-cases" will soon emerge, which could help in creating necessary precedents and standards in human rights protection.

In conclusion, it is obvious that the GFA struggles, on the one hand, with the controversy between the ethnic division of BiH and, on the other, with the new human rights system designed to protect individuals regardless of their ethnic background. The present author views this controversy as a challenge for stimulating and strengthening the GFA's human rights institutions and local judiciary and making them also responsible and competent for confronting the given political environment. A final point: the new human rights protection system should be interpreted as an overarching structure which could bridge and transcend the constitutional

---

[26] *See*, "The Lawyer's Code of Professional Responsibility", New York State Bar Association, Canon 2, EC 2-25: "A lawyer has an obligation to render public interest and pro bono legal service. A lawyer may fulfill this responsibility by providing professional services at no fee or at a reduced fee to individuals of limited financial means or to public service or charitable groups or organizations, or by participation in programs and organizations specifically designed to increase the availability of legal services. In addition, lawyers or law firms are encouraged to supplement this responsibility through the financial and other support of organizations that provide legal services to persons of limited means". Among many NGOs, engaging lawyers on a *pro bono* basis, the most experienced ones in the USA are the American Civil Liberties Union, Center for Constitutional Rights, and Children's Defence Fund (handling cases domestically), and the International Human Rights Law Group, Human Rights Watch, Lawyers Committee for Human Rights, and International League for Human Rights (with worldwide activities). In the United Kingdom, Amnesty International, Interights, and AIRE Centre have a worldwide reputation, while Justice takes up human rights cases domestically.

[27] A recent example is the response the International Human Rights Law Group, based in Washington D.C., is getting from local lawyers in BiH, regarding its regional project there. IHRLG launched the idea of working with local lawyers/advocates to help them initiate cases before both the Chamber and the Ombudsperson. They also offer assistance in organizing a scheme to provide free legal services to individuals, particularly women, who have been victims of human rights violations and who wish to file claims before the new protection system in Bosnia and Herzegovina.

settlement by enforcing the principles of universality and non-discrimination, and offer full support to individuals in their access to proclaimed human rights. The present author views this as the only alternative to the glorification and manipulation of group (national) rights, as well as an instrument for the civic cohesion of BiH.

NEDJO MILICEVIC

2. The Role and Relationship of the Constitutional and Non-Constitutional Domestic Human Rights Enforcement Mechanisms

From both historical and comparative perspectives it is clear that a primary function of a State's judicial system is the protection of human rights. As a constituent part of the apparatus of State, the judicial system must correspond in form to the nature of the specific state. However, factors determining characteristics of social function should never include such concerns as the need to complete statehood or quasi-statehood. This would be to subordinate and instrumentalise the primary function of protecting individual rights. Judicial systems exist to ensure the freedom of the human being, justice and equal protection of law – it is not their function to provide a confirmation of statehood.

The judicial organs are called on to protect human rights through both enabling and repressive measures, and they must, at all times, do so by means of reliable, transparent and consistent work practices. However, judicial bodies are only part of the overall social mechanism of realisation and protection of rights. Protection of human rights is the shared responsibility of the entire engine of the state, operating in the spheres of legislation, judiciary and the executive.

This human rights protection system should normally suffice. However, circumstances may arise whereby the three arms of government are inadequate to the scale of the task of ensuring and protecting rights, sometimes in circumstances whereby the weakness of one arm enfeebles another. Thus, a determination of whether a State's judicial system is adequate to its part in the shared responsibility will turn on an evaluation of the effectiveness within the context of the overall machinery of state. In this regard it is necessary to critically consider the current Constitutional and legal arrangements of Bosnia and Herzegovina as well as the key features of the state authorities.

M. O'Flaherty and G. Gisvold (eds.), Post-War Protection of Human Rights in Bosnia and Herzegovina, 13–25.
© 1998 *Kluwer Law International. Printed in Great Britain.*

Pursuant to the General Framework Agreement for Peace[1], Bosnia and Herzegovina[2] is a complex State with an especially elaborate structure. It comprises two Entities (the Federation of Bosnia and Herzegovina and Republika Srpska) each of which have, to a high degree, the features of Statehood. As a consequence, the central bodies of BiH are significantly weakened.

BiH has 13 operative constitutions: that of BiH (the GFA Constitution)[3], those of the two Entities and the constitutions of the ten cantons of the Federation. Organisation of authority in each of the Entities is significantly different. In Republika Srpska it is highly centralised and is constructed on only two levels (municipality and Republika Srpska bodies). On the other hand, Federation authorities perform on five levels: municipality, district, city, canton and Federation bodies.

A characteristic of the GFA Constitution is that the entire organisation of the State and its authorities is predicated on nationalistic considerations. In addition, the Constitution as a legal act presents itself as a pact (to the detriment of its normative features) in a manner whereby it seems to be ultimately an agreement between States. It thus lacks the features of a constitution as the legal act of one State. Accordingly, many of the issues and determinations of social relations which are normally considered to be obligatory elements of a State constitution are not defined with clarity or precision. The Constitution determines that the central bodies of BiH are weaker than those in any other State of the world. What authority they do have is invested by two means, (a) by succession and thus obligatory, (b) through what are termed, "additional competencies", to be determined by mutual consent.

Any consideration of the system for protection of human rights and fundamental freedoms must take account of two primordial considerations: first, the central BiH State is completely deprived of its classical judicial power (all of which is invested in the Entities), and, second, there are no provisions in the Constitution on property or contractual relations. The first point will be examined later in this chapter. With regard to the second, it must be acknowledged that property and contract are basic legal categories in any State, and that they profoundly influence all of social life and development. Does the silence of the Constitution of BiH mean that the Entities have full freedom in regulating property and contract. Could they then

---

[1] General Framework Agreement for Peace in Bosnia and Herzegovina, *initialed* Dayton, Ohio, 21 November 1995, *signed* Paris, 14 December 1995, 35 ILM 75 (1996) [hereinafter "GFA"].

[2] Bosnia and Herzegovina [hereinafter "BiH"] is one of the states formerly a part of the Socialist Federal Republic of Yugoslavia (SFRY), which existed until 1992. Post-1992, other former constituents of the SFRY, Serbia and Montenegro now comprise the state known as the Federal Republic of Yugoslavia [hereinafter "FRY" or "Serbia"].

[3] GFA, *supra*, Annex 4, (Constitution of Bosnia and Herzegovina) [hereinafter "BiH Constitution"].

develop systems which significantly differ, one from the other? Were such diverse systems to develop there would be created a set of objective limits for many social relations within BiH and the integrity of the State would be further compromised. If each Entity does not address the issues of property and contract in a complimentary and cooperative manner what meaning can be given the Constitution's stirring proclamation on "full freedom of movement of persons, goods, services and capital through Bosnia and Herzegovina"[4]. How can a regime be established ensuring the possibility of legal relations between individuals and legal subjects in each of the Entities?

The procedures of decision making in central bodies of the State are inefficient. They are also faced with the real possibility that veto powers will be exercised to ensure maintenance of the *status quo* and postponement of decisions until they are ineffective or irrelevant. In this regard, one should recall that the blocking of decisions is itself a form of decision making, often irrational, which can be imposed by a small number of participants in a decision making process, to the detriment of all.

Since a hierarchy of State authorities is almost entirely abolished in the new state system, the capacity of central authorities to impose their decisions is unclear: they lack a coercive constitutional basis to demand such implementation and instead rely on the goodwill of the Entities. This situation is at odds with the scientifically indisputable value of investing central authority with the competence to ensure implementation of what the various components of the State agree to be in the common interest. On observation of the small number of competencies left to the central authorities one must conclude that BiH society is in a state of partial disintegration. True, BiH required a high degree of decentralisation of authority because of both its multi-national character and demands of modernisation, but not to the extent that the State system is no more than the sum of its parts. At present, in law and society, the factors of disintegration are more powerful than those of integration.

The deetatisation of BiH demands an unavoidable decentralisation. However, there is not a corresponding deetatisation of Entities and cantons. There are thus created strong centres of regional authority which have a centrifugal impact with regard to affairs of State.

Both localistic and hegemonistic tendencies are at odds with the interests of the individual and the nation. While they may serve the interest of those in power they are disastrous for both democracy and economic prosperity. In BiH they are worse: they threaten the survival of the State. This State's constitutional construct, intended to create equality for peoples is a path to poverty. It seeks equality through establishment of a system of permanent crisis. In even the most decentralised of systems, where central Government has a very limited scope of action, it is still invested with

---

[4] BiH Constitution, *supra*, Art. I, ¶ 4.

sovereign authority. Not so in BiH; never before has there existed such a situation whereby decision-makers were deprived of the competency to ensure implementation of their decisions.

The constitutional law of BiH creates not only an irrational and inefficient system but may also incite new conflicts. In this regard one may observe that the political and legal systems are arranged in defiance of all accepted international best practice concerning management and decision-making. Thus, many key decisions for the State will be made at the level of Entities. Also, the decision-making system is open to massive and frequent blockages. Both situations are conducive to profound societal insecurity with all that this implies for maintenance of peace.

A central failure of the GFA is that it did not consistently apply the logic that BiH is a State of three constitutive nations. Instead, in an ill-considered and dangerous way it followed on the path of the Washington Agreement by creating divided or territorialised constituencies. In other words, though the Preamble to the Constitution declared that BiH is comprised of three constitutive nations, they are inserted within split constituencies. Thus, Bosniaks and Croats, but not Serbs, are acknowledged as constitutive of the Federation, and only Serbs have this status in Republika Srpska. This means that, in the current constitutional framework of the State the three nations are constitutive parts of BiH, but, simultaneously, each of them is not a constituent element of some 50% of the territory. Theoretically, such a situation might only be defensible on the basis that BiH was an association of States, a confederation or a union. Indeed, the situation propels BiH in that direction, with all that this implies for restriction on constitutional rights and freedoms and excacerbation of inequality.

The constitutional arrangement has the effect of completely depriving some persons of their human rights. The following three examples illustrate the point:

First, return of refugees and displaced persons is a basic pre-condition for the reintegration of BiH. Even if safe conditions for return are established many factors will ensure that this can never be fully accomplished. These people left or were expelled because they did not belong to a power-wielding nation in the region where they lived. Why should they now return when their second-class status has been given constitutional recognition? People will not forever accept their inferior status and its related deprivation of significant constitutional rights. There is thus a pressure on them to live in a territory/Entity where they belong to a constituent nation. This dynamic is sure to encourage peaceful continuation of ethnic separation and some kind of legalised ethnic cleansing.

Second, the *de facto* categorisation of first and second class citizens has drastic impact for realisation of voters' rights and access to functions of State authorities. According to the Agreement on Elections (Annex 3 of GFA), electoral rules must conform with the applicable international standards as applied in States with developed democracies. However, the

Constitutional division of the peoples of BiH into one or other of the two Entities creates fundamental violations of the Copenhagen Document of the CSCE Conference on Human Dimension of 1990[5]. Concretely, a citizen who is not a member of the constitutive nation of the particular Entity in which he resides can never be elected as a representative of that Entity to central bodies of the State or to certain functions within the Entity. Furthermore, for very many political offices there is stipulated a rule that membership comprise an equal number of persons from a constitutive nation(s) of an Entity and a certain number of "others". See, for example, the provisions of the Federation Constitution concerning the courts. It is stipulated that there should be an equal number of Croat and Muslim judges and that "others" should be adequately represented[6]. How can this tally with the provision that, "a right of every citizen to run for any political or public office, individually or as a representative of a political party or organisation has to be respected, without discrimination"[7]?

Third, the GFA in general, including the Constitution, pays more attention to issues of human rights then to any other matter. Fifteen international legal instruments are invoked (in the Federation Constitution the total is 21!), and Annex 6 is entirely devoted to the subject. This indicates that the signatories to the GFA were of the view that realisation and protection of human rights and fundamental freedoms is of primary social significance and that the war had been an appalling assault on such values. This admirable position is, however, already brought into question by the provisions of the new Constitution.

The Constitution explicitly proclaims that, "Bosnia and Herzegovina and both the Entities shall ensure the highest level of internationally recognised human rights and fundamental freedoms"[8]. Discrimination is banned, "on any ground such as language, religion and national origin"[9]. What can these provisions mean if other constitutional provisions effectively forbid members of certain nations from participating in certain State decision making or establish systems of unequal representation, as illustrated in the examples above?

The Constitution of the Federation stipulates that the official languages of the Federation are Bosnian and Croat and that the Latin is the official alphabet[10]. These languages and alphabet are thus also the official languages and alphabet for members of the Serb nation resident in the Federation. Of course the Constitution does provide for proclamation of further official languages – only, however, in circumstances agreed upon by a

---

[5] GFA, *supra*, Annex 3 (Agreement on Elections), Art. 1, ¶ 3.

[6] Constitution of the Federation of Bosnia and Herzegovina, *signed* Vienna, 18 March 1994, 33 ILM 740 (1994) [hereinafter "Federation Constitution"] at IV C, Art. 6(a).

[7] GFA, *supra*, Attachment to Annex 3 (Agreement on Elections), ¶ 7.5.

[8] BiH Constitution, *supra*, Art. II, ¶ 1.

[9] *Id.*, Art. II, ¶ 4.

[10] BiH Constitution, *supra*, Art. VI, ¶ 1.

majority of Bosniak and Croat delegates in the House of Peoples of the Federation[11]. The power to change the situation is thus placed in the hands of those who can have no reason to upset the status quo. The situation is similar in Republika Srpska where the language and alphabet in official use are Serbian and Cyrillic. Here, too, additional official languages can only be adopted in a manner determined by law[12]. Both Entities have thus adopted positions founded on inequality – with one nation discriminated against in the Federation and two in Republika Srpska.

The situation is no different with regard to symbols in the Entities: flags, coats of arms, seals, etc., all of these have nationalistic characteristics, but only of the national group which is constituent of the respective Entity.

In principle, it can be assumed that every modern State has a sophisticated and complex system of bodies and institutions, rules and instruments to protect and promote the rights of individuals and groups. An examination of such a system should have as its starting point the premise that the number and versatility of the mechanisms is intended to enhance capacity to overcome violations of rights. In other words, the sheer quantity of institutions and instruments need not be a problem: what is crucial, however, is that they efficiently relate to each other, mutually stimulate and animate – in other words, that they constitute one efficient system.

One can state that the system for protection of human rights in BiH, as presented in the GFA, is an ambitious one. The challenge is to determine how rights can be protected in a context of a large number of institutions and instruments and, moreover, the constitutional stipulation that the highest level of internationally recognised human rights protection should be ensured.

Another problem arises from acknowledgement of the principle that the modern development of civilisation requires that the rights of citizens throughout the territory are protected in as unified a manner as possible. BiH in no way meets the criteria for compliance with the principle. This situation and the problems it causes can be illustrated as follows:

1. The State of Bosnia and Herzegovina.

The State lacks a central regular judicial instance. What body then is responsible, for instance, to implement the provision of the BiH Constitution which states that a function of the central organs of the State is, "enforcement of international and inter-Entity criminal law enforcement, including relations with Interpol"[13]? And what does this provision mean,

---

[11] *Id.*, Art. VI, ¶ 3.
[12] Constitution of Republika Srpska, Article 7.
[13] BiH Constitution, *supra*, Art. III, ¶ 1(g).

given, not least, the varying versions in the unofficial translations[14]? In general, what are the roles and limits of activity of the Constitutional Court, Human Rights Chamber, Ombudsperson? Both now and in the long term, account must also be taken of other institutions with very important competencies regarding people's rights: the Commission for Displaced Persons and Refugees[15], the Commission for Preservation of National Monuments[16] and the Provisional Elections Commission[17]. How will they relate to, and overlap with, judicial bodies?

2. Federation of Bosnia and Herzegovina.

There are three levels of regular courts – municipal, cantonal and the Supreme Court. There are also the Constitutional Court, Human Rights Court and the institution of Ombudsmen.

3. Republika Srpska.

There are regular courts and a Constitutional Court.

Matters of regulation and adjudication of administrative law will be dealt with by responsible organs of the Federation and Republika Srpska. It is not at all clear what competencies, if any, central organs of the State will have in this regard. In any case, there seems to be no way to refer an administrative matter from the Entities to the central organs. The brief overview presented above clearly shows the inadequate attention paid to determining the judicial power of the State of Bosnia and Herzegovina, as well as the enormous differences between the Entities regarding institutions and instruments for protection of human rights.

Balanced application of laws and equal protection of rights in both Entities requires that the functioning and jurisdiction of judicial bodies should ensure a certain correlation between the instances in each Entity. The lack of such correlation in BiH is unjustifiable in that there is no obvious imperative for existence of two such diverse systems. For instance, to equate with the Federation, Republika Srpska needs an institution of Ombudsmen and a Human Rights Court. The international community obviously sees these institutions as very important for protection of human rights in the Federation. The argument is no less compelling for Republika Srpska.

---

[14] This provision of the Constitution of Bosnia and Herzegovina, Art. III, ¶ 1(g) is differently translated in each of the three unofficial translation done for and with the agreement of the three authorities of the State. In Bosnian: "enforcement of international and inter-Entity policies and regulations of criminal law provisions, including relations with Interpol." In Serbian: "implementation of criminal laws internationally and between Entities, including the relations with Interpol." In Croatian: "enforcement of international and inter-Entity criminal law, including the relations with Interpol."

[15] GFA, *supra*, Annex 7, Ch. II.

[16] GFA, *supra*, Annex 8.

[17] GFA, *supra*, Annex 3.

Divergence between the systems in the Entities can be seen as even greater once one goes beyond the names of various institutions and observes their mandates. Thus, both Entities have Constitutional Courts, but with greatly varying roles with regard to the protection of human rights. Concretely: The role of the Constitutional Court of Republika Srpska is primarily the abstract assessment of conformity of general acts with the law and Constitution and resolution of conflicts of responsibility between certain government bodies[18]. According to the Federation Constitution, "the main function of the Constitutional Court of the Federation is the resolution of disputes between Cantons, between Cantons and Federal authorities, between municipalities and their Cantons, between the institutions of the Federal authorities, between cities and their Cantons and between Federal authorities and municipalities and cities"[19]. It is both noteworthy and incomprehensible that this court has not the competence to assess the conformity of general acts with the law (it can however assess constitutional conformity of laws). This omission is particularly grave given the very extensive executive competencies of Cantons and municipalities.

The primary competency of the Constitutional Court of Bosnia and Herzegovina is, according to the Bosnian language translation, to "uphold this Constitution"; in the Serb translation, to "protect this Constitution"; in the Croatian translation, to "approve this Constitution"[20]. Resolution of disputes between Entities or between the State and an Entity or between institutions of State are part of the exclusive jurisdiction of the Constitutional Court[21]. The Court also has responsibility to assess whether decisions taken by an Entity to establish special relations with a neighbouring country are in accordance with the Constitution of BiH[22]. Another competence of the Constitutional Court is to determine compatibility with the BiH Constitution of any law or constitutional provision of an Entity[23]. The Court's competency to assess conformity of measures with the Constitution is limited to an examination of laws and does not extend to general acts or sub-legal regulations.

Special attention should be paid to the provision of the BiH Constitution whereby the Constitutional Court shall "have appellate jurisdiction over issues under this Constitution arising out of a judgement of any other court in Bosnia and Herzegovina"[24]. The Croatian language version refers to an "appeal responsibility". In the Bosnian version, the word "judgement" is replaced by the word, "opinion". Another translation problem lies in the

---

[18] Constitution of Republika Srpska, Art. 115.
[19] Federation Constitution, *supra*, IV C, Art. 10.
[20] BiH Constitution, *supra*, Art. VI, ¶ 3.
[21] *Id.*, Art. VI, ¶ 3(a).
[22] *Id.*, Art. VI, ¶ 3(a).
[23] *Id.*, Art. VI, ¶ 3(c).
[24] *Id.*, Art. VI, ¶ 3(b).

replacement of the term, "any court in Bosnia and Herzegovina" in the Croatian version with, "any court of the Entities". Given the importance of the jurisdictional issues these linguistic uncertainties are very worrying.

Ambiguities aside, this constitutional provision leads us to the conclusion that the appellate jurisdiction of the Constitutional Court of Bosnia and Herzegovina corresponds to the institution of the so-called constitutional complaint – a competence of many of the world's constitutional courts – whereby a complaint of violation of constitutional rights can be placed pursuant to exhaustion of all other judicial remedies. Such a double limitation for the appellate jurisdiction of the Constitutional Court of Bosnia and Herzegovina – that there be a violation of rights established in the Constitution and that all other legal remedies are exhausted – is necessary to avoid an anarchic system of legal protection.

But of which courts will the Constitutional Court have appellate jurisdiction. Will it extend to the regular courts of the Entities, the Entity constitutional courts, the Human Rights Court of the Federation, the Human Rights Chamber of Bosnia and Herzegovina? Clarification is required on these essential questions.

In favour of such an inclusive interpretation on this matter is the constitutional provision whereby the Constitutional Court of Bosnia and Herzegovina may strike down provisions of the Entity constitutions. An extension of the logic of such a provision would suggest that the power to strike down is intended to cover any act of any judicial body in the particular Entity. That said, the Constitutional Court of Bosnia and Herzegovina would need to act with the greatest of restraint in order not to undermine the authority and standing of the lower courts in the Entities. Similar restraint would be required in reviewing decisions of the human Rights Court of the Federation and the Human Rights Chamber.

The Human Rights Court of the Federation of Bosnia and Herzegovina has competence regarding, "all constitutional and legal provisions with regard to human rights or basic freedoms"[25]. Any verdict of a court of the Federation or of a canton may be referred to the Human Rights Court[26]. Decisions of the Human Rights Court are final and binding[27]. Also, the Constitutional Court of the Federation, the Supreme Court of the Federation or any cantonal court may refer a matter to the Human Rights Court, "if that issue addresses any matter within the competence of that court". Decisions of the Human Rights Court on such referrals are final and binding[28].

---

[25] Federation Constitution, IV C, Art. 19.
[26] *Id.*, IV C, Art. 20.
[27] *Id.*
[28] *Id.*, IV C, Art. 22.

The Human Rights Chamber can address cases of "alleged or apparent violations of human rights" or of discriminatory enjoyment[29]. All other remedies must first be exhausted[30]. The GFA stipulates that the Chamber must develop fair and effective procedures for the adjudication of applications, procedures in which, "appropriate written pleadings will be provided for and provision made for oral argument and presentation of evidence"[31]. Decisions of the Chamber are stated to be final and binding. Can it be subject to review? Given the following circumstances, it would appear that this is not the case: (a) decisions follow exhaustion of all other remedies; (b) they are adopted by a panel of seven members[32]; (c) they are adopted following a prescribed and instituted procedure and the reasoning is published[33]; (d) the reasoned decisions are sent not only to the parties but given general distribution and forwarded to the High Representative, the Secretary-General of the Council of Europe and the Organisation for Security and Cooperation in Europe[34].

There is urgent need for clarification of the competencies of the Commission for Displaced Persons and Refugees *vis à vis* the regular courts. The Commission is mandated to make decisions regarding, "every real property claim in Bosnia and Herzegovina where the property has not been voluntarily sold or otherwise transferred since 1 April 1992 and where the claimant does not enjoy possession of the property"[35]. Given that decision-making on property rights used to be in the competence of normal courts and is now so under existing law of Bosnia and Herzegovina, how should we proceed in the immediate future with regard to property of displaced persons and refugees? Perhaps the only workable solution is that competent bodies in Bosnia and Herzegovina amend relevant laws so that courts may not decide on real property matters which are within the jurisdiction of the Commission.

Similar issues arise with regard to property which, for reasons of culture, history, religion or ethnic significance, is considered to have the status of national monument. The Commission to Preserve National Monuments makes decisions in, "each individual case", which are "final and to be implemented in accordance with domestic law"[36]. It should be considered that competencies of regular courts be removed with regard to these matters.

---

[29] GFA, *supra*, Annex 6 (Agreement on Human Rights), Art. II.

[30] *Id.*, Art. VIII, ¶ 2 (a).

[31] *Id.*, Art. X, ¶ 1.

[32] *Id.*, Art. X, ¶ 2.

[33] *Id.*, Art. XI, ¶ 5.

[34] *Id.*

[35] GFA, *supra*, Annex 7 (Agreement on Refugees and Displaced Persons), Art. XI.

[36] GFA, *supra*, Annex 8 (Agreement on the Commission to Preserve National Monuments), Art IV.

The issue also arises with regard to decisions of the Provisional Election Commission which GFA define as final[37]. What is the role of the courts with regard to determination of legal validity of such decisions? Given that it is stipulated that elections be conducted entirely in accordance with rules of the Commission and that these rules are obligatory, "regardless of internal laws and regulations"[38], the regular courts should not intervene.

The normative system of protection of human rights in BiH presents features worthy of total support and others in need of explanation and clarification. Thus, one can only praise the proclamation contained in the Constitution of Bosnia and Herzegovina that the State and each Entity shall ensure the highest level of internationally recognised human rights and fundamental freedoms. It is, of course, primarily an aim or target to aspire to, in that its implementation is impeded by the brutal realities of the aftermath of a war in which fundamental rights and freedoms were brutally violated. Also worthy of praise are the new human rights protection institutions of BiH, such as the Human Rights Ombudsperson and the Human Rights Chamber. Inclusion of foreigners within membership of these institutions is a noteworthy and positive element.

Any analysis of the human rights protection system must however acknowledge that there are two completely separated systems on the level of the Entities and that there is a lack of institutions to equalise and integrate human rights protection. The Constitutional Court of Bosnia and Herzegovina and the Human Rights Chamber can only partially and inadequately fill this role. The problem is compounded by the lack of institutional correlation between the Entities and the resulting lack of basic conditions for equalised implementation of the law and for equality of rights of persons in each Entity.

The biggest problem facing institutional protection of human rights is the inadequate definition of respective and mutual competencies and the lack of machinery to adjudicate on jurisdictional conflicts. If the system is to perform its social function, considerable good will and professionalism will be required in order to elaborate appropriate rules of procedure which will address the problem. The unclear hierarchical relationships have special significance for BiH in that the other integrative forces of society or either enfeebled or entirely missing. To this situation we may also add the fact that BiH has considerable *lacunae* of substantive legal provisions. There is a similar lack of existing legal procedures for enforcement of human rights, with all that this implies for effective implementation of human rights obligations.

In addressing the range of problems the following might be considered: First, with regard to the scope of legislative activity of the Entities, it is realistic to assume that they will adopt differing legislative arrangements

---

[37] GFA, *supra*, Annex 3 (Agreement on Elections), Art. III, ¶ 3.
[38] *Id.*, Art. III, ¶ 1.

on a number of issues. Inevitably questions will arise as to which legislation is authoritative or concerning competency conflicts between authorities of the two Entities. Difficulties will most commonly arise in determining how the law of one Entity should be considered in proceedings occurring in the other Entity. This will, for instance, have an impact on the determination of the status of relationships, such as marriage and relationships between parents and children, etc. It will also have an impact on issues of inheritance, taxation, property and economic disputes. Resolving matters such as these must have as its starting point the provision of the Constitution of Bosnia and Herzegovina requiring "full freedom of movement of persons, commodities, services and capital throughout Bosnia and Herzegovina"[39].

An equal priority is the determination of the modalities to ensure compliance by the Entities with Bosnia and Herzegovina's international treaty obligations. The issue is exacerbated by the fact that almost all implementation of such obligations, enactment of legislation, etc., will be undertaken by the Entities. It is also necessary to clarify the competencies of Entity-based bodies and of Entity law concerning those legal acts and transactions which have an international element. Also, clarification is required for the rules on the recognition of foreign judicial and arbitration decisions.

Second, there is need for a further explication of the competencies of the Federation Court of Human Rights, the Human Rights Chamber and the Constitutional Court of Bosnia and Herzegovina. A mutual parallelism must be avoided and there is need for a selectivity appropriate to such levels of protection. To clarify: it is not in dispute that decisions on many constitutional rights and fundamental freedoms fall within the competency of all three institutions. What is at issue is how they can develop mutually useful and transparent jurisdictional clarity.

Third, a primary responsibility for the untangling of the myriad uncertainties falls to the BiH Parliamentary Assembly. The competency of this body is well-established in the BiH Constitution. On issues of criminal law the basis exists in the specific constitutional provision that the competence of institutions of BiH comprises, inter-alia, responsibility for "international and inter-Entity criminal law enforcement, including relations with Interpol"[40]. For all other matters, including protection of civil rights, a legal basis for intervention can be based on the constitutional provision regarding additional competencies: "Bosnia and Herzegovina shall assume responsibility for such other matters as are agreed by the Entities; are provided for in Annexes 5 through 8 to the General framework Agreement; or are necessary to preserve the sovereignty, territorial integrity, political independence, and international personality of Bosnia and Herzegovina.

---

[39] BiH Constitution, *supra*, Art. I, ¶ 4.
[40] *Id.*, Art. III, ¶ 1(g).

Additional institutions may be established as necessary to carry out such responsibilities"[41].

Ultimately, one must conclude that there is compelling and urgent need for the Entities to agree, either in principal or detail, that there be joint, BiH-based regulation of a range of issues concerning protection of human rights. Without this there will perpetuation of the absurdity of uneven protection of human rights in each of the Entities. Without it, the constitutional enshrining of human rights as supreme values of the State will remain no more than an unrealised and abstract aspiration.

---

[41] *Id.*, Art. III, ¶ 5(a).

3. Implications of the Special Status Accorded in the General Framework Agreement for Peace to the European Convention on Human Rights

I. INTRODUCTION

Respect for human rights forms one of the most important pillars of the civilian part of the General Framework Agreement for Peace in Bosnia and Herzegovina and its Annexes, signed in Paris on 14 December 1995[1]. In Article VII of the GFA the signatory parties recognise that the observance of human rights and the protection of refugees and displaced persons are of vital importance in achieving a lasting peace in Bosnia and Herzegovina[2]. In the context of this aim, the European Convention for the Protection of Human Rights and Fundamental Freedoms and the pertaining Protocols[3] has been given a prominent place in the GFA, inasmuch as the ECHR is directly referred to in a number of key provisions.

The ECHR is a Western European regional treaty for the protection of human rights and fundamental freedoms. It was drafted within the framework of the Council of Europe, a European organisation established shortly after the end of the Second World War. In the Preamble of the Statute of the Council of Europe, the Member States reaffirm their devotion to, *inter alia*, the rule of law; one of the principles which form the basis of all genuine democracy. The aim of the Council of Europe, set out in Article 1 of its Statute, is the achievement of greater unity between its European

---

[1] General Framework Agreement for Peace in Bosnia and Herzegovina, *initialed* Dayton, Ohio, 21 November 1995, *signed* Paris, 14 December 1995, 35 ILM 75 (1996) [hereinafter "GFA"].

[2] Bosnia and Herzegovina [hereinafter "BiH"] is one of the states formerly a part of the Socialist Federal Republic of Yugoslavia (SFRY), which existed until 1992. Post-1992, other former constituents of the SFRY, Serbia and Montenegro now comprise the state known as the Federal Republic of Yugoslavia [hereinafter "FRY" or "Serbia"].

[3] [European] Convention for the Protection of Human Rights and Fundamental Freedoms, 213 U.N.T.S. 221, 1 E.T.S. 5, *signed* 4 November 1950 [hereinafter "ECHR"].

M. O'Flaherty and G. Gisvold (eds.), Post-War Protection of Human Rights in Bosnia and Herzegovina, 27–69.
© 1998 *Kluwer Law International. Printed in Great Britain.*

Member States. This aim is to be pursued by discussion of questions of common concern and by agreements and common action in economic, social, cultural, scientific, legal and administrative matters and in the maintenance and further education of human rights and fundamental freedoms[4]. BiH applied for membership of the Council of Europe on 10 April 1995.

The ECHR was drafted in a period in which the memories of the atrocities committed by the Nazi regime during the Second World War were still fresh; it implicitly reflects the profound wish to ensure that such horrible events will not recur. This background explains a particularly striking feature of the ECHR, namely the right of individual petition. On the basis of this right, individuals may set the control and enforcement mechanisms foreseen in the ECHR into motion. The ECHR entered into force in 1950. Its substantive guarantees, which mainly concern classic civil and political rights, have been extended in the course of time by the adoption of the additional Protocols Nos. 1, 4, 6 and 7. The ECHR seeks to protect the enjoyment of fundamental rights and freedoms of individuals in their relations with public authorities. In principle it does not protect human rights and freedoms in relations between private parties.

Although the classical concept of "negative obligations" – an obligation that States refrain from interfering in the individual's enjoyment of human rights – appears to be predominant in the system of the ECHR, it has been recognised that the ECHR also includes "positive obligations" of a State in the sense that States should take appropriate measures in order to secure that individuals can effectively enjoy their rights protected under the ECHR[5]. These positive obligations do not, however, go so far as to impose an obligation to fully protect individuals against human rights violations committed by other private parties[6].

At present, the ECHR has been ratified by 34 member States of the Council of Europe[7], all of whom have recognised the right of individual

---

[4] For further details, *see* D. Gomien, D. Harris & L. Zwaak, *Law and Practice of the European Convention on Human Rights and the European Social Charter* (1996), at 11-14 [hereinafter "Gomien, Law and Practice"].

[5] *Cf. X. and Y.* v. *the Netherlands*, 91 Eur. Ct. HR (Series A) at 11-14, ¶¶ 21-30 (judgment of 26 March 1985); *Kroon and Others* v. *the Netherlands*, 297-A Eur. Ct. HR (Series A) at 56, ¶¶ 31-32 (judgment of 27 October 1994); *López Ostra* v. *Spain*, 303-C Eur. Ct. HR (Series A) at 54-56, ¶¶ 51-58 (judgment of 9 December 1994); *see also* No. 9348/81, Dec. 28.2.83, D.R. 32, at 190.

[6] For further details, *see*: E.A. Alkema, "The Third-Party Applicability of "Drittwirkung" of the European Convention on Human Rights", *in Protecting Human Rights: The European Dimension* (1988), at 33-45; D. Harris, M. O'Boyle & C. Warbrick, *Law of the European Convention on Human Rights* (1995), at 19-22 [hereinafter "Harris, Law of the European Convention"].

[7] Albania, Andorra, Austria, Belgium, Bulgaria, Cyprus, Czech Republic, Denmark, Estonia, Finland, France, Germany, Greece, Hungary, Iceland, Ireland, Italy, Liechtenstein, Lithuania, Luxembourg, Malta, the Netherlands, Norway, Poland, Portugal, Romania, San

petition. This right of individual petition allows the bodies established under Article 19 of this Convention, namely the European Commission of Human Rights and the European Court of Human Rights[8], which sit in Strasbourg, France, to examine individual applications in which it is alleged that in a particular case there has been a violation of one or more of the provisions of the ECHR by a State Party. Since the ECHR entered into force, it has acquired the reputation as being an effective instrument of international protection through the work of its control machinery: the European Commission of Human Rights, which receives applications and filters out the admissible cases, the European Court of Human Rights, which is competent to decide the merits of applications, and the Committee of Ministers, which has an autonomous decision-making power when a case has not been referred to the European Court and which further supervises the execution of judgments of the European Court. Such decisions are binding on the parties concerned.

As from their beginnings, the European Commission and the European Court have developed a substantial body of case law[9] in respect of the application of the rules of the ECHR. This jurisprudence is of particular relevance and interest to a practical application of the ECHR in BiH. To date, the European Commission has decided on the admissibility of more than 29,000 cases[10] and the European Court of Human Rights has rendered about 700 judgments and decisions[11].

The substantive provisions of the ECHR and its jurisprudence provide the member States with a set of continuously developing minimum rules to be respected. Of course any State may afford its citizenry a higher standard of protection but the ECHR seeks to secure that at least consistent mini-

---

Marino, Slovakia, Slovenia, Spain, Sweden, Switzerland, Turkey and the United Kingdom. Six Member States of the Council of Europe have signed, but not yet ratified the ECHR, namely Croatia, Latvia, Moldova, Russia, the Former Yugoslav Republic of Macedonia and Ukraine.

[8] These two organs will be replaced by a single Court when Protocol No. 11 to the ECHR will become operative, which is one year after the ratification of this Protocol by all Contracting States. To date, Italy, Poland, Portugal and Turkey have not yet ratified this Protocol.

[9] A selection of the Commission's case-law is published in the Series, *Decisions and Reports* (D.R.). Until 1996 the Court's judgments were published in Series A; from 1996 onward, the Court's judgments are published in annual *Reports of Judgments and Decisions* [hereinafter "Reports"].

[10] Only about 10% of the cases brought before the European Commission are in fact declared admissible. The vast majority of cases are rejected on various grounds; for further details, *see* European Commission of Human Rights, *Survey of Activities and Statistics 1996* (January 1997).

[11] This figure includes Article 50 judgments and decisions taken under Protocol No. 9 to the ECHR.

mum human rights standards are respected throughout the vast territory covered by the ECHR[12].

II. APPLICATION OF THE ECHR IN BOSNIA AND HERZEGOVINA

It is a fundamental principle of public international law that an international treaty only applies between the parties to it[13]. BiH has applied for membership of the Council of Europe, but so far has not been accepted. It is, therefore, not a party to the ECHR. However, the BiH authorities have committed themselves in the GFA to the applicability of the ECHR within the domestic legal system. Further, pursuant to the GFA, in case of conflict between national law and the provisions of the ECHR, the latter takes precedence. The fact that a non-member state of the Council of Europe has committed itself in this way presents a truly unique situation. The idea of basing constitutional human rights provisions in the former Yugoslavia directly on specified international instruments, including treaties drafted in the framework of the Council of Europe, existed in the 1991 "Carrington draft" which resulted from the European Community Peace Conference on Yugoslavia[14]. At present, the ECHR has been given a place, either explicitly or implicitly, in the constitutions which are in force in Bosnia and Herzegovina, both at the national level and at the level of the respective Entities, the Federation of Bosnia and Herzegovina and the Republika Srpska.

A. The Constitution of Bosnia and Herzegovina

Article II of the BiH Constitution contained in Annex 4 to the GFA explicitly states that the rights and freedoms set out in the ECHR shall apply directly in BiH and that these shall have priority over all other law. According to the wording of paragraph 5 of the same provision, all courts, agencies, governmental organs and instrumentalities operated by or within the Entities, shall apply and conform to the human rights and fundamental

---

[12] For further details on the general background of the ECHR and its pertaining control mechanisms: H.C. Krüger, "The European Commission of Human Rights", 1 HRLJ, No. 1-4; J. Velu & R. Ergec, *La Convention Européenne des Droits de l'Homme* (1990), at 37-61; Harris, Law of the European Convention, *supra*, at 1-36; Gomien, Law and Practice , *supra*; at 20-91; J. Frowein & W. Peukert, *Europäische Menschenrechtskonvention* (1996), at 1-26 [hereinafter, "Frowein, Europaische"].

[13] *See, e.g.*, I. Brownlie, *Principles of Public International Law* (1979), at 613 [hereinafter, "Brownlie, Principles"].

[14] C. Szasz, "The Protection of Human Rights Through the Dayton/Paris Peace Agreement on Bosnia", 90 AJIL 301, 306 (1996) [hereinafter "Szasz, Protection of Human Rights"]. On constitutional protection of human rights in BiH *see further*, Chapters 1, 2, and 4 of this volume.

freedoms referred to in paragraph 2 of Article II of the Constitution. Moreover, according to Article X of the BiH Constitution, no amendment to the Constitution may eliminate or diminish any of the rights and freedoms referred to in Article II or alter Article X itself. The ECHR has thus been given a solid place in the Constitution

Further, according to Article I of Annex 6 to the GFA, which specifically deals with the issue of human rights, the Parties – the State of Bosnia and Herzegovina and the two Entities, the Federation of Bosnia and Herzegovina and the Republika Srpska – "shall secure to all persons within their jurisdiction the highest level of internationally recognised human rights and fundamental freedoms", including the rights and freedoms provided in the ECHR and its Protocols and a number of other international agreements set out in the Appendix to Annex 6.

B. The Constitution of the Federation of Bosnia and Herzegovina

As originally proposed in the 1994 Washington Agreement, Article 6 of the Federation Constitution requires all Federation courts, administrative agencies and other governmental organs to apply and conform to the rights and freedoms provided in its Annex A, wherein the ECHR is explicitly mentioned.

C. The Constitution of the Republika Srpska

Until the adoption on 13 September 1996 of Amendments LIV to LXV to the Republika Srpska Constitution by its National Assembly, the scope of certain provisions of this Constitution dealing specifically with Human Rights and Freedoms were limited to citizens of the Republika Srpska[15]. Furthermore, apart from a rather obtuse reference contained in the former Article 68, the Constitution contained no provision expressly acknowledging the supremacy of the BiH Constitution.

The current Constitution contains no direct reference to the ECHR[16]. However, according to Amendment LVII to the Constitution, in case of conflict between the Constitution and the BiH Constitution, those provisions which are favourable for the citizen should be applied. In practice, this means that the protection afforded by Article II of the BiH Constitution, where it is stated that the rights and freedoms set out in the ECHR shall apply directly in Bosnia and Herzegovina and that these shall have

---

[15] *See, for instance*, Articles 10, 21, 23, 30 and 32 of the Constitution of the Republika Srpska as in force prior to the constitutional amendments adopted on 13 September 1996 by the National Assembly of the Republika Srpska.

[16] The only direct reference to the ECHR is made in Amendment LVII ¶ 3 to the Constitution of the Republika Srpska which provides that " ... Articles 13, 22, 23, 24, 25, 26, 28 and 30 of the Constitution ... are going to be applied in accordance with the corresponding ... Articles 8 to 11 of the European Convention (on Human Rights)".

priority over all other law, is guaranteed in the Constitution of the Republika Srpska, albeit indirectly.

III. PROTECTION MECHANISMS

Of course, the practical implementation of this far reaching commitment of the authorities of BiH can only be guaranteed through the establishment of adequate protection mechanisms to secure the protection of human rights and their effective functioning in practice. Under the GFA and the relevant laws at the level of the respective Entities, a number of such protection mechanisms have in fact been envisaged. Not all of them are currently functioning and, given their respective powers, when they are, overlapping jurisdictions and resultant difficulties, in particular in the Federation of Bosnia and Herzegovina, will be difficult to avoid[17].

A. Human Rights Protection Mechanisms at the National Level

1. The Constitutional Court
On the national level, the BiH Constitution (Annex 4 to the GFA) envisaged the creation of a Constitutional Court. This court is to be composed of nine members, three of whom will not be nationals of either BiH or a neighbouring state. The competence of this Court is set forth in Article VI of the BiH Constitution. It includes, *inter alia*, the determination of the compatibility of national laws with the ECHR and appellate jurisdiction over constitutional issues arising out of a judgment of any other national court. As Article II explicitly refers to the ECHR, such issues could include the direct application of the rights and freedoms guaranteed by the ECHR. Under Article VI of the BiH Constitution, the decisions of the Constitutional Courts shall be final and binding. So far, however, the Constitutional Court has not begun to function.

2. The Human Rights Commission
On a national level, the GFA further envisages the establishment of a special Human Rights Commission (Annex 6 to the GFA)[18]. This Commission consists of two parts, the Office of the Human Rights Ombudsperson, an Office held by one person who may not be a national of either BiH or a

---

[17] For further details, *see*, Venice Commission, *Opinion on the Constitutional Situation in Bosnia and Herzegovina with Particular Regard to Human Rights Protection Mechanisms*, (1996), 15-16 November 1996.

[18] For the historical background of this body, *see*, Szasz, Protection of Human Rights, *supra*, at 308-310.

neighbouring state[19], and the Human Rights Chamber, consisting of four-teen judges, eight of whom cannot be either BiH nationals or from a neigh-bouring state[20].

The Commission's task includes the examination of alleged or apparent violations of human rights as provided for in the ECHR and alleged or apparent discrimination in the enjoyment of any of the rights and freedoms provided for in the sixteen international instruments which are listed in the Appendix to Annex 6 to the GFA[21]. This Commission, which began work on 27 March 1996, enables private individuals who are victims of viola-tions of the provisions of the ECHR committed by one or more of the three Parties[22].

Pursuant to Article XI of Annex 6 to the GFA, the decisions of the Chamber shall be final and binding and the Parties shall fully implement the decisions by the Chamber. Annex 6 does not foresee any control mechanism as regards the implementation of decisions of the Human Rights Chamber.

As at 31 December 1996, 948 provisional complaints and 372 formal complaints had been lodged with the Office of the Human Rights Ombud-sperson. Of the formal complaints, 50 are directed against the State of Bosnia and Herzegovina, 134 against the Federation of Bosnia and Herze-govina and 152 against the Republika Srpska. The remaining cases are directed either against two or more Parties or against others. Most com-plaints concern property related issues[23].

B. Human Rights Protection Mechanisms at the Level of the Entities

Pursuant to Article III of the BiH Constitution, the Entities are obliged to maintain civilian law enforcement agencies operating in accordance with internationally recognised standards and with respect for the internation-ally recognised human rights and fundamental freedoms referred to in Article II of the Constitution, which explicitly mentions the ECHR.

---

[19] Pursuant to Article IV of Annex 6 to the GFA, the OSCE appointed Ms. G. Haller, a Swiss national, as Human Rights Ombudsperson for Bosnia and Herzegovina.

[20] The eight international members of the Human Rights Chamber, including the Presi-dent of the Chamber, were appointed by the Committee of Ministers of the Council of Europe. The national members of the Chamber were appointed by the Government of the Federation of Bosnia and Herzegovina (4 members) and by the Government of the Repub-lika Srpska respectively (2 members).

[21] The Human Rights Ombudsperson has an office in Sarajevo and in Banja Luka. The Chamber sits in Sarajevo.

[22] For further details, *see, Report on the Development of the Office of the Human Rights Ombudsperson for Bosnia and Herzegovina*, 4 September 1996; *and Report on the Activi-ties of the Human Rights Chamber for Bosnia and Herzegovina*, 5 November 1996.

[23] For further details, *see*, Human Rights Ombudsperson for Bosnia and Herzegovina – Sarajevo, Case Summary of 31 December 1996.

1. The Federation of Bosnia and Herzegovina
The Constitution of the Federation of Bosnia and Herzegovina provides for the creation of a number of bodies, which are competent to deal with human rights issues in the Federation, namely the Supreme Court, the Human Rights Court and the Federation Ombudsmen.

i. The Constitutional Court
Although the Federation has its own Constitutional Court, the competence of this court does not include human rights issues. It follows from Article 10, paragraph 3 in conjunction with Article 22 of Chapter IV C (The Judiciary) of the Federation Constitution that its Constitutional Court is to refer human rights issues arising in the course of proceedings before it to the Human Rights Court. The rulings of the Human Rights Court as regards such issues are binding on the Constitutional Court. Decisions by the Constitutional Court are final and binding.

ii. The Supreme Court
The role and competence of the Federation Supreme Court are delineated by Articles 14 to 17 of Chapter IV of the Federation Constitution. It shall consist of at least nine judges. It is the highest court of appeal of the Federation and is competent to examine appeals on all matters, except those within the jurisdiction of the Constitutional Court or the Human Rights Court. Its decisions are final and binding.

iii. The Human Rights Court
Articles 18 through 23 of Chapter IV C of the Federation Constitution contain the rules governing the Human Rights Court of the Federation. So far this court has not started to function. As a transitional arrangement[24], it will composed of seven members. Four of these individuals will be appointed by the Council of Europe's Committee of Ministers and will not be citizens of any state neighbouring BiH. The other three members shall include one Bosniac, one Croat and one Other. The competence of this Court includes any question concerning a constitutional or other legal provision relating to human rights or fundamental freedoms or to any of the instruments listed in the Annex to the Federation Constitution. This Annex contains the ECHR and twenty other Human Rights Instruments[25].

---

[24] *See* Constitution of the Federation of Bosnia and Herzegovina, *signed* Vienna, 18 March 1994, 33 ILM 740 (1994) [hereinafter "Federation Constitution"] IX, Art. 9.

[25] This list includes all but one of the instruments listed in the Appendix to Annex 6 of the GFA (not included is the 1992 European Charter for Regional or Minority Languages; the 1994 Framework Convention for the Protection of National Minorities was added to the list on 5 June 1996 by the adoption of Amendment XXVI to the Constitution). The list further includes five instruments not included in the Appendix to Annex 6, *i.e.* the 1948 Universal Declaration of Human Rights, the 1981 Declaration on the Elimination of all Forms of Intolerance and of Discrimination based on Religion or Belief, the 1990 Document

Appellants must complete the regular procedures before the competent courts in the Federation and then may file an appeal to the Human Rights Court, if their appeal concerns points falling within the specific competence of this court. The Human Rights Court is competent to examine cases begun after 1 January 1991; it is further competent to determine questions concerning matters within its competence which arise in the course of proceedings pending before the Constitutional Court, the Supreme Court or any Cantonal Court and which are referred to the Human Rights Court by these courts for a preliminary ruling. As already stated above, such rulings are binding on the requesting court.

iv. The Federation Ombudsmen
The Federation Constitution also governs the functioning of the Ombudsmen of the Federation of Bosnia and Herzegovina. Article 1, Chapter II B, commands that there shall be three Ombudsmen: one Bosniac, one Croat and one Other. This institution began to function in January 1995 following the appointment in 1994 for an initial period of at least three years of the first three Ombudsmen[26] by the OSCE in accordance with Article 9 of the Federation Constitution[27].

Article 4 of this same chapter states that the Ombudsmen shall independently carry out their functions, which includes the protection of the rights and freedoms set forth in, *inter alia*, the ECHR. In particular, they shall act to reverse the consequences of violations of such rights and freedoms, especially of ethnic cleansing[28]. Under Article 5, Chapter II B, they are competent to examine the activities of any institution of the Federation, Canton or Municipality or of any person which may impair the human dignity, rights, or liberties of another. They have a statutory right of access to all official documents, including secret ones, to attend judicial and administrative hearings as well as meetings of other organs, and to enter and inspect any place where persons are detained[29]. They may further initiate proceedings in competent courts and may intervene in any pending proceedings, including proceedings before the Human Rights Court. Finally, on the basis of Rule 37 (b) of the Rules of Procedure of the Human Rights Ombudsperson, the Federation Ombudsmen have a semi-direct

---

of the Copenhagen Meeting of the Conference on the Human Dimension of the OSCE, the 1990 Council of Europe Parliamentary Assembly Recommendation on the Rights of Minorities paras. 10-13, and the 1992 Declaration on the Rights of Persons belonging to National or Ethnic, Religious and Linguistic Minorities.

[26] Ms V. Jovanovic , Mr E. Muhibic, and Ms B. Raguz.

[27] For further details *see*, Institution of the Ombudsmen of the Federation of Bosnia and Herzegovina, *Annual Report on the State of Human Rights*, Sarajevo – February 1996; and *Semi-annual Report on the state of Human Rights*, Sarajevo – July 1996.

[28] Federation Constitution, *supra,* Chapter II B, Art. 2.

[29] Federation Constitution, *supra,* Chapter II B, Art. 7.

access to the Human Rights Chamber of the Human Rights Commission created pursuant to Annex 6 to the GFA.

v. The Federation Implementation Council

The Federation Implementation Council was established by the Federation of Bosnia and Herzegovina in May 1996. The Council has five members: the Federation President and Vice-President and three non-nationals, including the Principal Deputy of the High Representative. Any member of the Council, the Prime Minister of the Federation, the Federation Ombudsmen or the Human Rights Ombudsperson may bring cases before the Council to allege that any holder of a public office has violated the Federation Constitution or other Federation laws, including human rights and freedoms protected by the ECHR. The Council is competent to order the removal from office of the person concerned.

2. The Republika Srpska

i. The Constitutional Court

Articles 115 to 120 of the Constitution of the Republika Srpska set out the rules governing the Constitutional Court of the Republika Srpska. It is composed of seven members.

The competence of the Constitutional Court includes, *inter alia*, the determination of questions of the conformity with the Constitution of laws, other regulations and general enactments, as well as of conflicts of jurisdictions. It shall also issue opinions and suggestions to the highest constitutional bodies of the Republika Srpska and take other measures to ensure constitutionality and legality and the protection of freedoms and rights of citizens. The Constitution does not contain any provision to the effect that the Constitutional Court may examine the compatibility of laws with obligations arising from applicable international instruments, such as the ECHR. It is of course open to the Constitutional Court to examine whether a matter is contrary to the Human Rights and Freedoms set out in Chapter II of the Constitution.

Where the Constitutional Court finds a law, other regulation or enactment not in conformity with the Constitution, such a law, regulation or enactment automatically becomes null and void as from the date of the court's judgment[30]. Its decisions are binding and final. Proceedings before the Constitutional Court may be brought by the President of the Republic, the National Assembly and the Government of the Republika Srpska. Other bodies or State organs may institute constitutional proceedings insofar as the law may allow them to do so. The Constitutional Court may also examine a matter at its own motion. Private individuals do not, as such, have a right to take proceedings before the Constitutional Court, although,

---

[30] Constitution of the Republika Srpska, Art. 120.

according to the wording of Article 120 of the Constitution, they "can give an initiative", which can be understand as requesting permission to take constitutional proceedings.

ii. The Supreme Court
The role and competence of the Republika Srpska Supreme Court are found in Article 123 of the Constitution. As the highest court of law of the Entity, the Supreme Court exclusively shall secure the sole and universal enforcement of the law. The Supreme Court is the highest court of appeal in the Republika Srpska for civil, criminal and administrative cases. It may examine alleged violations of human rights norms in the context of civil, criminal and administrative procedures and insofar as those norms have been given a place in the legal order of the Republika Srpska. Its functioning may be compared to, for instance, the *Cour de Cassation* in France.

IV. Substantive Implications of the Applicability of the ECHR

Prior to discussing the substantive implications of the applicability of the ECHR in the specific situation in Bosnia and Herzegovina, one must consider the fundamental principles on which the ECHR is founded. Set forth in the Preamble to the ECHR, which forms an integral part of the ECHR[31], these principles include the rule of law. This principle is also outlined in the Preamble of the Statute of the Council of Europe[32] and in Article 3 of this Statute. The principle of the rule of law enshrines the notion of the supremacy of the law over State power, including limits on the authority States may exercise over individuals through the adoption of general laws. It encompasses the necessity of preventing uncertainty or arbitrariness in implementation of such laws and the separation of powers between the legislative, judicial and executive authorities. The rule of law defines as specifically as possible the fundamental rights and freedoms States must respect with regard to individuals within their jurisdiction.

Legality is another element of the principle of the rule of law. It implies that only previously adopted laws may be applied and, moreover, in principle, laws should not be applied retroactively. The scope and content of laws must be available to the public and sufficiently clear to allow one to foresee the consequences of non-compliance. Equally important, the principle of "lawfulness" implies that any exercise of State authority over

---

[31] *Golder* v. *United Kingdom*, 18 Eur. Ct. HR (Series A) at 16, ¶¶ 34-35 (judgment of 21 February 1975); *see also*, Brownlie, Principles, *supra*, at 626.

[32] "The Governments of ... reaffirming their devotion to the spiritual and moral values which are the common heritage of their peoples and the true source of individual freedom, political liberty and the rule of law, principles which form the basis of all genuine democracy ... ."

individuals is only acceptable insofar as such exercise is "in accordance with the law" or "prescribed by law", phrases to be found in several provisions of the ECHR, and insofar as the compatibility of the exercise of authority with the law is made subject to judicial control[33].

Another crucial element of the "rule of law" is the independence and impartiality of the judiciary. In determining disputes between individuals and disputes between the public authorities and individuals, the judiciary must function independent of a government. It must apply the laws duly enacted by the elected parliament in an unbiased manner[34] free from government influence. The judiciary is not meant to create laws, rather to apply the laws to specific situations in the course of public judicial proceedings. Public proceedings and independence are key to inspiring public confidence in the judiciary and in government[35].

It would go too far to discuss here and now all the substantive provisions of the ECHR[36] and their possible implications and effects as regards the current situation in Bosnia and Herzegovina. Therefore, a number of ECHR provisions have been selected, largely on the basis of certain problematic areas in BiH as reflected in, amongst other things, the subject matters of decisions and reports[37] of, and of complaints filed with, the Human Rights Ombudsperson for Bosnia and Herzegovina[38].

A. Article 3: The Right to Human Dignity

Article 3 of the ECHR provides that "no one shall be subjected to torture or to inhuman or degrading treatment or punishment." It is an absolute provision. In a recent case, the European Court held:

> Article 3, as the Court has observed on many occasions, enshrines one of the fundamental values of democratic society. Even in the most difficult of circumstances, such as the fight against organised terrorism and crime, the Convention prohibits in absolute terms torture or inhuman or

---

[33] *Cf.* No. 22942/93, Dec. 18.5.95 (unpublished).

[34] *Cf., Procola* v. *Luxembourg*, 326 Eur. Ct. HR (Series A) (judgment of 28 September 1995).

[35] *Cf., Hauschildt* v. *Denmark*, 154 Eur. Ct. HR (Series A) at 21, ¶¶ 46-48 (judgment of 24 May 1989); *Demicoli* v. *Malta*, 210 Eur. Ct. HR (Series A) at 18, ¶ 39 (judgment of 27 August 1991).

[36] There are a large number of books and other publications about the European Convention and the case-law. An extensive list containing a wide selection of these books and publications can be found in the recent extensive commentary on the ECHR: *See* Frowein, *Europaische, supra*, at 1023-1026.

[37] Human Rights Ombudsperson for Bosnia and Herzegovina, Decisions and Reports issued through 31 December 1996.

[38] Human Rights Ombudsperson of Bosnia and Herzegovina, Case Summary as of 31 October 1996.

degrading treatment or punishment. Unlike most of the substantive clauses of the Convention and of Protocols Nos. 1 and 4, Article 3 makes no provision for exceptions and no derogation from it is permissible under Article 15 even in the event of a public emergency threatening the life of the nation[39].

The reference is often invoked in complaints addressed to the European Commission of Human Rights in relation to a wide variety of situations concerning treatment perceived by complainants as being contrary to this provision. In the vast majority of such cases, underlying this perception is the idea that having been treated "unjustly" is inhuman and/or degrading[40], or in criminal cases that the sentence imposed is an inhuman and/or degrading punishment[41]. This idea is not supported by the case-law under this provision. Indeed, the interpretation given to this Article demonstrates that a rather high threshold applies. To come within the ambit of Article 3, ill-treatment must go beyond a certain level to attain a minimum level of severity, taking into account all the circumstances, including the duration of the treatment and its physical and mental effects[42].

The European Court examined Article 3 closely in the case of *Ireland* v. *the United Kingdom*. It held in that case that the word "torture" refers to deliberate inhuman treatment causing very serious and cruel suffering, that "inhuman treatment" is treatment causing "at least intense physical and mental suffering" and that a ill-treatment is "degrading" where is "arouses in their victims feelings of fear, anguish and inferiority capable of humiliating and debasing them and possibly breaking their physical or moral resistance"[43]. However, given the absolute character of Article 3 of the ECHR, it is not strictly necessary to make any distinctions once a treatment is found as falling within the scope of this provision. Insofar as distinctions are made, it has a moral rather than a legal value since the prohibition applies to all such forms of ill-treatment. Moreover, ill-treatment is not limited to physical abuse. The European Commission has held that a measure which does not involve physical ill-treatment but which lowers a person in rank, position, reputation or character can constitute "degrading treatment" provided it attains a minimum level of severity[44]. In *Ireland* v. *United Kingdom*, legislation specifying that nationals of the United Kingdom who had not been born in the United Kingdom or who had no ances-

---

[39] *Aksoy* v. *Turkey*, Eur. Ct. HR (judgment of 18 December 1996), to be published in *Reports* 1996, ¶ 62 (citations omitted).

[40] *Cf.* No. 8896/80, Dec. 10.3.81, D.R. 24, at 176.

[41] *Cf.* No. 5871/72, Dec. 30.9.94, D.R. 1 at 54.

[42] *Cf.*, *Ireland* v. *United Kingdom*, 25 Eur. Ct. HR (Series A) at 65, ¶ 162 (judgment of 18 January 1978).

[43] *Id.* at 66, ¶ 167.

[44] Nos. 4403/70-4419/70, 4422/70, 4423/70. 4443/70, 4476/70-4478/70, 4486/70, 4501/70 and 4526/70-4530/70 (joined), *East African Asians* v. *United Kingdom*, Comm. Report 14.12.73, D.R. 78, at 5.

tral connections with the United Kingdom no longer had a right of entry, was held not only racially discriminatory but also, given that some persons had been publicly subjected to this legislation and, thereby, their human dignity had been sufficiently mistreated, constituted degrading treatment[45].

Even a brief review of the caselaw under Article 3 would not be complete without mention of the concept of "administrative practice" developed under Articles 3 and Article 26 of the ECHR. Like the European Court and Commission, the Human Rights Commission and Chamber in BiH are obliged to verify that complainants have exhausted available effective remedies before they complain to either the Human Rights Ombudsperson or the Human Rights Chamber[46]. The European organs have exempted a certain category of complainants from this requirement. Those complaining of situations where *prima facie* evidence exists which establishes beyond reasonable doubt that the available remedies would be ineffective because of administrative practice of torture or ill-treatment need not demonstrate exhaustion of remedies[47]. The concept of "administrative practice" has been defined as "repetition of acts and official tolerance":

> By "repetition of acts" is meant a substantial number of acts of torture or ill-treatment which are the expression of a general situation. The pattern of such acts may be either, on the one hand, that they occurred in the same place, that they were attributable to the agents of the same policy or military authority, or that the victims belonged to the same political category; or, on the other hand, that they occurred in several places or at the hands of distinct authorities, or were inflicted on persons of varying political affiliations.

> By "official tolerance" is meant that, though acts of torture or ill-treatment are plainly illegal, they are tolerated in the sense that the superiors of those immediately responsible take no action to punish them or prevent their repetition; or that higher authority, in face of numerous allegations, manifests indifference by refusing any adequate investiga-

---

[45] Expulsion may also raise issues under Article 3 of the ECHR if there is a "real risk" of being exposed to a treatment contrary to this provision in the receiving State; *cf.*, *Vilvarajah and Others* v. *United Kingdom*, 215 Eur. Ct. HR (Series A) at 36, ¶¶ 107-108 (judgment of 30 October 1991).

[46] GFA, *supra*, Annex 6, Article VIII, ¶ 2 (a); Rules of Procedure of the Human Rights Ombudsperson of Bosnia and Herzegovina, Rule 21 (c).

[47] *Cf.* No. 8462/79, Dec. 8.7.80, D.R. 20 at 184; and Nos. 9911/82 & 9945/82, Dec. 15.3.84, D.R. 36, at 200. As regards the evidence, the European Court accepted that such proof "may follow from the coexistence of sufficiently strong, clear and concordant inferences or os similar unrebutted presumptions of fact. In this context the conduct of the Parties when evidence is being obtained has to be taken into account". *Ireland* v. *United Kingdom*, *supra*, at 64, ¶ 161.

tion of their truth or falsity, or that in judicial proceedings, a fair hearing of such complaints is denied[48].

This concept was further examined in the inter-state case of *Ireland* v. *the United Kingdom*, where the Court defined it as:

A practice incompatible with the Convention consists of an accumulation of identical of analogous breaches which are sufficiently numerous and interconnected to amount not merely to isolated incidents or exceptions but to a pattern or system, whereas such acts are tolerated in the sense that the superiors of those immediately responsible, although aware of such acts; a practice does not of itself constitute a violation separate from such breaches.

It is inconceivable that the higher authorities of a State should be, or at least should be entitled to be, unaware of the existence of such a practice. Furthermore, under the Convention those authorities are strictly liable for the conduct of their subordinates and cannot shelter behind their inability to ensure that it is respected[49].

Having regard to the specific ethnic aspects of the situation in BiH, these principles might provide guidance for the compatibility of certain legislation adopted and its application in practice. Although already declared null and void following the issuance of a Special Report by the Human Rights Ombudsperson[50], it would not have been totally inconceivable that the Decision of 28 November 1996, taken by the Brcko municipal authorities prohibiting patients from the Federation to be admitted to and medically treated in the Brcko General Hospital, would not only have been found discriminatory but also contrary to Article 3 of the ECHR, had this situation been examined by the European Court and/or Commission.

Another issue which sometimes surfaces in BiH is the treatment allegedly inflicted by police officers on detained persons. In this respect it is noteworthy to briefly mention the findings in the cases of *Tomasi* v. *France* and *Hurtado* v. *Switzerland*. In *Tomasi*, a person suspected of having killed a police officer was taken in detention, after which he alleged ill-treatment by police officers during his detention. He had already complained of this when he appeared before the investigating judge. When he was released, he was examined by four doctors. The doctors' certificates contained precise and concurring medical observations and indications of

---

[48] *The Greek case*, (inter-state application), Comm. Report 5.11.69, Yearbook 12, at 195-196.

[49] *Ireland* v. *United Kingdom*, *supra*, at 64, ¶ 159.

[50] Human Rights Ombudsperson for Bosnia and Herzegovina, *Special Report of 12 December 1996* (addressed to the Municipality and Mayor of Brcko).

dates for the occurrence of the injuries which corresponded to the period he had spent in custody. The Government was unable to explain the cause of his injuries, but maintained that they had not resulted from ill-treatment by police officers. The European Court rejected the Government's arguments. It concluded that the number and intensity of the blows inflected were sufficiently serious to render such treatment inhuman and degrading. The Court did not find it necessary to determine who had in fact caused the injuries. That they occurred during Mr Tomasi's detention apparently was sufficient to conclude that the State bore responsibility for Mr Tomasi's ill-treatment[51].

This finding seems to indicate that a State bears responsibility for ill-treatment of detainees, regardless of the question of who has inflicted such treatment[52], which, in turn, implies that public authorities are under an obligation to secure adequate mechanisms aimed at a effective prevention of the risk of ill-treatment of detainees. Such mechanisms could, for instance, include measures aimed at the prevention of detainees being assaulted by other detainees and adequate and fair disciplinary or other proceedings for staff of detention centres who are accused of ill-treatment. That such measures would imply the use of medical experts, whose independence and impartiality should be guaranteed, for the assessment of injuries, goes without saying.

The case of Mr Hurtado concerned the consequences of his violent arrest and his subsequent treatment in detention. In the course of his arrest, Mr. Hurtado was injured and his clothes were soiled. The Commission's Report found that no excessive or disproportionate force had been use by the police in his arrest, but that the authorities' failure to provide Mr Hurtado with clean clothes to replace those soiled as a result of his violent arrest to be humiliating and debasing and, thus, degrading within the meaning of Article 3 of the ECHR[53].

As a last subject to be considered under this provision as regards the particular situation in BiH, mention should be made of the repeated reports from various sources of ethnically motivated harassment by local police officers, other officials or private individuals and the subsequent failure of the police or the superiors of the officers involved to act upon knowledge of such harassment[54]. Harassment of this sort regularly results in either

---

[51] *Tomasi v. France*, 241-A Eur. Ct. HR (Series A) at 40, ¶¶ 107-116 (judgment of 27 August 1992).

[52] *See also, Ribitsch v. Austria*, 336 Eur. Ct. HR (Series A) (judgment of 4 December 1995).

[53] *Hurtado v. Switzerland*, Comm. Report 8.7.93, 280-A Eur. Ct. HR (Series A) at 9. In the subsequent proceedings before the European Court, this case was struck out by the Court following a friendly settlement reached between the parties.

[54] Such as, *inter alia*, the two reports issued by the Federation Ombudsmen on the State of Human Rights in the Federation of Bosnia and Herzegovina, the European Action

forcible evictions or "voluntary" departures of members of a given ethnic minority from their homes. Reports of such incidents indicate they occur throughout the territory of BiH. It cannot be excluded that the failure of the authorities to take appropriate steps to counter such practices may raise serious issues under Article 3 of the ECHR, particularly if incidents may be directly linked to public authorities. In cases where such practices have apparently included lethal violence the possibility of a violation of ECHR Article 2, encompassing the right to life, also arises[55].

B. Article 5 of the Convention; Liberty and Security of the Person

This provision of the Convention reads:

1.   Everyone has the right to liberty and security of person. No one shall be deprived of his liberty save in the following cases and in accordance with a procedure prescribed by law:

a.   the lawful detention of a person after conviction by a competent court;

b.   the lawful arrest or detention of a person for non-compliance with the lawful order of a court or in order to secure the fulfilment of any obligation prescribed by law;

c.   the lawful arrest or detention of a person effected for the purpose of bringing him before the competent legal authority on reasonable suspicion of having committed an offence or when it is reasonably considered necessary to prevent his committing an offence or fleeing after having done so;

d.   the detention of a minor by lawful order for the purpose of educational supervision or his lawful detention for the purpose of bringing him before the competent legal authority;

e.   the lawful detention of persons for the prevention of the spreading of infectious diseases, of persons of unsound mind, alcoholics or drug addicts or vagrants;

f.   the lawful arrest or detention of a person to prevent his effecting an unauthorised entry into the country or of a person against whom action is being taken with a view to deportation or extradition.

Council's Dayton Implementation Reviews, press releases of the Oslobodenje News Agency Sarajevo, and Reports issued by Human Rights Watch/Helsinki.

[55] *Cf.* No. 9348/81, Dec. 28.2.83, D.R. 32, at 190; and No. 16734/90, Dec. 2.9.91, D.R. 72, at 239.

2.   Everyone who is arrested shall be informed promptly, in a language which he understands, of the reasons for his arrest and of any charge against him.

3.   Everyone arrested or detained in accordance with the provisions of paragraph 1 (c) of this Article shall be brought promptly before a judge or other officer authorised by law to exercise judicial power and shall be entitled to trial within a reasonable time or to release pending trial. Release may be conditioned by guarantees to appear for trial.

4.   Everyone who is deprived of his liberty by arrest or detention shall be entitled to take proceedings by which the lawfulness of his detention shall be decided speedily by a court and his release ordered if the detention is not lawful.

5.   Everyone who has been the victim of arrest or detention in contravention of the provisions of this Article shall have an enforceable right to compensation.

Article 5 of the ECHR seeks to protect individuals from arbitrary arrest or detention, i.e. the protection of physical liberty in the classical sense. Its provisions apply to all within the jurisdiction of a State regardless of status and the list of permitted exceptions is exhaustive[56]. That is to say, where a person is deprived of his or her liberty on a ground not included in Article 5 paragraph 1, such a deprivation of liberty must be considered as contrary to this provision[57]. The question whether a person is deprived of his or her liberty must be answered on the basis of his or her concrete situation, whereas the difference between deprivation of and restriction upon liberty is merely one of degree or intensity, and not one of nature or substance[58].

The phrase "liberty and security of person" does not entail two different concepts, but is to be read as a whole[59]. As is apparent from the wording of Article 5, it does not only cover detention in a criminal context but also civil detention, such as compulsory admission to a mental hospital or the compulsory placement of a minor in a juvenile institution.

Article 5 of the ECHR contains certain guarantees intended to prevent States from enforcing, without due consideration, judgments or decisions which are not consistent with democratic principles, including respect for "the rule of law". It stipulates that a deprivation of liberty must be "lawful" and in accordance with "a procedure prescribed by law" and not merely that it be ordered by a "competent court". These phrases refer essentially

---

[56] *Cf. Engel and Others* v. *the Netherlands*, 22 Eur. Ct. HR (Series A) at 25, ¶¶ 57-59 (judgment of 8 June 1976).

[57] *Cf. Winterwerp* v. *the Netherlands*, 33 Eur. Ct. HR (Series A) at 16, ¶ 37 (judgment of 24 October 1979); and *Bouamar* v. *Belgium*, 129 Eur. Ct. HR (Series A) at 19, ¶ 43 (judgment of 29 February 1988).

[58] *Cf.* No. 12541/86, Dec. 27.5.91, D.R. 70, at 103.

[59] *Cf.* No. 10871/84, Dec. 10.7.86, D.R. 48, at 154.

back to domestic law, which is in the first place to be interpreted and applied by domestic courts but which must also be compatible with the Convention[60]. This means that domestic law itself must be in conformity with the ECHR, including the general principles expressed or implied therein, such as a fair and proper procedure, free from arbitrariness before an appropriate authority[61].

Paragraphs 2 – 4 of Article 5 of the ECHR contain procedural guarantees for persons who have been deprived of their liberty. Under Article 5 paragraph 2 it is required that such a person be promptly informed why he or she is detained, the term "promptly" implying at the moment of apprehension or immediately thereafter. This requirement also applies to all persons deprived of their liberty, including mentally ill persons forcibly committed to a mental hospital[62].

In particular, for a person arrested on suspicion of having committed a crime, the purpose of Article 5 paragraph 2 is to enable that person to challenge the reasonableness of the suspicion against him or her. It is not required that this information be given in a particular form or that the arrested person is provided with a complete case-file[63]. In the case of an arrest for security check purposes and not related to the existence of particular suspicions, information provided promptly as to the legal basis and the nature of the control is sufficient[64].

Paragraph 3 of Article 5 prescribes that anyone arrested on suspicion of having committed an offence be promptly brought before a judicial officer, who must be independent of the parties and who is competent to decide whether or not the detention is to be prolonged[65]. "Promptly" in this context does not mean "immediately" as under Article 5 paragraph 2, but according to the case-law under Article 5 paragraph 3, means that an arrested person must be brought before a judicial officer within a period of maximum four days[66]. By 1968, the European Court had already established the principle that an accused person in detention is entitled to have his case given priority and conducted with particular expedition. An accused is to be presumed innocent throughout the criminal proceedings against him or her and it is this principle which distinguishes the time requirements for matters relating to detention under Article 5 of the ECHR

---

[60] *Cf. Bozano* v. *France*, 111 Eur. Ct. HR (Series A) at 54, ¶¶ 54, 58 (judgment of 18 December 1986); and No. 17441/90, Dec. 4.9.92, D.R. 73, at 201.

[61] *Winterwerp* v. *the Netherlands*, *supra*, at 19, ¶ 45.

[62] *Cf. Van der Leer* v. *the Netherlands*, 170-A Eur. Ct. HR (Series A) at 13, ¶¶ 27-28 (judgment of 21 February 1990).

[63] *Cf.* No. 8098/77, Dec. 13.12.78, D.R. 16, at 111; No. 8828/79, Dec. 5.10.82, D.R. 30, at 93; and No. 9614/81, Dec. 12.10.83, D.R. 34, at 119.

[64] *Cf. McVeigh, O'Neill and Evans* v. *United Kingdom*, Comm. Report 18.3.81, D.R. 25, at 15; and No. 11539/85, Dec. 12.7.86, D.R. 48, at 237.

[65] *Cf. Brincat* v. *Italy*, 249-A Eur. Ct. HR (Series A) at 11, ¶¶ 20-21 (judgment of 26 November 1992).

[66] *Cf.* No. 19139/91, Dec. 30.3.92, (unpublished).

and for matters relating to the actual criminal procedure under Article 6 of the ECHR[67].

The right of a State to prolong pre-trial detention is not unlimited. As regards the question whether a period of pre-trial detention is "reasonable", the European Court has held that continued detention can be justified in a given case only if there are specific indications of a genuine requirement of public interest which, notwithstanding the presumption of innocence, outweighs the rule of respect for individual liberty. The persistence of reasonable suspicion that the person arrested has committed an offence is a condition *sine qua non* for the lawfulness of the continued detention, but after a certain lapse of time it no longer suffices unless there are relevant and sufficient grounds which continue to justify detention[68].

Regardless of the question whether a person's deprivation of liberty is in conformity with Article 5 paragraph 1 of the ECHR, the person concerned has the right under Article 5 paragraph 4 to take proceedings before a court in order to obtain a judicial determination of the lawfulness of his or her deprivation of liberty. This means that, in this respect, an examination under Article 13 (right to an effective remedy) is considered not necessary, Article 5 paragraph 4 being the *lex specialis*[69]. Such a judicial determination must be made speedily, in the course of fair proceedings[70], and must take place before a court competent to order a person's release where the deprivation of liberty is found to be unlawful[71].

The form and frequency of such proceedings depend on the grounds of detention. Where it concerns detention following a conviction, the required judicial control is considered to be incorporated in the original decision of the trial court[72]. Where it concerns forcible admission to a mental hospital, the form and frequency may be different from a case where it concerns pre-trial detention[73].

---

[67] *Wemhoff* v. *Germany*, 7 Eur. Ct. HR (Series A) at 22, ¶ 5, 27, ¶ 20 (judgment of 27 June 1968). The principle that detained persons are further entitled to special diligence has also been accepted as regards the length of proceedings under Article 6; *see Tomasi* v. *France*, *supra*, at 35, ¶ 84.

[68] *Cf. Scott* v. *Spain*, Eur. Ct. HR (judgment of 18 December 1996), to be published in *Reports* 1996, ¶ 74; *Yağci & Sargin* v. *Turkey*, 319-A Eur. Ct. HR (Series A) at 18, ¶ 50 (judgment of 8 June 1995); *and Van der Tang* v. *Spain*, 321 Eur. Ct. HR (Series A) at 17, ¶ 55 (judgment of 13 July 1995).

[69] *Cf.* No. 11256/84, Dec. 5.9.88, D.R. 57, at 47.

[70] *Cf. Winterwerp* v. *the Netherlands*, *supra*, at 24, ¶ 60; *see also* No. 15006/89, Dec. 10.12.90, D.R. 6,7 at 290.

[71] *Cf. Weeks* v. *United Kingdom*, Comm. Report 7.12.84, ¶¶ 101-105, 114 Eur. Ct. HR (Series A) at 49-50.

[72] *Cf. Iribarne Pérez* v. *Spain*, 325-C Eur. Ct. HR (Series A) (judgment of 24 October 1995); and No. 23888/94, Dec. 18.10.95, D.R. 83, at 48.

[73] *Cf. Toth* v. *Austria*, 224 Eur. Ct. HR (Series A) at 22-24, ¶¶ 80-87 (judgment of 12 December 1991); *Herczegfalvy* v. *Austria*, 244 Eur. Ct. HR (Series A) at 24-25, ¶¶ 74-78 (judgment of 24 September 1992); and *Wynne* v. *United Kingdom*, 294-A Eur. Ct. HR (Series A) (judgment of 18 July 1994).

Finally, Article 5 paragraph 5 of the ECHR guarantees an enforceable right to compensation for victims of unlawful detention under Article 5. An established breach of one of the provisions of Article 5 paragraphs 1-4 is thus required. Questions related to the availability of such compensation at the domestic level and the procedure to claim it were examined by the European Court in, for instance, the case of *Ciulla* v. *Italy*[74].

One important field of detention-related issues in BiH, which merits attention under this provision of the ECHR is that of the still detained or presumably detained prisoners of war and of persons detained on ethnical grounds for exchange purposes. One such case is currently pending before the Human Rights Chamber for Bosnia and Herzegovina[75]. The case concerns a catholic priest and his parents, who were deprived of their liberty prior to the entry into force of the GFA[76], but were offered as exchange for prisoners of war after the entry into force.

It may be clear from the wording of Article 5 paragraph 1 of the ECHR that detention for exchange purposes is not included in the exhaustive list contained in this provision. It is true that Article 5 may be derogated from in time of war or other public emergency. However, according to Article 15 of the ECHR, Contracting States are obliged to inform the Secretary General of any derogating measures and the reasons therefor[77]. It could have been envisaged to open a similar possibility for the Contracting Parties to Annex 6 to the GFA as a transitional arrangement for the duration of the state of imminent war danger. On the other hand, such a possibility would have seriously limited the practical effects of the applicability of the ECHR in BiH. To the present author's knowledge, there is no possibility foreseen for the Contracting Parties to Annex 6 to derogate from their obligations under the ECHR and consequently its provisions apply in full.

In these circumstances, the Contracting Parties may have a difficult task in establishing that prisoners of war and persons detained on ethnical grounds, who are currently still detained for exchange purposes, are so in conformity with Article 5 of the Convention. This would also include situations where it is established that persons have been apprehended by State authorities but who can no longer be traced[78]. The immediate release

---

[74] 148 Eur. Ct. HR (Series A) (judgment of 22 February 1989). *See* Article 5, ¶ 5; *Brogan & Others* v. *United Kingdom*, 145-B Eur Court HR (Series A) at 35, ¶¶ 66-67 (judgment of 29 November 1988); *Thynne, Wilson & Gunnell* v. *United Kingdom*, 190-A Eur. Ct. HR (Series A) at 81, ¶ 82 (judgment of 25 October 1990).

[75] Case No. CH/96/1, which is the same as Case No. 14/96, *Matanovi et al* v. *the Republika Srpska*, Human Rights Ombudsperson, Report 5.6.96.

[76] This means that their arrest and detention prior to this date cannot, *ratione temporis*, be examined by the Human Rights Commission under Annex 6 of the GFA and thus under Article 5 of the ECHR; *see*, Human Rights Chamber, Case No. CH/96/1, Dec. 13.9.96.

[77] On such measures taken by the United Kingdom; *Brannigan & McBride* v. *United Kingdom*, 258-B Eur. Ct. HR (Series A) at 48-57, ¶¶ 39-74 (judgment of 26 May 1993).

[78] *Cf. Cyprus* v. *Turkey*, Comm. Report 4.10.83, D.R. 72, at 5.

of such prisoners, whether or not through an exchange, would not automatically mean that they could no longer claim to be victims of a violation
of Article 5. Insofar as it would have been established by a competent body
that their detention had been contrary to the requirements of Article 5
paragraphs 1-4, only the award of compensation under Article 5 paragraph
5 of the ECHR could deprive them of the status of "victim".

C. Article 6 of the ECHR: Procedural Guarantees

Article 6 is one of the most invoked provisions of the Convention in the
Strasbourg proceedings, which is hardly surprising as it contains a set of
separate yet closely interrelated minimum requirements for "fair" proceedings. The scope of Article 6 paragraph 1 is, however, limited to those
procedures which entail a "determination of civil rights and obligations or
of any criminal charge" in the autonomous meaning given to these terms by
the Convention organs. Therefore, a qualification under domestic law of
proceedings as "civil", "criminal" or "administrative" does not automatically imply that such proceedings obtain a similar qualification in the
proceedings in Strasbourg[79]. Article 6 paragraphs 2 and 3 only concern the
procedural position of persons who have been "charged with a criminal
offence".

Article 6 of the ECHR provides:

1.   In the determination of his civil rights and obligations or of any
criminal charge against him, everyone is entitled to a fair and public
hearing within a reasonable time by an independent and impartial tribunal established by law. Judgment shall be pronounced publicly but the
press and public may be excluded from all or part of the trial in the interest of morals, public order or national security in a democratic society, where the interests of juveniles or the protection of the private life
of the parties so require, or to the extent strictly necessary in the opinion
of the court in special circumstances where publicity would prejudice
the interests of justice.

2.   Everyone charged with a criminal offence shall be presumed innocent until proved guilty according to law.

3.   Everyone charged with a criminal offence has the following minimum rights:

---

[79] *Cf.* No. 15058/89, Dec. 10.4.91, D.R. 69, at 306; and No. 15921/89, Dec. 1.7.91, D.R.
71, at 236.

a.   to be informed promptly, in a language which he under-stands and in detail, of the nature and cause of the accusation against him;

b.   to have adequate time and facilities for the preparation of his defence;

c.   to defend himself in person or through legal assistance of his own choosing or, if he has not sufficient means to pay for legal assistance, to be given it free when the interests of justice so re-quire;

d.   to examine or have examined witnesses against him and to obtain the attendance and examination of witnesses on his behalf under the same conditions as witnesses against him;

e.   to have the free assistance of an interpreter if he cannot understand or speak the language used in court.

For the sake of brevity, this chapter limits itself to indicating the most relevant concepts under this provision. Broadly speaking, these concepts include: access to a court; fair hearing (including equality of arms); proce-dure within a reasonable time; independent and impartial tribunal; public proceedings[80]. As regards rights protected by paragraph 3 of Article 6, the Convention organs have stated that the requirements of this paragraph are specific aspects of the right to a fair trial within the meaning of Article 6 paragraph 1 of the ECHR[81].

As an examination of the implications of the various requirements of Article 6 of the ECHR on those proceedings in Bosnia and Herzegovina, which would entail a "determination of civil rights and obligations or of any criminal charge" under the case-law relating to Article 6, can only be made on a case-to-case basis, it is not possible even to begin such an exer-cise in this chapter.

That, however, problems might exist in BiH under this provision be-comes apparent when considering a specific and relatively important category of cases which have been referred by the Human Rights Ombuds-person for Bosnia and Herzegovina to the Human Rights Chamber. This category of cases concerns the problems encountered by the purchasers of apartments sold to them by the former Yugoslav National Army; they are referred to as the "JNA apartment cases". According to the facts submitted by the complainants, they are precluded by law from challenging the deci-

---

[80] For a concise overview of the different elements of Article 6, *see*, D. Gomien, *Short Guide to the European Convention on Human Rights*, (1991), 34-51.

[81] *Cf. Poitrimol* v. *France*, 27-A Eur. Ct. HR (Series A) at 13, ¶ 29 (judgment of 23 No-vember 1993*); Lala* v. *the Netherlands*, 297-A Eur. Ct. HR (Series A) at 12, ¶ 26 (judgment of 22 September 1994); No. 20341/92, Dec. 6.1.93, D.R. 74, at 241; and 25062/94, Dec. 18.10.95, D.R. 83, at 77.

sion to nullify retroactively their purchase contracts with the Yugoslav National Army and – in certain cases – the decision to suspend judicial proceedings instituted in relation to these purchase contracts[82]. These problems touch upon two important elements of Article 6 paragraph 1 of the ECHR, namely the right of access to court and the right to a trial within a reasonable time. As at 31 December 1996, 21 "JNA apartment" cases have been referred to the Human Rights Chamber[83].

As regards the reasonable time requirement, the Convention organs have determined that the reasonableness of the length of proceedings must be assessed in the light of the circumstances of each case and having regard in particular to the following criteria: the complexity of the case, the conduct of the applicant and that of the competent authorities[84]. Persons held in detention are further entitled to special diligence[85]. Insofar as any delays would occur due to a structural backlog of cases, it has been held consistently that Article 6 paragraph 1 of the ECHR imposes on States the duty to organise their judicial systems in such a way that their courts can meet each of its requirements[86].

A further element to be mentioned in connection with Article 6 of the Convention, is the requirement under paragraph 3 (c) that anyone charged with a criminal offence is entitled to free legal aid. This is a very important requirement for a person facing criminal charges and possibly the imposition of a sentence. It includes two elements, namely the right of access to a lawyer and, if need be, to be appointed one free of charge.

As regards access to a lawyer in criminal proceedings, the European Court has stated that Article 6 of the ECHR is already applicable at the stage of the preliminary investigation into an offence by the police, as national laws may attach consequences to the attitude of an accused at the initial stages of police interrogation which are decisive for the prospects of the defence in any subsequent criminal proceedings. In such a situation, Article 6 requires that the accused be allowed to be assisted by a lawyer already at the initial stage of police interrogation. In the case of *John Murray* v. *the United Kingdom,* the Court held that to deny consultation with a lawyer, when adverse inferences may be drawn from one's silence during police interrogation, constitutes a violation of Article 6 of the

---

[82] *Cf.* Human Rights Ombudsperson, No. 6/96, Dec. 15.7.96; No. 27/96, Dec. 15.7.96; No. 18/96, Dec. 23.7.96; No. 72/96, Dec. 26.7.96; and No. 3/96, Dec. 27.9.96.

[83] Human Rights Ombudsperson for Bosnia and Herzegovina, Decisions and Reports issued through 31 December 1996.

[84] *Cf. Vernillo* v. *France*, 198 Eur. Ct. HR (Series A) at 18, ¶ 30 (judgment of 20 February 1991); *Kemmache* v. *France*, 218 Eur. Ct. HR (Series A) at 27, ¶ 60 (judgment of 27 November 1991); and *Pizzetti* v. *Italy*, 257-C Eur. Ct. HR (Series A) at 36, ¶ 16 (judgment of 26 February 1993).

[85] *Cf. Tomasi* v. *France, supra*, at 35, ¶ 84.

[86] *Cf. Tusa* v. *Italy*, 231-D Eur. Ct. HR (Series A) at 41, ¶ 17 (judgment of 27 February 1992).

ECHR. In this judgment the Court did not determine whether the lack of presence of a lawyer during police questioning (2 days) also constituted such a violation[87].

This principle implies that a person who is arrested and detained on suspicion of having committed an offence must be provided with adequate facilities to contact a lawyer upon his or her arrest. This principle further implies that contacts between a lawyer and an accused client are privileged, they must be enabled to communicate with each other without any supervision by the authorities of the prison or remand centre[88].

As regards the appointment of a legal aid lawyer, the European Court held in the case of *Croissant* v. *Germany*:

> It is true that Article 6 § 3 (c) entitles "everyone charged with a criminal offence" to be defended by counsel of his own choosing (see the Pakelli v. Germany judgment of 25 april 1983, Series A no. 64 , p. 15, § 31). Nevertheless, and notwithstanding the importance of a relationship between lawyer and client, this right cannot be considered to be absolute. It is necessarily subject to certain limitations where free legal aid is concerned and also where, as in the present case, it is for the courts to decide whether the interests of justice require that the accused by defended by counsel appointed by them. When appointing defence counsel the national courts must certainly have regard to the defendant's wishes ... . However, they can override those wishes when there are relevant and sufficient grounds for holding that this is necessary[89].

So far, the Convention organs have not determined the general question whether or not an accused may be obliged, after his or her conviction, to reimburse the costs of an appointed legal aid lawyer if he or she has the means to do so. In *Croissant* v. *Germany* both organs limited themselves to the facts of the case[90].

A State's obligation to provide free legal aid has also been recognised in cases concerning civil litigation, although according to the case-law on this point there is no right to free legal aid for every dispute relating to a "civil right" within the meaning of Article 6 paragraph. 1 of the ECHR[91].

---

[87] *John Murray* v. *United Kingdom*, Eur. Ct. HR, *Reports* 1996, at 54-55, ¶¶ 62-66 (judgment of 8 February 1996).

[88] *Cf. S.* v. *Switzerland*, 220 Eur. Ct. HR (Series A) at 15-15, ¶ 48 (judgment of 28 November 1991); *see also Campbell & Fell*, 80 Eur. Ct. HR (Series A) (judgment of 28 June 1984); *and Campbell* v. *United Kingdom*, 223 Eur. Ct. HR (Series A) (judgment of 25 March 1992).

[89] 237-B Eur. Ct. HR (Series A), at 32-33, ¶ 29 (judgment of 25 September 1992).

[90] *Id.* at 34-35, ¶¶ 33-38; and Comm. Report 7.3.91, at 41-42, ¶¶ 41-45.

[91] *Cf. Airey* v. *Ireland*, 32 Eur. Ct. HR (Series A) at 14-16, ¶¶ 26-28 (judgment of 9 October 1979); No. 11564/85, Dec. 4.12.85, D.R. 45, at 291; No. 10871/84, Dec. 10.7.86, D.R. 48, at 154; and No. 10594/83, Dec. 14.7.87, D.R. 52, at 158.

Both the European Commission and the Court have on numerous occasions indicated the important place which the right to a fair trial holds in a democratic society. The right of effective access to legal aid forms a part of this right. However, to take proceedings or to stand trial assisted by a lawyer could entail high costs. Given the difficult economic situation in Bosnia and Herzegovina and the vulnerability of certain groups in its society, such as detainees and members of ethnic minorities, the development of an adequate legal aid system, free of charge for those who cannot afford the services of a lawyer, is of crucial importance; not only for the persons concerned, but also for the development of human rights in Bosnia and Herzegovina by enabling those concerned to adequately argue their case or to defend themselves before the judicial authorities. It is inevitable that the difficult economic situation will affect the possibilities for the authorities of Bosnia and Herzegovina to comply with its obligations under Article 6 of the ECHR by developing and maintaining a legal aid system. Yet, given the importance of a fair trial, it is a crucial element in any legal system based on respect for human rights.

D. Article 8 of the ECHR: Right to Respect for Private and Family Life, Correspondence and Home

This provision of the ECHR reads:

1.   Everyone has the right to respect for his private and family life, his home and his correspondence.

2.   There shall be no interference by a public authority with the exercise of this right except such as is in accordance with the law and is necessary in a democratic society in the interests of national security, public safety or the economic well-being of the country, for the prevention of disorder or crime, for the protection of health or morals, or for the protection of the rights and freedoms of others.

As is clear from the text, Article 8 of the ECHR contains in principle a "negative obligation" for a State, namely to refrain from interfering unless there are justified grounds for so doing. However, the existence of "positive obligations" for States has been long recognised by the Strasbourg case-law[92].

Given the fact that, at the time of writing, it is still impossible to communicate, either by regular telephone or by mail, between the two Entities,

---

[92] *Cf. Airey* v. *Ireland, supra*, at 17, ¶ 32; *Keegan* v. *Ireland*, 290 Eur. Ct. HR (Series A) at 19, ¶ 49 (judgment of 26 May 1994); and *Kroon & Others* v. *the Netherlands, supra*, at 57, ¶ 36.

the question could arise whether the BiH authorities are under a "positive obligation" to secure the right to respect for correspondence within the meaning of Article 8 of the Convention, which includes communication by telephone[93], both in itself and in conjunction with Article 10 (right to receive and impart information)[94]. The case-law indicates that in determining whether or not such a positive obligation exists, regard must be had to the fair balance that has to be struck between the general interest and the interests of the individual[95].

As regards the current total absence of communication possibilities by regular mail and telephone between the Entities, which do not appear to have any technical causes as there are no major problems in communicating via these means with the rest of the world from either Entity, the authorities should define what "the general interest" is in their apparently implicit choice not to take the necessary steps to organise inter-Entity communication by mail and telephone. Following the authorities' definition and statement of the "general interest" in this field, it would be then for the authorities and, subsequently, for the competent human rights protection mechanisms to verify whether, in this implicit choice not to take necessary steps to organise inter-Entity communication channels by regular mail and telephone, a careful balance was struck between that general interest and the interests of the individuals.

Given the situation of minority groups in BiH, it is worth while having a closer look at the case-law under this provision as regards the rights of minorities, as there are links between minority rights and Article 8 of the ECHR. Apart from the mention of the word "minority" in Article 14 (prohibition of discrimination), the ECHR does not contain any direct reference to the position of minorities, or afford a specific protection of their fundamental rights and freedoms. The reason for this lack of a specific provision lies, most probably, in the idea that an effective protection of the human rights of individuals must also include an effective protection of fundamental rights and freedoms of minorities, regardless of the question whether it would be a linguistic, religious, ethnic or another kind of minority.

---

[93] Cf. *Kruslin & Huvig* v. *France*, 176-A Eur. Ct. HR (Series A) at 20, ¶ 26 and 176-B Eur. Ct. HR (Series A) at 52, ¶ 25 (judgments of 24 April 1990).

[94] According to the case-law, Article 8 is the *lex specialis* of Article 10 of the ECHR if it concerns communication of information or ideas. *Cf.* No. 23413/94, Dec. 28.11.95, D.R. 83, at 31.

[95] Cf. *B.* v. *France*, 232-C Eur. Ct. HR (Series A) at 47, ¶ 44 (judgment of 25 March 1992).

In 1973, a Council of Europe Committee of Experts on Minorities concluded that, from a legal point of view, there was no special need to made the rights of minorities the subject of a further Protocol to the ECHR. They also concluded that there was no major legal obstacle for the adoption of such a Protocol if it were considered advisable for other reasons. The issue of minority rights emerged again in 1990, when the Council of Europe Parliamentary Assembly recommended the Committee of Ministers to draw up a Protocol or separate Convention on the rights of national minorities. This initiative resulted in the Framework Convention for the Protection of National Minorities, which was opened for signature by the Council of Europe's Member States on 1 February 1995. Its implementation is to be done through national legislation and appropriate governmental policies. The implementation is to be monitored by the Committee on Ministers. To date 8 States have ratified this Convention[96] and 27 States have signed it, but not yet ratified. Six Member States of the Council of Europe have, so far, not signed this Convention[97]. It will enter into force as soon as 12 Contracting States have ratified it.

Sometimes, issues concerning members of minority groups are raised under Article 8 of the Convention. For instance in 1977, in a case brought by 48 Kalderas gypsies, the European Commission stated that a refusal to deliver a birth certificate can amount to infringement of the right to respect for family life[98]. In 1983, in a case brought by two Norwegian Lapps, the European Commission accepted that, under Article 8 of the Convention, a minority group is in principle entitled to claim respect for the particular life-style it may lead as being "private life", family life" or "home"[99]. However, in a later case, it held that members of a particular minority can only complain of measures affecting themselves, but not of measures affecting other members of the same minority[100].

Although the Commission restated its previous case-law that a traditional lifestyle of a minority may attract the guarantees of Article 8 as relating to the right to respect for "private life", "family life" and "home" in a case concerning caravan sites for gypsies, the Court did not follow that line, but limited the issue to interference with the right to respect for "home" without further examining the specific position of mobile home dwellers as a minority group[101].

A number of issues in relation to minorities could arise under Article 8 of the ECHR, such as, for instance, the right to respect for a forename and

---

[96] Cyprus, Estonia, Hungary, Moldova, Romania, San Marino, Slovakia and Spain.
[97] Andorra, Belgium, Bulgaria, France, Greece, and Turkey.
[98] No. 7823/77-7824/77, Dec. 6.7.77, D.R. 11, at 221.
[99] Nos. 9278/81 & 9415/81, Dec. 3.10.83, D.R. 35, at 30
[100] No. 12740/87, Dec. 7.8.88 (unpublished).
[101] *Buckley* v. *United Kingdom*, Eur. Ct. HR, (judgment of 25 September 1996), to be published in *Reports* 1996.

a family name[102], the right to education with due respect for differences in religious and philosophical convictions[103], the right to respect for sexual identity and orientation[104], the right to respect for a traditional life-style, right to be protected against defamatory remarks[105], right to respect for religious convictions in decisions awarding parental rights following a divorce[106], and the right not to be forcibly expelled from one's home and relocated[107].

This last right is directly linked to the right to respect for the "home", which touches upon one of the most pressing current problems in BiH. The war in Bosnia resulted not only in the destruction of many housing facilities, but also in an enormous group of displaced persons wishing either to return to their original homes or to build up a new life in their current place of residence. Families or persons who have remained in their homes throughout the war and who found themselves belonging to an ethnic minority after the cessation of the hostilities have often been evicted from their home even after the entry into force of the GFA by displaced persons belonging to the local ethnic majority. According to various reports, the police, in most cases, failed to act on complaints by members of an ethnic minority of being harassed by members of the local ethnic majority or of having been forcibly evicted from their home by refugees belonging to the ethnic majority[108]. In some cases it has even been alleged that the police or

---

[102] *Cf. Burghartz* v. *Switzerland*, 280-B Eur. Ct. HR (Series A) at 27-28, ¶¶ 22-24 (judgment of 22 February 1994); *Stjerna* v. *Finland*, 299-B Eur. Ct. HR (Series A) at 60, ¶ 37 (judgment of 25 November 1994); and *Guillot* v. *France* (judgment of 24 October 1996), to be published in *Reports* 1996.

[103] *Cf. Belgian Linguistic Case*, 6 Eur. Ct. HR (Series A) at 32-33, ¶¶ 6-7 (judgment of 23 July 1968); *Kjeldsen, Busk Madsen & Pedersen* v. *Denmark*, 23 Eur. Ct. HR (Series A) at 25-27, ¶¶ 51-53; *Efstratiou* v. *Greece*, Eur. Ct. HR (judgment of 18 December 1996), to be published in *Reports* 1996 at ¶ 25 May 1993, Series A no. 260-A, ¶¶ 26-28.

[104] *Cf. B.* v. *France*, 232-C Eur. Ct. HR (Series A) at 47-54, ¶¶ 43-63 (judgment of 25 March 1992); *Modinos* v. *Cyprus*, 259 Eur. Ct. HR (Series A) at 10-12, ¶¶ 16-26 (judgment of 22 April 1993); and *Laskey, Jaggard & Brown* v. *United Kingdom*, Eur. Ct. HR, (judgment of 19 February 1997), to be published in *Reports* 1997, ¶ 36, although in this last case, the Court appears to make the applicability of Article 8, as regards sexual activity, dependent on how persons conduct their sex life.

[105] No. 12664/67, Dec. 2.5.88 (unpublished). However, in a later case, No. 17439/90, Dec. 5.3.91 (unpublished), the Commission rejected a complaint lodged under Articles 9 (freedom of religion) and 14 of the ECHR related to a refusal to initiate criminal proceedings for blasphemy of the Islamic religion against the author and publisher of the book "Satanic verses".

[106] *Hoffman* v. *Austria*, 255-C Eur. Ct. HR (Series A) (judgment of 23 June 1993).

[107] *Cyprus* v. *Turkey* (inter-state cases), Comm. Report 10.7.76, ¶¶ 207-212; and Comm. Report 4.10.83, D.R. 72, at 5, ¶¶ 130-136.

[108] *See*, e.g., Institution of the Ombudsman of the Federation of Bosnia and Herzegovina, *Annual Report on the State of Human Rights*, Sarajevo – February 1996 *and Semi-annual Report on the state of Human Rights*, Sarajevo – July 1996; *Ongoing Ethnically-motivated Expulsions and Harassment in Bosnia*, 8 Human Rights Watch/ Helsinki Report No. 12(D) (August 1996), *No Justice No Peace*, 8 Human Rights Watch/ Helsinki Report No. 15 (D) at

other civil servants were involved in harassment of members of local ethnic minorities.

The case-law from Strasbourg as regards a situation where authorities themselves have been involved in harassment without any justification has become clear when the Court held, in the case *Akdivar and Others*, that the deliberate burning of homes and their contents by security forces whilst no justification for such acts was given by the authorities constituted a violation of both Article 8 of the ECHR and of Article 1 of Protocol No. 1 (right to respect for property)[109].

Another problem lies in the fact that a relatively large group of persons have "squatted" abandoned houses or apartments, because their own homes were destroyed or seriously damaged. A further problem is the application of the laws on abandoned accommodation in both Entities, on the basis of which refugees and displaced persons may obtain or already have obtained temporary permission to take up residence in accommodation declared "abandoned" pursuant to these laws, the so-called temporary right of use (*pravo privremenog koristenja*).

All these persons have problems related to their "home". On the basis of the case-law of the Convention organs, the concept of "home" is to be interpreted as the place where one has lawfully established oneself, either by having bought or rented it, with a view to take up permanent residence there, without having established, or the intention to establish, another residence elsewhere. It includes certain professional of business activities or premises. However, the extent to which business premises enjoy protection under Article 8 of the ECHR depends on the nature of the premises, the business activities exercised therein and the nature of the alleged interference[110].

On the basis of these principles, it appears that those persons who either have their home in private ownership, persons holding an occupancy right (*stanarsko pravo*) or persons holding a right to use accommodation (*pravo*

5-9, 12: (1996); *The Unindicted; Reaping the Rewards of "Ethnic Cleansing"*, 9 Human Rights Watch/ Helsinki Report No. 1 (D) at 52-55 (January 1997); Human Rights Ombudsperson, No. B11/96, Dec. 26.8.96 and Case No. 221/96, Dec. 12.12.96 (evictions in Bijeljina, Ugljevik and Lopare Municipalities); ICG Report 22 January 1997, at 1-2 (background situation in Brcko); EAC Dayton Implementation Review No. 13, 31 January 1997, at 3 under 1L (Mostar situation) and 1M (general situation displaced persons and refugees).

[109] *Akdivar & Others* v. *Turkey*, Eur. Ct. HR, (judgment of 16 September 1996), to be published in *Reports* 1996, ¶¶ 83-88.

[110] Cf. *Gillow* v. *United Kingdom*, 109 Eur. Ct. HR (Series A) at 19, ¶ 46 (judgment of 24 November 1986); *Niemitz* v. *Germany*, 251-B Eur. Ct. HR (Series A) at 34, ¶¶ 30-33 (judgment of 16 December 1992); *Buckley* v. *United Kingdom*, Eur. Ct. HR (judgment of 25 September 1996), to be published in *Reports* 1996, ¶ 54; *Loizidou* v. *Turkey*, Eur. Ct. HR, (judgment of 18 December 1996), to be published in *Reports* 1996, ¶ 66; No. 6202/73, Dec. 16.3.75, D.R. 1, at 66; No. 6148/73, Dec. 5.7.76, D.R. 9, at 19; No. 9327/81, Dec. 3.5.83, D.R. 32, at 187; No. 12474/86, Dec. 11.10.88, D.R. 58 at 94; and No. 23953/94, Dec. 6.9.95, D.R. 82, at 51.

koristenja stana) appear to have the strongest position under Article 8 as regards the right to respect for their "home", even if they have left these homes temporarily.

The persons holding a temporary right of use seem to be in a weaker position compared to the above categories and the question whether those who have squatted accommodation can claim any right under Article 8 of the ECHR in respect of their squatted homes is open to doubt to say the least. However, one can not exclude the possibility that, given the particular circumstances in BiH, also this last category would not remain wholly unprotected under Article 8 of the ECHR. In this respect, it should however be recalled that, according to the case-law of the European Commission, it is not contrary to Article 8 to evict persons from accommodation in which they themselves have no rights[111]. As regards harassment by private individuals in this context, the Commission has held that Article 8 of the ECHR may impose positive obligations on a State to protect the right to respect for home, which extend to providing protection against persistent and distressing harassment and deliberate persecution by another individual. However, the State is not obliged to provide a single, coherent remedy covering all heads of harassment[112].

It may be deduced from this decision that a State cannot ignore continuous harassment in the context of the right to respect for "home" and is obliged to offer adequate remedies when such situations occur. Insofar as it is established that the police and judicial authorities have turned a blind eye to such practices and the consequential effects thereof, it would be hardly surprising that this were to be found contrary to Article 8 of the ECHR.

Another obvious question which arises in this context, is whether the laws adopted by authorities of both Entities of Bosnia and Herzegovina on abandoned accommodation[113] are in conformity with this provision.

It is apparent that where a State, in the absence of the person who can claim a right to particular accommodation, allows or grants a right to another person to take up residence in that accommodation, there is an interference with the right to respect for "home" within the meaning of Article 8 of the ECHR. It is clear from the wording of Article 8 paragraph

---

[111] *Cf.* No. 11716/85, Dec. 14.5.86, D.R. 47, at 274.

[112] No. 20357/92, Dec. 7.3.94, D.R. 76, at 80.

[113] *See, e.g.*, The Law on Abandoned Apartments (*Zakon o napustenim stanovima* – concerns accommodation falling in the domain of so-called "social property" [*drustvena svojina*]) and The Law on Temporarily Abandoned Real Property Owned by Citizens during a State of War or Imminent War Danger (*Zakon o privremeno napustenim nekretninama u svojini gra ana za vrijeme ratnog stanja ili neposredne ratne opasnosti* – concerns privately owned accommodation) in the Federation of Bosnia and Herzegovina; and The Decree with Legal Force on the Settlement of Refugees and Other Persons on the Territory of the Republika Srpska (*Uredba o smjestaju izbjeglica i drugih lica na teritoriji Republike Srpske*) and the subsequent Law on the use of abandoned property (*Zakon o koristenju napustene imovine*) in the Republika Srpska. *See* Chapter 7 of this Volume.

2 of the ECHR and the pertaining case-law, that such an interference is not necessarily contrary to Article 8. There are however a number of conditions to be fulfilled. In the first place, the interference must be "in accordance with the law". This condition is a direct reference to the concept of legality, an important element of the "rule of law" principle.

In the *Sunday Times* case, the Court has ruled that the word "law" does not only refer to statutory rules, but also includes unwritten law and that the requirement implied by the expression "in accordance with the law" goes beyond mere conformity with legislation. The Court stated on this element:

> Firstly, the law must be adequately accessible; the citizen must be able to have an indication that is adequate in the circumstances of the legal rules applicable to a given case. Secondly, a norm cannot be regarded as a "law" unless it is formulated with sufficient precision to enable the citizen to regulate his conduct; he must be able – if need be with appropriate advice – to foresee to a degree that is reasonable in the circumstances, the consequences which a given action may entail[114].

This principle was formulated in connection with Article 10 of the ECHR (freedom of expression) which includes the same phrase in its second paragraph. This principle is considered as applying equally Article 8 issues[115]. It was further elaborated in *Malone*, where the Court stated:

> [T]he phrase "in accordance with the law" does not merely refer back to domestic law but also relates to the quality of the law, requiring it to be compatible with the rule of law ... The phrase thus implies – and this follows from the object and purpose of Article 8 – that there must be a measure of legal protection in domestic law against arbitrary interferences with by public authorities with the rights safeguarded by paragraph 1 [of Article 8] ... a law which confers a discretion must indicate the scope of that discretion, although the detailed procedures and conditions to observed do not necessarily have to be incorporated in rules of substantive law ... The degree of precision required of the "law" in this connection will depend upon the particular subject-matter ... it would be contrary to the rule of law for the legal discretion granted to the executive to be expressed in terms of an unfettered power. Consequently, the law must indicate the scope of any such discretion conferred on the competent authorities and the manner of its exercise with sufficient

---

[114] *Sunday Times* v. *United Kingdom*, 30 Eur. Ct. HR (Series A) at 31, ¶ 49 (judgment of 26 April 1979).
[115] *Cf. Silver & Others* v. *United Kingdom*, 61 Eur. Ct. HR (Series A) at 32-33, ¶ 85 (judgment of 25 March 1983).

clarity, having regard to the legitimate aim of the measure in question, to give the individual adequate protection against arbitrary interference[116].

Consequently, in cases concerning the application of the laws on abandoned accommodation, the first thing for the competent judicial authorities in Bosnia and Herzegovina would be to assess the compatibility of these rules with this requirement.

The second condition to be fulfilled is that the interference must have a "legitimate aim". That is to say at least one of the aims mentioned in Article 8 paragraph 2 of the ECHR. In the case of extreme shortage of housing accommodation, the aims of public safety, economic well-being of the country, prevention of disorder or the protection of health, or – in case there is a right to housing – the rights of others, could be argued.

The third condition to be met is that the interference must be "necessary in a democratic society". On this element, the Court has held that:

> ... the adjective "necessary" is not synonymous with "indispensable", neither has it the flexibility of such expression as "admissible", "ordinary", "useful", reasonable" or "desirable" ... the Contracting States enjoy a certain but not unlimited margin of appreciation if the matter of the imposition of restrictions, but it is for the Court to give the final ruling on whether they are compatible with the Convention ... those paragraphs of the Convention which provide for an exception to a right guaranteed are to be narrowly interpreted ...[117]

and that:

> The notion of necessity implies a pressing social need; in particular, the measure employed must be proportionate to the legitimate aim pursued. In addition, the scope of the margin of appreciation enjoyed by the national authorities will depend not only of the nature of the aim of the restriction but also on the nature of the right involved. In the instant case the economic well-being of [the respondent State] must be balanced against the applicants' respect for their "home", a right which is pertinent to their own personal security and well-being. The importance of such a right to the individual must be taken into account in determining the scope of the margin of appreciation allowed to the [State] ... the Court considers that [the respondent State] is better placed that the international judge to assess the effects of any relaxation of the housing controls. Furthermore, when considering whether to grant a licence [to

---

[116] *Malone* v. *United Kingdom*, 82 Eur. Ct. HR (Series A) at 32-32, ¶¶ 67-68 (judgment of 2 August 1984); *see also Buckley* v. *United Kingdom*, *supra*, at ¶ 76; and *Domenichi* v. *Italy*, Eur. Ct. HR (judgment of 15 November 1996), to be published in *Reports* 1996, ¶ 32.

[117] *Silver & Others* v. *United Kingdom*, *supra*, at 37-38, ¶ 97.

take up residence in specific accommodation], the Housing Authority could exercise its discretion so as to avoid any disproportionality in a particular case ... There remains, however, the question whether the manner in which the Housing Authority exercised its discretion in the applicants' case ... . corresponded to a pressing social need and, in particular, was proportionate to the legitimate aim pursued[118].

It has, however, been recognised that State intervention in socio-economic matters such as housing is often necessary in securing social justice and public benefit and that, in this area, the margin of appreciation available to a legislature in implementing social and economic policies, including in the field of housing may be a wide one[119].

It can be concluded from the above that States may adopt emergency legislation in the field of housing, as long as a fair balance is struck between the interests of the community as a whole and the rights of individuals and that such legislation is proportionate to the legitimate aim pursued. This will very probably be the most difficult question to answer in connection with the application of the laws on temporary use of abandoned accommodation in Bosnia and Herzegovina. However, one thing is clear. Article 8 paragraph 2 of the ECHR does not include the legitimate aim of the protection of the rights or interests of an ethnic majority in the field of housing or in any other field falling within the scope of Article 8 and it is doubtful that this would be accepted as "a pressing social need".

As a final word under Article 8 of the ECHR, attention should be drawn to the case-law relating to the control exercised by the authorities of the correspondence of detainees. This issue is, of course, closely linked with the defence rights of an accused protected by Article 6 of the Convention. The Court has held on several occasions that, in principle, contacts between accused and their lawyers are privileged[120]. As regards control by the authorities over letters between a lawyer and a detained accused, the Court has held that the authorities may only open a letter from a lawyer to a detainee where they have reasonable cause (i.e. the existence of facts or information which would satisfy an objective observer that a privileged channel of communication was being abused) to believe that it contains an illicit enclosure which the normal means of detection have failed to disclose. Moreover, the letter should only be opened for verification purposes and should not be read. Suitable guarantees preventing the reading of the letter should be provided, such as opening the letter in the presence of the

---

[118] *Gillow* v. *United Kingdom, supra,* at 22-23, ¶¶ 55-57; *see also Buckley* v. *United Kingdom, supra,* ¶¶ 74-76.

[119] *Cf. James & Others* v. *United Kingdom,* 98 Eur. Ct. HR (Series A) (judgment of 21 February 1986); *Mellacher & Others* v. *Austria,* 169 Eur. Ct. HR (Series A) (judgment of 19 December 1989); *see also,* No. 9327/81, Dec. 3.5.83, D.R. 32, at 187; 10825/84, Dec. 18.10.85, D.R. 52, at 198; and No. 16756/90, Dec. 12.1.91, D.R. 68, at 312.

[120] See also the comments in this respect under Article 6.

detainee[121]. In the case of *Campbell*[122], the Court further held that the opening of correspondence to detainees from the European Commission of Human Rights was contrary to Article 8 of the ECHR.

This case-law could have important implications for the control exercised by the authorities of Bosnia and Herzegovina over correspondence within the meaning of Article 8 of the ECHR between detainees and their lawyers and between detainees and the official human rights protection mechanisms functioning in Bosnia and Herzegovina, such as the Human Rights Commission under Annex 6 of the GFA. It follows from the principles that such contacts would be privileged.

The principles governing positive obligations and interferences with a protected right set out above (including lawfulness and proportionality) apply in an almost identical way in respect of the rights protected by Articles 9 (freedom of thought, conscience and religion), 10 (freedom of expression, to hold opinions and to receive and impart information) and 11 (freedom of peaceful assembly and association) of the ECHR. Article 11 of the Convention also protects the negative right of association, meaning that nobody should be forced to join a group or trade union if he or she does not want to[123].

E. Article 14 of the ECHR; Prohibition of Discrimination

Article 14 of the ECHR states:

> The enjoyment of the rights and freedoms set forth in this Convention shall be secured without discrimination on any ground such as sex, race, colour, language, religion, political or other opinion, national or social origin, association with a national minority, property, birth or other status.

The scope of this provision is, as is clear from the text, limited to the scope of the rights and freedoms protected by the Convention. This implies that discrimination as regards rights and freedoms falling outside the scope of the Convention is not contrary to the ECHR[124]. This is the obvious

---

[121]   *Cf. Campbell* v. *United Kingdom, supra,* at 18-21, ¶¶ 46-54.

[122]   *Id.,* at 21-22, ¶¶ 55-64.

[123]   *Cf. Sigurdur A. Sigurjónsson* v. *Iceland,* 264 Eur. Ct. HR (Series A) (judgment of 30 June 1993).

[124]   Such as, *inter alia,* linguistic freedom (cf. No. 10650/83, Dec. 17.5.85, D.R. 42, at 212; and No. 11100/84, Dec. 12.12.85, D.R. 45, at 20), economic and social rights, including the right to work (cf. No. 24088/94, Dec. 12.10.94, D.R. 79, at 138), determination of nationality (cf. No. 11278/84, Dec. 1.7.85, D.R. 43, at 216), asylum, residence permits, extradition and deportation (cf. No. 13654/88, Dec. 8.9.88, D.R. 57, at 287; No. 12068/86, Dec. 1.12.86, D.R. 51, at 237; No. 21808/93, Dec. 8.9.93, D.R. 75, at 264 and No.

reason why, in Article II, paragraph 2 of Annex 6 to the GFA, the scope of the prohibition of discrimination under Annex 6 has been extended to any of the rights and freedoms provided for in 15 other international instruments listed in the Appendix to Annex 6.

In most discrimination cases, the most difficult point for complainants is to prove a discriminatory treatment. It is only rarely that one comes across blatant discrimination. It is mostly camouflaged in the application of general measures, such as for instance the allocation of social housing. The case-law under Article 14 of the Convention could provide useful guidance for the interpretation of the term "discrimination " within the meaning of Article II, paragraph 2 of the Annex 6, since it is only the scope which differentiates it from the ECHR, not the prohibition of discrimination as such.

According to the case-law of the Strasbourg organs, not every difference in treatment of persons in "relevantly" similar situations constitutes "discrimination" within the meaning of Article 14 of the ECHR; and a measure which, as such, might be in conformity with the substantive right or freedom at issue may nevertheless be contrary to the prohibition of discrimination, if it applied in a discriminatory manner[125]. Most recently, in the *Van Raalte* case, the European Court restated the applicable principles as follows:

> For the purposes of Article 14 a difference of treatment is discriminatory if it has no objective and reasonable justification, that is if it does not pursue a legitimate aim or if there is not a reasonable relationship of proportionality between the means employed and the aim sought to be realised. Moreover the Contracting States enjoy a margin of appreciation in assessing whether and to what extent differences in otherwise similar situations justify a different treatment.

As the *Van Raalte* case concerned alleged discrimination based on sex, the Court added:

> However, very weighty reasons would have to be put forward before the Court could regard a difference in treatment based exclusively on the ground of sex as compatible with the Convention[126].

24015/94, Dec. 20.5.94, D.R. 77, at 144) and conscientious objection (cf. No. 17086/90, Dec. 6.12.91, D.R. 72, at 245).

[125] *Cf.* No. 22761/93, Dec. 14.4.94, D.R. 77, at 98; and No. 23419/94, Dec. 6.9.95, D.R. 82, at 41.

[126] *Van Raalte* v. *the Netherlands*, Eur. Ct. HR (judgment of 21 February 1997), to be published in *Reports* 1997, at ¶ 39; *see further*, *Schuller-Zgraggen* v. *Switzerland*, 263 Eur. Ct. HR (Series A) at 21-22, ¶¶ 64-67 (judgment of 24 June 1993); *Burghartz* v. *Switzerland*, 280-B Eur. Ct. HR at 28-30, ¶¶ 25-30 (judgment of 22 February 1994); and *Karlheinz*

Insofar as complainants were in a "relevantly" similar position to others with whom they sought to compare themselves, both the European Commission and the European Court have held several times, that a difference in treatment was not contrary to Article 14 of the ECHR, after having been satisfied that there was an objective and reasonable justification for this difference in treatment and that there was a reasonable relationship of proportionality between the means employed and the aim sought to be realised.

Such cases concerned, *inter alia*, the obligation of trainee lawyers to defend an accused without remuneration or reimbursement of expenses[127], proceedings to contest paternity of children born in wedlock[128], leasehold reform legislation aimed at protecting disadvantaged leaseholders[129], application of rules allocating a right to occupy accommodation[130], a decision that time spent in pre-trial detention pending appeal proceedings did not count towards service of the sentence imposed[131], the application of a law assigning to the State a large part of Church property[132], parental rights for children born out of wedlock[133], broadcasting facilities[134], and allocation of subsidies to schools[135].

To date, there are no indications in the case-law from which it could be deduced that States are under a positive obligation under Article 14 of the ECHR to secure the right to equal treatment by actively pursuing a policy of positive discrimination or to take certain measures to that effect in particular areas.

Schmidt v. *Germany*, 291-B Eur. Ct. HR (Series A) at 32-33, ¶¶ 24-29 (judgment of 18 July 1994).

[127] *Van der Mussele* v. *Belgium*, 70 Eur. Ct. HR (Series A) at 21-23, ¶¶ 42-46 (judgment of 23 November 1983).

[128] *Rasmussen* v. *Denmark*, 87 Eur. Ct. HR (Series A) (judgment of 28 November 1984).

[129] *James & Others* v. *United Kingdom*, 98 Eur. Ct. HR (Series A) at 44-46, ¶¶ 73-78 (judgment of 21 February 1986).

[130] *Gillow* v. *United Kingdom*, *supra*, at 25-26, ¶¶ 63-67.

[131] *Monnell & Morris* v. *United Kingdom*, 115 Eur. Ct. HR (Series A) at 26-27, ¶¶ 71-75 (judgment of 2 March 1987).

[132] *Holy Monasteries* v. *Greece*, 301-B Eur. Ct. HR (Series A) at 39-40, ¶¶ 91-94 (judgment of 9 December 1994).

[133] *McMichael* v. *United Kingdom*, 307-B Eur. Ct. HR (Series A) at 57-59, ¶¶ 94-99 (judgment of 24 February 1995); and No. 22920/93, Dec. 6.4.94, D.R. 77, at 108.

[134] *Cf.* No. 21472/93, Dec. 11.1.94, D.R. 76, at 129; and 24744/94, Dec. 28.6.95, D.R. 82, at 98.

[135] *Cf.* No. 23419/94, Dec. 6.9.95, D.R. 82, at 41.

F. Article 1 of Protocol No. 1 to the Convention; Respect for Property

The object and purpose of Article 1 of Protocol No. 1 is to protect individuals against arbitrary interferences in their property rights. It reads as follows:

> Every natural or legal person is entitled to the peaceful enjoyment of his possessions. No one shall be deprived of his possessions except in the public interest and subject to the conditions provided for by law and by the general principles of international law.

> The preceding provisions shall not, however, in any way impair the right of a State to enforce such laws as it deems necessary to control the use of property in accordance with the general interest or to secure the payment of taxes or other contributions or penalties.

The first question which arises under Article 1 of Protocol No. 1 is of course what is to be understood under the terms "property" and "possessions". According to the case-law under this provision, these terms include, *inter alia*, moveable and immovable property[136], under certain circumstances benefits from a social insurance scheme or pension fund[137], debts due to a creditor[138], the goodwill of a professional practice[139], company shares[140], an established right to inherit[141], earned income[142], a valid licence for exercising specific professional activities[143], a legitimate expectation to be able to realise real estate development plans[144], contractual rights[145] and patents[146].

The problems under Article 1 of Protocol No. 1 arise when a State interferes with "property" or "possessions", in the sense that it adopts

---

[136] *Cf.* No. 7456/76, Dec. 8.2.78, D.R. 13, at 40.

[137] *Cf.* No. 5849/72, Dec. 16.12.74, D.R. 1, at 46; No. 7624/76, Dec. 6.7.77, D.R. 19, at 100; No. 9776/82, Dec. 3.10.83, D.R. 34, at 153; and No, 10671/83, Dec. 4.3.85, D.R. 42, at 229.

[138] *Cf.* No. 7775/77, Dec. 5.10.78, D.R. 15, at 143; and No. 12164/86, Dec. 12.10.88, D.R. 58, at 63.

[139] *Van Marle & Others* v. *the Netherlands*, 101 Eur. Ct. HR (Series A) at 13, ¶ 41 (judgment of 26 June 1986); and No. 10438/83, Dec. 3.10.84, D.R. 41, at 170.

[140] *Cf.* No. 8588/79 & 8589/79, Dec. 12.10.82, D.R. 29, at 64; and No. 11189/84, Dec. 11.12.86, D.R. 50, at 121.

[141] *Cf.* No. 8695/79, Dec. 5.12.84, D.R. 39, at 26.

[142] *Cf.* No. 8410/78, Dec. 13.12.79, D.R. 18 at 216; No. 10438/83, Dec. 3.10.84, D.R. 41, at 170; and No. 10748/84, Dec. 7.10.85, D.R. 44, at 203.

[143] *Cf. Tre Traktörer AB* v. *Sweden*, 159 Eur. Ct. HR (Series A) at 21, ¶ 53 (judgment of 7 July 1989); *Fredin* v. *Sweden*, 192 Eur. Ct. HR (Series A) at 14, ¶ 40 (judgment of 18 February 1991).

[144] *Pine Valley Developments Ltd. & Others* v. *United Kingdom*, 222 Eur. Ct. HR (Series A) at 23, ¶ 51 (judgment of 29 November 1991).

[145] *Cf.* No. 12947/87, Dec. 12.7.89, D.R. 62, at 226.

[146] *Cf.* No. 12633/87, Dec. 4.10.90, D.R. 66, at 70.

certain measures affecting the scope of exercise of ownership rights. According to the case-law under Article 1 of Protocol No. 1, the provision:

> ... comprises "three distinct rules". The first, which is expressed in the first sentence of the first paragraph and is of a general nature, lays down the principle of peaceful enjoyment of property. The second rule, in the second sentence of the same paragraph, covers deprivation of possessions and subjects it to certain conditions. The third, contained in the second paragraph, recognises that the Contracting States are entitled, amongst other things, to control the use of property in accordance with the general interest, by enforcing such laws as they deem necessary for the purpose. However, the rules are not "distinct" in the sense of being unconnected: the second and third rules are concerned with particular instances of interference with the right to peaceful enjoyment of property. They must therefore be construed in the light of the general principle laid down in the first rule[147].

This approach implies three situations:

a. owners have the right to fully exercise their ownership rights, such as using, renting, selling or, if they wish to, destroying their property;

b. States may expropriate property, but only on one ground and only if it stays within the limits foreseen by law and with due respect for the general principles of international law; and

c. States may limit ownership rights, but only on two conditions and only when this is foreseen by law.

Here the important principles of legality and lawfulness appear once again. No interference is allowed, unless it is foreseen by, and in conformity with, domestic law, which in itself should be in conformity with the requirements of ECHR[148].

In the field of expropriation, whereby owners will irrevocably lose their ownership rights, a number of principles have been established in the Strasbourg case-law. First of all, a deprivation of ownership does not necessarily have to be a formal expropriation. The Court has recognised that certain situations, the creation of which is imputable to the State, amount to a *de facto* expropriation[149].

Secondly, the reference to the "public interest" in matters concerning deprivation of ownership relates to the justification and the motives for the taking of property by the State from private owners. The European Court held on this point that the taking of property effected for no other reasons

---

[147] *Cf. Mellacher & Others* v. *Austria, supra,* at 24-25, ¶ 42.

[148] *Cf. Lithgow & Others* v. *United Kingdom,* 102 Eur. Ct. HR (Series A) at 47, ¶ 110 (judgment of 8 July 1986).

[149] *Papamichalopoulos* v. *Greece,* 260-B Eur. Ct. HR (Series A) at 69-70, ¶¶ 42-45 (judgment of 24 June 1993).

than to confer a private benefit on a private party cannot be considered to be "in the public interest". This does not mean however that in order to be "in the public interest" property taken from a private owner should be put into use for the general public. The taking of property pursuant to a policy calculated to enhance social justice within the community may be described as being "in the public interest". As the fairness of legal rules governing contractual or property rights of private parties is a matter of public concern, legislative measures intended to bring about such fairness are capable of being "in the public interest", even if they involve the compulsory transfer of property from one individual to another[150].

The notion of "public interest" is considered as necessarily extensive and as leaving a certain margin of appreciation for States to frame and organise their policies in those fields considered as being in the public interest[151].

When pursuant to such a policy a person is deprived of his or her property, it should be determined whether such deprivation is in conformity with the principle of "lawfulness". It should further be determined whether the deprivation is proportionate to the aim pursued by examining whether a fair balance was struck between the protection of the right of property and the requirements of the general interest by considering the degree of protection from arbitrariness afforded by the relevant proceedings and by determining whether or not the private owner has to bear an individual and excessive burden[152].

The phrase "the general principles of international law" mentioned in Article 1 of Protocol No. 1 refers only to those principles of international law which protect foreign property against confiscation or against nationalisation or expropriation without adequate compensation being paid. It does not apply when a State expropriates its own nationals[153].

This does not, however, mean that a State is free to take property from its own nationals without having to provide compensation. As the Court has held, compensation terms are material to the assessment whether a fair balance has been struck between the various interests at stake and, notably, whether or not a disproportionate burden has been imposed on the person who has been deprived of his possessions. The taking of property without payment of an amount reasonably related to its value would normally constitute a disproportionate interference contrary to Article 1 of Protocol No. 1. It does not, on the other hand, guarantee a right to full compensation in all circumstances, as legitimate objectives of "public interest", such as pursued in measures of economic reform or measures designed to achieve

---

[150] *James & Others* v. *United Kingdom*, *supra*, at 30-31, ¶¶ 40-41.

[151] *Hentrich* v. *France*, 296-A Eur. Ct. HR (Series A) at 19, ¶ 39 (judgment of 22 September 1994).

[152] *Id.*, at 19-21, ¶¶ 40-49.

[153] *Lithgow & Others* v. *United Kingdom*, *supra*, at 47-50, ¶¶ 111-119.

greater social justice, may call for less than reimbursement of full market value[154].

The second paragraph of Article 1 of Protocol No. 1, relating to the limitations States may place on the use of property, is to be construed in the light of the principles contained in the first sentence of Article 1 of Protocol No. 1 set out above. Consequently, any interference must achieve a "fair balance" between the demands of the general interest of the community as a whole and the requirements of the protection of the individual's fundamental rights[155]. There is no fundamental difference between the concepts of "public interest" referred to in the first sentence and "the general interest" referred to in the second paragraph of Article 1 of Protocol No. 1[156].

As regards the condition of "securing the payment of taxes", the Court has held that the legislature of States, in passing laws aimed at the enforcement of tax debts, must be allowed a wide margin of appreciation, especially with regard to the question whether – and if so, to what extent – the tax authorities should be put in a better position to enforce tax debts than ordinary creditors are to enforce commercial debts. The Court further held that it would respect the legislature's assessment in such matters unless it would be devoid of reasonable foundation. A rule intended to facilitate the enforcement of tax debts was, in itself, found to clearly in the "general interest"[157].

The importance of Article 1 of Protocol No. 1 as regards the current situation in Bosnia and Herzegovina lies mainly in the field of housing. There are a number of situations where it is important. The first one concerns the situation of persons, who are the private owners of more than one house or apartment. Insofar as they would be compelled, pursuant to the application of a law which would be in conformity with the requirements of the principle of "lawfulness", to opt to live in one of their homes (whereas the other homes they own would be temporarily made available to homeless persons) there are no problems of incompatibility of such a measure with the relevant case-law of the Strasbourg organs[158].

A second situation is that of persons who now reside in one Entity and who have left their privately owned homes in the other Entity, either voluntarily in order to avoid belonging to a local ethnic minority, or involuntarily. Both categories could very likely face the same problem, namely

---

[154] *Id.*, at 50-51, ¶¶ 120-121.

[155] *Cf. Spadea & Scalabrino* v. *Italy*, 315-B Eur. Ct. HR (Series A) at 25-27, ¶¶ 28-41 (judgment of 28 September 1995).

[156] *James & Others* v. *United Kingdom, supra*, at 31, ¶ 43.

[157] *Gasus Dosier- und Fördertechnik GmbH* v. *the Netherlands*, 306-B Eur. Ct. HR (Series A) at 48-49, ¶¶ 60-61 (judgment of 23 February 1995).

[158] *Cf. Spadea & Scalabrino* v. *Italy, supra*, at 24-27, ¶¶ 26-41; *see also*, No. 6202/73, Dec. 16.3.75, D.R. 1, at 66; No. 10153/82, Dec. 13.10.86, D.R. 49, at 67; and No. 16756/90, Dec. 12.1.91, D.R. 68 at 312.

that they are unable to return to their home as, pursuant to the laws on temporary accommodation, these homes have been declared "abandoned" and are currently being used by other persons.

According to well-established case-law, the Convention is intended to safeguard rights that are "practical and effective". In situations of the present kind, it will have be ascertained whether the situation in which such owners find themselves amounts to a *de facto* expropriation[159].

On the basis of reports by various organisations and institutions active in Bosnia and Herzegovina[160], it could be argued convincingly that, at least for the time being, the chances for such persons to be allowed to return to their original privately owned homes are very small if not impossible. Whether these chances will improve in the future is still an open question, on which the answer to the question of whether or not such persons have a valid claim to have been *de facto* expropriated depends[161]. Maybe this question is premature, but it cannot be excluded that the issue will have to be addressed in the future by the competent authorities.

A third situation to be highlighted is that of those persons who have irrevocably lost their occupancy right (*stanarsko pravo*) in respect of accommodation through the operation of the respective laws on abandoned accommodation in both Entities when they did not return home in a timely fashion.

The first issue to be examined under Article 1 of Protocol No. 1 in this respect is the question whether an "occupancy right" (*stanarsko pravo* – a *sui generis* legal concept) constitutes a "possession" within the meaning of Article 1 of Protocol No. 1. There are certain arguments which could support such a finding, as it contains a number of patrimonial characteristics, in that it is granted for an indefinite period of time, it cannot be terminated except in certain specific circumstances foreseen in the Law on Housing Relations (*Zakon a stambenim odnosima*) of the former Socialist Republic of Bosnia and Herzegovina and it may be inherited. Furthermore, the financing for the construction of accommodation in respect of which occupancy rights were allocated came from taxes and/or social security contributions, part of which (*doprinos za stambenu izgradnju*) were allocated to the Housing Construction Contribution Fund (*Fond zajedni ke potrosnje – Dio za stambenu izgradnju*). So, although it cannot be equated with a building lease, a premium lease or a hereditary long lease, it could very well be found that this unique legal concept falls within the scope of Article 1 of Protocol No. 1, despite the absence of an easily measured economic value.

The answer to remaining questions regarding this category of persons is fully dependent on the findings by the competent authorities on the issue

---

[159] *Cf. Papamichalopoulos* v. *Greece, supra*, at 69, ¶ 42.
[160] *See* note 110, *supra*.
[161] *Cf. Loizidou* v. *Turkey, supra*, at ¶¶ 58-64.

addressed above. Assuming the answer to be affirmative, the possibility can not be excluded that the application of the laws on abandoned accommodation would not stand the test of Article 1 of Protocol No. 1.

CONCLUSION

The situation in Bosnia and Herzegovina is still far from resolved. Now the weapons are silent, it is possible to hear words again. It does not mean the struggle is finished. Only the tools have changed for more peaceful ones, which is a great and hopeful leap forward. What is crucial now, is the construction of a society which will be able to find its place in the European family. The European family has adopted certain values of which respect for human rights and fundamental freedoms in a society based on respect for the rule of law is one of the most important.

The international community has provided the authorities of Bosnia and Herzegovina with massive support, both in terms of finances and human expertise, in order to rebuild its society, to rebuild its multi-ethnic society which was once an example for many other States. A pillar of that support is the European Convention, but is no more than a tool. And primary responsibility for its application rests with the authorities of that State. For now, one can only but hope that, with assiduous application of that tool, Bosnia and Herzegovina will gain the seat which has already been reserved for it at the table of the European family.

MICHAEL O'FLAHERTY[1]

4. International Human Rights Operations in Bosnia and Herzegovina

INTRODUCTION

There are multiple international agencies and operations engaged in the promotion and protection of human rights in Bosnia and Herzegovina[2]. This chapter seeks to describe, comprehend, and assess the complex configuration, identify reasons for the manner of its development, locate it in the context of human rights provisions of the peace agreement, and evaluate the extent to which joint and several implementation of mandates has served to enhance the protection of human rights. The assessment of effectiveness is undertaken through examination of selected sectoral activities, including human rights monitoring, reporting, intervention and institution building. In each case, close attention is paid to the manner in which agencies co-ordinate their activities and otherwise co-operate with each other.

This chapter identifies significant successes and failures and proposes certain issues to be addressed as a matter of priority by the various organisations. It also draws attention to the successes, failures and considerable operational potential of the co-ordination mechanisms which have been developed. It is observed that these mechanisms must be further honed to, for instance, address the problems arising from the scale of involvement of local and international governmental and non-governmental actors in the human rights institution-building sectors.

Though the United Nations is present in BiH, it is not the "lead" international organisation with regard to issues of human rights. Its activities are not, therefore, the central concern of this chapter. The UN does, how-

[1] Thanks are due to Roland Salvisberg, Maria Stavropoulou and Greg Gisvold for commentating on drafts of this paper and to Peggy Hicks, Craig Jeness, Jim Ross and many others for generously giving of their time.

[2] Bosnia and Herzegovina [hereinafter "BiH"] is one of the states formerly a part of the Socialist Federal Republic of Yugoslavia (SFRY), which existed until 1992. Post-1992, other former consitutents of the SFRY have emerged as distinct states: Croatia, Slovenia, and the Federal Republic of Yugoslavia, comprised of former SFRY states Serbia and Montenegro.

ever, play an important role and its range of activities are identified, assessed and located within the matrix of international initiatives.

I. POLITICAL CONTEXT AND MANDATE

A. *The General Framework Agreement for Peace*

The Bosnia and Herzegovina Proximity Peace Talks, which took place in Dayton, Ohio, USA, from 1 to 21 November 1995, built upon previous agreements adopted in Geneva and New York in September 1995[3]. Both sets of talks occurred in a context of immense complexity. Much has been written of this elsewhere[4]. For purposes of the present paper it suffices to note the following issues, which had an impact on the manner in which the peace settlement addressed issues of human rights:

i.   Many interests were represented at the talks. There were three formerly warring parties, the Bosniaks[5], the Bosnian Croats and the Bosnian Serbs. Two of these were further represented in the context of their uneasy mutual alliance in the Bosniak/Bosnian Croat Federation[6]. Other key negotiating interests were the two "sponsor" States for the Bosnian Serbs and the Bosnian Croats, respectively Serbia and Croatia. The negotiations had, therefore, to seek to accommodate multiple and often inconsistent aims.

ii.   The negotiators were representative of the same regimes which had waged the conflicts since the beginning. Some of these regimes also continued to be led by or harbour persons indicted by the International Criminal Tribunal[7]. Factors such as these undermined the capacity of negotiators to address the past or establish conditions for reconciliation.

iii.   The forced displacement of people, "ethnic cleansing", had been a central war-aim of the Bosnian Serbs and Bosnian Croats[8]. A peace based on justice would call for voluntary return of displaced persons and a resultant reversal of the gains of war.

---

[3] Agreed Basic Principles, *adopted* September 8, 1995; Further Agreed Basic Principles, *adopted* September 26, 1995. These documes are reproduced in Office of the High Representative, *Bosnia and Herzegovina: Essential Texts* (Sarajevo, 1996).

[4] *See, e.g.*, Open Media Research Institute, *Transition*, Vol. 2, No. 14, July 1996.

[5] Persons of Bosnian Muslim origin.

[6] Established pursuant to the Washington Agreement of March 1994.

[7] Mr. Karazdic, for instance, was still at the head of the Bosnian Serb leadership and General Mladic led its armies.

[8] *See* Report of the UN Commission on Human Rights Special Rapporteur on the former Yugoslavia, UN Doc. E/CN.4/1996/9 (22 August 1995).

iv.   "Ethnic cleansing" and other war activities reached levels of barbarity not seen in Europe since the second world war. The wide publicisation of these practices contributed to a public concern that a peace settlement contain significant human rights guarantees.

v.   The hosts for the peace negotiations, the United States of America, wanted to speedily establish a peace that, *inter alia*, preserved the integrity of the Bosnian State, set the country on the path to a market economy and did not jeopardise the re-election chances of President Clinton.

vi.   Most of the negotiating parties had lost confidence in the capacity of the UN to implement or oversee a peace process. The view coincided with a concern of the US Congress that no US peacekeepers serve under a United Nations flag.

vii.   Unrestrained implementation of a *pax americana* was inhibited by the volatile nature of Russian support for the peace process. European States also wished for a European regional perspective in the peace agreement.

viii.   The peace talks coincided with a period in which NATO was seeking a new post cold war role[9].

ix.   Earlier proposed peace settlements had contained extensive human rights provisions[10]. Also, one of the models before the negotiators was the Washington agreement, under which the text of a Constitution was agreed for the Federation of Bosnia and Herzegovina which was replete with both substantive and procedural human rights references.

The eventual shape of the peace settlement was also significantly affected by the awkward, disjointed nature of the proximity talks methodology, as well as by an extreme time pressure, imposed by the negotiation hosts, which may have resulted in a lack of close attention to other than the central elements of the talks.

The peace settlement, the General Framework Agreement for Peace in Bosnia and Herzegovina[11], was initialled in Dayton and signed in Paris on 14 December 1995. It provided for the transfer of certain territories by belligerent parties, compliance with detailed provisions for withdrawal and

---

[9] For a recent analysis see, J. Gow, "Enlargement in the Balkan Mirror", War Report, No. 52 (June/July 1997).

[10] *See* P. Szasz, "The Protection of Human Rights Through the Dayton/Paris Peace Agreement on Bosnia", 90 AJIL 301 (April 1996) [hereinafter "Dayton/Paris Peace Agreement"].

[11] General Framework Agreement for Peace in Bosnia and Herzegovina, *initialed* Dayton, Ohio, 21 November 1995, *signed* Paris, 14 December 1995, 35 ILM 75 (1996) [hereinafter "GFA"].

partial de-mobilisation of forces, complete withdrawal of foreign forces and release of prisoners.

The GFA stipulated that BiH was to remain a unitary State. It was, however, to be divided in two entities which were to rob the central State of all but the most rump of authority. Thus, the Entities, the Federation of Bosnia and Herzegovina (established in the 1994 peace settlement between the Government and Bosnian Croat forces), with 51% of the territory, and Republika Srpska with 49%, were each given control of armies, police forces and the collection of revenue. National and Entity-based elections were to take place within a given time-frame. The agreement does insist on the rights of voluntary return to places of origin of refugees and displaced persons. However, this provision sits oddly with the Entity concept, whereby a significant proportion of displaced people is expected to return to areas under control of persons of the same ethnicity as those who perpetrated "ethnic cleansing". The GFA's frequent reference to and insistence on democratic principles is also at odds with such provisions for ethnisisation of public life in BiH as the reservation of certain central posts for persons of designated ethnic origin (e.g., Annex 4 of the GFA, the Constitution of Bosnia and Herzegovina, stipulates that the Presidency of Bosnia and Herzegovina must comprise one Bosniak and one Croat from the Federation and one Serb from Republika Srpska).

The GFA is suffused with direct references to human rights[12]. In Annex 4, the State and the Entities undertake to "ensure the highest level of internationally recognised human rights and fundamental freedoms"; the European Convention on Human Rights and its protocols are incorporated into domestic law and made directly applicable; a non-exhaustive list of 13 rights is enumerated; and, as in the earlier Constitution of the Federation of Bosnia and Herzegovina, the parties undertake to secure, without discrimination, the rights contained in 15 international instruments. Annex 6 also contains extensive human rights commitments. Within the Federation area the corpus of substantive human rights law is further complicated by continuing application of the provision of the Federation Constitution giving direct effect to 15 international instruments. The multiple source of human rights law present serious problems of interpretation and opens the door to endless damaging disputes over such matters as the identity and terms of applicable law. Thus, for instance, there is dispute over the applicable standard regarding the death penalty: whether it is the absolute ban in the 2nd Optional Protocol to the International Covenant on Civil and Political

---

[12] *See* P. Szasz, Dayton/Paris Peace Agreement, *supra*; M.O'Flaherty, "Human Rights and the General Framework Agreement for Peace in Bosnia and Herzegovina", *in* G. Alfredsson, G. Melander, B. Ramcharam, *Human Rights Monitoring Procedures: Festscrift for Jacob Moller*, (Deventer and Boston, forthcoming) [hereinafter "M.O'Flaherty, Human Rights and the GFA"]; Helsinki Citizens Assembly, *Dayton Continued in Bosnia and Herzegovina No. 1* (The Hague, 1997); and chapters elsewhere in this volume.

Rights or the partial ban contained in Protocol 6 to the European Convention on Human Rights[13].

The GFA and the various incorporated international instruments clearly obligate all public officials and courts to take appropriate action to implement the human rights provisions. At Annex 6, the GFA also creates a Human Rights Commission, comprising an Ombudsperson and the Human Rights Chamber. These institutions are called on to investigate and deliberate on cases of violations of the European Convention on Human Rights or of discrimination with regard to enjoyment of rights contained in those other human rights instruments listed in the Annex. The Federation Constitution had also established an Office of Ombudsmen to investigate allegations of human rights abuse in the Federation area; the GFA does not address its relationship to the Human Rights Commission. The GFA also does not establish an analogous Entity-based ombudsman mechanism for Republika Srpska. In Annex 7, the GFA establishes a Commission for Displaced Persons and Refugees, tasking it with deliberation on the property claims of dispossessed persons including determination of compensation claims. No provision is made regarding the source of compensation funds.

B. Implementing and Supervisory Organisations

International supervision of implementation of GFA is entrusted to several organisations. Pursuant to resolutions of the Security Council, a multinational military Implementation Force, operating under NATO command, was deployed. The original 53,000 person contingent was replaced in late 1996 by a 31,500 person Stabilisation Force[14]. As well as being tasked with supervision of implementation of the military aspects of the GFA, the force was accorded "the rights to fulfil its supporting tasks, within the limits of its assigned principal tasks and available resources, and on request" *inter alia* to help create secure conditions for implementation of other aspects of the peace agreement including free and fair elections, to assist in the activities of humanitarian missions, to prevent interference with freedom of movement and respond "appropriately" to violence to life or person. IFOR/SFOR has not played a prominent role with regard to direct promotion or protection of human rights. Its activities have been limited to such actions as provision of security to international police monitoring teams. It has also made legally qualified members available to participate in such

---

[13] Clarification on this matter may be provided by the Human Rights Chamber in the context of its deliberations on the legality of the death sentence imposed by a Sarajevo court on Mr. Stretko Damjanovic. *See* Office of the High Representative, Human Rights Coordination Centre, Human Rights Report 6-7 July, 1997.

[14] Hereinafter, respectively, "IFOR" and "SFOR". SFOR's mandate extends to June 1998 as confirmed by the North Atlantic Council, July 8, 1997.

institution-building activities as assessment of the needs of the judicial system[15] and analysis of jurisprudence.

The International Police Task Force[16] is an UNCIVPOL operation and is mandated to undertake law enforcement agency monitoring, re-structuring and training and monitoring of judicial organisations, structures and proceedings. The GFA stipulates that the IPTF must provide any credible information in its possession on human rights violations to the Human Rights Commission "or other appropriate organisations". In December 1996, the IPTF was mandated to undertake investigations of human rights violations carried out by the police. As of April 1997, the IPTF had an authorised strength of 1,900 officers, deployed in 54 locations. The size of the force, however, needs to be augmented. As of August, 1997, the Security Council had not yet granted it the 120 specialist human rights investigators it had requested at the end of 1996. As the Special Representative of the Secretary-General, Ambassador Eide, stated in April 1997 while "countries are fast and efficient in adding to our mandate, they are not equally generous, fast and efficient in adding to our resources"[17]. The IPTF is supported in its substantive work by 49 civil affairs officers of the UN mission[18]. In August 1997, UNMIBH also established a dedicated human rights office, led by a senior officer, to support IPTF's human rights related activities.

The UN High Commissioner for Refugees[19] is acknowledged in the GFA as the lead agency with regard to repatriation and relief of refugees and displaced persons. UNHCR maintains a team of protection officers spread thinly in the regions. During 1996 it also deployed officers charged with gathering and disseminating information on conditions for return, including information on human rights conditions. UNHCR's understanding of its role in addressing issues of human rights grew more narrow over the course of 1996. Thus, for instance, despite its concern to facilitate proper conditions for return, it stated in an October 1996 position paper that it had no mandate concerning strengthening of judicial institutions, monitoring of law enforcement officials or activities related to freedom of the press and freedom of expression[20].

The GFA tasks the Organisation for Security and Cooperation in Europe[21] with the adoption and putting in place of an elections programme whereby internationally supervised elections would be held at various

---

[15] *See* IFOR Office of the Legal Advisor, *A Report on the Legal System in Bosnia and Herzegovina* (October 1996).

[16] Hereinafter "IPTF".

[17] Address to the North Atlantic Council, Sarajevo, 18 April 1997.

[18] The UN Mission in Bosnia and Herzegovina [hereinafter "UNMIBH"].

[19] For general information on UNHCR activities in former Yugoslavia, please review the UNHCR website, located at http://www.unhcr.ch.

[20] UNHCR Position Paper on file with the present writer.

[21] Hereinafter "OSCE"; *see* http://www-osce.austria.eu.net.

levels of Government within a stipulated timeframe. National elections were conducted in September 1996. Despite an election campaign which was entirely compromised by human rights abuses and violations of international electoral standards, OSCE permitted all but the municipal elections to take place. The municipal elections of September, 1997, occurred too late for consideration here.

In view of the complexity of the peace agreement and the extent of international agency participation in its implementation, the GFA requests, "the designation of a High Representative[22], to be appointed consistent with relevant United Nations Security Council resolutions, to facilitate the Parties' own efforts and to mobilise and, as appropriate, co-ordinate the activities of the organisations and agencies involved in the civilian aspects of the peace settlement"[23]. The co-ordinating role of the High Representative regarding international organisations is stated in very deferential terms: "[t]he High Representative shall respect [the organisations'] autonomy within their spheres of operation while as necessary giving general guidance to them about the impact of their activities on the implementation of the peace settlement". For their part, they "are requested to assist (him/her) in the execution of his or her responsibilities by providing all information relevant to their operation in Bosnia and Herzegovina". The High Representative is also mandated to facilitate the resolution of disputes, participate in donor meetings, report to the Contact Group of States, the UN and, "other interested governments, parties and organisations". The High Representative's role regarding IPTF is limited to, "provision of guidance to and receipt of reports from the Force's Commissioner". The High Representative "[has] no authority over the IFOR and shall not in any way interfere in the conduct of military operations or the IFOR chain of command". Carl Bildt, a co-chairman of the International Conference for former Yugoslavia, was first appointed by the Peace Implementation Council as High Representative. He was replaced in May 1997 by Mr. Carlos Westendorp.

Given the extent of his responsibilities and the range of *lacunae* in the GFA which he had to address, the High Representative established an excessively modest presence in Bosnia and Herzegovina. Throughout 1996 he lacked sufficient technically qualified staff and failed to develop a presence outside Sarajevo adequate to the needs for regional and local coordination and co-operation among parties and international organisations. His office recognised this weakness and has consistently striven to address it. At the time of establishment of his office, Mr. Bildt appointed his Chief of Staff, a US diplomat, as Senior Deputy for Human Rights.

---

[22] *See* GFA, *supra*, Annex 10, Art. 1, ¶2; *see also* http://www.ohr.int.

[23] Pursuant to the provisions of GFA, the mandate of the High Representative derives from the Conclusions of the Peace Implementation Conference of 8-9 December 1995 and UN Security Council resolution 1031 of 15 December 1995.

That person delegated almost entirely this human rights responsibility to a senior staff member, who served as the Human Rights Advisor to the High Representative. The High Representative's role in co-ordinating human rights activities is discussed below.

The principal reference point in the GFA for deployment of civilian human rights operation is Annex 6, Article XIII, which provides that:

i.   the parties shall promote and encourage the activities of non-governmental and international organisation for the protection and promotion of human rights;

ii.   the parties join in inviting the United Nations Commission on Human Rights, the OSCE, the United Nations High Commissioner for Human Rights, and other inter-governmental or regional human rights missions or organisations to monitor closely the human rights situation in Bosnia and Herzegovina, including through the establishment of local offices and the assignment of observers, rapporteurs, or other relevant persons on a permanent or mission-by-mission basis and to provide them with full and effective facilitation, assistance and access;

iii.   the parties shall allow full and effective access to non-governmental organisations for purposes of investigating and monitoring human rights conditions in Bosnia and Herzegovina and shall refrain from hindering or impeding them in the exercise of these functions;

iv.   all competent authorities in Bosnia and Herzegovina shall co-operate with and provide unrestricted access to the organisation established in this Agreement, to any international human rights monitoring mechanisms established for Bosnia and Herzegovina, to the supervisory bodies established by any of the international agreements listed in the Appendix to this Annex, to the International Tribunal for the former Yugoslavia, and to any other organisation authorised by the UN Security Council with a mandate concerning human rights or humanitarian law[24].

The breadth of invitation is unprecedented in peace agreements. Among its many notable elements are the clear coverage of both monitoring and institution building activities, the reference to NGOs, the provision of an open ended permission for the conducting of missions, opening of offices, etc., and reference to the Human Rights Treaty Bodies (the "supervisory bodies" referred to at paragraph 4). The implications of such broad and inclusive terms may be further appreciated, given the inclusion among the GFA's signatories of two non State parties, the Federation of Bosnia and Herzegovina and Republika Srpska.

---

[24]   *See* GFA, *supra*, Annex 6, Art. XIII.

A further mandate for action to promote human rights can be found in Annex 7 of the GFA, which addresses issues of refugees and displaced persons. Article III of the Annex accords full and unrestricted access to UNHCR, ICRC, UNDP and "other international, domestic and non-governmental organisations relevant to refugees and displaced persons" with a view towards undertaking "other activities vital to the discharge of their mandates and operational responsibilities", such as "protection functions and the monitoring of basic human rights and humanitarian conditions"[25].

Unlike earlier proposed peace settlements[26] and the existence of applicable models in peace agreements adopted elsewhere, the GFA does not contain elaborated provisions for any single international civilian human rights operation. This absence of directive guidance has facilitated the deployment of a number of distinct missions.

The principal operation in BiH remains that of OSCE. It is tasked with both monitoring/investigation/intervention activities as well as a democratisation/civil society development programme. These activities are somewhat artificially and unhelpfully conducted in two entirely distinct functional departments, respectively termed "human rights" and "democratisation"[27]. OSCE has a national network of offices undertaking both categories of activities. In September 1997, there were 30 human rights and 34 democratisation officers deployed in local, regional, and headquarters postings. This figure is not sufficient to the needs of as ambitious a pro-

---

[25] GFA, *supra*, Annex 7, Art. III.

[26] "The idea of establishing a special international human rights monitoring mechanism for Bosnia was first mentioned in the Cutileiro Principles, which would have established both a seven-member Mixed Commission for Human Rights with four appointed by the EC chairman and a Monitoring Mission drawn entirely from the Community. The precursor to the [Vance Owen Peace Plan] proposed that [the International Conference for the Former Yugoslavia] establish an International Commission on Human Rights for Bosnia and Herzegovina with wide powers to investigate and hear complaints. The [Vance Owen Plan] itself called for the establishment by the UN Secretary-General of an International Human Rights Monitoring Mission, whose functions were specified in some detail. The *Invincible* Constitutional Agreement merely foresaw the establishment of such a UN mission, without venturing any details". P. Szasz, Dayton/Paris Peace Agreement, *supra*, at 30-31; *see also*, Anonymous, "Human Rights in Peace Negotiations", 18 Hum. Rts Q. 249 (1996).

[27] The division tends to distract attention from the central role of human rights discourse with regard to all issues of promotion of democracy. The marginalisation of attention to the universal human rights standards may facilitate a process whereby programmes of democratisation can become vehicles for implementation of the objectives of one particular State or for promotion of idiosyncratic conceptions of the relative values of various human rights (by, for instance, prioritising promotion of civil and political over social and economic rights, or by interpreting freedom of expression as a right paramount to all others). *See generally* S. Talbott, "Democracy and the National Interest", Foreign Affairs (November/December 1996), at 47-63.

gramme as that assumed by OSCE[28]. The OSCE Office for Democracy and Human Rights (ODIHR), based in Warsaw, is also active in promoting human rights institution building activities.

The UN High Commissioner for Human Rights/Centre for Human Rights[29] has had a small field presence in Bosnia and Herzegovina since early 1994. During 1996, the international staff usually numbered 7 persons. UNHCHR/CHR activities since the conclusion of the GFA have encompassed three general areas. The first encompasses support for the mandates of the UN Commission on Human Rights Special Rapporteur, Mrs. E. Rehn, and the UN Expert in charge of the Special Process on missing persons in former Yugoslavia (whose mandate was terminated in April 1997). The mandate of the Special Rapporteur[30] includes reporting periodically on the human rights situation in the countries of the region (now including Bosnia and Herzegovina, Croatia, and the Federal Republic of Yugoslavia) and to issue recommendations to the Commission on Human Rights, the General Assembly, OSCE and the High Representative. Her reports are tabled at the Security Council. The second involves provision of expert advisors to the Office of the High Representative, though no more than two advisors have ever been deployed at any one time. And the third relates to undertaking training for international police and civilian human rights monitors. In 1996, an extensive programme of IPTF training was implemented and brief seminar activities were implemented with OSCE. Notwithstanding the need, no significant training programmes have, as yet, been implemented in 1997.

The European Community Monitoring Mission (ECMM) has been deployed in BiH since 1992 on the basis of memoranda of understanding negotiated with the Government. It has a wide-ranging monitoring mandate on behalf of a number of western European States and does address issues of human rights and civil society. ECMM works closely with OSCE. There are some 80 monitors deployed.

The Council of Europe, exceptionally for an organisation without a field presence capability, has an office in Sarajevo. The three-person team facilitates the Council in carrying out tasks assigned to it in the GFA, such as appointment of certain Office holders, as well as implementation of a programme of technical co-operation with a view to eventual membership by BiH of the Council and ratification of the European Convention on

---

[28] *See* OSCE Mission to Bosnia and Herzegovina, "Democratisation Program, Strategies and Activities for 1997", OSCE Doc. REF.SEC/70/97 (describing the OSCE democratisation programme for 1997).

[29] Hereinafter "UNHCHR/CHR".

[30] *See* K. Kenny, "Formal and Informal Innovations in the United Nations Protection of Human Rights: The Special Rapporteur on the Former Yugoslavia", 48 Austrian J. Pub. and Int'l L. 19 (1995); F. Gaer, "UN-Anonymous: Reflection on 'Human Rights in Peace Negotiations'", 19 Hum. Rts. Q. 1 (1997).

Human Rights. Activities include human rights training, legislative review and the strengthening of judicial and political institutions[31].

The European Union will play an increasingly important role in human rights institution building activities, through, inter-alia, the future management and disbursal of funds from the PHARE programme[32].

There are also a myriad international human rights institution building activities being conducted at any one time, by such bodies as the US Agency for International Development, SIDA, Open Society Fund, American Bar Association, National Democratic Institute, International Institute for Democracy and Electoral Assistance, International Human Rights Law Group, USIS, and various UN bodies, including the UNDP, UNICEF, UNESCO and the UN Crime Prevention and Criminal Justice Division. Human rights monitoring activities are conducted by organisations such as International Crisis Group, Balkan War Report , European Action Council for Peace in the Balkans, Open Media Research Institute, International Helsinki Committee and Human Rights Watch. Account should also be taken of the UN human rights treaty bodies. Their role is discussed elsewhere in this chapter.

The multiplicity of organisations addressing issues of human rights is such that a heavy onus falls on the High Representative to introduce and sustain effective co-ordination mechanisms. His office has attempted to address the issue from the moment of its inception. There are three principal mechanisms for coordination: the Human Rights Coordination Centre, the Human Rights Task Force and the meetings of the Principal Officers of the Main International Implementing Partners[33].

The Human Rights Coordination Centre[34] initiative, located in the office of the High Representative in Sarajevo, is staffed by a small team of High Representative staff and part-time liaison officers made available by OSCE, IPTF, UN Civil Affairs and ECMM. UNHCHR/CHR has undertaken to place human rights experts in the office on a full-time basis; five were originally envisaged but this figure was never reached. The HRCC is tasked with the maintenance of effective information exchange and policy-development mechanisms of participating organisations in the fields of human rights monitoring, intervention and institution building. Democratisation activities come within its remit and both of the relevant OSCE departments participate in its activities. Since early 1997, the HRCC is managed by a Steering Board which meets weekly and is comprised of senior officers of these organisations as well as representatives of UNHCR,

---

[31] *See* Council of Europe, *Council of Europe Action in Bosnia and Herzegovina, Programme of Activities 1997* (Strasbourg, 1997).

[32] At the time of writing of the present paper, a PHARE programme for Bosnia and Herzegovina was being devised by a Danish consultancy organisation, Dialogue Development.

[33] The High Representative and the directors of SFOR, IPTF, UNMIBH, OSCE [hereinafter "the Principals"].

[34] Hereinafter "HRCC".

the European Union, the Council of Europe and SFOR. The Steering Board is chaired by the High Representative's Human Rights Advisor.

The HRCC has had difficulty in developing methodologies for participation in its work of the many groups, including NGOs, active in the human rights sector. It attempts to involve relevant organisations in its activities on an issue by issue basis. In February 1997, a consortium of NGOs, denominated the NGO Council, was invited to nominate a representative to join the Steering Board. Only in May did it nominate OXFAM to be its representative. As of early August, that NGO had still not taken its place at the Steering Board table. The HRCC exists only at the level of headquarters in Sarajevo and is not adequately supported by regional or local coordination structures[35].

The Human Rights Task Force meets irregularly and is chaired by the High Representative or his Senior Deputy. It comprises the principal officers of HRCC participating organisations as well senior representatives of significant human rights organisations or institutions. Members of this group include the UN Special Rapporteur, the various Ombudspersons, and a representative of the Human Rights Chamber. Neither local nor international NGOs are represented; they are, however, sometimes invited to participate in "informational sessions". The Task Force follows an agenda agreed upon by the HRCC Steering Board and is intended to decide on major policy issues in a manner whereby they impact immediately on the work programmes of the Principals.

The HRCC and/or the Task Force increasingly channel major urgent human rights concerns to the regular meetings of the Principals. The device is employed when a top-level intervention is required, such as a joint demarche, joint senior missions, intervention with the heads of external organisations, or development of major inter-agency programmes (such as that which facilitated freedom of movement for voters in the elections of 1996). The Principals may and do, of course, also address human rights issues of their own volition.

A number of *ad hoc* coordination bodies have also been established to address particular human rights problems, such as freedom of movement and tracing of missing persons, where it is seen as essential by the Principals or by the States members of the GFA Peace Implementation Council that they be addressed in a focused, ongoing and high level manner. These groups tend to develop with little or no reference to existing initiatives and tend not to be driven by the human rights operations.

---

[35] Useful local co-ordination initiatives have occurred – for instance in Banja Luka: the "Human Rights Working Group"– but these efforts have been *ad hoc* and inadequately integrated into existing Human Rights Coordination Centre structures.

II. EVALUATING THE IMPLEMENTATION OF
HUMAN RIGHTS COORDINATION IN BOSNIA AND HERZEGOVINA

The value of the human rights coordination system may be assessed in the light of its successes. This chapter's examination of activities, sector by sector, will permit the undertaking of such an evaluation.

A. *Planning, recruitment, training and doctrine*

OSCE had never before mounted such an operation and did not formally draw on the experience derived from previous similar operations of other organisations. Staff are all seconded by Governments and initial recruitment criteria focused on senior experience as lawyers, judges, etc., rather than on the necessary field skills. Actually, staff members have come from many different professional backgrounds and include persons beginning their careers. A minority of staff have either formal or field-acquired prior human rights skills. In-service training has been inadequate and, in 1996, the efforts of UNHCHR/CHR to provide training were largely subverted by a poorly developed OSCE training policy. Management of the OSCE operation have grown much more receptive to issues of training and, in 1997, have begun to address deficiencies . Throughout 1996, the OSCE mandate to supervise elections impacted negatively on its human rights activities. At the level of logistics it resulted in interminable secondment of human rights officers to tasks related to preparation or implementation of elections. In terms of integrity of mandate it associated the operation with a series of election-related decisions which paid inadequate regard to issues of human rights[36].

As an UNCIVPOL operation, IPTF drew on the considerable experience of UN peacekeeping operations, benefiting thereby from the services of well-qualified legal officers, UN civil affairs officers, and senior police officers who had served in other field missions. Recruitment, as always, was by secondment, and special human rights qualifications were not specified. During 1996, IPTF did, however, benefit from an ambitious and well received training programme of UNHCHR/CHR. As of September 1997, however, a training programme for those police deployed since conclusion of that training programme (a majority of the force) had not been implemented. IPTF has requested deployment of 120 officers with advanced human rights skills. Pending their deployment, organisational changes, including appointment of senior police and civilian UNMIBH personnel with human rights responsibility, have enhanced the profile of human rights in IPTF activities.

---

[36] A primary exemplar of this problem remains the recommendation that elections proceed despite evidence of endemic abuses of the election campaign process.

During the war, UNHCHR/CHR had an important role in primary human rights monitoring on behalf of the Special Rapporteur; however, with deployment of major monitoring operations, this function disappeared. UNHCHR/CHR has still to fully address implications of its change in status for its own work practices[37]. The GFA also provided UNHCHR/CHR with opportunities to provide technical assistance for IPTF training and the work of the HRCC. The training programme was deployed and efficiently implemented in 1996 but as of September 1997 a follow-up programme is still awaited. The scale of support given to the HRCC never met anticipated levels. Negotiations are ongoing for extension of the UNHCHR/CHR's technical co-operation activities. Recruitment to the field operation is done at headquarters level with little consultation of field management and not all staff are appropriately qualified. The CHR has never undertaken in-service training for members of the field operation. The activities of the UNHCHR/CHR field operation were subject to independent evaluation in early 1997, the findings of which have not been made public.

A number of the personnel servicing the High Representative's coordination mechanisms are experienced human rights professionals. Their numbers are, not however, commensurate with the scale of tasks to be accomplished. One issue which has never been addressed is that of reflecting on or providing guidance regarding issues of field operation planning, deployment, staff recruitment or training. The HRCC has also had little input into decisions on who is deployed to liaise with it. The HRCC has, however, facilitated guest-participation of human rights officers in the training activities undertaken by HRCC member organisations or elsewhere.

B. Administrative and Logistical Support and Security

All of the human rights operations suffer from deficient logistical and administrative support. One consequence is that the operational potential of, for instance, IPTF and OSCE has never been fully exploited. Each of the organisations has significantly improved its procedures for the securing of information . The HRCC has assisted in this regard by drawing attention to inappropriate practices within organisations (such as, for instance, the hiring by an IPTF station in early 1996 of the local police chief's daughter as an interpreter).

Security of the personnel of civilian mission has not been perceived as a major problem in the post-GFA period, though there have been isolated incidents of intimidation. Local staff of international organisations are also occasionally subject to harassment. The various human rights operations

---

[37] For instance, it has yet to identify the precise role of the one office which it has maintained outside Sarajevo, located in the principal city of Republika Srpska, Banja Luka.

have access to security guidance given by SFOR and have, for instance, acted on the advice to temporarily withdraw from Republika Srpska on at least two occasions in 1996. No organisation has systematically implemented obligatory training courses for civilian personnel with regard to the very serious problem of land-mines.

IPTF is an unarmed force and thus relies heavily on security provided by SFOR in carrying out hazardous tasks such as night patrols in tense locations, conducting of searches for long barrelled weapons, and raids on police stations, such as those in Republika Srpska in August 1997. It has expressed concern that the this year's reduction in the size of the military force has impacted negatively on its ability to function and that IPTF activities will become untenable if and when a military force withdraws.

C. Investigation, Intervention and Effectiveness

With so many co-existing monitoring operations, there is a high likelihood that human rights incidents will be reported and monitored by more than one organisation. Indeed, the situation in BiH persistently provides examples of incidents which have received the simultaneous attention of multiple operations, including occasions (such as during the 1996 elections) where the monitors are so thick on the ground as to get in the way of each other. Multiple monitoring may not only be wasteful but also can provide widely varying, conflicting and confusing accounts. Problems can also arise of multiple and mutually compromising interventions, especially at local level.

The High Representative's coordination mechanisms continue to address the issue in a vigorous fashion. The HRCC serves as an information clearing house and attempts to distill the essence of multiple reporting. Where the information remains confused or inadequate, it tasks appropriate organisations with further investigation. On occasion, when it is considered that local monitors require assistance, it has deployed teams of experienced investigators who report back to the HRCC (and participating organisations) both on the incident at issue and on how the local monitoring methodologies might be improved. A survey of recommendations made in 1996 indicated a high level of implementation of its recommendations regarding improved methodology.

The HRCC has also addressed some aspects of the issue of more effective intervention. One initiative, discussed below, has been its campaign to educate international staff about the existing domestic remedies and how they might be employed strategically. Another has been promoting inter-agency knowledge of and access to the various methods by which IPTF can have sanctions imposed on local police officers (these sanctions are of great importance in a society where some 70% of all human rights violations are perpetrated by the police). The HRCC has also facilitated the increasingly employed device of the issuing of joint *demarches* by the

Principals. The Principals have also been successfully encouraged to develop strategies for inclusion of human rights considerations into deci-sion-making relating to economic assistance ands reconstruction.

At the end of 1996, in the context of preparation of cases to be submitted by the Special Rapporteur directly to the senior member of the Presidency, Mr.Izetbegovic, it was considered that human rights investigations were still not of a consistently acceptable standard. It was decided to upgrade the HRCC support by establishment of a dedicated specialised monitoring and response unit. The team's capacity received its first test when, in February 1997, it joined with IPTF to undertake a major investigation of reports of grave police abuses in Mostar[38]. The co-operative and thorough nature of that investigation is seen as having accorded it a particular authority. The investigation findings were endorsed by the UN Security Council on 11 March 1997[39].

Improvements in the human rights monitoring and intervention environ-ment have been among the principle achievements of the HRCC. It has not, however, fundamentally addressed the issue of wasteful multiple primary reporting and, while it has ensured a certain coordination of high level interventions, it has not had consistently similar success at local level (not least because of the lack of HRCC-linked structures outside Sarajevo). The HRCC has also not yet undertaken the important task of systematically assessing the effectiveness of interventions and of issuing recommenda-tions to HRCC organisations based on its findings.

D. Addressing the Issues of Refugees and Internally Displaced Persons

The war in BiH resulted in displacement of some 2,100,000 people. Each of the Entities accommodates large populations which have been internally displaced. Republika Srpska also houses Serbs displaced from Croatia. While over 250,000 people have now returned to areas where they are part of the local ethnic majority, authorities in each of the Entities and in Croa-tia have successfully obstructed all but token voluntary return to areas controlled by people of different ethnicity to the returnees. Obstruction of return[40] is partly accomplished by a range of human rights abuses[41], such as various forms of police harassment and limitations on freedom of move-ment, as well as application of discriminatory legislation. Displacement also gives rise to human rights problems in the manner by which internally

---

[38] *See* International Crisis Group, *Grave Situation in Mostar: Robust Response Required* (Sarajevo, 13 February 1997) (overview of the situation in Mostar during that period).

[39] *See* UN Docs. S/1997/201, S/1997/204, and S/PRST/1997/12.

[40] For an exhaustive independent analysis, see International Crisis Group, *Going No-where Fast: Refugees and Internally Displaced Persons in Bosnia and Herzegovina* (Sara-jevo, April 1997).

[41] *See generally* M. Stavropoulou, "Bosnia and Herzegovina and the Right to Return in International Law" elsewhere in this volume.

displaced groups may, in the regions to which they have been relocated, engage in campaigns of harassment of members of minority ethnic groups in these regions. This phenomenon is illustrated by campaigns of harassment waged against Muslims living in the Teslic region of Republika Srpska, perpetrated, to a significant degree, by refugees from the Krajina region of Croatia, and by Bosnian Croats against Muslims in West Mostar.

The scale of displacement-related human rights abuses is such that each of the organisations must address the issue on a constant basis as an issue of both monitoring and institutional reform. They must also recognise that their work in building a just democratic society will be doomed if it is constructed on the basis of the distorted demographics which have been brought about by the war and the policies of "ethnic cleansing". Promotion of voluntary return is therefore an essential element in the human rights agenda for BiH. The various organisations remain more or less true to this ideal. Attempts at the coordination of human rights monitoring and intervention are described elsewhere in this chapter. One return-related institution building activity on which there has been effective HRCC-based coordination has been the campaign for reform of laws regulating ownership and possession of abandoned property. Another significant coordinated return-related project is the Reconstruction and Return Task Force, under the auspices of UNHCR, which links agencies dealing with both these issues. It has an important role to play in facilitating common positions by such disparate organisations as UNHCR, the World Bank and the European Commission.

Occasionally, peace implementation organisations, such as SFOR and IPTF, are accused of dealing with return issues in a manner which gives priority to the concerns of current local populations in areas targeted for return or which lays undue emphasis on security conditions. These are possible perspectives for analysis of such incidents as the imposition of burdensome formalities on Muslim internally displaced persons who have attempted to exercise their right to return to homes located just inside the Inter-Entity Boundary Line (the IEBL) in Republika Srpska (termed, "the zone of separation").

The Office of the High Representative has given its full support to a grassroots initiative of displaced persons, "The Coalition for Return", and has encouraged other international organisations to support it as a model of "citizen-empowerment" to counteract the obstructive policies of local authorities[42].

At the highest level of policy development, UNHCR occasionally convenes a humanitarian affairs working group of the Peace Implementation Council, with membership from the main peace implementing agencies. On an operational level, the human rights community maintains ongoing close

---

[42] *See* Conclusions of the London Peace Implementation Conference, held 5 December 1996, reproduced on the Office of the High Representative website, http://www.ohr.int.

contact with UNHCR and it participates in The HRCC activity. UNHCR also, in 1993, signed a memorandum of understanding with UNHCHR/CHR on the exchange of information. This facility has been moribund for some time. Reductions in UNHCR staffing levels since GFA have greatly limited its capacity to address human rights issues. As already noted, it has also defined its human rights mandate in rather narrow terms.

E. Internal and Public Reporting.

In the early days of the various missions there were serious problems of internal reporting. Staff at OSCE headquarters, for instance, frequently complained that field offices were forwarding neither adequate nor appropriately formatted information. IPTF suffered similar problems with regard to human rights-sensitive information. In one notorious and well-publicised incident, an IPTF station reported to regional headquarters that there were indicted war criminals serving in the local police station; however, the regional headquarters did not deem the information worthy of transmittal to Sarajevo. UNHCHR/CHR had no effective mechanism for regular periodic transmittal of pertinent information. Each of the organisations improved considerably during 1996. OSCE implemented an efficient and well conceived system of weekly reports; IPTF made serious efforts to develop a human rights reporting chain; UNHCHR/CHR implemented and sustained a system of monthly activity reports.

The HRCC is a very effective channel for the sharing of internal reports among participating agencies. Based on the internal reports, the HRCC has also developed a daily human rights report, in English and local languages. Though open to criticism regarding its journalistic approach, the report does draw attention to the major daily occurrences and, over time, clearly demonstrates the pattern of human rights abuses. It receives very wide distribution, including to diplomatic missions, journalists, and NGOs . This report is distributed world-wide by means of email[43]. A weekly edition also receives wide distribution, distributed to interested local parties, including journalists and NGOs and is posted on the High Representative's website[44]. Another publication, the Bulletin of the High Representative, which is distributed in hard copy and on the website, also addresses significant human rights issues. OSCE is developing its public reporting and now has a monthly democratisation newsletter, also available by email, and, in abridged form on its website[45]. Among the actors who issue regular public UN reports on the human rights situation are the Special Rapporteur[46], the

---

[43] For further information, *see* OHR website, http://www.ohr.int.

[44] *Id.*

[45] Information may be found on the OSCE Bosnia and Herzegovina Mission's website, http://www-osce.austria.eu.net.

[46] Posted on the UNHCHR homepage: http://www.unhchr.ch.

High Representative[47] and the Special Representative of the UN Secretary-General.

Development of public reporting has been a significant success of the co-ordinated missions in BiH. Work still remains to be done in promoting popular access to the material through such devices as speedily translating material into local languages and promoting awareness of and facilitating information on access to the UN reports. The obscurity of some such reports is illustrated by the manner in which a report of the Special Rapporteur on preparations for the 1996 elections[48], issued two months before polling day, received no media attention whatsoever, even though it constituted an official, strident, and systematic criticism of the range of electoral abuses[49]. The press officers of the various organisations have also failed to exploit the periodically significant presence of world media in a manner which might draw useful attention to issues of human rights.

F. The Relationship Between Monitoring and Institution Building

Both OSCE and the Office of the High Representative address issues of monitoring and institution building in a disjunctive way. OSCE deals with monitoring in its human rights branch and institution building primarily in its democratisation branch. The High Representative has undertaken significant institution-building activity (such as law reform, support for institutions of State, a number of civil society-related projects, etc.) without reference to the office of its human rights advisor. The absence of the human rights teams from a range of the institution-building activities may result in a lack of sustained reference to the range of applicable international human rights instruments. It also impedes development of a proper synergy between concerns of monitoring and institution building.

As 1996 progressed, an enormous number of human rights/civil society institution-building activities were commenced in BiH, implemented by the various agencies participating in the HRCC as well as a host of other bodies, including those listed earlier. First efforts were commonly characterised by considerable overlapping of activity, wasted resources and badly-designed projects. There were also serious institution-building needs which were not being addressed (such as the promotion of NGO activity outside certain major population centres). In response to the need for coordination, various sectoral steps were taken, such as an IPTF initiative to co-ordinate rule of law projects and an effort by the American Bar Association to facilitate information exchange on law reform activities.

---

[47] Posted on his homepage: http://www.ohr.int.

[48] UN Doc. E/CN.4/1997/5 (27 June 1996, but erroneously dated 17 July 1996).

[49] Broader issues are raised in this regard, concerning a widespread lack of understanding of the existence or functioning of mechanisms of the UN Commission on Human Rights.

The HRCC, however, was slow to become involved, primarily because it had become preoccupied with issues of human rights monitoring. The HRCC was also not well attuned to issues of institution building because its membership excluded so many bodies active in the field.

Late in 1996, the HRCC took its first serious steps to both co-ordinate institution building and promote best practice, including developing appropriate linkages with monitoring activities. In the context of a necessarily cumbersome mechanism which sought to facilitate the participation of all relevant local and international actors, it drew up a lengthy list of areas in urgent need of co-ordinated action. The first was the promotion of enhanced and strategic referral of cases of human rights abuse to the existing domestic mechanisms (such as the Human Rights Chamber and the Federation Ombudsmen) rather than immediately to the political leadership. A first step in this regard was the facilitation of a process whereby members of the various mechanisms met together for the first time to clarify the mutuality of their mandates and offer guidance on strategic referral. Such meetings ultimately led to the publication of a referral guide[50] which was widely distributed by OSCE. The action taken on this matter can be deemed a success both in terms of improving the practice of human rights monitors and strengthening the indigenous human rights institutions.

In 1997, the HRCC's capacity to address issues of institution building was strengthened by the establishment of specialist units dealing with issues such as promotion of the rule of law, human rights education and NGO support. International organisations focusing on institution-building activities, such as the Council of Europe and the European Union, were also invited to sit on its Steering Board. As has already been noted, the NGO Council has not actively taken advantage of the invitation to participate which was extended to participate in the Steering Board's activities. At the time of this writing, it may be observed that the new structures have somewhat promoted the status of institution building *vis a vis* monitoring activities in the HRCC. The latter, however, continue to receive the predominant attention of HRCC management, a fact which may be partly because the HRCC chief, who also serves as the High Representative's Human Rights Advisor, is obliged to address an endless litany of human rights emergencies. It is also relevant that the preponderance of HRCC staff experience is in issues of monitoring and emergency intervention.

The HRCC has yet to turn its attention to many of the institution-building sectors or to develop proper working relationships with the full range of implementing agencies. In this regard, it must continually struggle with the issue of the correct parameters for its concern. Where does a human rights competency begin and end? When is an issue of civil society support or democratisation not a matter for the human rights specialists? In

---

[50] OSCE, *Guidelines for Processing Human Rights Violations in the Field, Volume I* (Sarajevo, 1997).

this regard, it must be acknowledged that pragmatism, if nothing else, will always dictate that there be sectoral activities best left outside the human rights coordination mechanisms (for instance, in the law reform area, it is hard to envisage a useful role for the HRCC with regard to, for example, technical development of commercial law or narcotics trafficking provisions). To the extent that organisations or sectoral activities at left out of the co-ordination mechanisms it is important that means be found whereby influence can be brought to bear to ensure that those excluded categories respect the fundamental human rights imperatives. This is, for instance, perhaps the most useful way to address issues concerning activities in BiH of the international financial institutions.

G. Institution Building

1. Police

Bosnia and Herzegovina has a multitude of police forces[51], all over-staffed and most of which, during and since the war, primarily served the interests of one or other ethnic group. To the extent that police have received training, it was in the pre-war communist force and with no attention paid to issues of community policing. The vast majority of human rights abuses continue to be perpetrated by members of the police in a context of effective impunity. Police reform is accordingly a matter of high priority for BiH.

IPTF has a mandate to train and promote organisational reform, which includes a programme of downsizing and a vetting system whereby incompetent or miscreant officers may be excluded. Training activities carried out primarily by IPTF personnel were somewhat *ad hoc* in 1996. However, close attention is now being paid to development of the curricula in police academies. International funding is available to assist local police in upgrading their systems and equipment. So far, the IPTF programme has been partially implemented. Only in late in the summer of 1997 did elements of the police forces in Republika Srpska agree to participate. The change of heart occurred in the context of an international determination to insist on compliance of Republika Srpska with the GFA. The President of the Entity, Mrs. Plavsic, also encouraged compliance of the police with the GFA obligations in the context of her currying of international support in her power struggle with Mr. Karajdic. The manner by which IPTF asserted its

---

[51] At least, this is so in the Federation, where each canton has one or more separate forces. Across Bosnia and Herzegovina, however, a problem arises in terms of just what constitutes a police force. The GFA foresees the interpretative issue and gives the IPTF a mandate to deal with all organisations with a "mandate including law enforcement, criminal investigations, public and State security, or detention and judicial activities". GFA, *supra*, Annex 11, Art. VII.

authority in the region, initially through forced entry into police stations, also demonstrated the importance for their work of close protective support provided by SFOR[52].

Except for *ad hoc* and uncoordinated initiatives, such as a regionally organised OSCE training for police chiefs in February 1997, the various civilian human rights operations are not closely involved in the police training programmes. In this regard, UNHCHR/CHR, notwithstanding its dealings with police in other countries, has persistently failed to exploit opportunities to participate in the process of developing and implementing the human rights components of training modules. The police vetting mechanism is watched closely by the civilian operations and they co-operate with IPTF in attempting to use it as a form of sanction for perpetrators of human rights abuses.

2. Prisons

BiH has some 14 long-term detention facilities for civilian prisoners. The principal problem for prisoners is the excessive length of pre-trial detention. Though reform of prison conditions is obviously required, this does not presently warrant priority attention from the international community. The UN Crime Prevention and Criminal Justice Division is now implementing a training programme for prison personnel.

3. Judicial Reform

The war left BiH with appalling problems in the administration of justice. There were three court systems (one in Republika Srpska and two in the Federation) which had no dealings with each other; many of the best judges, court officials and law students had left the country or were otherwise occupied; adoption of new Constitutions both before and in the context of the GFA, together with the patchwork development of law and wartime regulations, had created a legal chaos; and many court buildings were either destroyed or severely damaged. Miscarriages of justice occur frequently, particularly where defendants belong to ethnic-minority groups or are indigent. A particular problem, which still occurs sporadically, is the trying of persons on war-crime charges in contravention of rules agreed between the Government authorities and the International Criminal Tribunal in The Hague.

The international community's judicial monitoring activities are well co-ordinated. In the context of HRCC activities, UNHCHR/CHR has put in place an effective system of inter-agency co-operation to ensure that judicial processes which are sensitive from a human rights point of view are observed and reported in a professional manner, and that requirements for institutional change are addressed. A number of local and international

---

[52] *See* Office of the High Representative, *OHR Bulletin*, No. 58 (26 August, 1997) (regarding the IPTF's assertiveness in Republika Srpska).

NGOs, such as the Helsinki Committee on Human Rights and the International Human Rights Law Group, participate in these activities. Monitoring activities extended in 1997 to review of the process of appointment of judges; and in May 1997, HRCC organisations jointly issued a strong denunciation of the process in parts of the Federation. The HRCC also continues to attempt to open inter-Entity channels on such issues as collection of evidence, receipt of testimony and mutual recognition of the qualifications of advocates: with only little success to show so far.

Other institution-building requirements are being addressed to a greater or less extent by a wide range of international organisations and NGOs. Activities include assistance in law reform, training of lawyers and judges, development of a judge's manual and a reference manual on international standards for independence of the legal profession, enhancing capacity of the judges and lawyers' associations and the university law schools, and development of free legal aid schemes. Good work is being done, but there continue to be serious deficiencies.

Much more coordination is required. The manner in which a number of organisations, including IPTF, SFOR, and the UN Crime Prevention and Criminal Justice Division, conducted identical surveys of the justice system is an example of wasted resources. It is also clear that a number of organisations, including some which otherwise participate in the HRCC, are unwilling to assist HRCC in promoting collaborative activities in the sector. IPTF, for example, without organisational reference to the HRCC, persists in assuming to itself the co-ordinating role regarding every aspect of reform of the criminal justice system[53]. Also regrettable is the manner in which a number of schemes of free legal aid for indigent defendants are being developed without adequate mutual reference to and outside existing HRCC structures[54].

Inconsistent attention is now paid to the need for projects to be sustainable in the long term. This criticism may be directed at the funding and management components of those actual and proposed systems of legal aid which are devised by international organisations. It is also apparent in the manner whereby projects are largely implemented by international staff and local capacity is thus not being adequately developed. In addition, poor planning sometimes results in unsuitable project methodology and content. This was well-illustrated by the failure of a joint OSCE/Council of Europe scheme in 1996 to bring together at one seminar all the judges of the country. No Republika Srpska judges made the journey to the venue in the Federation – an eventuality which could have been anticipated and addressed. Those judges who did attend were presented with a programme of very uneven quality. A second and more successful attempt in 1997 dem-

---

[53] See the IPTF contribution to a HRCC background paper on rule of law activities, 6 May, 1997 (on file with the present writer).
[54] *Id.* (OSCE and UNHCR contributions),

onstrated that the organisers had learned much from the first experience. In general, projects would benefit from systematic evaluation and impact assessment.

4. Official Human Rights Institutions[55]

This paper has already made reference to the plethora of human rights mechanisms created pursuant to the various peace initiatives: the Human Rights Chamber, the Ombudsperson for Bosnia and Herzegovina, the Federation Ombudsmen, the Commission for Displaced Persons and Refugees (Real Property Commission). To these may be added the Constitutional Court of Bosnia and Herzegovina and the still un-established Human Rights Court of the Federation. Account should also be taken of the Election Appeals Sub-commission and the regular courts, all of which have competence to address human rights issues.

The various international organisations interact with the human rights institutions in a number of ways. First, nomination of some or all of the various institutions (other than lower level courts) is upon appointment by designated international organisations. Thus, for instance, OSCE appoints the Federation Ombudsmen and the International Ombudsperson. The Council of Europe appoints members of the Human Rights Chamber. Second, certain organisations have undertaken to provide medium to long term financial support to certain of the institutions. Third, this chapter has already described the manner in which the organisations, acting through the HRCC, have successfully promoted inter-institution discussion and encouraged development of strategies for strategic referral. Fourth, various initiatives have been taken to promote implementation of decisions of the institutions. These have included the making of strong statements by the Principals in support of the Ombudsmen and the undertaking of joint missions by the Federation Ombudsmen and the UN Special Rapporteur. Early in 1997, the Federation Ombudsmen reported that initiatives such as these did promote the process of implementation of decisions[56]. Fifth, representatives of some of these institutions have participated in the activities of the Human Rights Task Force. They are also occasionally invited to meetings of the HRCC Steering Board. During 1996, certain institutions also participated on a regular basis in specific projects at the HRCC. One project in which they played a substantial part was the campaign to tackle the myriad legal problems relating to occupancy of domestic property. New HRCC structures are intended to ensure that they are invited to similarly participate in all other activities relevant to their competencies

---

[55] *See also* M.O'Flaherty, Human Rights and the GFA, *supra*.

[56] Ombudsmen of the Federation of Bosnia and Herzegovina, *Annual Report on the Situation of Human Rights for 1996* (Sarajevo, March 1997) [hereinafter "Federation Ombudsmen 1996 Report"].

This brief survey does indicate that there is a high degree of beneficial contact between these institutions and the international human rights organisations which promotes immediate and long term sustainability of the institutions and integrates them more effectively into the range of activities of the international organisations. More, however, is possible. There is need for still more sustained efforts to promote implementation of the decisions of institutions through such actions as joint *demarches* by the Principals.

Enthusiastic support for the institutions should, however, be nuanced in a manner which encourages and supports efforts of the regular courts to address issues of human rights. Thought needs to be given also to the manner by which the provision of funding to the institutions does not create a level of dependence which will cause problems when the international organisations withdraw.

There is another task for the international organisations: the undertaking of constructive appraisal of the work of the institutions. The various bodies are presently developing in a context of little or no public scrutiny or analysis; they require, however, the benefit of hard criticism (even if delivered in a context of great confidentiality). The present writer is, for instance, concerned that attention is not being drawn to the manner in which the work practices of the Ombudsperson for Bosnia and Herzegovina may be overly formalistic and ill-suited to the post-war realities of the country[57]. Another institution, the Election Appeals Sub-commission seems to have escaped all criticism despite its neglect for principles of due process of law in its activities at the time of the 1996 elections[58].

---

[57] The Ombudsperson has, for instance, chosen to develop a working methodology, closely modelled on that of the European Commission on Human Rights, which, in its complexity and legalism, poses daunting obstacles for the non-lawyer. Office of the Human Rights Ombudsperson for Bosnia and Herzegovina, *First Annual Report* (Sarajevo, April, 1997). By comparison, the Federation Ombudsmen operate a flexible, readily accessible and informal methodology which integrates well in the local cultural and social context. *See* Federation Ombudsmen 1996 Report, *supra*.

[58] It presented itself as a judicial body but persistently failed to comply with such elements of judicial due process as provision of an effective right of defence or of a right of appeal against imposition of serious penalties. For a self-assessment by the EASC of its own activities, see Election Appeals Subcommission, *Report to Head of Mission* (Sarajevo, 4 October 1996) (copy on file with the present writer).

5. Non-Governmental Organisations[59]

Pre-war BiH did not have a community of local human rights NGOs. A small number developed during the war, notably the Human Rights Centre in Tuzla and the human rights department of the Tuzla Citizens' Forum, both of which have undertaken extensive training and human rights promotional activities. In Sarajevo, with ongoing support of the Open Society Fund, a Law Centre was developed which addresses issues of human rights institution building. There is now an Helsinki Committee for Human Rights in Sarajevo and Bijeljina in the Republika Srpska which focuses its attention on monitoring and human rights education. There are very many other voluntary groups which address issues of human rights monitoring or institution building as part of their range of activities, such as women's organisations and bodies, including civil groups, which represent the interests of sectors of society. The Coalition for Return also sees its campaign as a human rights one. Most of the groups active with regard to human rights participate in an initiative called "the Citizens' Alternative Parliament".

The human rights NGOs are increasingly professional in approach. They have been fortunate in being led by highly competent Bosnian nationals. The principal groups have also benefited from international linkages with such bodies as the International Helsinki Committee and Helsinki Citizen's Assembly. The NGOs are, however, very unevenly distributed in the country, with the preponderance in such centres as Sarajevo and Tuzla. There is an almost complete lack of NGOs addressing human rights issues in all of the Croat-controlled parts of the Federation and many locations in Republika Srpska. Another problem for the NGO community is its very heavy reliance on international financial assistance. Large sums are being distributed by the aid agencies of a number of States – often in an inefficient manner which fails, to promote organisational sustainability[60].

A vast number of international NGOs are active in Bosnia and Herzegovina, many addressing issues of civil society, including human rights. The major international human rights monitoring NGOs, however, maintain only a modest or no presence in the country. They nonetheless wield influence. Groups such as Amnesty International and Human Rights Watch have attracted a lot of attention for their interventions and manage to maintain international media attention on such issues as the failure to arrest indicted war criminals. The Lawyers' Committee for Human Rights and the Open Society Institute[61] have issued commentaries on such matters as

---

[59] *See generally* I. Smillie, *Service Delivery or Civil Society: Non-Governmental Organisations in Bosnia and Herzegovina* (CARE Canada, December 1996); Dialogue Development, *Survey of Bosnian Civil Society Organisations* (April 1997); Helsinki Citizen's Assembly, *Dayton Continued in Bosnia and Herzegovina 2* (Banja Luka, 1997).

[60] One donor agency is, for instance, funding 200 civil society development projects of 70 organisations or groups in just one municipality.

[61] Under the auspices of its Forced Migration Projects.

the property and citizenship legal regimes, which have influenced the work of the Office of the High Representative and others promoting law reform. One NGO, the International Crisis Group, has had remarkable success, through both public interventions and discreet lobbying, in raising media attention and influencing policy development on a number of human rights and other issues. BiH has provided this group with the opportunity to demonstrate the extent of real influence which can be wielded by an international voluntary group which is well endowed, present, and visible in the country and supported by a politically influential board

The international human rights operations have shown some sensitivity to the need to work with and support the development of local NGOs. Support comes in a number of ways. Some HRCC organisations, especially OSCE and the Office of the High Representative, have NGO support programmes which provide technical assistance, advice on how to approach the donor community and practical assistance in such matters as safely moving people across the Inter-Entity Boundary Line to attend gatherings. Relevant local NGOs have also participated in certain sectoral activities of the HRCC. They are, for instance, very active in the project addressing problems relating to property. The NGOs are also present in the coordination groups for law reform and promotion of the rule of law. In addition, most HRCC information is now distributed to local NGOs. Information provided by them is also channelled through the HRCC and features regularly in the daily Human Rights Report. NGOs are often the primary source for reports of the Special Rapporteur and international organisations. As mentioned already, however, NGOs have yet to show real interest in participating as members in the activities of the Human Rights Steering Board.

Some of the most important initiatives to assist the local NGO community are developed outside HRCC structures by international NGOs. This was the case, for instance, with the opening in May 1997 of the NGO Information and Support Center in Bosnia and Herzegovina. During the summer of 1997, an NGO/IO consortium[62] began developing a project to establish a technical and legal support service for local civil society focused NGOs, the Bosnian NGO Law, Education and Advocacy Project (LEA).

There is still much that the international human rights operations can do to promote the NGO sector. A first goal should be to encourage development of NGOs in neglected regions. A second would encompass a continuing search for ways to integrate effectively the local and international NGOs into the work of the HRCC, even in face of a lack of enthusiasm from NGOs themselves. There is a related need to encourage coordination in the voluntary sector itself. Despite the important initiatives for informa-

---

[62] Open Society Fund, The International Rescue Committee, World Bank, and The International Council of Voluntary Agencies.

tion sharing facilities in the NGO community, insufficient coordination and co-operation among local and international NGOs, with resultant waste and mis-direction of resources, remains. It is also important that the donor community work in a more collaborative manner. The HRCC has already attempted to address this issue, though in a somewhat half-hearted manner.

One further and essential challenge for the international human rights operations is to involve local groups in development and implementation of institution building programmes. For reasons including short-term planning and the desire for immediate results, far too many of these are currently carried out by directly by the international groups in a manner which suggests that they will collapse as soon as the internationals leave. The matter gives current cause for concern regarding, for instance, the development of legal aid projects, and the many inter-Entity dialogue initiatives[63].

An encouraging recent development has been the establishment of the Democracy Foundation of Bosnia and Herzegovina. This body, run by a widely representative and gender-balanced board comprising Bosnian nationals, intends to begin the process of "re-patriating" the range of civil society projects which are currently being implemented by international organisations. The international group promoting the project, the International Institute for Democracy and Electoral Assistance (International IDEA), has exhibited a model methodology whereby it undertakes extensive consultation and resolves to withdraw as soon as possible while leaving in place a mechanism for non-directive international support.

6. Human Rights Education

Three organisations with well-established roles regarding human rights education, UNESCO, UNICEF, and the Council of Europe, are present in BiH. Other international organisations with a training mandate include IPTF with regard to the local police forces. Major human rights operations, principally OSCE, have also shown a concern to address the issue. Little has yet been achieved. The lack of progress is not surprising for a number of reasons.

The war totally disrupted the various target groups, such as children in the school system, and professionals organised into associations. Schools have to be re-built, teachers return, and basis text books be printed and distributed. Many professional bodies have yet to re-constitute or establish themselves. Also, greatly complicating the re-establishment of an educational and professional system is the Entity division, which requires that almost every strategic goal be achieved by a process of parallel implementation of two programmes. It took some time for the international community to acknowledge the full extent of division and realise that common

---

[63] Whereby, meetings are facilitated between groups of professionals from each of the Entities.

strategy for BiH was so often futile. Much time was wasted and planning discarded in 1996 because of a failure to grasp this reality.

The range of education needs is vast and goes well beyond the scope of activities of the human rights component of any international operation. Thus, for instance, at least four departments of the Office of the High Representative, have a legitimate interest in education issues. In such a context it is difficult for the human rights components to argue that their concerns must be implemented on a priority basis. It is no less difficult to argue against those who would, and do, impede development of a human rights curriculum for schools on the basis that it must be developed over a number of years as part of an integrated school programme.

With regard to the human rights education of children, UNICEF should be in a position to lead the process of developing and implementing a HRCC-centred plan which addresses the entire range of issues and actors and which has the rights of the child as its corner-stone. Experience in BiH has not demonstrated that UNICEF is yet likely to take on the role. During 1996, it developed its country programme and action plan with unseemly haste and minimal reference to political circumstances[64]. Since then, it appears to have undertaken little meaningful consultation with the main human rights organisations or their co-ordination mechanisms.

There have been some educational achievements. Reference has already been made to the activities of IPTF and the UN Crime Prevention and Criminal Justice Division. The Council of Europe and OSCE grow ever more effective in implementing trainings for judges, lawyers and politicians and UNESCO is developing courses in civil education for children. Relying extensively on Bosnian national staff, OSCE has also made real efforts to undertake voter-education in preparation for the 1996 elections. Despite endless technical problems and in the absence of published scientific evaluations, this campaign seems to have had some success in reaching its target groups[65].

One success for the co-ordinated efforts of the HRCC organisations (together with a number of local and international non-governmental groups) was the establishment of the University of Sarajevo Centre for Human Rights. Many groups had proposed that a Centre be established and there was originally a danger that competing interests would destroy the idea. In this context, HRCC organisations took the lead in co-ordinating development of the project. The Centre opened in December 1996 and is being encouraged to become a truly local institution with a capacity for research, training and dissemination of materials. It has already organised a

---

[64] It negotiated the plan with the "caretaker" central government prior to the 1996 elections and without adequate reference to the fundamental constitutional reform whereby almost all matters concerning promotion of the rights of children would be addressed at the level of the Entities.

[65] This tentative assessment is based on anecdotal indications.

number of training activities for Sarajevo university students and has commenced collaboration in a number of research projects of European human rights institutes. In July 1997, it implemented an ambitious human rights training module at Tuzla Summer University, which brought together third-level students from all parts of the country[66]. It was originally hoped that the Centre could be a pan-Bosnian institution; however, because of the Entity-based nature of the organisation of education, this is now clearly untenable, and thus the HRCC is faced with the need to encourage development of a similar facility in Republika Srpska.

The number of NGO-generated human rights education projects is increasing. These are typically in such sectors as "citizen-empowerment" and human rights skills for NGO activists[67]. Implementation of these programmes would benefit from enhanced coordination and information exchange among NGOs and between them and the international human rights operations. The HRCC has a role to play in this regard and it has commenced the compilation of an ongoing survey of all such activities.

H. The Human Rights Treaty Bodies[68]

As has already been observed, the GFA invites intervention of the various supervisory bodies of human rights treaties, including the treaty bodies under each of the six principal UN human rights instruments[69]. The invitations are unprecedented and present treaty bodies with opportunities to undertake their monitoring and technical assistance activities outside the normal methodologies such as examination and commentary on periodic reports submitted by the State. Since treaty bodies normally have competence only to deal with sovereign Governments, it is also noteworthy that the invitation obligates non-State parties (the Entities).

The HRCC has recognised the significance for long term monitoring and institution building of active involvement by the treaty bodies and, in 1996, co-ordinated the preparation of submissions to two of them, the Committee on the Elimination of Racial Discrimination and the Committee on the Rights of the Child. These efforts met with limited success[70].

---

[66] This project has been promoted by a Dutch student NGO, YSY.

[67] For reference to the training of lawyers, see Part II above.

[68] The Human Rights Committee, the Committee on Economic, Social and Cultural Rights, The Committee Against Torture, the Committee on the Elimination of Racial Discrimination, the Committee on the Elimination of Discrimination Against Women, the Committee on the Rights of the Child.

[69] *See* M.O'Flaherty, "Treaty Body Innovation and Bosnia and Herzegovina", *in* J. Crawford and P. Alston (eds.), *The Treaty Bodies faced with States of Emergency: The Case of Bosnia and Herzegovina* (Cambridge, forthcoming).

[70] Both Committees did devote time to addressing issues specific to Bosnia and Herzegovina, but have yet to intervene forcefully. *See* further Chapter 11 of this volume.

I. Addressing The Past

The wars in former Yugoslavia have left a bitter legacy of hate, fear and anger. There are multiple local and international responses, many of which involve the international human rights operations. One of the most significant steps towards addressing the past and promoting reconciliation would be the establishment of conditions for voluntary return of displaced persons. The roles of the international human rights operations have been detailed elsewhere in this paper.

The elections were conceived of as an opportunity to provide the democratic base on which a just future might be built. The 1996 elections served no such purpose and, in the context of massive violation of the rules applicable to democratic campaigning, returned to power the leaders who had waged the war. OSCE's mishandling of the elections compromised its integrity and damaged the reputation of all parts of its operation, including the human rights and democratisation programmes.

Determination of the fate of the approximately 18,000 missing persons is an important element in creating conditions for reconciliation. This classic role of ICRC[71] was undertaken by a number of actors in Bosnia and Herzegovina[72]: the UN Commission on Human Rights appointed an expert on the issue; the Special Rapporteur became involved; the US administration funded a high-level international commission; and ICRC itself developed programmes. Lack of co-operation from the local authorities (why should it be assumed that authorities would cooperate in the investigation of war crimes in which they may be implicated?) has contributed to the substantial failure to determine the fate of the majority of missing persons. Attempts at coordination of the various international initiatives has tended to occur within the Office of the High Representative but outside the HRCC structure.

The ongoing failure of the International Criminal Tribunal for former Yugoslavia[73] to be given custody of indicted war criminals is well documented elsewhere[74]. As of June 1997, only 8 of the 74 indictees were in custody. The international human rights operations have persisted in attempting to address the issue; IPTF has on a number of occasions publicly shamed IFOR/SFOR by drawing attention to the manner in which information passed to the troops on sighting of indictees was not acted upon. The Principals, spurred on by the Human Rights Task Force and the HRCC,

---

[71] For general information on their activities in former Yugoslavia, please consult the International Committee of the Red Cross website, http://www. icrc.ch.

[72] *See* Chapter 5 of this volume.

[73] For general information on Tribunal activities, please consult the UN website, http://www.unorg/icty. An excellent ongoing source of independent information on Tribunal activities is the email publication, *Tribunal Update* – available by subscription from the Institute for War and Peace Reporting (majordom@osa.ceu.hu).

[74] *See, e.g.*, Chapter 10 of this volume.

have continued to devise and implement strategies to encourage indictees to surrender. One current stratagem is to get third States to refuse to give entry or transit visas to any such person. It was further agreed in June 1997 that municipalities in which indicted persons held public office would be denied all economic aid. The HRCC maintains close contact with the Tribunal, often channelling to it information relevant to its mandate of which it would not otherwise be aware.

Locally tried war-crimes cases, may also, if carried out with full respect for due process of law, contribute to the process of reconciliation. Agreements between the International Tribunal and the authorities in BiH (the so-called "Rules of the Road" adopted in Rome 18 February 1996) stipulate that persons may be held for trial in BiH only if the Tribunal first certifies that there is sufficient evidence on which to proceed *and* decides to relinquish jurisdiction. The terms of the agreement were persistently violated in 1996. Consistent HRCC monitoring and intervention has led to a substantial reduction in violations by the Federation in 1997. Republika Srpska, however, refuses all co-operation. The HRCC has also frequently harried the Tribunal into addressing such issues in a timely manner. The HRCC trial-monitoring project has given priority to the monitoring of local war crimes trials.

A number of small scale community-reconciliation projects have been initiated in various locations in BiH with support from the Office of the High Representative and OSCE. These well intentioned projects, targeted as they are at the current local populations, have perhaps been implemented on the false premise that a community can be reconciled prior to correction of the distorted demographics which result from "ethnic cleansing".

There is ongoing reflection on the usefulness of establishing some form of Truth Commission for BiH[75]. The wide-ranging consultations, which are being conducted in an open and thorough manner, seek to address such difficult problems as the appropriate operational model for a country in which those elements which led to or perpetuated the war are still in place. The various human rights operations are integrated into the process of reflection.

The Special Rapporteur has been mandated by the UN Commission on Human Rights to compile an overview of the human rights situation in former Yugoslavia since 1991, with a view to, *inter alia*, the promotion of reconciliation. She is currently in the process of devising a project whereby the report can be drafted.

---

[75] Thus, in July 1997, a roundtable of interested persons from all parts of Bosnia and Herzegovina and from HRCC participating organisations, was convened in Strasbourg by a consortium comprising The US Institute for Peace, OSCE (ODIHR) and the Council of Europe. *See* Chapter 12 of this volume.

The process of addressing the past will require that the human rights operations intensify the imposition of pressure for arrest of indicted war criminals; continue to monitor compliance by local authorities with agreements reached with the International Tribunal; persist in encouraging the Tribunal to itself follow the agreed procedures; and, strive to co-ordinate and ensure the appropriateness of the range of reconciliation initiatives. It also falls to the human rights missions to persist in insisting both publicly and within their own organisations, that the past can only ultimately be addressed and reconciliation promoted if conditions are created whereby the displaced are given a real opportunity to return home in safety.

CONCLUSION

Human rights missions deployed in Bosnia and Herzegovina are confronted by a dauntingly difficult local situation. They must deal with multiple parties, Bosniak, Bosnian Croat, Bosnian Serb, and others, in various configurations, some of which, such as the Federation partnership, are fragile and shallow. Difficulties are compounded by the continuing control wielded by the war-mongers, the extent to which war criminals remain at large, and the failure to reverse the effects of such war crimes as "ethnic cleansing". The constitutional and other arrangements of the GFA compound the local complexities by establishing State structures and systems which actually subvert the pursuit of justice and the promotion of reconciliation. While the GFA contains extensive, important, and innovative human rights provisions, these present complications because of their sheer abundance and lack of mutual coherence.

The task of the international community is further complicated by the existence of a multiplicity of mandates. In the fields of human rights monitoring and intervention, there are a number of international operations with overlapping assignments. Regarding institution building, the situation is even more complex, given the vast array of international and local governmental and non-governmental bodies which wish to be involved. Within this welter of activity, the international human rights operations' efforts to chart courses of useful activity have been further complicated by the GFA's failure to designate a lead agency for either all or part of the human rights tasks, or to accord a strongly-termed coordination role to the High Representative.

The urgent need for operational models of co-operation and coordination led to the High Representative's office establishing the HRCC and its associated mechanisms. These, notwithstanding ongoing need for development, have had some success. The principal achievements have been in the fields of human rights monitoring, intervention and public reporting, with regard to all of which there have been ongoing improvements in the joint and several activities of OSCE, IPTF, the Office of the High Representative, and other HRCC participating organisations. The international organisations have fewer successes to show in the various fields of human rights institution building. The main achievements have been with regard to support for the various State human rights institutions and for the local NGO community. Reform of the police and judicial systems, however, has yet to bear any significant fruit. The work of human rights education remains in its infancy. With regard to the addressing of the past a range of impediments block any real progress – though the HRCC and its related coordination mechanisms have maintained persistent pressure on such matters as inducement of the surrender of persons indicted by the International Tribunal. While lack of significant progress in the institution building sectors has multiple causes, essayed elsewhere in this chapter, one of the most important of the responses must be a strengthening of the HRCC system.

Optimal institution building efforts require co-operation of the myriad of interested agencies. Given the multiple competencies and sovereign mandates of the various actors, this co-operation can not be based on the model of a strong lead agency. Instead, a participative and horizontal form of co-operation model, such as that underlying the HRCC, must be encouraged. Many organisations present in BiH have yet to fully accept the merits of supporting the model. Thus, for instance, some organisations, already part of the HRCC, still only make partial use of its services and occasionally act unilaterally in a fashion which undermines or impedes attempts to develop multi-agency strategic programmes. Other actors, such as the NGO and donor communities, have not yet acknowledged the need for close co-operation either in general, or between the inter-governmental and non-governmental sectors in particular.

The HRCC must itself develop if it is to attract the confidence and support of the human rights community. It needs to demonstrate that it can consistently gain the attention at the top levels of policy making among the international peace implementation organisations. In this regard, the internal HRCC management structure should be reviewed with a view to raising the profile and standing of the HRCC. One possible action in this regard would be a separating of the functions of the HRCC director and human rights advisor to the High Representative with a concomitant granting to the HRCC director of participation in the meetings of the Principals. Such a move would obviously have implications with regard to the level of seniority at which appointment was made to the post of the HRCC director. Separation of the roles of the High Representative's Human Rights Advisor and the HRCC director might also free the director to spend less time in addressing the day to day emergencies which, inevitably, demand the attention of the current incumbent of the combined posts. A less radical restructuring of the HRCC might involve the appointment of a second HRCC (co-) director, whereby the two directors would divide up management responsibility for human rights monitoring and institution building activity within the HRCC and the Office of the High Representative.

On an operational level, the HRCC needs to integrate and expand existing regional coordination so that its impact is not just felt at headquarters level in Sarajevo. It also need considerably more personnel with experience in such fields as the management of multi-agency co-operation, and, with regard to institution building, the undertaking of needs assessment and provision of technical co-operation.

Enhanced implementation of all aspects of the mandates of the human rights missions present in BiH will also require concerted efforts by each agency to address its own internal organisational deficiencies. For instance, IPTF still awaits the specialist officers to requested in 1996 and has yet to provide human rights training for officers deployed in 1997. UNHCHR/CHR is handicapped by a lack of policy guidance or of appropriate levels of administrative and managerial support from its headquarters and, as a result, it misses many opportunities to fulfill an important role as a provider of expert services and training. OSCE has been hampered by the organisational nexus between election support and human rights. Also, though a novice in deploying a substantial human rights mission, it has picked up many of the bad habits of other human rights operations, regarding such matters as recruitment policy and lack of adequate in-service training (though 1997 has given indications of significant improvements). The Council of Europe finds itself profoundly implicated in the institution building sector, but lacks the capacity for sustained field work.

Many of the HRCC organisations, as well other governmental and non-governmental actors, need to further professionalise their activities. Too much work continues to smack of amateurism. In the fields of institution building, for instance, it is commonplace to find poorly planned projects, which lack sustainability components, fail to integrate local skills and resources, or do not incorporate systems of evaluation or impact assessment. Meeting the challenge of professionalisation may require fundamental re-evaluation of recruitment methods and systems of project and personnel management as well as the maintenance of in-service training programmes. There is a role for the HRCC to help organisations to meet these needs and to promote generally compliance with standards of best practice.

Reform of the various organisations and their closer co-operation will not alone bring a culture of human rights to BiH. An array of local and international circumstances will determine ultimate success or failure in that ambition. Reform and co-operation will however, greatly increase the odds of any future evaluation of the international operation concluding that all was done that could be done.

MANFRED NOWAK

5. Disappearances in Bosnia-Herzegovina[*]

I. FACTS CONCERNING DISAPPEARANCES

By the end of 1996, some 20,000 persons were missing in Bosnia and Herzegovina (BiH), i.e. more than in most other countries of the world[1]. The majority of the missing are civilians, and between 80 and 90% are men of Muslim origin. While all Bosnian parties caused disappearances, there is no doubt that the Bosnian Serb forces and their allies, the Yugoslav National Army (JNA) and Serb paramilitary forces, are responsible for more than 80% of all disappearances. A first wave of disappearances occured in Eastern Bosnia between April and September 1992 in the context of military attacks and "ethnic cleansing" operations carried out by the JNA and Serb paramilitary forces (especially Arkan's, Seselj's and the White Eagles) against the Muslim population in cities and towns at the river Drina (e.g. Zvornik, Visegrad, Foca) or close to it (e.g. Bratunac, Rogatica, Srebrenica, Vlasenica). A second wave of disappearances with the same political background occurred in the Bosnian Krajina (Western BiH) between May and August 1992, most prominently in the region of Prijedor.

Most of the missing persons were last seen in one of the notorious concentration camps established by Bosnian Serb forces, such as "Omarska", "Trnopolje", "Manjaca" or "Keraterm". During 1993 and 1994, the number of new disappearances dropped significantly. The Bosnian Croat army (HVO) is responsible for some hundred disappearances of Bosnian Muslims in Herzegovina during 1993. The last and most notorious wave of disappearances occured in Eastern Bosnia after the conquest by Bosnian Serb forces of the UN declared "safe areas" of Srebrenica and Zepa in July 1995[2]. Between 6000 and 7000 Muslims are still missing from this region,

---

[*] *Editors' note:* This chapter was completed before the author resigned as UN Expert on Disappearances in Former Yugoslavia. His resignation statement is herewith as an Annex to the chapter.

[1] This is an estimate based on information provided by the Bosnian parties, associatons of family members of missing persons, the ICRC and the UN special process on missing persons in the former Yugoslavia. UN Doc. E/CN.4/1997/55.

[2] *Cf.* Jan Willem Honig & Norbert Both, *Srebrenica – Record of a War Crime* (1996).

M. O'Flaherty and G. Gisvold (eds.), *Post-War Protection of Human Rights in Bosnia and Herzegovina*, 107–121.
© 1998 *Kluwer Law International. Printed in Great Britain.*

and most of them are believed to be victims of arbitrary executions and mass killings by Bosnian Serb forces, and are buried in many mass graves located in this area.

Although many disappearances, on all sides are the direct result of the armed conflict, there is no doubt that the systematic policy of "ethnic cleansing" is the major reason for the vast amount of disappearances, particularly among the civilian population. Whether enforced or involuntary disappearances as defined and prohibited by the 1992 UN Declaration on the Protection of All Persons from Enforced Disappearance[3], were committed as part of a planned and systematic strategy in the context of "ethnic cleansing" operations cannot be answered on the basis of the data presently available but further research on the root causes of disappearances is currently being carried out[4].

II. MISSING PERSONS AND THE PEACE PROCESS

The General Framework Agreement for Peace[5] of 14 December 1995[6], together with UN Security Council resolutions 1022, 1031 and 1037 (1995), constitute a solid legal and political basis for achieving a lasting and sustainable peace in Bosnia and Herzegovina[7]. The Presidents of Serbia, Croatia and BiH as well as the Bosnian parties and the Contact Group agreed upon a comprehensive peace-keeping and peace-building operation with a strong and efficient international military presence (IFOR and its successor SFOR)[8] and a strong link between the military and civil-

---

[3] G.A. Res. 47/33 (1992), 18 December 1992, Preamble.

[4] The Vienna based Association for the Promotion of the Ludwig Boltzmann Institute of Human Rights (BIM), with the financial assistance of the Government of the Netherlands, conducts a research project in support of the UN special process on missing persons aimed at investigating the root causes, the precise extent and circumstances of the phenomenon of disappearances in the former Yugoslavia.

[5] General Framework Agreement for Peace in Bosnia and Herzegovina, *initialed* Dayton, Ohio, 21 November 1995, *signed* Paris, 14 December 1995, 35 ILM 75 (1996) [hereinafter "GFA"].

[6] The GFA consists of the General Framework Agreement for Peace in BiH and 11 Annexes thereto. *Cf.* James Sloan, "The Dayton Peace Agreement: Human Rights Guarantees and their Implementation", 7 EJIL 207 (1996).

[7] Bosnia and Herzegovina is one of the states formerly a part of the Socialist Federal Republic of Yugoslavia (SFRY), which existed until 1992. Post-1992, other former constituents of the SFRY, Serbia and Montenegro now comprise the state known as the Federal Republic of Yugoslavia [hereinafter "FRY" or "Serbia"].

[8] In resolution 1031 (1995) of 15 December 1995, the UN Security Council, acting under Chapter VII of the UN Charter, authorized for a period of 12 months the establishment of a Multinational Military Implementation Force (IFOR) in accordance with Annex 1A of the Dayton Peace Agreement. IFOR in fact acted under NATO command and was composed of more than 53,000 troops from 16 NATO nations, 12 Partnership for Peace nations, and 8 other nations. As of 20 December 1996 the UN Security Council in resolution 1088 (1996)

ian components of peace-building, including the protection of human rights. In Article VII of the GFA all parties recognized that "the obsevance of human rights and the protection of refugees and displaced persons are of vital importance in achieving a lasting peace". Annex 4 of the GFA enacted the present Constitution of BiH which contains a comprehensive bill of rights. In particular, the rights of the European Convention on Human Rights (ECHR) and its Additional Protocols are directly applicable in BiH and its two Entities, the Federation of BiH and the Republika Srpska (RS), have priority over all other law including the Constitution and are not even subject to constitutional amendment. Annex 4 also established the Constitutional Court of BiH as the guardian of the Constitution and its bill of rights[9]. In addition, Annex 6 established the Human Rights Commission for BiH composed of an Ombudsperson and a 14 member Human Rights Chamber with the authority to investigate human rights complaints and to decide in a final and binding manner whether any of the Bosnian parties violated its human rights obligations.

The major human rights focus of the GFA, therefore, aims at building efficient institutions for the monitoring and protection of human rights in BiH after the entry into force of the GFA. The experience of 1996 shows, however, a huge gap between theory and practice and a lack of enforcement of human rights by both the Bosnian parties and the international community[10].

In a situation of genocide and other most serious and systematic human rights violations, as the people of BiH went through between 1992 and 1995, the link between peace-building and human rights must also have a retrospective dimension. A lasting and sustainable peace needs, first of all, reconciliation among the people and the three ethno-religious communities, and reconciliation can only be achieved on the basis of serious and genuine attempts to establish the truth about the horrors of the past and to bring at least the main perpetrators to justice. This is a major lesson taught by other situations of gross and systematic human rights violations in the world[11].

Unfortunately, the GFA does not pay much attention to this important aspect and prerequisite of the peace-process. It only reaffirms the important role of the International Criminal Tribunal for the former Yugoslavia[12], but

---

of 12 December 1996 established for a period of 18 months a multinational Stabilization Force (SFOR) as the legal successor of IFOR to fulfil the role specified in Annex 1A and Annex 2 of the Dayton Peace Agreement.

[9] *Cf.* Sienho Yee, "The New Constitution of Bosnia and Herzegovina", 7 EJIL 176 (1996).

[10] *See* Chapters 1, 2 and 4 of this volume.

[11] *E.g.*, the situation in South Africa or Guatemala where Truth Commissions played an important role. *See also* Priscilla B. Hayner, "Fifteen Truth Commissions – 1974 to 1994: A Comparative Study", 16 Hum. Rts Q. 597 (1994). (*See also* Chapter 12 of this volume.)

[12] Hereinafter ICTY. *Cf.* John R.W.D. Jones, "The Implications of the Peace Agreement for the International Tribunal for the former Yugoslavia", 7 EJIL 226 (1996).

does not establish other institutions, such as a Truth Commission. With respect to the problem of missing persons, only Article 5 of Annex 7 stipulates that the Bosnian parties should provide information on all persons unaccounted for through the tracing mechanisms of the International Committee of the Red Cross[13]. No measures in case of non-compliance are foreseen. In other words, the GFA treats the huge and politically highly sensitive problem of some 20,000 missing persons as a purely humanitarian issue to be solved only by the good offices of the ICRC rather than recognizing it as one of the major unresolved human rights issues with important political implications. More human rights oriented efforts of the international community such as the UN Special process on missing persons in the territory of the former Yugoslavia, are not even mentioned in the GFA.

III. MAIN INSTITUTIONS CONCERNED WITH MISSING PERSONS[14]

A. National Institutions

All three ethnic communities established institutions which maintain lists of missing persons and which are the major bodies negotiating the release of prisoners or the exchange of mortal remains exhumed from mass graves: the BiH State Commission for the Tracing of Missing Persons which has close links to the Bosniac (Muslim) side of the Federation, the Office for the Exchange of Prisoners and Missing Persons of the Croation side of the Federation, and the RS State Commission for the Exchange of Prisoners of War and Missing Persons. Unfortunately, the policy of reciprocity which originated in the exchange of prisoners during the war still dominates their appoach of negotiation, both at a bilateral level and in the framework of the ICRC-chaired Working Group on Missing Persons.

B. International Institutions

The ICRC is the main organisation entrusted by international humanitarian law with the tracing of persons missing from armed conflicts. In 1995, the ICRC began systematically to collect tracing requests from the famillies of missing persons and, on 12 June 1996, it launched a tracing campaign by, *inter alia*, publishing a book with the names of missing persons on its file and inviting the families to react to the information contained in the book and to submit further tracing requests[15]. By the end of 1996, three editions of the book were published, and the number of family tracing requests had increased to more than 16,000. The ICRC also facilitates the negotiations

---

[13] Hereinafter "ICRC".
[14] *Cf.* UN Doc E/CN.4/1997/55.
[15] ICRC, *Missing Persons on the Territory of Bosnia and Herzegovina*, (Geneva, 1996).

among the Bosnian parties in the framework of the ICRC-chaired Working Group on Missing Persons.

The UN Special Process on missing persons in the territory of the former Yugoslavia was established on 9 March 1994 by Commission on Human Rights resolution 1994/72 and extended by resolutions 1995/35 and 1996/71. It is entrusted to one expert member of the UN Working Group on Enforced or Involuntary Disappearances, the author of the present chapter, and aims at determining the fate and whereabouts of the missing and at alleviating the suffering of their relatives. The Expert is supported by the field operation of the UN High Commissioner for Human Rights and reports annually to the Commission[16]. In order to establish a division of labour with the ICRC, the Expert in 1996 reduced his own efforts of registering and transmitting family tracing requests and concentrated his activities on facilitating the excavation of mass graves and exhumation of mortal remains. This includes fund raising for a comprehensive programme of forensic activities, as requested in UN Commission on Human Rights resolution 1996/71 of 23 April 1996.

The Office of the High Representative was established under Annex 10 of the GFA with the task of monitoring the implementation of the peace settlement, of coordinating the activities of civilian implementation and of maintaining liaison with IFOR[17]. The OHR actively fulfilled its coordination role by, *inter alia*, offering its services and meeting rooms to all institutions involved, by chairing the Expert Group on Exhumations and Missing Persons and by facilitating the process of inter-party exhumations through the establishment of the Joint Forensic Expert Commission on Exhumation.

These institutions closely cooperated with or were supported by other international organizations or institutions, such as ICTY, the UN High Commissioner and the UN Special Rapporteur on Human Rights in the former Yugoslavia, UNHCR, IFOR/SFOR, and the International Police Task Force (IPTF) established by UN Security Council resolution 1035 (1995) of 21 December 1995 in accordance with Annex 11 of the GFA. Some non-governmental organizations (NGOs) actively supported the joint efforts of tracing missing persons, in particular Bosnian associations of family members of missing persons, the Boston-based organization Physicians for Human Rights (PHR) and the Vienna-based Association for the Promotion of the Ludwig Boltzmann Institute of Human Rights (BIM).

---

[16] UN Docs. E/CN.4/1995/37, E/CN.4/1996/36, E/CN.4/1997/55.

[17] Carl Bildt, former Swedish Prime Minister, became the first High Representative and established his Office [hereinafter, OHR].

C. Special Coordination and Negotiation Bodies

The ICRC-chaired Working Group on Missing Persons was formally established on 30 March 1996 in accordance with Article 5 of Annex 7 of the GFA. It is the major body for negotiations on missing persons among the Bosnian parties. Up to the end of 1996, the Working Group held a total of 9 sessions at the OHR in Sarajevo. The UN Expert on missing persons, representatives of the Federal Republic of Yugoslavia (FRY), the Republic of Croatia and of the Governments of the Contact Group, as well as representatives of associations of families attend as observers. Although the Working Group presently acts as the main channel of information on missing persons between the Bosnian parties, the negotiations are usually highly politicized and based on the principle of reciprocity. Consequently only few cases can be considered clarified as a result of the Working Group's efforts, most of whom were dead and identified after exhumation.

On 22 February 1996, the Expert Group on Exhumations and Missing Persons was established in order to coordinate the efforts of all international actors involved in exhumation activities. It is chaired by the OHR and is presently composed of ICRC, the UN Expert on missing persons, the UN High Commissioner on Human Rights, the UN Special Rapporteur on Human Rights, ICTY, IFOR/SFOR, IPTF, UNTAES, PHR, BIM, a representative of the US Government, and a representative of the ICMP (see *infra*). Up to the end of 1996 it held a total of 15 meetings, usually in Sarajevo, agreed on common guidelines and minimum standards for professional exhumations, approved of a budget for a comprehensive programme of forensic activities, entrusted PHR and BIM with the task of establishing an *antemortem* data base (AMDB) on missing persons, coordinated a programme of international forensic experts seconded by Governments aimed at assisting and monitoring exhumations and autopsies carried out by the Bosnian parties, and established a Joint Forensic Expert Commission on Exhumation for the purpose of facilitating inter-party exhumations. Apart from considerable progress in establishing a comprehensive AMDB, the actual results of the Expert Group in facilitating, coordinating and organizing exhumations for the purpose of clarifying the fate and whereabouts of missing persons were, however, far from satisfactory during 1996.

The Joint Forensic Expert Commission on Exhumation was established on 25 June 1996 at a meeting of the Bosnian parties in Banja Luka convened by the OHR after extensive discussions in the Expert Group on Exhumations and Missing Persons on how to actively involve the Bosnian parties in a joint exhumation process. The Forensic Expert Commission consists of two forensic pathologists from each party and is entrusted to organize and conduct those inter-party exhumations agreed upon by the parties. Because of major political problems this joint "Banja Luka exhumation process" was in fact stalled during most of the summer months, and joint exhumations were only conducted at five sites. Altogether, the mortal remains of less than 400 bodies were exhumed.

On 11 October 1996, the International Commission on Missing Persons in the former Yugoslavia (ICMP) was officially established on the initiative of the US-Government and in conformity with a proposal made by the UN expert on missing persons in his last report[18]. It is chaired by former US Secretary of State Cyrus Vance and is composed of high representatives of the Bosnian parties, the FRY, the Republic of Croatia, and six further well-known international personalities. The High Representative, the UN expert on missing persons and high-level representatives of ICTY, ICRC, IFOR IPTF, UNTAES, PHR and the Mine Action Centre (MAC) act as advisors. The ICMP established an office in Sarajevo and identified priority areas for future action, including political pressure on all parties concerned, support to families and survivors, and financial assistance to forensic activities and other relevant projects aimed at bringing a solution to the problem of missing persons.

IV. IN SEARCH OF A SOLUTION TO THE PROBLEM OF THE MISSING

Any evaluation of progress depends, of course, on the yardstick. What do we mean if we speak of a solution to the problem of the missing persons? Most of the families, as in other countries with disappearances, continue to hope that their loved ones are still alive and held somewhere in secret detention. The ideal solution, in their opinion, is therefore to get them back alive. Although it cannot be excluded that some of the missing persons might still be held in secret detention – and there are, indeed, all kind of rumours concerning secret detention places in Serbia and the RS which are not easy to be verified or falsified – there are strong indications that the great majority of the missing are in fact victims of arbitrary executions and are buried in one of the many suspected mass graves in BiH.

What is a solution to these cases? Can we consider them clarified if the authorities concerned allege that they died in armed conflicts? Probably not. How much proof would the authorities have to produce? According to the working methods of the UN Working Group on Enforced or Involuntary Disappearances[19] a case is usually considered clarified if the Government alleges the death of the person concerned and the source – either the family or an NGO acting on its behalf – agrees. In most cases families would not agree to an assumption of death unless the Government produces convincing evidence. This does, however, not mean that families have in any case a veto power. There are cases in which the Working Group considers them clarified despite objections by the source. The

---

[18] *Cf.* UN Doc. E/CN.4/1996/36, ¶ 81.
[19] *Cf.* UN Doc. E/CN.4/1996/38, Annex I (p. 91).

working methods of the ICRC are similar although in certain cases they seem somewhat less strict.

As a general rule one might, therefore, conclude that Governments must prove beyond reasonable doubt that a missing person is dead in order to consider a given case clarified. In BiH the situation is more complicated since there is not just one Government accountable. In addition to the three Bosnian parties, families often hold the Government of the FRY, sometimes also the Government of Croatia, responsible for disappearances. Even if the authorities of different Bosnian parties would agree about the fate of a missing person, the families might not be convinced. That is why in BiH, where we have strong indications and evidence about a huge number of mass graves without reliable information on who is buried there, the excavation of mass graves, exhumation and identification of mortal remains seems in most cases the only proper method to proof, beyond reasonable doubt, the fate and whereabouts of missing persons[20].

The clarification of the fate and whereabouts of missing persons, alive or dead, is, however, not the only solution to the problem of the missing. Under the UN Declaration on the Protection of All Persons from Disappearance, Governments are also obliged to thoroughly investigate every individual case of disappearance, to bring the perpetrators to justice and to pay compensation to the victims or their families. In BiH, families also regularly claim their right to a decent burial. In other words, the exhumation of mortal remains from a mass grave or of unburied mortal remains, such as in the Kravice region[21], might not only serve the purpose of identification but also to hand the body back to the families for a decent burial according to their religious customs. This causes another controversial issue. According to certain customs, the mortal remains shall be buried at a site close to the place of residence of the person concerned. Since there is still no freedom of movement across the Inter-Entity Boundary Line (IEBL) in BiH, and since most family members of missing persons are internally displaced, the implementation of the right to a decent burial creates considerable political and practical problems.

To sum up: a solution to the problem of missing persons, which is a major precondition for reconciliaion and a lasting peace in BiH, might consist in the clarification of the fate and whereabouts of the missing, through the disclosure of all relevant information by all authorities concerned, the release of all remaining secret detainees and the exhumation of mortal remains in a thorough investigation of the phenomenon of disappearances (the "right to know the truth"), in bringing the major perpetrators to justice, in paying compensation to the victims and their families, in

---

[20] *Cf.* also the report of the UN expert on missing persons to the 1996 UN Commission on Human Rights, UN Doc. E/CN.4/1996/36, ¶ 78.

[21] *Cf.* UN Doc E/CN.4/1997/55

permitting a decent burial close to the former place of residence and similar measures.

V. PROGRESS ACHIEVED

If the yardstick for an evaluation of the progress achieved is a solution to the problem of the missing as outlined above, very little progress has been made in 1996. Notwithstanding the joint efforts of various national and international institutions and coordination bodies involved, only very few missing persons could be found alive, and not more than a few hundred of the roughly 20,000 cases of missing persons could be clarified through means of exhumation and identification[22]. There are no reports about any thorough investigations, any indictments or judicial sentences for enforced disappearances, any compensation or decent burials close to the former place of residence.

The reasons for these shortcomings are manifold and directly related to the present political situation and lack of human rights in BiH. First of all, the authorities concerned are not willing to disclose all relevant information because the pressure on them is not strong enough, because such information might be used againts their leaders as evidence before ICTY or in other criminal investigations, and because the negotiations are still dominated by the philosophy of reciprocity. This, of course, has to do with the present political reality. BiH is a divided country, and the main perpetrators of enforced disappearances and other crimes against humanity are in fact still in power.

In addition, serious exhumations were only carried out by ICTY (with the full support of what was then IFOR) and by the Bosnian parties on their own territory[23]. Such exhumations are, however, only of limited value to the goal of clarifying the fate and whereabouts of the missing. ICTY conducts exhumations exclusively for the purpose of collecting evidence for indictments or trials and, therefore, only needs samples. ICTY neither has the intention nor the mandate nor the means to excavate mass graves in order to identify all mortal remains discovered. The Bosnian parties, on the other hand, are interested to clarify the fate and whereabouts of missing persons, but in principle only of "their own" ones. Very few Bosnian Serbs, Croats or Muslims are, however, buried on the territory under control of "their own" authorities, and most of these mass graves – in particular on territory which was handed over in accordance with the GFA – have in fact already been excavated. There is only very limited interest by the Bosnian parties in inter-party exhumations. With sufficient pressure from the international community, some inter-party exhumations might continue

---

[22] *Cf.* UN Doc. E/CN.4/1997/55.
[23] *Id.*

in 1997, but definitely not longer than the philosophy of reciprocity permits, i.e. as long as there are mutual interests of "exchanging bodies". Most mass graves of Bosniacs are, however, in the RS without an equivalent on the territory of the Federation. As long as BiH remains a *de facto* divided State without freedom of movement across the IEBL this situation will not change.

This suggests the final and most decisive reason for the obvious failure to reach a solution to the problem of missing persons in BiH: the lack of political will on the part of the international community. That the clarification of the fate and whereabouts of missing persons is still regarded by most Governments and politicians as an obstacle rather than a precondition to the peace-process is shown most bluntly by the lack of relevant provisions in the GFA or by the extremely vague language of resolution 1996/71 of the UN Commission on Human Rights (in particular paragraph 34). Other evidence can be found in the reluctance of donor Governments to make sufficient funds available to the programme of forensic activities, the refusal of IFOR to provide proper support and security to exhumations beyond those conducted by ICTY, and the non-existing link between economic assistance and serious efforts to solve the problem of missing persons.

During the summer of 1996, there were, however, also certain signs by some western Governments to take the fate of the missing somewhat more seriously. While the recommendation of the UN Expert on missing persons to establish a multilateral high level commission on missing persons did not prompt any positive reaction by the US or any other Government in the UN Commission on Human Rights in April 1996, President Clinton, only two months after, announced the creation of a very similar "International Commission on Missing Persons in the former Yugoslavia" and authorized immediately $2 million (US) for this purpose.

Other western Governments in autumn indicated their interest in exhumations and made some funds available for the pogramme of forensic activities. Even the ICRC, which had been extremely sceptical towards exhumations by the international community, reversed its policy and announced in November a strong interest in this issue by, *inter alia*, assuming the role of custodian for the *antemortem* database on missing persons. This database which is in the process of being established by two NGOs, PHR and BIM, with the financial assistance of the European Union and the Netherlands, is a major precondition for larger-scale exhumations. The collection of the relevant data through interviews with family members of missing persons indicates that, at least for the roughly 6500 persons missing from Srebrenica, a comprehensive programme of exhumations can be carried out already in 1997 under the condition that the international community provides the necessary political, financial and military support.

VI. Conclusions

The fate and whereabouts of some 20,000 missing persons, predominantly Muslim men who disappeared in 1992 and 1995 in the course of "ethnic cleansing" operations carried out by Bosnian Serb forces, the JNA and Serb paramilitary groups, remains one of the most sensitive and politicized human rights problems of the past which needs to be solved in order to achieve a lasting peace. The victims are not only the missing persons themselves, but also more than 100,000 family members most of whom are refugees or internally displaced persons presently living on the territory of the Federation. These families, in accordance with international human rights and humanitarian standards, demand from the authorities of BiH, the Federation, the RS, the FRY and the international community the implementation of their right to know the truth and to get their loved ones back, either alive or through the means of exhumations.

So far, the authorities concerned and the international community have made very little progress in clarifying the fate and whereabouts of missing persons and reaching a solution to the problem of disappearences. Although an impressive number of national and international institutions and coordination mechanisms have been entrusted with the task of solving the issue of the missing much remained lipservice. A clear political will to effectively tackle this problem seems to be lacking on all sides.

Since BiH is still a *de facto* divided country with the nationalistic leaders of the war-time in power, and without freedom of movement, a breakthrough in solving the problem of missing persons can only be achieved with strong pressure from, as well as political and financial support of, the international community. As far as political pressure is concerned, the ICMP might have enough political authority to force the national authorities to disclose the relevant information. The donor community should pay more attention to the problem of missing persons and make financial and technical assistance for economic reconstruction and development conditional on the willingness of national authorities to release detainees, disclose information on the missing and cooperate with the relevant international mechanisms in their efforts to clarify the fate and whereabouts of missing persons.

In addition, the international community should provide the necessary funds and support to carry out a comprehensive programme of forensic activities. In 1997, such activities should focus on missing persons from Srebrenica for whom most *antemortem* data have already been collected. In order to avoid further filibustering by the Bosnian parties, most excavations of mass graves, exhumations and identifications of mortal remains shall be carried out by international teams of forensic experts seconded by Governments and assisted, if they so wish, by Bosnian experts. International exhumations need to be well coordinated, financed beforehand through contributions to the UN voluntary fund, and can only be conducted if SFOR provides full military support and security to the forensic experts working in the field.

ANNEX

UN Special Process on Missing Persons in the former Yugoslavia
Final Statement by Manfred Nowak
Expert
Fifty third Session of the Commission on Human Rights

Geneva, 26 March 1997

Mr Chairman,
    This is my last report to this Commission on the fate and whereabouts of missing persons in the territory of the former Yugoslavia. As of today, I resign from a mandate which this Commission and the Chairman of the UN Working Group on Enforced Disappearances has entrusted upon me in 1994. My resignation is, unfortunately, not due to the fact that the fate and whereabouts of many thousands of missing persons in the region were clarified. On the contrary, the number of missing persons has significantly increased during those three years, and the families are still waiting in vain for an answer from the authorities concerned and the international community on the fate of their loved ones. My resignation is rather based on the experience that there is not sufficient political will to establish the fate of the missing by all possible means, including exhumation and to create an unambiguous mandate of the special process based on a clear division of labour with the ICRC and other relevant organizations. But let me stress again my deep conviction that a solution to the problem of disappearances is a major precondition for justice and a sustainable peace in the region. Let me first give you a short summary of the situation of missing persons in Croatia and in Bosnia and Herzegovina as outlined in my third written report to the Commission (UN Doc E/CN.4/1996/55), and then the reasons for my resignation.
    In Bosnia and Herzegovina, some 20,000 persons are still missing. The great majority are Bosnian men of Muslim origin who became victims of "ethnic cleansing" operations carried out by the JNA, Serb paramilitary groups and Bosnian Serb forces between May and September 1992 and after the fall of Srebrenica and Zapa in July 1995. Among the missing are also Bosnian Muslims, victims of "ethnic cleansing" operations carried out by Bosnian Croat forces during 1993 in Herzegovina as well as a limited number of combatants and civilians of all three ethnic communities who disappeared as a result of various armed conflicts between 1992 and 1995. Although there is not yet enough evidence to prove that systematic acts of enforced disappearances as defined in the UN Declaration on the Protection of All Persons from Enforced Disappearance were committed as a planned strategy similar to, e.g., the practice of the former military Government in Argentina, there is ample evidence to prove that most missing

persons are victims of a systematic policy of "ethnic cleansing" above all by Bosnian Serb forces.

In the Republic of Croatia, some 5,000 persons are still missing. This includes more than 2,500 Croatian civilians and combatants who became victims of "ethnic cleansing" operations by the JNA and Serb paramilitary group in late 1991, above all in Eastern Slavonia; up to 1,000 JNA soldiers allegedly still missing as a result of the armed conflict in 1991; and up to 2,000 Croatian Serb civilians who allegedly disappeared as a result of operations "Flash" and "Storm" carried out by the Croatian Army in May and August 1995. The information provided on missing Serbs is, however, far less detailed and reliable than the information available on missing Croats.

Mr. Chairman, let me now turn to the reasons for my resignation.

1. Lack of adequate support for exhumation

In view of the fact that most of the missing persons have most probably been killed, in my last report to the Commission I drew the attention of the international community to the urgent need for excavating mass graves and exhuming and identifying the mortal remains found therein (UN Doc E/CN.4/1996/36, paragraphs 74–79). I stressed in this report that "the primary responsibility for carrying out these tasks remains with the authorities under whose jurisdiction a suspected mass grave falls". I added, however, that "if the authorities concerned are not willing to carry out the excavation, then the task will fall to international organizations and mechanisms, including the special process". Most suspected mass graves are located in the territory of the Republika Srpska, and the Bosnian Serb authorities are not willing to open them unless there is a specific interest of reciprocity *vis-à-vis* the Federation authorities. If we wish to tell the women of Srebrenica or other families of missing persons the truth and facilitate a decent burial of their loved ones, then the international community should take the lead by organizing such exhumations with the assistance of Bosnian and international teams of forensic experts. Mere pressure on the Bosnian parties is in my opinion not sufficient as the experience of last year clearly demonstrates. Such undertakings are, however, expensive and depend on the full political and financial support of the international community as well as on the military and logistical support of peacekeeping forces in the field, in particular SFOR. In May 1996, I drew up a budget for a comprehensive programme of forensic activities which amounted to roughly 6 million US$. After numerous fundraising appeals and meetings with potential donors, voluntary contributions amounting to little more than 300,000 US$, i.e. some 5% of the required funds, have been received in the respective UN voluntary fund. IFOR consistently refused to provide the required security to forensic experts in the field. Although SFOR shows more willingness to support these "humanitarian exhumations", major problems, such as the de-mining of suspected mass graves, remain unresolved. I wish to express my gratitude to those Governments that actively supported my approach and/or made financial contributions but I have to state that this support is not sufficient to carry out a comprehensive programme of forensic activities as requested by the Commission in its resolution 1996/71.

2. Lack of coordination among international actors in the field
With the entry into force of the Dayton Peace Agreement a number of new institutions were added to those already active in the former Yugoslavia. The Office of the High Representative was entrusted to coordinate their activities. Consequently, an Expert Group on Exhumations and Missing Persons was established under the auspices of the High Representative. Although much time was spent with these coordination efforts, there was no lead agency concept and division of labour which could have solved problems arising from overlapping mandates of the Special process on missing persons and other institutions, such as ICRC and the ICRC-chaired Working Group on Missing Persons, the UN Special Rapporteur on Human Rights in the former Yugoslavia, the International Criminal Tribunal in the former Yugoslavia, and others. To some extent, these coordination problems were the result of the vague mandate of the Special Process as defined in Commission resolution 1995/71. In my written report I therefore requested the Commission "to define this mandate as unambiguously as possible" but unfortunately, I did not receive any positive response. On 21 March 1997, the International Commission on Missing Persons in the Former Yugoslavia (ICMP, to many better known as the "Blue Ribbon Commission"), which was established on the initiative of the US Government, held its first full meeting in Zagreb. Since this Commission seems to have the full support of many key Governments, it might be more successful in coordinating the various actors.

3. Lack of cooperation from the Federal Republic of Yugoslavia (FRY)
From the very beginning the Government of the FRY refused to cooperate with the Special Process – originally because it had been established as a joint mandate with the former Special Rapporteur, Mr Mazowiecki, later for other reasons. Since I am deeply convinced that the answers to many questions of families of missing persons, both in Croatia and in Bosnia and Herzegovina, should be provided by the FRY authorities, the non-cooperative attitude of Belgrade remains a major reason for the lack of progress in clarifying the fate and whereabouts of missing persons in the region. Again, the International Commission on Missing Persons might be more successful in overcoming this obstacle.

Mr. Chairman, the issue of missing persons is one of the most difficult human rights problems to solve – not only in the former Yugoslavia. Most of the work that might lead to a reconciliation process between the families of missing persons and those who are responsible for the disappearances still needs to be done. But let me conclude by also stressing the progress achieved during last year. First of all, Governments today are much less reluctant towards exhumations as a means of clarifying the fate of missing persons than one year ago when I first made such a recommendation. Secondly, most clarifications of last year are in fact the result of exhumations carried out, in particular, by the respective authorities in Croatia and Bosnia and Herzegovina. Finally, a high-level multilateral commission on missing persons involving all relevant parties in the former Yugoslavia, as recommended in my last year's report, has recently been established. I wish the International Commission on Missing Persons much success in its efforts to shed light on the fate of the missing and encourage the families to actively cooperate with this Commission. I thank the families for their trust and cooperation with me and would be grateful to the donors who responded to my fundraising appeals if the funds so far received could be made directly available to the associations of families of missing persons in Croatia and in Bosnia and Herzegovina.

Thank you, Mr. Chairman.

MARIA STAVROPOULOU

6. Bosnia and Herzegovina and the Right to Return in International Law

One of the tragic consequences of all wars is the resultant large population movements. The war in the former Yugoslavia has been no exception to this principle. In contrast to other wars, however, forced population movements in Bosnia have been a central aim of the fighting parties. "Ethnic cleansing", as the practice of forcing people out of their homes to create ethnically homogenous areas became known, has uprooted more than half of the population of Bosnia and Herzegovina[1].

When the war is over, one immediate question is how to manage the return of the displaced to their homes, where, hopefully, they can resume their lives. While the existence of a right to return to one's own country is a rather uncontroversial issue in international law, the right to return to one's area of origin is less clear. Return to one's home and area of origin is prone to becoming the subject of political compromises in the aftermath of an "ethnic cleansing" war. In addition, return may become less a question of a "right" and more one of lack of other alternatives, especially when guarantees for physical safety and adequate protection of human rights are weak. All these issues exist in post-Dayton Bosnia, where they affect profoundly hundreds of thousands of refugees and internally displaced persons.

---

[1] It is estimated that in Bosnia and Herzegovina alone there still are 1.2 million internally displaced persons and that 1.3 million refugees have fled to third countries. U.S. Agency for International Development, Former Yugoslavia Situation Report # 5 (September 5, 1996). An estimated seventy percent of Bosnia's pre-war population of 4.4 million has been uprooted by the war.

M. O'Flaherty and G. Gisvold (eds.), Post-War Protection of Human Rights in Bosnia and Herzegovina, 123–140.
© 1998 Kluwer Law International. Printed in Great Britain.

I. THE RIGHT TO RETURN TO ONE'S OWN COUNTRY

A. Human Rights Law

Human rights law is unequivocal on the right of an individual, outside of national territory, to return to his or her country[2]. The right has been recognised in article 13(2) of the Universal Declaration of Human Rights[3]. It has been further guaranteed *a contrario* in article 12(4) of the International Covenant on Civil and Political Rights (ICCPR)[4] and has been incorporated in the Convention on the Elimination of All Forms of Racial Discrimination[5] and the Convention on the Rights of the Child[6]. Regional instruments have also guaranteed this right[7]. For instance, the Fourth Protocol to the European Convention for the Protection of Human Rights and Fundamental Freedoms prohibits in article 3(2) the deprivation of the right to enter the territory of the State of which a person is a national[8]. The right has been subsequently reaffirmed in inter-governmental and academic conferences and United Nations resolutions[9].

---

[2] Views of the human rights doctrine are also more or less uniform on this issue. *See, e.g.*, William Frelick, "The Right of Return", 2 IJRL 442 (1990); Guy S. Goodwin-Gill, "The Right to Leave, the Right to Return and the Question of a Right to Remain", *in* Vera Gowlland-Debbas, (ed.), *The Problem of Refugees in the Light of Contemporary International Law Issues 93* (1996); Hurst Hannum, *The Right to Leave and to Return in International Law and Practice* (1987).

[3] Universal Declaration of Human Rights, G.A. Res. 217 A (III), UN Doc. A/810 (1948), at 78 [hereinafter Universal Declaration].

[4] "No one shall be arbitrarily deprived of the right to enter his own country". International Covenant on Civil and Political Rights, 999 UNTS 171, *adopted* 16 December 1966 [hereinafter "ICCPR"].

[5] International Convention on the Elimination of All Forms of Racial Discrimination, 660 UNTS 195, *adopted* 21 December 1965 [hereinafter "Race Convention"].

[6] Convention on the Rights of the Child, G.A. Res. 44/25, UN Doc. A/44/49 (1990) [hereinafter CRC].

[7] For instance, see African (Banjul) Charter on Human and People's Rights, *adopted* 27 June 1981, OAU Doc. CAB/LEG/67/3 rev.5, *reprinted in* 21 ILM. 58 (1982), *entered into force* 21 October 1986 [hereinafter "African Charter"]; American Convention on Human Rights, O.A.S. Treaty Series No. 36, 1144 UNTS 123, *entered into force* 18 July 1978, [hereinafter "American Convention"].

[8] Protocol No. 4 to the European Convention for the Protection of Human Rights and Fundamental Freedoms, Securing Certain Rights and Freedoms other than Those Already Included in the Convention and in the First Protocol thereto, *signed at* Strasbourg on 16 September 1963, *entered into force* 2 May 1968, Council of Europe Treaty Series No. 46 [hereinafter Fourth Protocol to the ECHR].

[9] World Conference on Human Rights: Vienna Declaration and Programme of Action, held at Vienna, 14-25 June 1993, UN Doc. A/CONF.157/23, Part I, ¶ 23; CSCE Concluding Document of the Vienna Meeting on the Follow-up to the Conference, 15 Jan. 1989, *reprinted in Council of Europe, Human Rights in International Law: Basic Texts* (1991), ¶ 20; Recommendations of the OAU/UNHCR Symposium on Refugees and Forced Population Displacements in Africa, EC/1994/SCP/CRP.7/Add.1, 21 September 1994; Strasbourg Declaration on the Right to Leave and Return, *adopted on* 26 November 1986, *reprinted in*

While the "right to return" in general is firmly embedded in human rights law, its exact scope and modalities of implementation are less clear[10]. The right is linked with citizenship, which itself is a concept fraught with ambiguities, inasmuch as it is enjoyed primarily, though not perhaps exclusively, by citizens. Article 12(4) of the ICCPR, for instance, guarantees the right to return to one's "own" country, as opposed to the country of which she is a national. This distinction indicates that the protection extends to persons who have such a strong attachment to a state that they view it as their "own" or home country. The longer one stays, the stronger the claim to this protection may become; refugees and stateless persons, who no longer have a country of their own to which they can return, have an even clearer such claim. The same is true of permanent alien residents or children of immigrants born in the country concerned[11].

A further question relates to whether a refusal to grant entry into a country to one of its nationals can ever be permissible. At first blush, it would appear that article 12(4) prohibits only "arbitrary" deprivations of one's right to return. However, it has been observed, on the basis of an examination of the *Travaux Preparatoires*, that the only acceptable ground for refusing entry to a national would be that exile has been lawfully imposed as punishment for some crime[12]. Even so, one commentator suggests, exile will nevertheless be arbitrary if no State wishes to receive the expelee, since no other State apart from the State of nationality is obliged to

---

AJIL 432, 435 (1987). *See, e.g.,* Sub-Commission on Prevention of Discrimination and Protection of Minorities Resolutions 1994/24 (26 August 1994), resolution 1995/13 (18 August 1995) and resolution 1996/9 (23 August 1996) (affirming the right of refugees and displaced persons to return, in safety and dignity, to their country of origin and/or within it to their place of origin or choice). Numerous resolutions have been adopted with regard to the right to return of various refugee groups. *See, e.g.,* G.A. Res. 194 (III), UN Doc. A/810, (1948), at 24, ¶ 11 (regarding the return of Palestinians to their homes). With regard to the former Yugoslavia in general and Bosnia and Herzegovina specifically, various Security Council resolutions have been adopted which affirm the right of all displaced persons to return voluntarily to their homes of origin, such as Resolution 947, U.N. SCOR, 49th Year, 3434th meeting at 41, ¶ 7, UN Doc. S/INF/50 (1994) and Resolution 1009, U.N. SCOR, 50th Year, 3563d meeting at 2, ¶ 2, UN Doc. S/RES/1009 (1995) and resolution 941, U.N. SCOR, 49th Year, 3428th meeting at 30, ¶ 3, UN Doc. S/INF/50 (1994).

[10] *See* Goodwin-Gill, *supra*, at 101 (noting that instances in which return has been denied are generally part of broader persecution contexts); Kay Hailbronner, "Comments on the Right to Leave, Return and Remain", *in* Vera Gowlland-Debbas, *supra*, at 109, 116 (discussing the problems of nationality and refusal by the State of origin to admit its citizens).

[11] Manfred Nowak, "U.N. Covenant on Civil and Political Rights," *in CCPR Commentary* (1993), at 220.

[12] *Id.* at 218-219. See M. J. Bossuyt, *Guide to the "Travaux Preparatoires" of the International Covenant on Civil and Political Rights,* (1987), at 260.

accept him/her[13]. In modern practice, however, whether as a matter of law or fact, such exile is deemed highly unlikely to occur[14].

Lastly, though permitted from the other rights guaranteed by article 12 in limited circumstances, derogation of the right to return is not allowed. ICCPR article 12(4) (right to return) is not referred to article 12(3), which is the paragraph allowing for lawful restrictions on the right to freedom of movement and choice of residence to protect national security, public order, public health or morals or the rights and freedoms of others. It follows, therefore, that the right to return may not be restricted on such grounds.

B. International Humanitarian Law

International humanitarian law regulating inter-state armed conflicts contains detailed provisions elaborating on the repatriation of prisoners of war[15] and protected persons (internees[16] and other aliens[17]) during or after the cessation of hostilities. Repatriation must not be delayed after the general closure of hostilities; it may be obligatory even before hostilites are over. For instance, in case of evacuation of protected persons from occupied territory, it is stipulated that they will be transferred back to their homes as soon as hostilities in their area have ceased[18]. Article 85(4)(b) of Protocol I declares the deliberate and unjustifiable delay in the repatriation of civilians as a grave breach of the Geneva Conventions and the Protocol[19].

---

[13] Jean-Marie Henckaerts, *Mass Expulsion in Modern International Law and Practice* (1995), note 26 and accompanying text at page 81 (citing Paul Weis, *Nationality and Statelessness in International Law,* 45-47 (1979)).

[14] United Nations Department of Economic and Social Affairs, Study of the Right of Everyone to be Free from Arbitrary Arrest, Detention and Exile, UN Doc. E/CN.4/826/Rev.1 (1964), ¶¶ 788-822.

[15] Geneva Convention relative to the Treatment of Prisoners of War, 75 UNTS 135, 12 August 1949, arts. 110 and 118 [hereinafter "Third Geneva Convention"].

[16] Geneva Convention relative to the Protection of Civilian Persons in Time of War, 75 UNTS 287, 12 August 1949, arts. 132-135 [hereinafter "Fourth Geneva Convention"].

[17] *Id.* arts. 35-36.

[18] Fourth Geneva Convention, *supra,* art. 49(2).

[19] *See* Protocol Additional to the Geneva Conventions of 12 August 1949, and relating to the Protection of Victims of International Armed Conflicts (Protocol I), 1125 UNTS 3, *adopted* 8 June 1977, art. 85.

II. THE RIGHT TO RETURN TO ONE'S AREA OF ORIGIN

A. Human Rights Law

There is no general rule that displaced persons no longer residing in their areas of habitual residence and their usual homes have an explicit right to return to them beyond the exercise of their freedom of movement and choice of residence, as recognised in human rights instruments. Similarly, refugees and other nationals have a right to return to their country, but not an explicit right to return to their areas of habitual residence. The right to freedom of movement and choice of residence has been enshrined in article 13(1) of the Universal Declaration[20], in article 12(1) of the ICCPR[21], and in regional human rights instruments[22]. These instruments, however, permit states to derogate from these rights and to place restrictions on their exercise[23]. So, for instance, article 12(3) of the ICCPR provides that the freedom of movement and choice of residence "shall not be subject to any restrictions except those which are provided by law, are necessary to protect national security, public order (*ordre public*), public health or morals or the rights and freedoms of others, and are consistent with the other rights recognised in the present Covenant". The application of such restrictions must be prescribed by law and based one of the enumerated grounds justifying limitations. Further, any such legal restriction must respond to a pressing public or social need, pursue a legitimate aim, and be proportionate to that aim[24]. It has been suggested that restrictions to article 12(3) must be enacted by the appropriate legislature and that the law must be accessible to all those subject to it and have an adequate degree of certainty. In addition, any restrictions must be "necessary" to achieve one of the purposes of interference, allowing for scrutiny on the basis of an objective minimum standard[25]. The principle of proportionality as well as the right to an effective remedy are also of relevance in this context.

Clearly, return to one's area of habitual residence can be restricted in grave cases of political or military threat to the entire nation, in order to protect "national security", or in all cases of lawful deprivation of personal liberty necessary to protect "public order". The "public health" exception would provide only rarely a ground for restriction on return as it would have to involve a particular sort of emergency, such as an epidemic or

---

[20] Universal Declaration, *supra*.

[21] ICCPR, *supra*.

[22] Fourth Protocol to the ECHR, *supra*, Article 2(1); African Charter, *supra*, article 12(1); of the American Convention, *supra*, article 22(1).

[23] *See* also American Convention, *supra*, article 22(3) and (4); African Charter, *supra*, article 12(2); Fourth Protocol to the European Convention, *supra*, articles 2(3) and (4).

[24] "The Siracusa Principles on the Limitation and Derogation Provisions in the International Covenant on Civil and Political Rights", 7 Hum. Rts Q. 237 (1985).

[25] Nowak, *supra*, at 209-211.

water contamination. The "public morals" exception should provide no justification for restrictions. The protection of the "rights and freedoms of others" might justify a certain delay in the exercise of the right to return, if taking into account any property rights acquired by third parties, whether lawfully or in the interest of equity, is necessary.

Restrictions on return are the exception to the rule, however, and thus may not be of a permanent nature; ultimately, return to one's home area should be permissible even where initially restricted. The above apply *mutatis mutandis* to the somewhat different (i.e., more detailed) formulation of the permissible restrictions on the freedom of movement provided for in article 2 of the Fourth Protocol to the ECHR[26]. Technically, return is a form of the exercise of the freedom of movement. For a person displaced by war, however, returning home is more: it is the resumption of a life torn apart and is directly related to the enjoyment of the entire range of human rights, in particular economic, social and cultural rights and the right to participate in political affairs. From this perspective, therefore, the standard of scrutiny of the necessity and proportionality of any restrictions imposed on one of the grounds specified in article 12(3) should be higher than would otherwise be the case.

Return of displaced persons and refugees to their areas of habitual residence is also a corrective measure, applicable to instances of discrimination and associate practices such as "ethnic cleansing." Human rights bodies and mechanisms of the United Nations have specifically demanded the reversal of "ethnic cleansing" by allowing return to occur[27]. Refusal to allow return, where such refusal is, in effect, a continuation of invidiously discriminatory practices, is unlawful. Use of the "restrictions" permissible pursuant to article 12(3) or lawful derogation from article 12 should not save such refusal, as to do so would violate the peremptory norm of non-discrimination[28].

---

[26] Fourth Protocol to the European Convention, *supra*.

[27] Report of the Committee on the Elimination of Racial Discrimination, U.N. GAOR, 50th Sess., Supp. No. 18, ¶ 219, UN Doc. A/50/18 (1995) (urging "the immediate reversal of ethnic cleansing, which must begin with the voluntary return of displaced people"). *See also* General Recommendation of the Committee concerning the rights of refugees and persons displaced on the basis of ethnic criteria, adopted at its 49th session, UN Doc. CERD/C/49/CRP.2/Add.9. *See also* Sixth Periodic Report submitted by Mr. Tadeusz Mazowiecki, Special Rapporteur on the situation of human rights in the territory of the Former Yugoslavia, UN Doc. E/CN.4/1994/110, (21 February 1996), at ¶¶ 283-293; report submitted by Ms. Elizabeth Rehn, Special Rapporteur on the situation of human rights in the territory of the former Yugoslavia, U.N. doc. E/CN.4/1996/3, (14 March 1996), at ¶ 61. *See also* note 9, *supra*.

[28] The legal framework of the protection of minorities is also relevant in this context. *See* Framework Convention for the Protection of National Minorities, *opened by* the member States of the Council of Europe on 1 February 1995, *in* Framework Convention for the Protection of National Minorities and explanatory report (1995).

Where obstruction of return cannot be attributed to the State, but only to non-state actors, these may incur individual liability under international law where their acts constitute recognised international crimes. More importantly, however, in such a case, the State is expected to take measures to the best of its ability to prevent any such obstructions and to bring to justice those responsible. In that vein, the State is expected to undertake steps to prevent policies that effectively discourage return, such as incitement to racial hatred, as provided for in articles 2, 20(2) and 26 of the ICCPR[29].

B. International Humanitarian Law

International humanitarian law does not contain any provisions with regard to the return of internally displaced persons, save with regard to situations of occupation. Article 49(2) of the Fourth Geneva Convention states that persons who have been evacuated during an occupation "shall be transferred back to their homes as soon as hostilities in the area in question have ceased."

III. REPATRIATION OF REFUGEES AND INTERNALLY DISPLACED PERSONS IN SAFETY AND DIGNITY

The "right to return" implies a choice as to whether to exercise the right or not. In cases of refugee movements, however, the issue frequently is whether and how soon return can be encouraged, if not "imposed," instead of remaining an option of the refugee. The legal situation varies, depending on whether the persons concerned are refugees in the wider sense of the term (i.e., asylum seekers, holders of asylum, *de facto* refugees or persons enjoying "temporary protection"), or whether they are internally displaced[30].

---

[29] *See* Human Rights Committee General Comment No. 3, (1981), *reprinted in* Note by the Secretariat, Compilation of General Comments and General Recommendations adopted by Human Rights Treaty Bodies, UN Doc. HRI/GEN/1/Rev.1 (1994), 29 July 1994.

[30] For the working definition of the term "internally displaced" see Report of the Representative of the Secretary-General on internally displaced persons, UN Doc. E/CN.4/1996/52/Add.2, ¶ 8. *See also* Report of the Representative of the Secretary-General on internally displaced persons, UN Doc. E/CN.4/1995/50, ¶¶ 116-127 (discussing critically the working definition).

A. Repatriation of Refugees

The repatriation of refugees (in particular in cases of mass displacement) is considered by UNHCR as the best solution to a refugee movement[31] and preferable to settlement in the country of asylum or a third country[32]. Such repatriation, however, must be voluntary, the result of the individual refugee's free and informed decision-making[33]. Particular safeguards are required to ensure that a refugee woman's decision to repatriate is voluntary and special standards govern UNHCR's practice with respect to the voluntary repatriation of refugee children[34].

Repatriation of a refugee to a country where safety and dignity cannot be guaranteed, however, amounts to *refoulement* and is strictly prohibited under universal and regional refugee instruments[35]. Article 33(1) of the 1951 Refugee Convention provides that "[n]o Contracting Party shall expel or return ("*refouler*") a refugee in any manner whatsoever to the frontiers of territories where his life or freedom would be threatened on account of his race, religion, nationality, membership of a particular social group or political opinion"[36]. UNHCR's Executive Committee has consistently reaffirmed the significance of the principle of *non-refoulement* to refugees[37]. Similarly, repatriation to a country where fear exists that the returnee may be subjected to torture is also prohibited under article 3(1) of the Convention Against Torture[38], and has been interpreted by the Human Rights Committee to violate both the right to freedom from torture as

---

[31] United Nations High Commissioner for Refugees, Executive Committee Conclusions No. 18 (XXXI) Voluntary Repatriation (1980) and No. 40 (XXXVI) Voluntary Repatriation (1985).

[32] See however Tim Allen, "The United Nations and the Homecoming of Displaced Populations," in 301 Int'l Rev. of the Red Cross 340, 340-353 (1994) (noting that enthusiasm for repatriation is not warranted in the absence of information about what has happened to those refugees who have returned home in the past).

[33] *See* UNHCR Handbook, *Voluntary Repatriation: International Protection* (1996) [hereinafter "Handbook"].

[34] Executive Committee Conclusion No. 73 (XLIV) Refugee Protection and Sexual Violence (1993); UNHCR, Refugee Children: Guidelines on Protection and Care (1994), at 138-144

[35] Organisation of African Unity Convention Governing the Specific Aspects of Refugee Problems in Africa, 10 September 1969, article II(3), 1001 UNTS 45, *ratified by* 41 States on 1 February 1996. *See generally*, Guy S. Goodwin-Gill, *The Refugee in International Law*, 2d ed., (1996), AT 117-171.

[36] Convention relating to the Status of Refugees, 189 UNTS 137, *adopted* 28 July 1951. Conclusions of the Declaration of Cartagena of 1984, *in* Annual Report of the Inter-American Commission on Human Rights 1984-1985, OEA/Ser.L/V/II.66, doc. 10 rev. 1, 1 October 1985, ¶ 5.

[37] Executive Committee Conclusion No. 6 (XXVIII) Non-Refoulement (1977), Executive Committee Conclusion No. 25 (XXXIII) General (1982).

[38] Convention against Torture and Other Cruel, Inhuman or Degrading Treatment or Punishment, 23 ILM 1027 (1984), as modified 24 ILM 535 (1985), at 197.

formulated in article 7 of the ICCPR and the right to life[39]. The European Court of Human Rights has reached a similar interpretation with regard to the prohibition of inhuman treatment under the ECHR (article 3)[40]. This fact is particularly important to those enjoying "temporary protection", as opposed to asylum, inasmuch as it remains unclear to what extent the principles of *non-refoulement* and voluntary repatriation apply[41].

When a refugee can avail herself of the protection of his/her own State, she ceases technically to be a refugee and thus loses the interim protection of the 1951 Refugee Convention and the principle *of non-refoulement* (as soon as the cessation clauses provided for in article 1 C of the Convention can be applied and invoked). This change in status occurs as a matter of course upon voluntary repatriation (in the sense, however, of re-establishment, not a mere instance of return), but may also take place through other means, such as the renewal of the national passport[42]. Nevertheless, in certain cases compelling reasons may support the continuation of refugee status for some individuals, even when circumstances indicate that most refugees from a given country cannot refuse to re-avail themselves of the protection of their own country following the necessary change of circumstances there. This may be the case where, for example, a refugee has suffered such atrocious forms of persecution as to be mentally and psychologically unable to repatriate[43].

In addition to being voluntary, any repatriation involving the international community must be conducted under circumstances that provide for guarantees for the returnees' safety and dignity. These guarantees may include the returnees' physical safety at all stages during and after their return, respect of family unity, a reduction to a minimum of border crossing formalities, permission for refugees to bring their movable possessions when returning, and respect for school and planting seasons in the timing of repatriations and freedom of movement[44]. It may further require the establishment of conditions of a self-sustainable livelihood and of prospects of an eventual social, economic, cultural and political re-integration.

---

[39] Human Rights Committee General Comment No. 20, ¶ 9, *reprinted in* Note by the Secretariat, Compilation of General Comments and General Recommendations, *adopted by* Human Rights Treaty Bodies, UN Doc. HRI/GEN/1/Rev.1 (29 July 1994); views on Communication No. 469/1991 (*Charles Chitat Ng* v. *Canada*), UN Doc. CCPR/C/49/D/469/1991, (7 January 1994), *adopted* 5 November 1993.

[40] *Cruz Varas Case*, Judgement of 20 March 1991, Series A, No. 201, at ¶ 69 (quoting *Soering Case*, Judgement of 7 July 1989, Series A, No. 161, ¶ 91).

[41] *See* Goodwin-Gill, *The Refugee in International Law*, *supra*, at 276. The UNHCR Executive Committee in Conclusion No. 74 (XLV) General (1994) has clearly linked "temporary protection" with "safe return when conditions permit to the country of origin."

[42] *See generally* James Hathaway, *The Law of Refugee Status*, (1991), at 189-205.

[43] This has been recognised by the Executive Committee of UNHCR in Conclusion No. 65 (XLII) (1991).

[44] *See* Handbook, *supra*, at 12.

B. The Return and Resettlement of Internally Displaced Persons

No human rights instrument expressly provides internally displaced persons legal protection against being forcibly returned to places where their safety cannot be guaranteed[45]. However, a protection of this nature flows from the right to life and the right to physical and mental integrity, as guaranteed *inter alia* in articles 6 and 7 respectively of the ICCPR and articles 2(1) and 3 of the ECHR. It is also a consequence of the right to freedom of movement, as discussed above, which encompasses the right not to be moved against one's own will.

C. Alternative Solutions

Where repatriation of a refugee is not possible, settlement in the country of asylum or a third country may be envisaged. UNHCR has used resettlement as a means of protection and of offering a refugee a durable solution in the absence of other solutions in sight, even though it considers it as the "last resort." Special security concerns and the situation of "vulnerable groups," in particular women at risk, torture victims, the physically or mentally handicapped and certain medical and family reunion cases, have in the past triggered resettlement[46]. Resettlement and local integration of refugees, however, are rare once voluntary repatriation processes have been initiated.

For internally displaced persons, settlement in another part of their own country is not a legal problem by virtue of the right to freedom of movement and choice of residence. Where return to one's area of origin is either practically impossible for security or sustainability reasons or psychologically too taxing for the individual concerned, such settlement may be the only available durable solution. In such a case, it may require special measures, such as financial support and allocation of land. Of course, the potential exists that settlement in another area inside the country may in effect complete the process of "ethnic cleansing". However, such concerns must be balanced against the right of the displaced to resume their normal lives as soon as possible and to put an end to their uprootedness. At the same time, claims that certain groups cannot return to areas where they would constitute an ethnic or other minority because their safety cannot be guaranteed must be scrutinised to ensure they are not being invoked for political reasons, rather than in the best interests of the displaced. Attempts to discourage return interfere with the right to return, as described above.

Finally, seeking and receiving asylum in a third country is another option for internally displaced persons which must remain open throughout their internal displacement.

---

[45]   UN Doc. E/CN.4/1996/52/Add.2, *supra*, ¶ 248.

[46]   *See* Goodwin-Gill, *The Refugee in International Law*, *supra*, at 278.

IV. THE GENERAL FRAMEWORK AGREEMENT FOR PEACE
IN BOSNIA AND HERZEGOVINA[47]

Both the Constitution of Bosnia and Herzegovina (Annex 4 of the General Framework Agreement) and the Agreement on Human Rights (Annex 6) list the right to liberty of movement and residence among the fundamental rights and freedoms which the Parties have agreed to secure to all persons within their jurisdiction. In fact, the inclusion of "full freedom of movement" of persons (as well as goods, services and capital) in article I of the Constitution and the stipulation that "[n]either Entity shall establish controls at the boundary between the Entities" is one of the most distinctive characteristics of the agreement to end the Bosnian conflict.

With regard to nationality, the BiH Constitution provides that all persons formerly citizens of the Republic of Bosnia and Herzegovina[48] until the entry into force of the Constitution continue to enjoy this citizenship and would not be arbitrarily deprived of it[49]. It follows that refusal to grant entry to the state following arbitrary deprivation of such nationality would not be lawful[50].

In addition, Annex 7 (Refugees and Displaced Persons) contains detailed provisions on the process of return of refugees and displaced persons, which are in effect an expression of the right to return as analysed above and of the need to secure non-discriminatory protection of human rights and appropriate conditions of safety and economic, political and social viability. Thus, article I of Annex 7 (and article II (5) of the Constitution) enunciates the right of all refugees and displaced persons "freely to return to their homes of origin" and the obligation of the Parties to the GFA to accept these persons. Special reference has been made to the restoration of property rights, physical integrity and freedom from any persecution or discrimination, and specific provisions regarding the implementation of these rights has been included in paragraph 3 of article I. Furthermore, the GFA leaves free the choice of final destination, recognising the right of the displaced to settle in other areas rather than their area of origin if they so wish. In such cases the displaced will have, presumably, to respect earlier

---

[47] Proximity Peace Talks, Wright-Patterson Air Force Base, Dayton, Ohio, November 1-21, 1995, UN Doc. ICFY/INFORMAL/4 Job no. GE.95-64240. *See also* Paul C. Szasz, "The Protection of Human Rights Through the Dayton/Paris Peace Agreement on Bosnia", 90 AJIL 301, 301-315 (1996) (describing the human rights provisions included in the Dayton Peace Agreement).

[48] A constituent state of the former Socialist Republic of Yugoslavia.

[49] General Framework Agreement for Peace in Bosnia and Herzegovina, *initialed* Dayton, Ohio, 21 November 1995, *signed* Paris, 14 December 1995, 35 ILM 75 [hereinafter "GFA"], at Annex 4, Art. I(7).

[50] For a detailed discussion of the new citizenship law of Bosnia and Herzegovina, see Open Society Institute, "Forced Migration Projects," *in Citizenship Law in Bosnia & Herzegovina* (May 1996).

property claims of returnees originating from the area to which they wish to permanently settle[51].

The Agreement specifically provides that the Parties shall not compel returnees "to remain in or move to situations of serious danger or insecurity, or to areas lacking in the basic infrastructure necessary to resume a normal life"[52]. Presumably, the provision applies not only to refugees who have returned to BiH from third countries, but also to the internally displaced in BiH, since to argue otherwise would contravene international human rights law[53]. It would have been technically better if internally displaced persons had been explicitly included in the formulation of article I(4); otherwise, the provision is a significant expression of a principle of "internal *non-refoulement*", and the first of its kind in peace agreements and human rights instruments.

However, the GFA lacks a similar provision with regard to *non-refoulement* and repatriation from states other than the parties to the GFA's different annexes. While the GFA stipulates the right of refugees "freely to return" and calls on states that have accepted refugees to promote return in accordance with international law in co-ordination with UNHCR, it does signify this return to be "early"[54]. Nevertheless, it does not stipulate any deadline or other specific time-frame for the return and repatriation.

At the same time, the GFA is silent on solutions to displacement within BiH other than repatriation, return and establishment. According to UNHCR, more than 60% of the over 566,000 refugees currently in the Federal Republic of Yugoslavia may prefer to remain in that country and be locally integrated, while tens of thousands of the Bosnian Croat refugees in Croatia may also wish to settle permanently there. As discussed below, however, many Bosniac refugees in Western Europe may be unable to return to BiH[55].

The GFA also provides for the establishment of a Commission for Displaced Persons and Refugees. This Commission's mandate, however, is limited to receiving and deciding any claims for the return of, or compensation for, real property in BiH[56]. Unquestionably an important issue, adjudication of property claims is not the only hindrance to return in BiH. For this reason, the human rights institutions provided for in other parts of

---

[51] GFA, *supra*, Annex 7, Art. I(4).

[52] GFA, *supra*, Annex 7, Art. I(4) (emphasis added)

[53] *See* note 45 above and accompanying text.

[54] GFA, *supra*, Annex 7, Art. I(1) (emphasis added); *Id.*, Art. I(5).

[55] UNHCR's Strategy for Bosnia and Herzegovina and the Region for 1997 and 1998, UNHCR Special Operation for Former Yugoslavia, 11 October 1996.

[56] The work of the Commission may be further constricted by the lack of appropriate funding. *See* Commission for Real Property Claims of Displaced Persons and Refugees, Appeal for Funds to Enable the Commission to Operate from September 1996 to December 1997 (1996), on file with the present author.

the GFA will have a crucial impact on the process of return and repatriation.

V. RETURN TO AND WITHIN POST-GFA BOSNIA[57]

Reality on the ground in BiH is different from the one envisaged in the GFA and international human rights instruments. Due to real or orchestrated security problems and lack of rapid progress in the reconstruction of the country, return of refugees and displaced persons remains the exception rather than the rule one year after the GFA's signing. In March 1996, UNHCR hoped to help return home over two million BiH refugees by December 1997; however, it soon complained that none of the parties were honouring their obligations in terms of return and, thus, the return process was very slow. Only 250,000 had returned to their areas of original residence by November 1996 and most of those were internally displaced persons returning to areas inhabited by the ethnic majority to which they belonged, or to the Zone of Separation, which is administered and heavily patrolled by IFOR[58]. As the U.N. Secretary-General has stated in his report to the Security Council in October 1996, "increasingly, contrary to the letter and spirit of the [GFA], the Inter-Entity Boundary Line (IEBL) has acquired the status of a *de facto* border for people and goods"[59].

The threat of violence has been a key deterrent to repatriation and return. On some occasions violence has been specifically used to discourage or avert the reestablishment of the displaced, and has been serious enough to induce the NATO-led peace forces (IFOR) to prepare to deal with violent incidents, as displaced families would try to return to their homes across ethnic lines[60]. Preliminary visits by community representatives to assess whether it would be safe to return have often been obstructed by local authorities, especially in the Republika Srpska, in spite of specific agreements signed by all parties addressing the issue of such visits. In some cases, "spontaneous demonstrations" are organised by the current inhabitants that "oppose" the return of the displaced[61]. In other cases, visits

---

[57] The observations in this section are based on a visit to Bosnia by the present author in October 1996.

[58] Remarks by Sadako Ogata, United Nations High Commissioner for Refugees, at the Carnegie Council on Ethics and International Affairs, New York, 1 November 1996, copy on file with the present author.

[59] UN Doc. S/1996/820 (1 October 1996), ¶ 41.

[60] As reported by Reuters from Sarajevo, "Violence Expected as Refugees Return Home", on 20 April 1996, and from Geneva, "UN Warns of Conflicts over Homecomings", on 19 April 1996.

[61] *See* Periodic report submitted by Ms. Elisabeth Rehn, Special Rapporteur on the situation of human rights in the territory of the former Yugoslavia, UN Doc. E/CN.4/1997/5 (17 July 1996), at ¶ 19.

organised and negotiated by UNHCR have been outright refused, and fears are voiced that the displaced may try to take matters in their own hands, forcing their way back and provoking greater levels of violence. Even within the Federation itself, "Muslims and Croats have hardly seen any reintegration"[62].

Politics continue to meddle with the right to return: While the BiH government has declared its preference for the return of the displaced to their areas of original residence, the Republika Srpska authorities discourage return of ethnic Serbs to the territory of the Federation, as well as return of Bosniaks and Croats inside the Republika Srpska[63]. The Croat authorities are also known to have obstructed the return of Bosniaks in Mostar, and of Serbs in north-western Bosnia on several occasions.

Other deterrents to freedom of movement include the lack of public or private transportation facilities across the IEBL and the lack of agreements regarding identity documents and licence plates. Lack of available housing and resources is yet another obstacle to return and repatriation; so too land mines, unexploded ammunition and the booby traps spread throughout the territory of Bosnia and Herzegovina, including the cities. Discriminatory treatment of minority members and returnees in employment, housing and medical car, lack of clear commitments from the political leadership, nationalistic statements in the media and the existence of secret lists of war criminals pose additional problems. Property laws passed during the war by all the parties to the conflict to deal with "abandoned property" were not repealed until October 1996, despite being in conflict with the specifications of the GFA and having a discriminatory effect *vis à vis* displaced persons and returnees.

To worsen matters, new evictions accompanied by violence have on occasion taken place even after the GFA: for instance, a hundred and fifty persons are estimated to have been forced from Serb territory and another fifty from the Croat side of Mostar[64]. Between twenty and sixty thousand Serbs fled the Serbian suburbs of Sarajevo in March 1996, when the city came officially under Federation control, while as late as September 1996 others had to be evacuated from Banja Luka amidst fears for their security[65]. There have been also ongoing reports of illegal evictions of Bosniacs from Mostar. In fact, it is unclear whether return movements are greater than new displacements occurring *since* the Dayton Peace Agreement.

---

[62] Sadako Ogata, "UNHCR in Bosnia: An Uphill Struggle 11 Months after Dayton", 44 NATO Review 17 (November 1996).

[63] UN Doc. E/CN.4/1997/5, *supra*, ¶ 28.

[64] *Id.*, ¶ 29.

[65] *See* UN Doc. E/CN.4/1996/63, *supra*, ¶ 35; *cf.* Sadako Ogata, "Remarks made at the Contact Group Meeting, Moscow, 23 March 1996", *in A Selection of Speeches and Statements by Mrs. Sadako Ogata*, vol. I, (1996), at Ch. 15 [hereinafter "*A Selection of Speeches*"].

It is also possible that the return process itself may be a cause of delay in further repatriations and returns. For instance, it is now widely recognised that even within the Bosnian-Croat Federation, many of the Croats and Muslims who once lived in mixed communities in Central Bosnia are trapped in a complex web of return, resettlement and allocation of property that prevents them from returning home in the near future.

Matters became more complicated as the elections of 14 September 1996 approached. The OSCE, which oversaw the elections, made an effort to allow the exercise of voting rights outside the municipality of one's original or actual residence, so as not to be seen as condoning "ethnic cleansing"[66]. Nevertheless, on the day of the election, the great majority of the displaced did not return to their home areas to vote; in addition, others took advantage of the election rules to vote in areas where the showing of an ethnic majority was strategically important[67]. Subsequently, and in preparation for the municipal elections, the OSCE amended the rules to restrict registration of voters outside their area of original or present residence.

Where returns across the IEBL are taking place – mostly within the zone of separation – they are accompanied by extra-ordinary processes, such as inter-ethnic competition as to which community will build up more roofs to prove ethnic presence and control, especially in areas where the borders remained undefined by GFA, in particular the Brcko corridor. It is now recognised that for some refugees repatriation will not be possible at all: in the cases of many "mixed marriage" families, for instance, settlement in "majority areas" will not be an option; the same is true for individuals seriously traumatised by their experiences during the war. Some internally displaced persons may require humanitarian resettlement outside Bosnia even at this stage of post-Dayton peace, in particular children with severe medical or psychological problems[68].

Despite indications that repatriation was less than smooth in the first ten months of the GFA's implementation, western governments were preparing to order large numbers of Bosnian refugees and persons under "temporary protection" to return back. Germany, which hosts the largest number of Bosnian refugees in Western Europe (an estimated 320,000), has declared its will to commence with repatriation within the last six months of 1996,

---

[66] OSCE Press release: Provisional Election Commission: Rules for Election – No Sanctioning of Ethnic Cleansing, April 27, 1996.

[67] Only an estimated twenty thousand crossed the IEBL to vote. Department of Humanitarian Affairs, Bosnia and Herzegovina, Report No. 9, 26 September 1996. *See also* International Crisis Group, *Elections in Bosnia and Herzegovina* (22 September 1996).

[68] Elizabeth Rehn, Special Rapporteur for the Situation of Human Rights in the Territory of the Former Yugoslavia, Presentation to the Committee on the Rights of the Child Concerning Bosnia and Herzegovina (24 September 1996) (on file with the author).

in the face even of considerable political opposition[69]. UNHCR has clearly denounced efforts by western governments to resort to massive repatriations of Bosnians and to the lifting of "temporary protection"[70], and has warned that the designation of certain areas as targets for repatriation assistance, which were selected on the basis of their level of destruction, should not be considered as a pronouncement of their "safety" and should not be used as a pretext for enforced returns[71].

Over the past year, UNHCR, IFOR, and a score of other inter-governmental agencies have been strenuously urging the authorities in BiH to abide by their Dayton commitments. UNHCR, in particular, which was assigned the "lead agency" role in the humanitarian relief efforts during the war, continues today to provide large amounts of material assistance to BiH displaced and war-affected populations. UNHCR is also heavily engaged n reconstruction and rehabilitation work. But, UNHCR is also playing a key role in negotiating assessment visits and promoting the return of the refugees and displaced persons to their homes. In addition, it has been actively monitoring the process of return, as have many other organisations as well[72]. UNHCR's role is a particularly delicate one, as it has to balance three sets of seemingly irreconcilable objectives. First, it must promote repatriation while not simultaneously encouraging the lifting of "temporary protection." Second, it must invest in schemes of return that hold the promise of success, without at the same time acquiescing to patterns of emphasis on return primarily to "majority areas" (which, in the end, would mean *de facto* ethnic segregation); and third, advocating for return, while simultaneously trying to secure other alternative solutions

---

[69] Bayern besteht auf rascher Flüchtlingsrückkehr, Süddeutsche Zeitung, 19 September 1996. To that effect, Germany and Bosnia were reported in early November 1996 to have concluded a treaty regulating the return of all Bosnian refugees living in Germany. Until June 1997 only single people and couples without children would return. Reported by Human Rights Information Network on 11 November 1996.

[70] *See, e.g.,* Sadako Ogata, Statement at the Humanitarian Issues Working Group of the Peace Implementation Conference, Geneva, 13 May 1996, *in A Selection of Speeches, supra. See also* IFOR Press Conference, Sarajevo, September 29, 1996, Reply by Kris Janowski, UNHCR Spokesman, to questions re UNHCR's position on Germany's plan to deport Bosnian refugees, reported by the Human Rights Information Network on 30 September 1996.

[71] Department of Humanitarian Affairs, Report No. 9, *supra.*

[72] Such as: IFOR, which has been a key factor in separating the former warring factions; the ICRC; the IPTF and the Civil Affairs officers of the United Nations Mission in Bosnia and Herzegovina (UNMIBH); the officers of the UN High Commissioner for Human Rights; the Office of the High Representative and its Human Rights Coordination Centre; the European Community Monitoring Mission; and the OSCE Mission to Bosnia and Herzegovina. *See, e.g.,* ICRC Report on the Situation of the Kuplensko-Returnees in the Area of Velika Kladusa/Cazin (Zagreb, 1 March 1996); Human Rights Watch, *No Justice No Peace: The United Nations International Police Task Force's Role in Screening Local Law Enforcement* (28 September 1996); UN Doc. S/1996/820, *supra.*

less palatable to the international community. This situation is one of the legacies of the GFA.

VI. CONCLUDING REMARKS

Arguments over whether the law is sufficient to deal with the different "categories" of victims of forcible dipslacement and armed conflicts have raged over the past few years. Various initiatives have already been launched to strengthen the law where it is perceived to be weak or unclear[73]. In post-Dayton BiH some of the grey areas in international law, especially as they pertain to internally displaced persons and their right to return (or not) to their home areas, have been clarified by the GFA. While such clarification is welcome in terms of the overall development of international law, it should not obscure the fact that other, equally important provisions of international human rights and refugee law remain fully in force and applicable both to the parties to the GFA and to third countries, even where not mentioned in the GFA.

The real test may appear in the form of a vicious circle for the BiH government: how to ensure rapid economic development of the country so as, *inter alia*, to mitigate any renewed risks of conflict, while at the same time fulfill an obligation to absorb hundreds of thousands of returnees who can only strain its fragile economy. While the GFA[74] entrusts to the international community the monitoring of the protection of human rights of returnees and displaced persons and with providing material assistance with the repatriation process, it does not specify what is to happen to the return process if conditions necessary to return are not met. Moreover, in the likely event that such conditions are indeed not met, it is safe to expect that prospective returnees will be reluctant to repatriate and will avoid doing so by whatever means, frustrating the efforts of host governments to "solve" the refugee problem.

Ironically, the GFA runs the risk of being labelled as the ultimate endorsement of "ethnic cleansing," unless the right to return is fully implemented. The situation on the ground in Bosnia will determine whether this is the case[75]. In the meantime, careful assessment of the conditions in different regions of Bosnia will be necessary to decide on the feasibility of any return and repatriation processes. Before repeating the truism that

---

[73] The most serious efforts include a compilation and analysis of legal norms pertaining to internally displaced persons, included in UN Doc. E/CN.4/1996/52/Add.2, *supra,*, and a Declaration on Minimum Humanitarian Standards elaborated by a number of scholars and currently under review by Governments, *reprinted in* UN Doc. E/CN.4/1996/80/Add.3, 11 March 1996.

[74] GFA, *supra*, Annex 7.

[75] Paolo Raffone, Derrière la façade éléctorale – Le cauchemar des réfugiés bosniaques, Le Monde Diplomatique, Septembre 1996.

return is the best solution for refugees, it should at this stage be taken into account that the right to return means different things to people whose ideas about the country and community they might return to vary significantly and may have been seriously altered over the past few years.

ELENA POPOVIC

7. The Impact of International Human Rights Law on the Property Law of Bosnia and Herzegovina

I. INTRODUCTION

Soon after the military aspects of the General Framework Agreement for Peace in Bosnia and Herzegovina were successfully implemented, it became clear that the future of the peace process would depend on the safe and orderly return of refugees and displaced persons[1]. The GFA itself recognized the fact that "[t]he early return of refugees and displaced persons is an important objective of the settlement of the conflict"[2]. However, in the time since it was signed, very little has been done to carry out obligations set forth by its Annex 7. In addition, property laws which were adopted during the war remain in effect throughout the country despite being clearly "discriminatory in intent or effect."

To a large extent, the decision of refugees and displaced persons to return home will depend on whether there is a shelter to return to, that is, on their ability to reacquire possession of their property. In recognition of this fact, the GFA's Annex 7 provides, in its very first article, that refugees and displaced persons "shall have the right to have restored to them property of which they were deprived in the course of hostilities since 1991 and to be compensated for any property that cannot be restored to them." The GFA envisioned the Commission for Displaced Persons and Refugees to receive and decide claims for the return or just compensation of real property in Bosnia and Herzegovina[3]. By the end of 1996, almost a year after the signing of the GFA, resolution of property problems in Bosnia has barely begun. The Commission has just started receiving property claims.

---

[1] General Framework Agreement for Peace in Bosnia and Herzegovina, *initialed* Dayton, Ohio, 21 November 1995, *signed* Paris, 14 December 1995, 35 ILM 75 (1996) [hereinafter "GFA"].

[2] GFA, *supra*, Annex 7, Art. I(1)

[3] GFA, *supra*, Annex 7, Art. VII.

M. O'Flaherty and G. Gisvold (eds.), Post-War Protection of Human Rights in Bosnia and Herzegovina, 141–156.
© 1998 *Kluwer Law International. Printed in Great Britain.*

Generally, there are two types of evictions – entirely illegal ones[4], and those which in different ways implicate legal elements[5]. Violation of the right to property is the most significant human rights problem in both Entities – the Federation of Bosnia and Herzegovina and the Republika Srpska – of Bosnia and Herzegovina[6]. In the first half of 1996, for example, out of 1,927 cases that the Ombudsmen of the Federation of Bosnia and Herzegovina considered, 64.06% were property related[7]. In the Republika Srpska, independent sources indicate that 70% of all cases pending before civil law courts in Banja Luka alone concern property. The full scope of the problem is difficult to assess because most violations remain unreported. Evictions continue in the Banja Luka region, West Mostar, Central Bosnia, the Bihac pocket, and the Sarajevo suburbs – everywhere where ethnic minorities still exist – apparently in an effort to finish the process of ethnic cleansing. Not rarely, victims of evictions are political opponents as well.

To complete the picture, "[a]n estimated half of the housing has been damaged and about 6 percent destroyed in the Federation of Bosnia and Herzegovina ... . Detailed estimates of damage are not available yet for the Republika Srpska (RS) but are likely to be comparable in certain regions"[8]. Given the above, one cannot overemphasize the importance of the resolution of property problems in Bosnia and Herzegovina and of the protection of the right to property.

II. RIGHT TO PROPERTY IN THE GENERAL FRAMEWORK AGREEMENT

The first mention of the right to property in the GFA is found in its Annex 4 containing the Constitution of Bosnia and Herzegovina. Article II(3) enumerates human rights guaranteed, the right to property included. To ensure the highest level of internationally recognized human rights and fundamental freedoms, the Agreement lists treaties applicable in Bosnia

---

[4] Those have more frequently happened during the war. Such evictions were carried out through different means – from violent campaigns of ethnic cleansing in which whole communities are forced to flee, to very subtle pressure to leave.

[5] An example in the Republika Srpska would be the application of the Law on the Use of Abandoned Property. In the Federation, such evictions were carried out pursuant to annulment of contracts on purchase of apartments that had belonged to the former Yugoslav National Army.

[6] Bosnia and Herzegovina [hereinafter "BiH"] is one of the states formerly a part of the Socialist Federal Republic of Yugoslavia (SFRY), which existed until 1992. Post-1992, other former constituents of the SFRY, Serbia and Montenegro now comprise the state known as the Federal Republic of Yugoslavia [hereinafter "FRY" or "Serbia"].

[7] *See,* Institution of the Ombudsman of the Federation of Bosnia and Herzegovina, Semi-annual Report on the State of Human Rights, Sarajevo, July 1996, Statistics for 1996.

[8] World Bank, Technical Annex, Bosnia and Herzegovina, Emergency Housing Repair Project, Report NO. T-6937-BIH, July 8, 1996, at 1 [hereinafter "Technical Annex"].

and Herzegovina[9]. It is difficult, however, to determine what would be the highest level of international standards with respect to the right to property. There is little mention of this right in international law. In the optimistic spirit following the end of the World War II, the right to property found a place in the 1948 Universal Declaration of Human Rights, Article 17 of which provides that "[e]veryone has the right to own property alone as well as in association with others. No one shall be arbitrarily deprived of his property". But, as a consequence of ideological differences in the Cold War era, the right to property was left out of both the International Covenant on Civil and Political Rights and the International Covenant on Economic, Social and Cultural Rights[10].

The situation is more clear with respect to the European Convention for the Protection of Human Rights and Fundamental Freedoms, which the GFA specifies is directly applicable in Bosnia and Herzegovina[11]. The GFA provides that the ECHR shall have priority over all other law in Bosnia and Herzegovina. Article 1 of the First Protocol to the ECHR provides that

> Every natural or legal person is entitled to the peaceful enjoyment of his possessions. No one shall be deprived of his possessions except in the public interest and subject to the conditions provided for by law and by the general principles of international law.
>
> The preceding provisions shall not, however, in any way impair the right of a State to enforce such laws as it deems necessary to control the use of property in accordance with the general interest or to secure the payment of taxes or other contributions or penalties.

Although it contains the term "possessions", this article in substance guarantees the right to property[12].

Annex 6 of the GFA, which deals with human rights, reiterates principles laid down in the Constitution. The Constitution gives refugees and displaced persons the right to have restored to them property which was taken from them in the course of the hostilities since 1991 and to be compensated for any such property that cannot be restored to them[13]. Similarly, Annex 7 further guarantees this right, listing a number of conditions necessary for the safe and dignified return of refugees. In order to demonstrate a

---

[9] GFA, *supra*, Art. III, Annex 4, (Constitution of Bosnia and Herzegovina), Art. II, ¶ 1 [hereinafter Constitution].

[10] *See* International Covenant on Civil and Political Rights, 999 UNTS 171, *adopted* 16 December 1966 [hereinafter "ICCPR"]; International Covenant on Economic, Social and Cultural Rights, 993 UNTS 3, *adopted* 16 December 1966 [hereinafter "ICESCR"].

[11] GFA, *supra*, Annex 6, Art. I; [European] Convention for the Protection of Human Rights and Fundamental Freedoms, 213 UNTS 221, 1 ETS 5, *signed* 4 November 1950 [hereinafter "ECHR"].

[12] *Marckx* v. *Belgium*, 2 EHRR 350 (1979).

[13] Constitution, *supra*, Art. II, ¶ 5, repeated in GFA, *supra*, Annex 7, Art. I(1)

commitment to full respect for human rights and fundamental freedoms of all persons within their jurisdiction and to create without delay conditions suitable for the return of refugees and displaced persons, it binds the Parties to immediately undertake certain confidence building measures, including "the repeal of domestic legislation and administrative practices with discriminatory intent or effect"[14]. To implement the right to property, Annex 7 also establishes a Commission for Displaced Persons and Refugees to decide claims for return of property or compensation instead of return. The Commission, which began work on March 14, 1996, is composed of nine commissioners – three from the international community and six from BiH, four from the Federation of Bosnia and Herzegovina and two from the Republika Srpska.

III. RIGHT TO PROPERTY IN THE POSITIVE LAW OF BOSNIA AND HERZEGOVINA

The right to property is governed by different enactments of each Entity comprising BiH. It is likely to stay that way as the regulation of property issues remains within the legislative competence of the Entities[15]. Laws and regulations limiting property rights, passed during the war, remain in effect almost a year after the signing of the GFA, though they should have been repealed as discriminatory. In addition, local authorities enforce those enactments arbitrarily, taking into account political and ethnic considerations. These laws continue to pose a great obstacle to the return of refugees and displaced persons.

A. *Federation of Bosnia and Herzegovina*

The Law on Basis of Ownership Relations was enacted in 1995 to regulate the basic issues of property rights in Bosnia and Herzegovina, and, thereby, to replace the former Yugoslav Law on Basic Property Rights[16]. The Basic Law regulates: definition of ownership, limits on ownership, object of property rights, definition of real property, adverse possession, occupation, abandoned property, etc. It guarantees the right to property in a manner consistent with the ECHR and its Protocols[17]. It holds that

---

[14] GFA, *supra*, Annex 7, Art. I(3).

[15] "All governmental functions and powers not expressly assigned in this Constitution to the institutions of Bosnia and Herzegovina shall be those of the Entities." Constitution, *supra*, Art. III.3(a), Art. III, ¶ 1 and Art. IV, ¶ 4.

[16] *Zakon o osnovama vlasnickih odnosa*, S.l.RBiH no. 37/95 of 2 October 1995 [hereinafter "Basic Law"].

[17] Open Society Institute/Forced Migration Projects, Property Law in Bosnia and Herzegovina, New York, March 1996, at 4 [hereinafter "Property Law"].

Ownership rights can be limited or taken away only in the public interest and in accordance with the Constitution, in a way and under conditions prescribed by law. The owner has the right to full compensation for the rights thus limited or taken away. The above provision is not applicable to situations in which the property has been limited or lost due to the illegal behavior of the owner[18].

The Annex 7 Commission is charged with deciding claims for *real* property only. Having said so, it is important to note that the Basic Law defines real property to include "real property by destination"[19]. This definition is in accordance with the European legal tradition. As the main property problem in Bosnia and Herzegovina is property left behind by those who were fleeing persecution or fighting, it is worth mentioning that the Law considers property to be abandoned only if the owner has, beyond doubt, expressed his/her free will not to own the property at issue anymore[20].

In addition to the Basic Law, there are several other enactments worth mentioning regarding property rights, in particular those concerning repatriation of refugees and displaced persons. These include: the Decree with the Force of Law on Temporary Abandoned Real Property under Private Ownership during the State of War or the State of Immediate War Danger, the Law on Abandoned Apartments, and the Tenancy Law. Some of these enactments regulate issues already covered by the Basic Law, and, thus, are *lex specialis – derogat legi generali*.

1. Private Ownership

The Decree with the Force of Law on Temporary Abandoned Real Property under Private Ownership during the State of War or the State of Immediate War Danger was adopted in May 1993[21]. As the title indicates, the 1993 Decree was meant to regulate an issue which emerged during the course of the war, and to regulate it temporarily. Notwithstanding the wording, the consequences might be long lasting, if not permanent[22].

The Decree defines abandoned property as any property that has not been used by its owner since April 30, 1991; it further empowers a competent authority to declare such property abandoned. An exception is provided for the property which an owner has assigned to someone for use[23]. This exception is compatible with the general definition of aban-

---

[18] Basic Law, *supra*, at Art. 4.

[19] Real property by destination is a movable thing that follows the same legal regime as the main thing (real estate) as, by virtue of law or of owner's will, its purpose is to further the use of the real property. *See* Basic Law, *supra*, at Art. 5.

[20] Basic Law, *supra*, at Art. 50.

[21] *Uredba sa zakonskom snagom o privremenom napustenim nekretninama u svojini gradjana za vrijeme rata ili u slucaju neposredne ratne opasnosti*, S.l.RBiH no. 11/93 of 10 May 1993 [hereinafter "1993 Decree"].

[22] Property Law, *supra*, at 11.

[23] 1993 Decree, *supra*, at Art. 5.

doned property found in the Basic Law, which requires a demonstration of undoubtable free will to abandon. However, in war conditions it seems to be unjustifiable as it discriminates against those who were fleeing immediate danger and had no time to arrange such transactions, unlike those who had foreseen their plight and ensured that their property would not be considered abandoned. Notwithstanding the title, the Decree states that movable things belonging to real property are also abandoned.

The municipality, which governs the property after it has been declared abandoned, can assign it to a beneficiary for use for a period of one year, with a possibility of extending the usage on the beneficiary's request, if justifiable reasons so require. Through the assignment of property, a beneficiary does not become an owner, nor do his rights resemble ownership rights. He is only entitled to *usus* and cannot dispose of property by any means, nor can he change or burden the property in any way. A temporary beneficiary must treat the property with due care (*"dobar domacin"*), and is liable to the municipality for all damages.

At the same time, however, the owner of property declared abandoned is deprived of his ownership rights. This outcome is particularly troubling given the presumption of abandonment created by the Decree, which states that property is considered abandoned simply because the owner has not been using it since April 30, 1991. Ownership rights are absolute rights that grant an owner the right to use the property in the way he deems appropriate, including the right not to use the property. The owner may appeal the decision declaring his property abandoned. Success in such an appeal is possible, but not automatic or even likely. "There is no provision in the Decree that would consider an owner's appeal, or any other legal action launched by the owner, as an expression of his/her interest and will to use the property, i.e., as evidence of his/her will *not* to abandon"[24].

Although the 1993 Decree does not mention owner's rights while the property is considered abandoned or assigned to someone, it is clear that the intent is to deprive the owner of any rights during that time. "Otherwise, it would be hard for the municipality to govern the property, and in particular, assign it to someone else, if the owner could dispose of it"[25]. The only mention of an owner's rights in the 1993 Decree refers to the situation in which an owner returns to the municipality in which his property is located. "Upon return to territory of the municipality in which his property is located, the owner can at any time launch a request to get all or part of his possessions back"[26]. Actual possession is to be transferred to the owner within three days from the date of the request. If the property was assigned to a beneficiary, he would have eight days from receipt of the decision to give up the property. In practice, property is being returned to

---

[24] Property Law, *supra*, at 11.
[25] *Id.*, at 10.
[26] 1993 Decree, *supra*, at Art. 25.

the owner upon the return and request without major problems, although the terms set up by the Decree are rarely being met.

Despite this procedure, the 1993 Decree remains problematic. It fails, for example, to address situations involving owners returning to Bosnia and Herzegovina, but not to the territory of the municipality where his/her property is located. It does not regulate what happens if the owner does not return at all. Moreover, the 1993 Decree is clearly contrary to Article 1 of the First Protocol to the ECHR inasmuch as it deprives an owner of the right to property.

The right to peaceful enjoyment of one's possessions guaranteed by the Protocol has been elaborated in decisions of the European Court of Human Rights, most notably in *Sporrong and Lonnroth* v. *Sweden* and *Lithgow*[27]. Article 1 of the First Protocol to the ECHR sets forth three principles: the right to peaceful enjoyment of property, the right that deprivation of possessions will only occur subject to certain conditions, and that States Parties to the Protocol are entitled to control the use of property in accordance with the general interest by enforcing such laws as they deem necessary for the purpose[28]. The second and third of these principles must be construed in the light of the general principle established by the first rule[29].

It may be argued that Bosnia and Herzegovina has enacted the Decree in order to control "the use of property" as it had to deal with the overwhelming number of displaced persons. However, the issue is whether such a control represents "a fair balance between the protection of the right to property and the requirement of the general interest"[30]. There must be a reasonable proportionality between the means employed and the aim pursued[31]. This is not the case here as the Decree infringes not only upon *usus*, but *abusus* as well, and therefore amounts to a deprivation of property. "[R]estriction on the use of private possessions must leave the owner at least a certain degree of freedom."[32] Under the 1993 Decree, that freedom is available only if the owner decides to return to the municipality where the property is located; it is unavailable indefinitely if the owner decides not to return or decides to return to some other locale.

2. Tenancy Rights

Given that the transition from socialism in Yugoslavia was halted by the war, some relics of the former socialist regime still play an important role in BiH. One of these remaining instutions were apartments held pursuant to a scheme of tenancy rights[33]. Guaranteed by constitutions of the former

---

[27] A/52, 5 EHRR 35 (1983); A/102, 8 EHRR 329 (1986).
[28] *Sporrong and Lonnroth* v. *Sweden, supra.*
[29] *Lithgow, supra.*
[30] Property Law, *supra.*
[31] *Mellacher and others* v. *Austria*, A/169, 12 EHRR 391 (1990).
[32] Property Law, *supra.*
[33] Also referred to as occupancy rights.

state and its republics, tenancy rights were *sui generis*, involving elements of both personal (contractual relation) and property rights (elements of ownership). There is no similar legal institution in comparative law or international law.

During the socialist regime, an employee would qualify for an apartment after a certain period of employment and fulfillment of certain requirements. Such apartments remained socially-owned property (that is, State property) but a holder of tenancy rights had rights very similar to those of an owner. For this reason, these rights were referred to as "quasi-ownership rights". A holder of tenancy rights could use the apartment in ways similar to an owner, able to rent, modify, and exchange the apartment. Upon the death of the holder of tenancy rights, the rights over the apartment could be transferred to another member of the household. Unlike an owner, a holder of tenancy rights had to pay rent, utilities and some other fees. A holder of tenancy rights had to look after the apartment with due care ("*dobar domacin*"), and was responsible for all daily changes and repairs[34]. Tenancy rights are therefore a property right and thus provisions of the GFA and ECHR regarding property rights apply[35].

There were approximately 1,295,000 housing units in Bosnia and Herzegovina. Overall, nearly 80% of these units were privately owned, though over half of the units in larger cities were socially owned property[36]. Sarajevo, for example, possessed some 80,000 socially owned apartments, just over half of the city's apartments[37]. During the transition from socialism, the privatisation of socially owned property began in the former Yugoslav republics; in Bosnia, privatisation included purchase of apartments under tenancy regime. However, privitisation was halted by the war. In short, after the war, in most urban areas apartments under tenancy regime remain the only shelter available for the return of refugees and displaced persons.

During the war, the Law on Abandoned Apartments, enacted on 15 June 1992, regulated the disposition of socially-owned apartments[38]. Under the 1992 Law, a holder of tenancy rights temporarily lost the right to use the apartment if he and other members of the household abandoned the apartment after April 30, 1991[39]. The 1992 Law defines an abandoned apartment as "abandoned by the holder of tenancy rights and members of his/her household who had permanently lived in the apartment, and since has not been temporarily used by them". The 1992 Law does not set forth time

---

[34] *See* Property Law, *supra.*

[35] Office of the High Representative, Law on Abandoned Apartments: Compliance with the provisions of the Dayton Peace Agreement and the International Instruments referred therein, at 4 [hereinafter "Abandoned Apartments"].

[36] Technical Annex, *supra*, at 1.

[37] World Bank, *Emergency Housing Repair Project*, at 7.

[38] *Zakon o napustenim stanovima*, S.l.RBiH no. 6/92 of 15 June 1992, 8/92, 16/92, 13/94, 36/94, 9/35, and 33/95 of 10 September 1995 [hereinafter,"1992 Law"].

[39] Abandoned Apartments, *supra*, at Art. 1.

limits or an event after which apartments may be declared abandoned. As a result, almost a year after the GFA apartments are still being declared abandoned.

Exceptions exist, such as the case of an apartment abandoned under pressure by forces pursuing ethnic cleansing goals, or because of the threat of immediate danger because of the war, or because the apartment itself was demolished, burned, damaged by the war. The wording of this exception provision may cause certain doubts and give rise to arbitrary application. For example, is an apartment in Sarajevo under the control of the Bosnian Government abandoned if the holder of tenancy rights fled the daily shelling of the city? If not, what criteria guide the regulation's application? The exception could easily swallow the rule. The GFA has imposed territorial division and underwritten new legislative competence. A narrow interpretation of the exception provision might encompass only those apartments in areas transferred post-GFA from the Serb to Federation control. Yet another exception exists in Article 3 of the 1992 Law, which excludes from its reach apartments in which the holder of tenancy rights began to use it within 7 days (if the tenancy holder is a displaced person) or 15 days (if the tenancy holder is a refugee) after the effective date of the Law.

Although the remainder of the 1992 Law deals with apartments defined as abandoned on the basis of non-use, Article 1 specifies that for the purposes of this Law an abandoned apartment is also an apartment in which arms and/or ammunition were found for which there is no permit issued to the holder of tenancy rights, as well as an apartment that has been used for illegal activities. In addition, a competent defense authority may launch an initiative with the competent municipal or city authority to have certain apartments previously owned by the Yugoslav National Army declared abandoned.

Once an apartment has been declared abandoned, a competent body may assign it for temporary use to "an active participant in a struggle against the aggressor on the Republic or to a person left homeless because of the immediate war danger"[40]. This person becomes a temporary beneficiary and can use the apartment for a maximum of one year after the proclamation of the end of the state of immediate war danger, which is still in place. The procedure and conditions for assigning abandoned apartments were prescribed by the Criteria for Assigning Abandoned Apartments to Temporary Beneficiaries[41].

Prior to giving possession of an apartment to a beneficiary, a competent authority shall seal the apartment, evidence the belongings and register the apartment in special records of abandoned apartments. If these conditions

---

[40] *Id.*, Art. 7, ¶ 1.
[41] Kriteriji za dodjelu napustenih stanova na privremeno koriscenje, S.l.RBiH no. 9/92 of 12 July 1992 and 9/93 of 29 April 1993 [hereinafter "Criteria"].

are not fulfilled, the apartment cannot be assigned, and decision on assigning it, if exists, is null. In a number of cases, these requirements were not fulfilled for different reasons (for example lack of sealing material), but apartments have been assigned in spite of that. The 1992 Law makes explicit that the beneficiary enjoys, *to the extent possible*, the rights of the holder of tenancy rights as regulated by the Tenancy Law[42]. It does not specify any parameters to this limitation, aside from prohibiting the exchange of the apartment.

As noted above, tenancy rights were quasi-ownership rights. Ultimate ownership rights were of society through the employer. Accordingly, the 1992 Law does not regulate the rights of a holder of tenancy rights while the apartment is considered abandoned in a manner similar to that of the 1993 Decree on Abandoned Real Property with respect to ownership rights. Article 10 provides that in order to continue the use of tenancy rights, a holder of tenancy rights must *start using* the apartment in 7 days (if s/he is displaced person in Bosnia) or 15 days (if a refugee outside Bosnia) after the proclamation of the end of the war. If not, the apartment is considered permanently abandoned and the holder of tenancy rights permanently loses his tenancy rights upon the decision of a competent authority. The end of the war was proclaimed on December 22, 1995. Even if refugees and displaced persons could have returned within such a short period of time, given the long and uncertain procedure to retake possession, it is unlikely that they could have actually started using the apartment as the 1992 Law requires. Application of this article resulted in thousands of apartments being declared permanently abandoned. The actual number of such apartments is difficult to determine, but the estimates (based on the May 1996 official figure of 6,000 apartments) range from 8 to 12 thousand, the vast majority of which belonged to Serbs and Croats.

Pursuant to this article, the 1992 Law imposes preclusive time limitations after the proclamation of the end of the war for return of displaced persons and refugees in order to retain tenancy rights. Under the Tenancy Law, a holder of tenancy rights would lose tenancy rights if he did not justifiably use the apartment for six months continuously. Given that holders of tenancy rights had no ownership rights over apartments, such terms might be justifiable. The apartments were socially owned property during the previous regime and are State property now as part of a transitional arrangement. Thus, as owner, the State may argue that it is entitled to dispose of it by any means. By definition, however, a socially owned apartment was owned in part by the tenancy right holder. "As an example, immediately before the war, a couple who had worked 25 years might have paid up to 75,000 DMs for the right to occupy a socially owned apartment"[43]. In addition, the transition in BiH was halted by the war, prevent-

---

[42] *Zakon o stambenim odnosima*; S.l.RBiH no. 14/84.
[43] OSCE, Special Report, at 15.

ing many from purchasing the apartments they had in possession under tenancy regime.

Having noted that tenancy rights should be considered property rights, everything said in regard to compliance of the 1993 Decree with the First Protocol to the European Convention for the Protection of Human Rights and Fundamental Freedoms is applicable here. As the 1992 Law, like the Decree, was enacted to enable the State to deal with flow of displaced persons, it could, again, argue that the 1992 Law is simply a means of controling the use of property to which the State is entitled in the general interest. More so possibly, as laws controlling the use of property are especially called for and usual in the field of housing, which in modern societies is a central concern of social and economic policies[44]. However, "the control" imposed by the 1992 Law, and in particular by its Article 10, amounts to full deprivation of the right to property and, thus, does not strike a balance between the general interest, and the rights of an individual. As such, the 1992 Law, as well as the 1993 Decree, is an obstacle to the repatriation of refugees and displaced persons, and, therefore, contrary to the GFA.

In addition to the 1993 Decree and the 1992 Law, contracts on the purchase of apartments formerly owned by JNA have been annulled by yet another decree with the force of law[45]. Given the retroactive effect, this action is not only contrary to the principle of legal certainty but also infringes upon vested rights, in this case ownership rights, and thus indisputably violates the GFA and ECHR. In practical terms, it widens the scope of the application of the Law on Abandoned Apartments.

B. Herzeg-Bosna

Although formally dissolved, the self-proclaimed Croatian Republic of Herzeg-Bosna continues its existence and functions, including its self-styled legal system. This system maintains a comprehensive set of decrees and regulations concerning real property, and in particular regarding expropriation and confiscation.

The Decree on Abandoned Apartments defines abandoned property, exceptions, and assignment to temporary beneficiary in wording similiar to the 1992 Law described above. However, the Decree temporarily terminates property rights of both holders of tenancy rights and owners, and, thus, equally covers socially and privately owned apartments, houses, and resort houses. An apartment determined abandoned may be assigned for temporary use to a member of the Croatian Defense Council or other persons who has become homeless in the course of the war, for at least one

---

[44] *Spadea and Scalabrino* v. *Italy*, Series A, No 315-B; Application No 23/1994), European Court of Human Rights (1996) 21 EHRR 482 (1995).
[45] S.l.RBiH no. 50/95.

year after the proclamation of the end of the state of immediate war danger[46].

According to the Decree on Takeover of the Yugoslav National Army and the Federal Department of National Defense Assets, apartments which belonged to the former Yugoslav National Army and the Federal Department of National Defense, are now considered property of Herzeg-Bosna. In addition, the Decree on Takeover and Transition of the Property of the Enemy to the Croatian Community of Herzeg-Bosna provided for confiscation of the property of Serbian and Montenegrin citizens and legal persons as well as the property of "citizens of Bosnia and Herzegovina who participated ... in activities of the enemy".

Real property regulations of the Croatian Republic of Herzeg-Bosna represent a flagrant disregard of the GFA inasmuch as they practically impede the right of displaced persons to return to their homes. As such, they represent a final act of the policy of ethnic cleansing. For reasons similiar to those discussed above with regard to the 1993 Decree and the 1992 Law, these "Herzeg-Bosna" Decrees also violate the ECHR.

C. Republika Srpska

The Law on the Use of Abandoned Property was adopted only after the signing of the GFA[47]. Its Article 1 cynically implies that this timing was by design to accommodate refugees and displaced persons and to protect the property of those who left. It covers both real and movable property, private ownership, and tenancy rights. Without even mentioning it, the Law suspended tenancy rights; it refers to holders of these rights simply as "users"[48].

By virtue of another provision, opportunity is made available for arbitrary application because the criteria and time after which property is not being used are not specified:

> "Real and movable property that have been abandoned by their owners or by the holders of the right to use, are considered abandoned. Whether property is abandoned is to be ascertained in each particular case, during the making of inventory and registering abandoned property"[49].

In addition, the Law does not regulate a procedure for declaring property abandoned, making the arbitrary application even more possible.

---

[46] *Hrvatsko vijece odbrane* [hereinafter "HVO"].
[47] *Zakon o koriscenju napustene imovine*, S.g.RS no. 3/96 of 27 February 1996 [hereinafter "RS Law"].
[48] *See* In light of the Law on Transfer of Socially Owned Property to State Ownership, S.g.RS no. 4/93, 29/94, 31/94, 9/95 and 19/95, at Article 59.
[49] RS Law, *supra*, Art. 2, ¶ 1.

The Republika Srpska "protect[s] and govern[s]" abandoned property through the Ministry for Refugees, Displaced Persons and Commission on Refugee Housing and other republic and municipal bodies. Abandoned property may be assigned for an indefinite period of time for use to refugees and displaced persons, those who became homeless in the course of the war, families of killed solders, war veterans, and certain professionals. In addition, unlike the laws and decrees in the Federation, the Law allows for accommodation of refugees, displaced persons and those homeless in apartments and buildings with more than 15 square meters of "surplus of living space" per a member of the household, until adequate accommodation is provided[50]. This provision applies where owners or users have not fulfilled a military or working duty, or where members of the owner's or user's household have left the territory of the Entity. From situations arising from the application of the said provision, a number of illegal evictions have occurred.

Again, unlike the regulations in the Federation which only implicitly limit the right of an owner to dispose of property, Article 49 of the Law explicitly makes null and void all contracts on renting, using or keeping the real property concluded after 6 April 1992 between the owner and another person. Further, the Law bans disposal of ownership via proxy by persons who left the Republika Srpska after the same date. An owner of abandoned real property located in the Federation or in one of the states which have emerged from the former Yugoslavia may, however, exchange that property for the property in the Republika Srpska whose owners are in possession of that property, provided approval of the competent body is secured. This provision was apparently envisioned as likely to encourage resettlement of the few remaining Muslims and Croats in the Entity, who would eventually trade their property to leave for the territory controlled by their respective ethnic group.

Article 39 of the Law, which regulates the rights of an owner after permanently returning, raises yet another issue. After his permanent return, an owner has the right to have his property restored or to be compensated for it in accordance with settlements the Republika Srpska arrived at with the Federation or Croatia, respectively. The property should be restored within 15 days upon owner's return, unless it has been assigned for temporary use. In the latter case, longer terms are foreseen: 30 days after a temporary beneficiary returns to his property, or 60 days from the payment of the compensation for property the temporary beneficiary deserted and for possible expenses he incurred in the course of using the property in question.

A condition of permanent return in order to use and dispose of one's property already unjustifiably limits ownership rights which include the right not to use the property at all. Additional conditions applied in in-

---

[50] *Id.*, Art. 17.

stances where property is assigned to a temporary beneficiary further limit ownership rights. These conditions restrict owner's rights on the basis of circumstances that are purely beyond his influence: willingness and ability of the temporary beneficiary to return to his property, and willingness of the Federation, or in some instances Croatia, to restore or compensate property of the temporary beneficiary. Moreover, the return of property is conditioned on reciprocity. The Republika Srpska Law's Article 42 permits exclusion of the provision on restoration of property if similar regulations do not exist in the Federation or Croatia. Not only do such conditions limit the right to return, but, in the former case, a principle of reciprocity more applicable to dealings between States is applied within the single State of Bosnia and Herzegovina. Lastly, it is worth noting that, although Article 39 refers to a "user" as well, it in effect does not deal with restoration of property to a holder of occupancy rights. This amounts to a full deprivation of property rights of a holder of tenancy rights.

All these provisions clearly violate basic principles of Annex 7 to the GFA as they infringe upon the right to return, and more clearly the provision on repeal of legislation and administrative practices which are discriminatory in intent or effect as they favor an ethnic majority. Furthermore, they are contrary to the Constitution of Bosnia and Herzegovina and the European Convention for the Protection of Human Rights, which has become an integral part of the Bosnian legal system which guarantees right to property. It also opposes principles of vested rights and legal certainty well rooted in the European legal tradition.

IV. THE COMMISSION FOR REAL PROPERTY CLAIMS

Annex 7 to the General Framework Agreement for Peace regulates issues concerning refugees and displaced persons. It not only sets forth a number of rights and principles regarding their safe and voluntary return, but also establishes a mechanism to deal solely with one particular right – property. Thereby, the GFA recognizes the importance of property rights in finding durable solutions for uprooted people. The mechanism established by this annex, a Commission, "shall receive and decide any claims for real property in Bosnia and Herzegovina, where the property has not voluntarily been sold or otherwise transferred since April 1, 1992, and where the claimant does not now enjoy possession of that property. Claims may be for return of the property or for just compensation in lieu of return"[51].

The Commission for Displaced Persons and Refugees was later rightly renamed the Commission for Real Property Claims of Displaced Persons and Refugees. The GFA's Annex 7 charges this body with deciding claims for return or compensation for dispossession of real property resulting from

---

[51] GFA, *supra*, Annex 7, Art. XI of Annex 7.

the conflict in BiH. By doing so, the Commission is to build confidence between the entities and among the divided populations, and to contribute to creating conditions conducive to the return of displaced persons and refugees. However, Annex 7 also states that "[a]ny person requesting compensation in lieu of return who is found by the Commission to be the lawful owner of that property shall be awarded just compensation as determined by the Commission"[52]. It should be noted that such an unconditional option to choose compensation might induce refugees not to return to their places of origin[53]. Individuals might elect to stay in a territory controlled by their ethnic group and seek compensation for property left behind, which would cement the ethnic cleansing committed during the war[54]. Such a blank option for compensation is contrary not only to the basic principles of the GFA, but to another provision of the same annex which empowers the Commission not to "recognize as valid any legal property transaction, including any transfer that was made under duress, in exchange for exit permission or documents, or that was otherwise in connection with ethnic cleansing"[55].

The Commission has the competence to promulgate its own rules and regulations, taking into consideration local legal tradition. Although the Commission has not yet promulgated any such rules, it has adopted a principle to disregard all laws and regulations that do not stand up to international standards. In application, this principle should include all the regulations described above, save the Law on Basis of Ownership Relations. In promulgating rules, the Commission should address the compatibility of the said regulations with the principles of the GFA and with the European Convention for the Protection of Human Rights and Fundamental Freedoms and its protocols.

Commission decisions are final. Annex 7, however, contains no detailed provisions regarding the execution and enforcement of such decisions. This may prove to be a serious obstacle to the work of the Commission, and may undermine not only the credibility of the Commission, but also the peace process as a whole.

---

[52] *Id.*, Art. XII, ¶ 2.

[53] *See* Forced Migration Projects, The Commission for Displaced Persons and Refugees. Options and Issues, New York, February 1996.

[54] For example, the commissioners representing the Republika Srpska have said a couple of times that their only interest in the work of the Commission is the issue of compensation.

[55] GFA, *supra*, Annex 7, Art. XII, ¶ 3.

V. CONCLUSION

War-time regulations in both Entities were adopted because of the over-whelming number of displaced persons in need of shelter. At present, these laws are not only an obstacle to repatriation of refugees and displaced persons, but also represent a blatant disregard of the obligation to repeal domestic legislation and administrative practices with discriminatory intent or effect. Those regulations provide a quasi-legal frame for deprivation of property. As these regulations and their application are discriminatory, they represent a final act of ethnic cleansing. Therefore, they not only violate the rules and principles of international law, but the basic notions of morality and justice as well.

SUSANNE MALMSTROM

8. The Relevance of International Human Rights Law for the Development of Economic, Social and Cultural Policy in Bosnia and Herzegovina.

Following the signing of the General Framework Agreement for Peace[1] there has been a focus on the realization of civil and political rights, highlightened by the process leading up to the elections. In order to rebuild Bosnia and Herzegovina[2] into a modern and stable democracy, it is important to consider all human rights in a broad and comprehensive manner.

The denials of human dignity occur both through violation of civil and political rights and through violation of economic, social and cultural rights. Respect for all rights and positive action for their realization are necessary elements for guaranteeing human dignity. The international community has increasingly agreed that all human rights must be considered in context with each other. Recent international treaties such as the Convention on the Rights of the Child[3] and the Convention on the Elimination on All Forms of Discrimination against Women[4] include civil and political rights as well as economic, social and cultural rights. Additionally, at the World Conference on Human Rights in 1993, 171 Governments stated that all human rights are universal, indivisible, interdependent and interrelated[5].

The neglect of economic, social and cultural rights has often proved to be the root cause of many conflicts, i.e. discrimination of minorites in the

---

[1] General Framework Agreement for Peace in Bosnia and Herzegovina, *initialed* Dayton, Ohio, 21 November 1995, *signed* Paris, 14 December 1995, 35 ILM 75 (1996) [hereinafter "GFA"].

[2] Bosnia and Herzegovina [hereinafter "BiH"] is one of the states formerly a part of the Socialist Federal Republic of Yugoslavia (SFRY), which existed until 1992. Post-1992, other former consitutents of the SFRY have emerged as distinct states: Croatia, Slovenia, and the Federal Republic of Yugoslavia, comprised of former SFRY states Serbia and Montenegro [hereinafter "FRY" or "Serbia"].

[3] Convention on the Rights of the Child, GA res. 44/25, UN Doc. A/44/49 (1989).

[4] Convention on the Elimination of All Forms of Discrimination Against Women, 1249 UNTS 13, *adopted* 18 December 1979 [hereinafter "Women's Convention"].

[5] World Conference on Human Rights: Vienna Declaration, UN Doc. A/CONF.157/24 (part I) (1993), ¶ 5 [hereinafter "Vienna Declaration for Action"].

M. O'Flaherty and G. Gisvold (eds.), Post-War Protection of Human Rights in Bosnia and Herzegovina, 157–172.
© 1998 *Kluwer Law International. Printed in Great Britain.*

access to education, work and housing quite often constitues the pre-stage of armed conflicts. This paper will focus on the human rights obligations imposed on the BiH government and the Entities in the sphere of economic, social and cultural rights by virtue of the GFA. These obligations set limits and directions for domestic policy choices, meaning that there are certain restrictions placed on the democratic forces in determining the content of laws and in allocating resources for economic, social and cultural purposes. International human rights treaties elevate economic, social and cultural rights and policies above political preferences. These fundamental needs and the guarantee of human dignity are not at the mercy of changing governmental policies. It is not possible to devise generalized and meaningful policy guidelines on all matters. A selection of issues which are, in the opinon of this author, of particular importance to the broader issue of the realisation of economic, social and cultural rights in BiH are highlighted in in this chapter.

I. Overriding Principles and Obligations

Economic, social and cultural rights have been elaborated and amplified in a number of universal and regional instruments which apply in BiH by virtue of the GFA. In article 2(2) of the BiH Constitution, which is annex 4 of the GFA, it is stated:

> The rights and freedoms set forth in the European Convention for the Protection of Human Rights and Fundamental Freedoms[6] and its Protocols shall apply directly in Bosnia and Herzegovina. These shall have priority over all other law.

The Constitution also enumerates in article 2(3) rights which are protected, *inter alia*, freedom of association, the right to education and the right to property. Furthermore, in the Annex to the Constitution is a listing of international and regional human rights conventions which shall apply in Bosnia and Herzegovina. The following are the most relevant for the development of economic, social and cultural policies; the International Covenant on Economic, Social and Cultural Rights[7], the International Covenant on Civil and Political Rights[8], the Convention on the Elimination of all Forms of Discrimination against Women[9], the International Conven-

---

[6] [European] Convention for the Protection of Human Rights and Fundamental Freedoms, 213 U.N.T.S. 221, 1 E.T.S. 5, *signed* 4 November 1950 [hereinafter "ECHR"].

[7] International Covenant on Economic, Social and Cultural Rights, 993 UNTS 3, *adopted* 16 December 1966 [hereinafter "ICESCR"].

[8] International Covenant on Civil and Political Rights, 999 UNTS 171, *adopted* 16 December 1966 [hereinafter "ICCPR"].

[9] Women's Convention, *supra.*

tion on the Elimination of All Forms of Racial Discrimination[10], the Convention on the Rights of the Child[11], the International Convention on the Protection of the Rights of All Migrant Workers and Members of Their Families[12], the European Charter for Regional or Minority Languages[13], and the Framework Convention for the Protection of National Minorites[14].

The BiH government should develop measures to ensure the promotion and protection of human rights using the above-mentioned instruments and the BiH Constitution as a framework for this purpose. In order to implement human rights on a national level amending relevant legislation, the adoption of new legislation or the change of administrative pratices will be necessary. Additionally, the formulation of a long-term set of policies designed to ensure full and lasting compliance with international obligations will be required. As a starting point a few overriding principles and obligations can be dervied from these instruments which shall penetrate all legislation, policies and development programmes.

Internationally, the most comprehensive and important instrument for our purposes is the Covenant on Economic, Social and Cultural Rights, which in article 2 outlines the general legal obligations[15]. It provides for progressive realization and acknowledges contraints due to the limits of available resources. It also imposes various obligations which are of immediate effect. Among such obligations two are of specific importance: the requirement "to take steps" in order to meet the minimum core obligations and the principle of non-discrimination. But, what does the obligation "to take steps" involve?

It is often stated that all economic, social and cultural rights must be provided by the State. It may lead to high costs and bureucracy, but the individual must equally be the active subject of all economic, social and cultural development[16]. In order for the individual to be in the position to ensure satisfaction of his or her needs, the Government must seek to create an atmosphere where it is possible. It requires that personal resources,

---

[10] Convention on the Elimination of All Forms of Racial Discrimination, 660 UNTS 195, *adopted* 21 December 1965 [hereinafter "Race Convention"].

[11] Convention on the Rights of the Child, *supra*.

[12] International Convention on the Protection of the Rights of Migrant Workers and their Families, GA res. 45/158, UN Doc. A/RES/45/158 (1990) [hereinafter "Migrant Workers Convention"].

[13] European Charter for Regional or Minority Languages, ETS 148 (1992) [hereinafter "European Language Charter"].

[14] Framework Convention for the Protection of National Minorites, Council of Europe, ETS 157 (1994) [hereinafter "Framework Convention for National Minorites"].

[15] *See* General Comment No. 3 of the Committee on Economic, Social and Cultural Rights at its Fifth session, UN Doc E/1991/23 (1990) [hereinafter "General Comment No. 3"]. *See also* P. Alston, *The International Covenant on Economic, Social and Cultural Rights, Manual on Human Rights Reporting* (1991), at 39-78.

[16] Declaration on the Right to Development, *adopted* 4 December 1986, GA res. 41/128 (1986), Art. 2.

whether it is land, capital or labour, must be protected by the Government, in order for the individual to have freedom of action and freedom to use the resourses in relation to others. Additionally, the Government has an obligation to assist and to fulfil the basic needs[17].

Legislative measures can perhaps be singled out as one of the most appropriate means of ensuring the realization of economic, social and cultural rights. Legislative measures alone, however, may be insufficient in the absence of political will. Additionally, among the measures which might be considered appropriate is the provision of judicial remedies with respect to rights which can be considered justiciable[18]. The content of State obligations under the Covenant on Economic, Social and Cutural Rights was further elaborated by a group of experts in the so-called Limburg Principles[19]. Among them is the following:

> Although the full realization of the rights recognized in the Covenant [on Economic, Social and Cultural Rights] is to be attained progressivly, the application of some rights can be made justiciable immediately while other rights can become justiciable over time[20].

A number of issues are capable of immediate judicial application, *inter alia*, non-discrimination, fair wages, the right to form trade unions, the right to strike, and free primary education. In addition to taking certain legislative measures, the Government has the obligation to ensure, at the very least, minimum essential levels of each of the rights, "a minimum core obligation". Thus, for example, a State party in which any significant number of individuals are deprived of essential foodstuffs, of essential primary health care, of basic shelter and housing or of the most basic forms of education is, prima facie, failing to discharge its obligations under the Covenant[21].

It must be noted that any assessment as to whether a State has discharged its minimum core obligation must also take account of resourse constraints within the country concerned. The Government must thus take the necessary steps "to the maximum of its availble resources"[22]. The

---

[17]   *See* A. Eide, "Economic, Social and Cultural Rights as Human Rights", *in* A. Eide, C. Krause, and A. Rosas (eds.), *Economic, Social and Cultural Rights, A Textbook* (1995), at 36-40 [hereinafter "Eide, Krause, and Rosas, *Economic, Social and Cultural Rights*"]; A. Eide, "Future Protection of Economic and Social Rights in Europe", *in* A. Bloed, L. Leicht, M. Nowak, and A. Rosas (eds.), *Monitoring Human Rights in Europe, Comparing International Procedures and Mechanisms*, at 187-219 (discussions of the division of state obligations into three levels: respect, protection, and fulfillment).

[18]   General Comment No 3, *supra.*

[19]   The Limburg Principles on the implementation of the International Covenant on Economic, Social and Cultural Rights, UN Doc. E/CN.4/1987/17 (1986) [hereinafter "the Limburg Principles."].

[20]   *Id.*, ¶ 8.

[21]   General Comment No 3, *supra.*

[22]   ICESCR, *supra*, Art. 2(1).

phrase "its available resources" refers to both the resources of the BiH government and those available from the international community, through assistance and co-operation. In order for a State party to be able to attribute its failure to meet at least the minimum core obligations to a lack of availble resources, it must demonstrate that every effort has been made to use all resources that are at its disposition in an effort to satisfy, as a matter of priority, those minimum obligations. Therefore, at a minimum, the obligation to take steps involves the drawing up of a detailed plan of action for the progressive achievement of economic, social and cultural rights.

While adopting policies, it is essential to engage the population in the formulation, planning, implementation and evaluation of national strategies, policies and programmes of economic and social development[23]. Legislative and regulatory frameworks, institutional arrangements and consultative mechnisms should be established to ensure the effective participation of all the elements of society. The Government must give due priority to those social groups living in unfavourable conditions by giving them particular consideration. Policies and legislation should correspondingly be designed to benefit disadvantaged social groups and vulnerable groups, in need of special protection, *inter alia*, migrant workers, women, minorites and children. In drawing up a national action plan identifying steps to improve the human rights situation, it is important to accomplish overall human rights co-ordination. The importance of developing and adopting specific human rights strategy cannot be overstated. The existence of a strategy signifies that some form of assessment has been carried out, and that there is a set of targets which the government has identified and against which its performance can be measured[24].

For the purpose of examining and measuring compliance, bench-marks or indicators should be identified. Indicators require the establishment of mechanisms whereby human rights standards are translated into the practice of governmental bodies[25]. A system for the gathering of information statistics must be construed, in order to identify bench-marks for the evaluation of achievements. It is essential that the information can be seperated in order to look at the situation of specific groups, i.e. women or ethnic minorities.

The other overriding principle, the principle of non-discrimination and equality is the starting point in making economic, social and cultural rights operational. The principle was spelled out already in the Charter of the United Nations. In article 1(3) it is stated " ... promoting and encouraging

---

[23] Copenhagen Declaration and Programme of Action, UN Doc. A/CONF.166/9 (Annexes I and II) (1995), ¶ 85 (b); Declaration on Social Progress and Development, GA res. 2542 (XXIV) (1969), Art. 15 (a); Report of the Working Group on the Right to Development on its third session, UN Doc. E/CN.4/1995/27, ¶ 91.

[24] K. Tomasevski, "Indicators," *in* Eide, Krause, and Rosas, *Economic, Social and Cultural Rights, supra*, at 397.

[25] *Id.*

respect for human rights and for fundamental freedoms for all without distinction as to race, sex, language, or religion." Article 55 (c) calls for a promotion of, " ... universal respect for, and observance of, human rights and fundamental freedoms for all without distinction as to race, sex, language or religion". Furthermore, the principle is set forth in articles 1 and 2 of the Universal Declaration of Human Rights, article 1 of which reads: "All human beings are born free and equal in dignity and rights"[26]. This principle is also protected in a number of the instruments listed in the GFA, *inter alia*, article 14 of the European Convention, articles 2(1) and 26 of the Covenant on Civil and Political Rights, article 2(2) of the Covenant on Economic, Social and Cultural Rights, article 1 of the Convention on Elimination on All Forms of Racial Discrimination and article 1 of the Convention on Elimination on All Forms of Discrimination against Women.

This principle is of immediate implementation and not subject to progressive realization. In the light of the above-mentioned provisions, discrimination may be understood[27] to cover any distinction, exclusion, restriction or preference which is based on such grounds as race, colour, sex, language, religion, political or other opinon, national or social origin, property, birth or other status, and which has the purpose or effect of nullifying or impairing the recognition, enjoyment or exercise by all persons, on equal footing, of economic, social and cultural rights. The grounds specified in the international instruments are not exhaustive, since they prohibit discrimination as to "other status". The BiH Constitution enumerates association with national minority in conformity with the European Convention[28].

International instruments and a provision in the Constitution are not sufficent. In order to combat discrimination effectively, the principle must apply to all legislative measures taken and to all adminstrative policies and other public programmes. A sound national legislative foundation is therefore indispensable. As part of that, discrimination issues should be made justiciable, i.e. able to be brought before a court, not only at the level of the Constitutional Court of Bosnia and Herzegovina. In addition to legislation

---

[26] Universal Declaration of Human Rights, *adopted* 10 December 1948, UN Doc A/810, at 71 (1948), Art. 1 [hereinafter "Universal Declaration"].

[27] The definition of discrimination has been further developed in context of other human rights treaties. *See* General Comment No. 18, Human Rights Committee, UN Doc. HRI/GEN/1/Rev.1, at 26 (1994) [hereinafter "General Comment No. 18"].

[28] *"Non-discrimination*: The enjoyment of the rights and freedoms provided for in this Article or in the international agreements listed in Annex I to this Constitution shall be secured to all persons in Bosnia and Herzegovina without discrimination on any ground such as sex, race, color, language, religion, political or other opinon, national or social origin, association with national minority, property, birth or other status." GFA, *supra*, Annex 4 (Constitution of Bosnia and Herzegovina), Art. II(4) [hereinafter "Constitution"].

and administrative measures, appropriate policy measures must be undertaken.

The prohibition of discrimination entails the elimination of both *de jure* and *de facto* discrimination by public authorites, by the community at large, and by private persons or bodies[29]. Elimination of *de facto* discrimination is much more difficult and requires more far reaching means than enacting laws recognising equality. Positive action and affirmative advancement of disadvantaged groups is necessary. In article 2(2) of the Convention on the Elimination of All Forms of Racial Discrimination, it is formulated as follows:

> [I]n the social, economic, cultural and other fields, special and concrete measures to ensure the adequate development and protection of certain racial groups or individuals belonging to them ... ".

In other words, the Government must take affirmative action in order to eliminate the conditions which perpetuate the discrimination. Such action may involve granting for a limited time to the part of the population concerned certain preferential treatment in specific matters as compared with the rest of the population. As long as such action is needed to correct discrimination in fact, it is a case of legitimate differentiation[30].

II. PROGRAMMATIC GUIDELINES FOR IMPLEMENTATION ON A NATIONAL LEVEL

The international monitoring mechanisms, including reporting and complaint procedures, are complementary in relation to the domestic protection of human rights. National judicial mechnisms and legal remedies are not sufficient to effectively protect economic, social and cultrual rights. This chapter should therefore be seen in the broader context, which in addition to legislative measures, discusses programmes and policies for removing obstacles for the realisation of economic, social and cultural rights. The overriding principles and obligations listed above apply of course to all of the discussed topics. The issues will be highlighted under the following headings: culture, education, housing, work, social security, and health. The issues of property rights and minority rights have not been focused upon since they are dealt with elsewhere in this book.

A. Culture

Article 15 of the Covenant on Economic, Social and Cultural Rights recognises that there is a right to take part in cultural life. The right to exercise

---

[29] General Comment No. 18, *supra*, ¶ 9.

[30] *Id.*, ¶ 10.

this right without discrimination is protected in, *inter alia*, article 5(e)(vi) of the Convention on Elimination of All Forms of Racial Discrimination and article 13 (c) of the Convention on Elimination of All Forms of Discrimination Against Women. Participation in cultural life includes both the right to artistic, literary and scientific creation and the right to enjoy the benefits so created. This right is closely interrelated to other rights, for example, the right to freedoms of expression, information, religion and assembly. The Government is obliged to respect the freedom of the individual to assert and to develop her or his preferred cultural orientation.

The Government should establish institutional infrastructure for the implementation of policies to promote popular participation in culture such as cultural centres, museums, libraries, theatres, cinemas and traditional crafts and arts, promotion of awareness and enjoyment of the cultural heritage of national ethnic groups and minorites[31]. Article 27 of the Covenant on Civil and Political also protects the right of persons belonging to minorites, in community with other members of their group, to enjoy their own culture. This right has been broadly interpreted in the case-law of the Human Rights Committee, extending the protection to the material case necessary for maintaining and developing the culture of minority groups[32].

B. Education

The right to education is explicitly enumerated in article II (3)(l) of the BiH Constitution[33]. Consequently, all courts, governmental organs or agencies, Entity-operated organ or agency, shall apply and conform with it in accordance with article II(6) of the Constitution[34]. Additionally, the right is protected in a number of instruments applicable in BiH by virtue of the GFA. What this right to education includes must be seen towards the background of article 13 of the Covenant on Economic, Social and Cultural Rights, article 2 of Protocol No. 1 of the European Convention[35] and other applicable human rights instruments protecting the right to education, *inter alia*, article 5(e)(v) of the Convention on the Elimination of All Forms of Racial Discrimination, articles 5(a) and (b), 10, and 14(2)(d) of the Con-

---

[31] Guidelines regarding the form and content of reports to be submitted by State Parties. UN doc. E/1991/23 [hereinafter "Guidelines for States Parties Reports"].

[32] *See* G. Alfredsson and A. de Zayas, "Minority Rights Protection by the United Nations", 14 Hum. Rts. J. 1, (1993).

[33] The Constitution of Bosnia and Herzegovina is printed in Annex 4 to the GFA. Constitution, *supra*.

[34] *"Implementation.* Bosnia and Herzegovina, and all courts, agencies, governmental organs, and instrumentalities operated by or within the Entites, shall apply and conform to the human rights and fundamental freedoms referred to in paragraph 2 above". Constitution, *supra*, Art. II(6).

[35] ECHR, *supra*.

vention on Elimination of All Forms of Discrimination against Women, and article 28 of the Convention on the Rights of the Child.

The right to education has many diffrent dimensions. Among the obligations covered by the right to education there are a number of issues which should be implemented immediately. The Government shall guarantee equal access to education. History shows that education systems have frequently been used to systematically discriminate against i.e. women,and ethnic and religious minorities, thus denying specific groups of society equal participation in the political, social and economic life of the community. Therefore, equal opportunity and equal access to education are extremely important in the process of rebuilding a country for the future. In addition to international instruments guaranteeing non-discrimination in the field of education[36], article 2 of Protocol No.1 of the European Convention in combination with article 14 of the European Convention guarantees equal access to existing educational institutions. It was affirmed in the *Belgian Linguistic* case of the European Court of Human Rights which imposes an obligation to guarantee "to persons subject to the jurisdiction of the Contracting Parties the right, to avail themselves of the means of instruction existing at a given time"[37].

Primary education shall be compulsory and available free to all[38]. The immediate implementation of this right is underlined by obliging a Government that has not satisfied the obligation, within two years "to work out and adopt a detailed plan of action for the progressive implementation, within a reasonable number of years, to be fixed in the plan, of the principle of compulsory education free of charge for all"[39]. This does not necessarily mean that all schools must be govermental, the right could also be guaranteed by private schools or a combination of private and public.

Additionally, Governments shall guarantee equal access to secondary and higher education. In order not to deny equal access to certain group of society, there is a strong argument in favour of making secondary and higher education free and supplying finacial assistance in case of need. The United Nations Development Programme's 1991 Human Development Report asserts that "offering the most basic services free permits greater equality of opportunity and fulfils a Government's responsibility to provide for its citizens' basic human rights"[40]. It suggests that (a) primary education is a basic right and should be free and that (b) there is a strong case for

---

[36] Race Convention, *supra*, at Art. 5(e)(v); Women's Convention, *supra*, Art. 10; ICESCR, *supra*, Art. 13.

[37] *Case Relating to Certain Aspects of the Laws on the Use of Languages in Education in Belgium*, Eur. Ct. H.R. 6 (Ser. A) (1968) at 31.

[38] ICESCR, *supra*, Art.13(2)(a).

[39] ICESCR, *supra*, Art. 14.

[40] United Nations Development Programme, Human Development Report 1991, at 9 [hereinafter "Human Development Report"].

making secondary education free as well, for reasons of equity and pro-
ductivity benefits[41].

Another aspect of the right to education is the right of parents which is
protected in article 2 of Protocol No. 1 of the European Convention. It
reads in part: " ... the right of parents to ensure such education and teaching
in conformity with their own religious and philosophical convictions".
Similar protection for parents rights are found in a number of international
human rights instruments, *inter alia*, article 13(3) of the Covenant on
Economic, Social and Cultural Rights and article 14(2) of the Convention
on the Rights of the Child.

There is also an obligation to provide for human rights in education[42].
Article 1 (3) of the United Nations Charter calls for the promotion and
encouragement of respect for human rights and fundamental freedoms[43].
The value and usefulness of human rights knowledge and education can
not be stressed enough. It is the foundation for the enjoyment of and respect for all rights and freedoms. In order to underline this importance, the
Commission on Human Rights proclaimed a Decade for Human Rights
Education starting on 1 January 1995[44]. The right to human rights education was originally formulated in article 26(2) of the Universal Declaration
of Human Rights:

> Education shall be directed to the full development of the human per-
> sonality and to the strengthening of respect for human rights and funda-
> mental freedoms. It shall promote understanding, tolerance and friend-
> ship among all nations, racial or religious groups, and further the
> activites of the United Nations for the maintenance of peace.

Similar formulations are contained in article 13 (1) of the Covenant on
Economic, Social and Cultural Rights, article 29(1)(b) of the Convention
on the Rights of the Child and article 7 of the Convention on the Elimination of all Forms of Racial Discrimination.

A Government has an obligation to draw up a national programme for
education. In doing so, Governments should provide for indicators to
measure improvements over time. In the field of education, typical indicators to be applied in a cross-temporal perspective are i.e. literacy rates,
primary, secondary and tertiary enrolment ratios, completion and drop-out

---

[41] *Id.* at 67.

[42] For a comprehensive overview of the right to human rights education, see G. Alfredsson, "The Right to Human Rights Education," *in* Eide, Krause, and Rosas, *Economic,
Social and Cultural Rights*, *supra*, at 213-227.

[43] To achieve international co-operation in solving international problems of an economic, social, cultural, or humanitarian character and in promoting and encouraging respect
for human rights and for fundamenatal freedoms for all without distinction as to race, sex,
language, or religion. Charter of the United Nations, T.S. 993, 3 Bevans 1153, *adopted* June
26, 1945, Art. 1(3).

[44] Commission on Human Rights res. 1994/51, UN Doc. E/CN.4/1994/51 (1994).

rates, primary pupil-teacher ratio and public expenditure on education as a percentage of the country's gross national product, of total public expenditure or in comparison to the expenditure, for example, for military purposes[45].

C. Housing

Considering the extraordianary situation in BiH, where a great part of the population lives outside its borders currently unable to return, the lack of housing and the extensive destruction of infrastructure emerge as major problem areas. A wide variety of international instruments applicable in Bosnia and Herzegovina protect different aspects of the right to housing[46], but article 11(1) of the Covenant on Economic, Social and Cultural Rights is the most important when combined with the work of the monitoring body. The Government should accordingly pursue effective legislation and policies aimed at creating conditions for ensuring the full realization of the right to housing. It should improve the availability of affordable and adequate shelter for all. As both the Commission on Human Settlement and the Global Strategy for Shelter to the Year 2000 have stated: ''Adequate shelter means ... adequate privacy, adequate space, adequate security, adequate lighting and ventilation, adequate basic infrastructure and adequate location with regard to work and basic facilites – all at a reasonable cost''[47].

The Government should adopt a national housing strategy which, as stated in paragraph 32 of the Global Strategy for Shelter[48], "defines the objectives for the development of shelter conditions, identifies the resources available to meet these goals and the most cost-effective way of using them and sets out the responsabilities and time-frame for the implementation of the necessary measures"[49]. A national shelter strategy must spell out clear operational objectives for the development of shelter conditions both in terms of the construction of new housing and the upgrading and maintenance of existing housing stock, infrastructure and service[50].

Many of the measures that will be required involve resource allocations and policy initiatives of a general kind. However, the role of legislative measures should not be underestimated in this context. The Committee on

---

[45] M. Nowak, "The Right to Education," *in* Eide, Krause, and Rosas, *Economic, Social and Cultural Rights, supra*, at 200.

[46] Race Convention, *supra*, at Art.5(e)(iii); Convention on the Rights of the Child, *supra*, Art.27; Women's Convention, *supra*, Art.14(2); Migrant Workers Convention, *supra*, Art. 43.

[47] General Comment No. 4 of the Committee on Economic, Social and Cultural Rights, UN Doc. E/1992/23 (1992) [hereinafter "General Comment No. 4"].

[48] GA res 43/181, UN. doc. A/43/8/Add.1 (1988) [hereinafter "GA res 43/181"].

[49] General Comment No. 4, *supra*.

[50] GA res 43/181, *supra*.

Economic, Social and Cultural Rights considers, that the following issues, among others are suitable for legal action: (a) legal appeals aimed at preventing planned evictions or demolitions through the issuance of court-ordered injunction; (b) legal procedures seeking compensation following an illegal eviction; (c) complaints against illegal actions carried out or supported by landlords (whether public or private) in relation to rent levels, dwelling maintenance, and racial or other forms of discrimination; (d) allegation of any form of discrimination in the allocation and availability of access to housing; and (e) complaints against landlords concerning unhealthy or inadequate housing conditions[51].

Objectives must be set for the construction of new housing and for the upgrading and maintenance of the existing housing stock in terms both of the scale of the activites and of the housing standards to be met[52]. Governmental support should mainly be allocated to the most needy population groups. The Government should provide detailed information about homeless persons and families, those inadequately housed and without ready access to basic amenities, those living in 'illegal' settlements, those subject to forced evictions and low-income groups, in order to measure achievements.

D. Work

The right to work includes "the right to the opportunity to gain his living by work which he freely chooses or accepts"[53]. In the reporting guidelines to the Covenant on Economic, Social and Cultrual Rights, reference is made to ILO Convention No. 122[54] concerning Employment Policy. It recommends that, to encourage economic growth and development, the Government shall have an active policy designed to promote full, productive and free choice of employment.

> Such a policy should aim at ensuring that (a) there is work for all who are available for and seeking work; (b) such work is as productive as possible; (c) there is freedom of choice of employment and the fullest possible opportunity for each worker to qualify for, and to use his skills and endowments in, a job for which he is well suited, irrespective of race, colour, sex, religion, political opinion, national extraction or social origin[55].

---

[51] General Comment No. 4, *supra*, ¶ 17.

[52] GA res 43/181, *supra*.

[53] ICESCR, *supra*, Art. 6.

[54] [ILO] Convention (No. 122) Concerning Employment Policy, 569 U.N.T.S. 65, *entered into force* July 9, 1965.

[55] *Id.* Art. 1(2).

Measures should be adopted to improve economic opportunities through the elimination of legal, social, cultural and practical obstacles. The Government shall guarantee freedom from forced labour through legislative or regulatory measures. The Universal Declaration declares that "Everyone has the right to work, to free choice of employment ... "[56]. This latter phrase implies a freedom from forced labour. Similar wordings are found in a number of international instruments, *inter alia*, article 6(1) of the Covenant on Economic, Social and Cultural Rights. The right is emphasized further in in article 4(2) of the European Convention on Human Rights: "No one shall be required to perform forced or compulsory labour". Reference can also be made to article 8(3) of the Covenant on Civil and Political Rights.

The Government should safeguard and promote respect for basic workers' rights, including, *inter alia*, the right to form trade unions, the right to bargain collectively, and the right to equal remuneration for work of equal value. The most detailed and comprehensive standards in this field are the conventions of the International Labour Organisation. The protection of the right to form trade unions is found in, *inter alia*, article 22(1) of the Covenant on Civil and Political Rights, article 8 of the Covenant on Economic, Social and Cultural Rights, and article 11(1) of the European Convention. Two important ILO conventions for the protection of workers' rights are the Freedom of Association and Protection of the Right to Organise Convention[57] and the Right to Organise and Collective Bargaining Convention[58].

The Government should ensure the provision of a healthy and safe workplace. Among other human rights treaties, the Covenant on Economic, Social and Cultural Rights recognizes the right of just and favourable conditions of work[59]. In the guidelines on reporting[60] reference is made to certain ILO Conventions: the Minimum Wage-Fixing Convention[61], the Equal Remuneration Convention[62], the Weekly Rest (Industry) Convention[63], the Weekly Rest (Commerce and Offices) Convention[64], the Holi-

---

[56] Universal Declaration, *supra*, Art. 26(1).

[57] [ILO] Convention (No. 87) Concerning Freedom of Association and Protection of the Right to Organise, 68 U.N.T.S. 17, *adopted* 9 July 1948.

[58] [ILO] Convention (No. 98) Concerning the Application of the Principles of the Right to Organise and Bargain Collectively, 96 U.N.T.S. 257, *adopted* 1 July 1949.

[59] ICESCR, *supra*, Art. 7.

[60] Guidelines for States Parties Reports, *supra*.

[61] [ILO] Convention (No. 131) Fixing a Minimum Wage, 825 UNTS 77, *adopted* 22 June 1970.

[62] [ILO] Convention (No. 100) Concerning Equal Remuneration for Men and Women for Work of Equal Value, 165 UNTS 303, *adopted* 29 June 1951.

[63] [ILO] Convention (No.14) Concerning Weekly Rest (Industry) Convention, 38 UNTS 187, *adopted* 17 November 1921.

[64] [ILO] Convention (No. 106) Concerning Weekly Rest (Commerce and Offices), 325 UNTS 279, *adopted* 26 June 1957.

days with Pay Convention (Revised)[65], the Labour Inspection Convention[66], the Labour Inspection (Agriculture) Convention[67], and the Occupational Safety and Health Convention[68].

The Government should establish a system of minimum wages which covers all groups of wage earners. The Universal Declaration states in art 23(3) that "everyone who works has the right to just and favourable remuneration ensuring for himself and his family an existance worthy of human dignity, ... ". The above-mentioned ILO Convention on Minimum Wage-Fixing should be noted. The Government should also strengthen labour market information systems, particularly the development of appropriate data and indicators on employment, underemployment, unemployment and earnings, as well as the dissemination of information concerning labour markets, including as far as possible, work situations outside formal markets[69]. All such data should be disaggregated by, gender, age, ethnic group, etc.

E. Social security

There is a right to be protected economically by the Government under certain conditions. Article 11(1) of the Covenant on Economic, Social and Cultural Rights guarantees the right to an adequate standard of living which also relates to social assistance and other need-based forms of social benefits. Additionally, article 9 of the Covenant on Economic, Social and Cultural Rights states that the Government should "recognize the right of everyone to social security, including social insurance". A more detailed description of the content of this right is found in the guidelines for reporting under the Covenant on Economic, Social and Cultural Rights[70]. There the following issues are specified: medical care, sickness benfits, unemployment benefits, old-age benefits, emploment injury benefits, family benefits, maternity benefits, invalidity benefits and survivors' benefits. The same issues are found in the principal International Labour Organisation instrument in this field, the Social Security (Minimum Standards) Convention[71].

---

[65] [ILO] Convention (No. 132) Concerning Holidays with Pay (Revised), 883 UNTS 97, *adopted* 24 June 1970.

[66] [ILO] Convention (No. 81) Concerning Labour Inspection, 54 UNTS 3, *adopted* 11 July 1947.

[67] [ILO] Convention (No. 129) Labour Inspection (Agriculture) Convention, 812 UNTS 87, *adopted* 25 June 1969.

[68] [ILO] Convention (No. 155) Occupational Health and Safety and the Working Environment, 1331 U.N.T.S. 279, *adopted* 22 June 1981.

[69] Copenhagen Programme of Action, *supra* (Annex II), ¶ 54(b).

[70] U.N doc. E/C.12/1991/1 (1992).

[71] [ILO] Convention (No. 102) Concerning Social Security (Minimum Standards), 210 UNTS 131, *adopted* 28 June 1952.

The Convention on the Elimination of All Forms of Discrimination against Women identifies several forms of social security that must be provided to women without discrimination with regard to retirement, unemployment, sickness, invalidity, old age[72] and the right to family benefits[73]. This, in turn, entails the identification of gender-specific needs and obstacles. The Government is obliged to take preventive measures and introduce a prohibition and impose sanctions against discrimination on the basis of pregnacy, maternity leave and dissmissals on the basis of marital status[74]. Also, the Government has an obligation to provide material assistance and support programmes, particularly with regard to nutrition, clothing and housing, to parents under article 27 of the Convention on the Rights of the Child, even though the responsibility for the material well-being of the child rests primarily with his or her parents.

The right to social security should be made justiciable and be made subject to appeal to administrative courts or to other legal remedies. Article 6 (1) of the European Convention reads: "In the determination of his rights and obligations or of any criminal charge against him, everyone is entitled to a fair and public hearing within a reasonable time by an independent and impartial tribunal established by law ... ". In the *Schuler-Zgraggen* case, the European Court on Human Rights stated that "the general rule is that Article 6 (1) [of the European Convention] does apply in the field of social insurance, including even welfare assistance"[75]. Article 6 thus imposes an obligation to provide for procedural protection and a fair trial for individuals challenging alleged violations of their social rights.

F. Health

The right to health is enumerated in a number of international conventions[76], i.e. the Covenant on Economic, Social and Cultural Rights which in article 12(1) provides for "the right of everyone to the enjoyment of the highest attainable standard of physical and mental health". The obligation to implement the right to health is an obligation to achieve progressively the full realization of the right. However, some aspects of the right to health are of immediate implementation.

The Government has the obligation to immediately take the necessary steps for: (a) provision for the reduction of the stillbirth-rate and of infant mortality and for the healthy development of the child; (b) the improvement of all aspects of environmental and industrial hygiene; (c) the pre-

---

[72] ICESCR, *supra*, Art. 11(1).

[73] *Id.* Art. 13.

[74] *Id.* Art. 11(2).

[75] *Schuler-Zgraggen* v. *Switzerland*, Eur. Ct. H.R. 263 (ser. A) (1993).

[76] Convention on the Rights of the Child, *supra*, Art. 24(1); Women's Convention, *supra*, Arts. 12 and 14(2); Race Convention, *supra*, Art. 5(e)(iv).

vention, treatment and control of epidemic, endemic, occupational and other diseases; and (d) the creation of conditions which would assure to all medical service and medical attention in the event of sickness[77]. The Government should guarantee access to free primary health care. WHO has elaborated, in its programme Primary Health Care for All by the Year 2000, the means to achieve the highest attainable standard of living. This approach is described in the Alma-Ata Declaration[78] with its emphasis on preventive health measures. such as immunization, and on maternal and child care.In addition to primary healthcare, the UNDP Human Development Report suggests that low-income families and children under five should have access to hospital care[79].

III. Conclusion

When taken seriously, international monitoring efforts aimed at the protection of human rights should serve to influence and even shape domestic policy choices. There is a need for a coherent approach to human rights, and to considering all the rights in context with each other and keeping in mind their universality and indvisibility. The international instruments should not bee seen as limitations, but as guidelines in building an equal and stable society. The Limburg Principles, specifically No. 65, should be remembered:

> The systematic violation of economic, social and cultural rights undermines true national security and may jeopardize international peace and security. A State responsable for such violations shall not invoke national security as a justification for measures aimed at surpressing opposition to such violations or at perpetrating repressive practices towards its population"[80].

---

[77] ICESCR, *supra*, Art.12(2).

[78] World Health Organization/United Nations Children's Fund International Conference on Primary Health Care: Declaration of Alma-Ata, *adopted* 12 September 1978; *see* Report of the International Conference on Primary Health Care, Alma-Ata, "Health for All" Series, No. 1 (WHO, Geneva 1978).

[79] Human Development Report 1991, *supra*, at 67.

[80] Limburg Principles, *supra*, ¶ 65.

CHRISTINE CHINKIN

9. Strategies to Combat Discrimination Against Women

I. WOMEN'S RIGHTS AND THE GENERAL FRAMEWORK AGREEMENT

The General Framework Agreement for Peace in Bosnia and Herzegovina[1] and its twelve accompanying Annexes pay greater attention to the guarantee of fundamental human rights and freedoms than any previous international peace agreement[2]. The parties must carry out their relations consistent with the principles of the Helsinki Final Act and the Organization for Security and Co-operation in Europe[3]. Part VII of the Helsinki Final Act affirms respect for a wide range of human rights, including freedom of thought, conscience and religion "without distinction as to race, sex, language or religion"[4]. In 1990, a European political commitment was made to human rights as the "first responsibility of government" and as an essential safeguard against "an over-mighty state"[5]. Accordingly Article VII of the GFA states that

> Recognizing that the observance of human rights ... [is] of vital importance in achieving a lasting peace, the Parties agree to and shall comply fully with the provisions concerning human rights set forth in Chapter One of the Agreement at Annex 6, as well as the provisions concerning human rights set forth in Chapter One of the Agreement at Annex 7.

---

[1] General Framework Agreement for Peace in Bosnia and Herzegovina, *initialed* Dayton, Ohio, 21 November 1995, *signed* Paris, 14 December 1995, 35 ILM 75 (1996) [hereinafter "GFA"]. Bosnia and Herzegovina [hereinafter "BiH"] is one of the states formerly a part of the Socialist Federal Republic of Yugoslavia (SFRY), which existed until 1992. Post-1992, other former consitutents of the SFRY have emerged as distinct states: Croatia, Slovenia, and the Federal Republic of Yugoslavia, comprised of former SFRY states Serbia and Montenegro.

[2] *Cf.*, J. Sloan, "The Dayton Peace Agreement: Human Rights Guarantees and their Implementation", 7 EJIL 207 (1996).

[3] GFA, *supra*, Art. I.

[4] Conference on Security and Co-operation in Europe, Final Act, 14 ILM 1293 (1975).

[5] Charter of Paris for a New Europe: A New Era of Democracy, Peace and Unity, 21 November 1990, 30 ILM 190 (1991).

M. O'Flaherty and G. Gisvold (eds.), Post-War Protection of Human Rights in Bosnia and Herzegovina, 173–194.
© 1998 *Kluwer Law International. Printed in Great Britain.*

International human rights obligations can only be effectively implemented at the domestic level. This truism is especially crucial in a federal structure where the central authority lacks political or moral authority over all constituent parts. Accordingly, Bosnia and Herzegovina, as well as the two Entities that comprise the State, the Federation of Bosnia and Herzegovina and the Republika Srpska[6], must ensure the 'highest level of internationally recognized human rights and fundamental freedoms' in all matters within their competence[7]. The GFA established an institutional framework, in the form of the Human Rights Commission for Bosnia and Herzegovina, to effectuate this goal[8]. The GFA incorporates the European Convention for the Protection of Human Rights and Fundamental Freedoms and its Protocols[9] as direct law in BiH with priority over all other law and enumerates specific rights and, thereby, gives greater specificity to human rights obligations[10]. BiH is required to become (or remain) a party to listed United Nations and regional human rights instruments[11], and is

---

[6] GFA, *supra*, Annex 4, Art. I(3) (Constitution of Bosnia and Herzegovina) [hereinafter Constitution].

[7] The federal structure bestows residual governmental power upon the Entities. *See, e.g.*, Constitution, *supra*, Art. III (3) (a).

[8] Constitution, *supra*, Art. II (1).

[9] [European] Convention for the Protection of Human Rights and Fundamental Freedoms, 213 UNTS 221, ETS 5, *signed* 4 November 1950 [hereinafter "ECHR"].

[10] Constitution, *supra*, Art. II (2) and (3).

[11] Constitution, *supra*, Art. II (7). Fifteen agreements are listed in Constitution, Annex I: the International Covenant on Civil and Political Rights, 999 UNTS 171, *adopted* 16 December 1966 [hereinafter "ICCPR"]; the International Covenant on Economic, Social and Cultural Rights, 993 UNTS 3, *adopted* 16 December 1966 [hereinafter "ICESCR"]; the Convention on the Prevention and Punishment of the Crime of Genocide, 78 UNTS 277, *adopted* 9 December 1948 [hereinafter "Genocide Convention"]; the Geneva Conventions on the Protection of Victims of War, 75 UNTS 31, 85, 135, and 187, signed 12 August 1949 and the Protocols I and II, 1125 UNTS 3 and 609, *entered into force* 7 December 1978 thereto; the Convention on the Status of Refugees, 189 UNTS 137, *adopted* 28 July 1951, and its Protocol, 606 UNTS 267, *adopted* 31 January 1967 [hereinafter "Refugee Convention"]; the Convention on the Nationality of Married Women, 309 UNTS 65, *adopted* 29 January 1957; the Convention on the Reduction of Statelessness, 989 UNTS 175, *adopted* 30 September 1961; the Convention on the Elimination of All Forms of Racial Discrimination, 660 UNTS 195, *adopted* 21 December 1965 [hereinafter "Race Convention"]; the Convention on the Elimination of All Forms of Discrimination Against Women, 1249 UNTS 13, *adopted* 18 December 1979 [hereinafter "Women's Convention"]; the Convention against Torture and Other Cruel, Inhuman or Degrading Treatment or Punishment, 23 ILM 1027 (1984), as modified 24 ILM 535 (1985) [hereinafter "Convention Against Torture"]; the European Convention against Torture and Other Cruel, Inhuman or Degrading Treatment or Punishment, ETS 126, 27 ILM 1152 (1988); the Convention on the Rights of the Child, GA res. 44/25, UN Doc. A/44/49 (1989); the International Convention on the Protection of the Rights of Migrant Workers and their Families, GA res. 45/158, UN Doc. A/RES/45/158 (1990); the European Charter for Regional or Minority Languages, ETS 148 (1992); and the Framework Convention for the Protection of National Minorites, Council of Europe, ETS 157 (1994).

internationally responsible for their implementation[12]. All competent national authorities are bound to co-operate with international monitoring bodies, whether established explicitly with respect to BiH, or operating under their respective treaty mandates[13]. BiH became a party to a number of these treaties through succession in 1993[14]. It is therefore formally bound by the body of human rights law that is integrated into the domestic structures for the construction of the post-conflict State.

The future guarantee of human rights in BiH is handicapped by the lack of a human rights culture or infrastructure prior to the break-up of the former Socialist Federal Republic of Yugoslavia. Although the SFRY allowed personal freedoms not experienced elsewhere in Eastern Europe, no democratic tradition in the course of relations between State and individual[15]. Nevertheless, in 1990 the SFRY headed the eligibility list of former socialist States for membership in the Council of Europe with the required commitment to the European Convention on Human Rights. It has been contended that the role of women is economically and symbolically crucial to the political transformation in Eastern Europe essential to such membership, but that women's interests are being sacrificed to the transformation[16].

There are similarities between the position of women in Bosnia and Herzegovina with those elsewhere in Eastern Europe and lessons can be learned from their experiences. There are also distinctions, the most evident being the armed conflict conducted with rampant disregard for all human rights, including those asserted as peremptory norms of international law, such as the right to life and bodily integrity. In the transformation of a communist state and the reconstruction of a civil society in the aftermath of devastating destruction, emphasis must be on imbuing a respect for the individual and group rights of the members of the different communities. But, where individuals are identified as members of groups there is less space for the recognition of their individual rights. In this environment the rights of women are unlikely to be accorded a high prior-

---

[12] A federal state is internationally responsible for human rights abuses committed by a constituent element. *Toonen* v. *Australia*, Human Rights Committee, Communication No. 488/1992, UN Doc. CCPR/C/50/D488/1992, 4 April 1994.

[13] Constitution, *supra*, Art. II (8).

[14] Bosnia and Herzegovina succeeded to several of the multilateral treaties mentioned in above: the ICCPR, ICESCR, the Refugee Convention and its Protocol, the Convention on the Nationality of Married Women, the Women's Convention, the Convention Against Torture, and the Convention on the Rights of the Child on 1 September 1993. It succeeded to the Genocide Convention on 29 December 1992 and the Race Convention on 16 July 1993.

[15] Z. Pajic, "The Former Yugoslavia", *in* H. Miall (ed.), *Minority Rights in Europe: the Scope for a Transnational Regime* (1994), at 56.

[16] N. Funk and M. Mueller, *Gender Politics and Post-Communism* (1993), at 2 [hereinafter "Funk and Mueller"].

ity. Even in states with a tradition of human rights protection, women's rights are not easily secured.

Enjoyment of the constitutionally guaranteed rights and freedoms in Bosnia and Herzegovina is to be ensured to all persons "without discrimination on any ground", including sex[17]. Other than this prohibition of discrimination, no reference is made to particular factors that might prejudice the effective assurance of women's rights within BiH[18]. Women did not participate in the talks at Dayton, Ohio that producted the GFA, despite acceptance of the desirability of such a strategy only weeks earlier at the Fourth United Nations World Conference on Women[19]. The GFA does not allude separately to women, nor to any reasons for special attention to be paid to their circumstances. The emphasis upon the goal of reconciliation between the "constituent peoples" of the Republic of Bosnia and Herzegovina[20], subsumes women without acknowledgment that their experiences of conflict and its aftermath may well differ from those of men, and that their needs and priorities in reconstruction may also differ. Women remain largely invisible in the reports of the Special Rapporteur of the United Nations Commission on Human Rights on the Situation of Human Rights in the Territory of the Former Yugoslavia, which fail to consider that listed human rights abuses can have a different impact on women[21].

The present writer argues that the prohibition of discrimination on the grounds of sex in the application of the rights guaranteed by the GFA is insufficient to hold out to women the same vision of human rights protection offered to men. After outlining the international standards articulated for the protection of women's rights, the present author argues that existing deficiencies within human rights law that undermine its effectiveness for securing women's rights in all States may be especially detrimental in the context of women in BiH; therefore, it is necessary that national and international agencies responsible for the implementation of human rights in BiH pay special attention to the situation of women.

---

[17] Constitution, *supra*, Art. II (4).

[18] The remarkable inattention paid to women's issues other than abortion in post-communism and in elections in particular' is remarked upon in N. Funk and M. Mueller. *See* Funk and Mueller, *supra*, at 12.

[19] Beijing Declaration and Platform for Action, UN Doc. A/CONF.177/20 and A/CONF.177/20/Add. 1 (1995), ¶ 142 [hereinafter "Beijing Platform"].

[20] Constitution, *supra*, at Preamble

[21] *See, e.g.*, "Situation Of Human Rights Abuses in the Territory of the Former Yugoslavia", UN Doc. E/CN.4/1996/63 (1996) [hereinafter "Human Rights Abuses in the Former Yugoslavia"]. The omission of any women's groups is striking in the Annex of the Programme of Meetings of the Special Rapporteur.

II. INTERNATIONAL LAW AND THE GUARANTEE OF WOMEN'S RIGHTS

The constitutional prohibition of discrimination and its positive corollary, the commitment to equality between men and women, is required by BiH membership of the UN and its commitment to the international and regional human rights treaties contained within Annex 4. Article 14 of the European Convention is representative:

> The enjoyment of the rights and freedoms set forth in this Convention shall be secured without discrimination on any ground such as sex, race, colour, language, religion, political or other opinion, national or social origin, association with a national minority, property, birth or other status[22].

This provision is limited, however, inasmuch as it is linked to the rights enumerated in the Convention. Unlike Article 26 of the International Covenant on Civil and Political Rights, it is not a free-standing assertion of equality before the law[23]. But, unlike the European Convention, the ICCPR is not given priority in the BiH constitution.

Recognition came early within the UN human rights system that the general legal prohibition of discrimination did not prevent persistent global discrimination against women in all fields of life[24]. The need for a specialised Convention amplifying those areas in which women are most disadvantaged by systemic discrimination was accepted[25]. The Convention on the Elimination of All Forms of Discrimination Against Women was the most significant legal achievement of the UN Decade for Women, which was held from 1975-85[26]. BiH's accession to the Convention in 1993 and the inclusion of the Convention in the GFA are important from the perspective of ensuring a legal commitment to guaranteeing women's rights[27].

The explicit goal of the Women's Convention is to achieve equality for women based on the recognition that full global development and international peace and security require maximum participation of women on equal terms with men[28]. The Convention draws upon women's experiences to specify where gender-based discrimination has the most adverse impacts

---

[22] *Cf.*, European Social Charter, 525 UNTS 89, *entered into force* 26 February 1965, Art.14.

[23] *See* ICCPR, *supra.*

[24] *The United Nations and The Advancement of Women, 1945-1995*, (United Nations Blue Books Series, Volume VI 1995).

[25] The Convention on the Nationality of Married Women is a single issue non-discrimination treaty. The Women's Convention, in contrast, is partially modeled upon the first, broad non-discrimination treaty, the Race Convention of 1966.

[26] *See* Women's Convention, *supra.*

[27] Constitution, *supra*, Art. II (7) and Annex 1. The Former Yugoslavia was a party to the Women's Convention.

[28] Women's Convention, *supra*, at Preamble.

upon women. It requires the suppression of trafficking in women and exploitative prostitution (Article 6) and details the rights of rural women (Article 14). Other provisions require states to take appropriate measures to ensure equal participation of women in public decision- and policymaking (Articles 7 and 8); equality in nationality laws and in the administration of justice (Articles 9 and 15); equality in and access to education, employment, and health services (Articles 10-12); equality in other areas of economic and social life (Article 13); and equal rights within the family (Article 16).

Unlike the general human rights instruments, the Womens Convention defines as well as condemns discrimination against women[29]. It imposes obligations upon parties to take positive steps to eliminate it in national laws, policies and constitutions, and to ensure the practical realisation of this objective. Parties are obliged to undertake "appropriate measures" in all fields for the "full development and advancement of women". The consequences of past discrimination are redressed by allowing for positive discrimination (or affirmative action) during a transitional phase until equality is achieved. In addition, the Convention recognises that formal, legal measures are insufficient for the accomplishment of this goal and accordingly requires parties to take appropriate measures to change attitudes with respect to sexist stereotyping and the assumption of the inferiority of one sex over the other[30].

III. MONITORING AND IMPLEMENTATION OF HUMAN RIGHTS

The UN human rights system has developed a number of mechanisms for implementing and monitoring the articulated standards. The Economic and Social Council has developed procedures through its resolutions[31]. Also, the Commission on Human Rights may examine complaints from individuals which reveal consistent patterns of human rights abuses[32]. The potential of this competence is limited by practical restrictions and generally confined to circumstances in which a majority of UN member states have concerns regarding a human rights violation, for example apartheid in South Africa[33]. The Commission also has a procedure to handle complaints

---

[29] The definition found in Article I of the Women's Convention resembles that in the Race Convention. The UN Human Rights Committee General Comment 18 (37th session 1989) notes these definitions in defining discrimination. *See* ICCPR, *supra*, Art. 26.

[30] Women's Convention, *supra*, Arts. 1-5.

[31] ECOSOC Res. 1235 (XLII), UN Doc. E/4393 (1967) and 1503 (XLVIII), UN Doc. E/4832/Add.1 (1970). Res. 1503 is supplemented by Resolution 1 (XXIV), UN Doc. E/CN.4/1070 (1971), of the Sub-Commission on the Prevention of Discrimination and Protection of Minorities.

[32] ECOSOC Res 1235.

[33] I. Brownlie, *Basic Documents in Human Rights* (3rd ed. 1992), at 15.

from individuals and non-governmental organisations which can result in an investigation by an ad hoc committee[34]. However, this procedure has weaknesses of its own, including procedural technicalities, time-consuming processes and a dependence upon the political will of the Commission to pursue complaints. Systematic discrimination against women has never inspired such widespread concern or political will. The Commission on the Status of Women can examine confidential communications that appear to reveal a "consistent pattern" of "discriminatory practices against women". But, it can only make recommendations to ECOSOC and this procedure remains under utilised[35].

BiH is subject to the monitoring provisions of the UN human rights treaties and the European Convention[36]. Different mechanisms have been devised, although only one has been made applicable to the Women's Convention. The Committee on the Elimination of Discrimination Against Women established under the Women's Convention has 23 independent experts who receive initial and periodic reports from States parties on their progress in realising their obligations under the Convention[37]. CEDAW scrutinises these reports in advance of a public presentation by a State representative. CEDAW may question and comment on the report, but has no power to enforce any conclusions. Under this system, States parties summarise their on-going Convention performance; inadequacies in such performace can come to light during the public session. However, so short is the time allotted the CEDAW session that few reports can be adequately considered[38].

Other human rights treaty bodies have greater monitoring powers than CEDAW. The Human Rights Committee, the Committee against Racial Discrimination and the Committee against Torture, for example, are competent to receive complaints from one State party of non-compliance by another[39]. A individual complaint procedure under the ICCPR's First Optional Protocol, the Race Convention and the Convention against Torture exists to supplement this inter-State complaint[40]. This procedure allows an individual to complain of a violation of the relevant treaty, provided all local remedies have been exhausted. In response, the respec-

---

[34] ECOSOC Res. 1503.

[35] ECOSOC Res. 1983/27. *See* L. Reanda, "The Commission on the Status of Women", *in* P. Alston (ed.), *The United Nations and Human Rights* (1992), at 265, 297-300.

[36] "UN human rights treaties" include the ICCPR, the ICESCR, the Race Convention, the Women's Convention, the Convention against Torture, and the Convention on the Rights of the Child. *See* Chapter 11 of this volume.

[37] Women's Convention, *supra*, Art. 17.

[38] The Women's Convention, Article 20, allows CEDAW normally to meet for two weeks annually. The General Assembly noted with approval the amendment extending this time adopted by states parties at their 8th meeting, 22 May 1995. GA Res. 50/202 (1995).

[39] ICCPR, *supra*, Art. 41; Race Convention, *supra*, Art. 11; Convention Against Torture, *supra*, Art. 21.

[40] Race Convention, *supra*, Art. 14; Convention Against Torture, *supra*, Art. 22.

tive Committees have quasi-judicial investigative powers and can make a non-binding determination of violation.

It has been argued that CEDAW's weaker implementation powers indicate that the international community attaches less importance to the Women's Convention than other human rights treaties[41]. Accordingly, the Beijing Platform for Action supports the process initiated by the Commission on the Status of Women for the drafting of an optional protocol to the Women's Convention allowing for a right of individual petition[42]. The Commission is now considering an optional protocol, but it will likely be many years before such a development eventuates.

The prohibition of sex-based discrimination in the general human rights treaties could be utilised as a counter to CEDAW's procedural deficiencies. For example, BiH's acceptance of ICCPR's First Optional Protocol allows individual Bosnian women to claim discrimination with regard to the rights guaranteed by the ICCPR, or under Article 26, the general equality clause[43]. Similarly, other human rights bodies should be alert to gendered abuses when reviewing States' reports and drafting general comments and recommendations on the appropriate interpretations of their respective Conventions. Unfortunately, such gender awareness has not been frequent. It has been suggested that the Women's Convention has created a separate body of women's rights outside the mainstream of human rights development[44]. This marginalisation has been enhanced by the historical association of the Women's Convention with the Commission on the Status of Women, rather than the Commission on Human Rights and by the servicing of CEDAW by the Division for the Advancement of Women, rather than the Centre for Human Rights. Recognizing that this duality impedes the adequate implementation of women's human rights, the Beijing Conference urged their integration throughout the UN system[45].

Accession to the ECHR will bind BiH to its procedural, as well as substantive, provisions[46]. It could become subject to both inter-State and

---

[41] A. Byrnes, "The 'Other' Human Rights Treaty Body: The Work of the Committee on the Elimination of Discrimination Against Women", 14 Yale JIL 1 (1989).

[42] Beijing Declaration and Platform for Action, *supra*. The Vienna Conference on Human Rights had recommended that CSW and CEDAW examine the feasibility of an optional protocol providing a right of individual petition. United Nations World Conference on Human Rights: Vienna Declaration and Programme of Action, 25 June 1993, 32 ILM 1661 (1993), UN Doc. A/CONF.157/23 (Part II), ¶ 40 [hereinafter "Vienna Declaration and Programme for Action"].

[43] Bosnia and Herzegovina accepted the First Optional Protocol on 1 March 1995.

[44] H. Charlesworth, "What are 'Women's International Human Rights'?" *in* R. Cook, *Human Rights of Women* (1994), at 58.

[45] Beijing Platform for Action, *supra*, ¶ 231.

[46] Bosnia and Herzegovina applied for membership of the Council of Europe on 10 April 1995.

individual complaints[47]. The constitutional priority accorded to the European Convention requires the Bosnian courts to apply the jurisprudence of the European Court and Commission[48]. A number of cases from this body of precedent are especially relevant to the situation of women there. For example, in *Cyprus* v. *Turkey*, the European Commission determined that rape of Cypriot women by Turkish military personnel could be imputed to Turkey, the occupying power, and constituted inhumane treatment contrary to Article 3 of the ECHR[49]. The Vienna Programme of Action reaffirmed this decision, stating that "violations of the human rights of women in situations of armed conflict are violations of the fundamental principles of international human rights and humanitarian law"[50]. At Beijing, it was stressed that all such violations, including rape, require a "particularly effective response". The relevance to the BiH situation is apparent. The case also illustrates the advantages of the inter-State complaint procedure which eliminates the need for a named victim and allows scrutiny of systematic State abuse.

The ECHR allows petitions to be made by NGOs as well as individuals[51]. This broad concept of standing lessens the pressure upon individual victims of abuse. The procedure provides opportunities for authoritative interpretations of the ECHR and for the development of general principles of human rights law that can be advantageous to women. The European Court of Human Rights, for example, has ruled upon classic direct discrimination. In *Abdulaziz, Cabales and Balkandali* v. *UK*, the Court held that a British law imposing strict requirements upon women in the UK before their foreign spouses could join them violated privacy rights and were discriminatory[52]. The court noted that discrimination requires 'weighty' justifications, none of which were found in this case. In *Airey* v. *Ireland*, the Court held that respect for family life under Article 8 may necessitate positive action by a State, including provision of legal aid for an indigenous wife seeking judicial separation from her violent husband[53]. The Court held that, as Article 8 does not define the concept of a family, single parent families must be accorded the same respect as two parent families. Ensuring such respect includes acting so as to allow those concerned to lead a normal family life. Positive steps were also required in *Marckx* v. *Belgium*, where laws concerning the status of illegitimacy were

---

[47] ECHR, *supra*, Arts. 24 and 25.

[48] The Eleventh Protocol to the ECHR created a single-tiered system by removing the European Commission. ECHR, Protocol No. 11, E.T.S. 155, 33 ILM 960 (1994).

[49] Applications No. 6780/74 and No. 6950/75 (10 July 1976).

[50] Vienna Declaration and Programme for Action, *supra*, ¶ 38; Beijing Platform for Action, *supra*, ¶ 132.

[51] ECHR, *supra*, Art. 25.

[52] 94 ECHR (Series A) (1985).

[53] 32 ECHR (Series A) (1979).

challenged[54]. Finally, in *X and Y* v. *the Netherlands*, the Netherlands was held to be in breach of the Convention for the failure of its criminal law to provide legal redress to a 16 year old intellectually disadvantaged child who had been sexually abused[55]. The Court held that the positive obligations required to uphold respect for family life may include measures in the sphere of individual relations. This statement extends international responsibility for failure by the State to secure the guaranteed rights and freedoms for everyone under its jurisdiction to some private actions. The case did not directly address women's rights but could be applied by analogy, for example, to the failure of a State to apply its criminal law to prosecute private acts of violence inflicted upon women[56].

European Convention jurisprudence on women's reproductive rights is less clear. In *Open Door Counselling Ltd and Dublin Well Woman Centre Ltd* v. *Ireland*, the right to freedom of expression was held to prevent the Irish government from lawfully stopping women in Ireland receiving information about English abortion services[57], but in *Bruggemann and Scheuten* v. *Germany*, the Commission held that the right to privacy does not guarantee a woman's right to abortion[58]. The efficacy of the individual complaint procedure for tackling systemic power imbalance and structural sexism has also been queried[59].

IV. THE EFFECTIVE GUARANTEE OF WOMEN'S RIGHTS?

Despite the prohibition on discrimination against women in the GFA, the prospects for effective attainment of women's legal rights remain weak. Factors related to the unlikeliness attaining this goal include inadequacies within existing human rights law and to the particular situation of women within Bosnia and Herzegovina. Experience elsewhere shows that women's human rights are rarely given sufficient national priority or resources. Without attention to these problems, the guarantees of the GFA are unlikely to have a positive impact upon women's lives in the reconstruction of Bosnia and Herzegovinan society.

When determining priorities for the guarantee of rights, a note of caution must be expressed. Women's experiences throughout the conflict varied greatly depending upon such distinguishing features as national identity,

---

[54] 31 ECHR (Series A) (1979).

[55] 91 ECHR (Series A) (1985); *see also Costello & Roberts* v. *UK*, 9 EHRR 112 (1995).

[56] In *Whiteside* v. *UK*, the European Commission found the state potentially responsible for failure to protect the woman applicant against harassment. However local remedies had not been exhausted. Application No. 20357/92; 18 EHRR C.D. 126 (1994).

[57] 246 ECHR (Series A) (1992).

[58] 21 YB ECHR 638.

[59] A. Bayefsky, "The Principle of Equality and Non-Discrimination in International Law", 11 Hum. Rts Q. 1 (1990).

class, economic circumstances, urban or rural residence, family situation, age, employment and physical attributes. Some women were militarily active, while others participated in peace movements. Some stayed in the same place throughout the war, while ethnic cleansing or the physical destruction of their homes forced others to leave, many on more than one occasion. Thousands suffered severe physical and sexual abuse, or have relatives and friends who did so. Women survivors know of the brutal deaths of family and friends, or remain unaware of their fate. Many have cared alone for children whose childhood has been destroyed by war, and for elderly people. Women's options may be constrained by their many different and still changing circumstances and no outsider can presume to make judgments as to the most important aspects of women's rights in Bosnia and Herzegovina. At all times women in Bosnia and Herzegovina must be seen and treated as agents, not subjects, in the reconstruction of their society.

A. The Primacy of Civil and Political Rights

To some, the collapse of Eastern European socialism is indicative of the triumph of western political philosophy, and of its commitment to civil and political rights as the ideological underpinning to capitalism and the free market[60]. Western liberal theory has traditionally favoured civil and political rights over economic and social rights. Thus, the Universal Declaration of Human Rights has only five articles dedicated to economic and social rights, but has thirty articles related to civil and political rights. Although economic and social rights have been termed "survival and development rights"[61], the mandatory language of the ICCPR contrasts significantly with the more limited obligation to "take steps ... with a view to achieving progressively the full realization of the rights" in the International Covenant on Economic, Social, and Cultural Rights[62]. The latter also has weaker monitoring provisions compared with its civil and political rights counterpart[63].

---

[60] *Cf.*, M. Thornton, *Dissonance and Distrust Women in the Legal Profession* (1996), at 23 ("The notion of public good became intertwined with, and indistinguishable from, the needs of capitalism").

[61] D. Parker, "Resources and Child Rights: An Economic Perspective", *in* J. Himes (ed.), *Implementing the Convention on the Rights of the Child* (1995), at 33.

[62] ICESCR, *supra*, Art. 2 (1). ICCPR imposes the immediate obligation 'to respect and ensure' the Covenant's rights. ICCPR, *supra*, Art. 2 (1). *See* Chapter 8 of this volume.

[63] The Human Rights Committee was established by the ICCPR, in Article 28(1), while the Economic, Social and Cultural Committee was formed in 1986 by ECOSOC. There is no right of individual complaint under the ICESCR, but a right is available through adherence to the First Optional Protocol to the ICCPR. First Optional Protocol to the ICCPR, 999 UNTS 171, *adopted* 19 December 1966.

Despite the assertion at the 1993 Vienna World Conference on Human Rights of the indivisibility and interdependence of all human rights, the priority accorded to civil and political rights remains and is embodied in the GFA. The European Convention, a catalogue of civil and political rights with comparatively strong implementation procedures, is directly applicable in BiH law, but the European Social Charter is not. The Organisation for Security and Co-operation in Europe, one of the most active intergovernmental agencies in BiH, emphasises pluralistic democracy, the rule of law and human rights, which involve civil and political rights. Out of the thirteen rights enumerated in the BiH Constitution only one is drawn from the ICESCR. The BiH Constitution postulates "the protection of private property and the promotion of the market economy"[64]. The Preamble to the Agreement establishing the European Bank for Reconstruction and Development avows human rights protection, but again it is limited to civil and political rights. Unusually, the Women's Convention embraces both civil and political and economic and social rights, reflecting the particular significance of the latter to women[65]. Nevertheless, economic rights are unlikely to be accorded priority when set against the many instruments favouring civil and political rights that have been incorporated into the GFA and the preferred political ideology.

Civil and political rights are to be accorded without discrimination. The legal guarantees of equality and democracy entitle women to the opportunity to participate in the public arena on the same terms as men and to be accorded the same legal protection there. However, trends elsewhere towards democratization, good governance and open political participation have not increased the numbers of women in political life. At Beijing, it was noted that in some countries undergoing "fundamental political, economic and social changes" numbers of women in national legislative and decision-making bodies had in fact decreased. The September 1996 elections in BiH resulted in the election of only a minute proportion of women. Local elections have not yet been possible in BiH. Yet, public life is not limited to elections. Women's participation in continuing dialogue and dispute resolution processes, including those involving the Human Rights Commission established pursuant to the GFA, must also be ensured. International support to women's NGOs must include preparing local women to take on such roles. Unequal participation in all aspects of public life undermines the substance of democracy and lessens the likelihood of women's interests being taken seriously[66].

---

[64] Constitution, *supra*, at Preamble.

[65] The Convention on the Rights of the Child continues this conjunction of rights.

[66] *Cf.*, Beijing Platform for Action, *supra*, ¶ 181, ("Women's equal participation in decision-making ... can be seen as a necessary condition for women's interests to be taken into account. Without the active participation of women and the incorporation of women's perspective at all levels of decision-making, the goals of equality, development and peace cannot be achieved.").

Of significant importance among women's interests are concerns for the guarantee of adequate economic and social conditions. Enhanced civil and political rights have little relevance for women without reference to the economic, social and cultural context in which they operate. In BiH, as elsewhere in Eastern Europe, the commitment to civil and political rights is precisely to uphold economic structural change. The transition to the free market elsewhere in Eastern Europe has had its social costs, including widespread impoverishment, higher crime rates and corruption fostered by the institutional vacuum created by the dismantling of government structures. Communist ideology provided extensive social benefits. These benefits, however, were tainted inasmuch as they were "threaded through authoritarian structures that denied the worth of the individual"; nevertheless, they were relied upon[67].

In what has been called "a changing definition of human rights" in Eastern Europe, governments have retreated from assuring previously accepted economic rights[68]. Women in Eastern Europe have borne the brunt of many of these changes through reduced access to public housing, employment and health care. Decreased availability and increased costs of child care facilities are other restraints upon women's choices.

In BiH, where state-building, economic transition and reconstruction are occurring in the wake of war, the effects might be especially detrimental for women. Socialist commitment to women's formal equality ensured their high participation in the paid workforce, albeit at lower pay than men and largely segregated in 'feminised' areas of employment in positions of little authority[69]. The war in Bosnia forced women and men out of their pre-war professional and private lives. In many areas of Bosnia while able men were militarily engaged, women struggled to survive in the face of the deliberate destruction of civilian life, including housing and other essential services. The legitimation of the two Entities in the GFA appears to have resulted in thousands of people unwilling to return to their previous homes, even where they remain intact. Care must be taken to ensure women's equal treatment in restoration of property or payment of compensation, especially where families have been split or destroyed[70].

Another factor is the traditional role of women as carers of children, the sick, wounded (including those suffering psychological harm) and elderly. The Special Rapporteur of the United Nations Commission on Human Rights on the Situation of Human Rights in the Territory of the Former Yugoslavia has emphasised the urgent need for rehabilitative measures for children traumatised and physically injured by the war, who require expert

---

[67] Funk and Mueller, *supra*, at 2.

[68] K. Tomasevski, "Human Rights in Eastern Europe", *in* P. Baeker, H. Hey, J. Smith and T. Swinehert (eds.), *Human Rights in Developing Countries* (1994).

[69] *E.g.*, textiles, office work, health and education. Funk and Mueller, *supra*, at 7.

[70] GFA, *supra*, Art. VII.

psychological, educational and medical care[71]. Much of this social burden is likely to fall heavily on women. The European Social Charter secures the right of mothers and children to appropriate social and economic protection[72]. This right is problematic inasmuch as it identifies women through motherhood; but, it nevertheless accords some assurance that the European Convention on Human Rights, with its civil and political rights orientation, does not. The potential charge on women of addressing the needs of children could become empowering if the function is respected as a national priority, with provision of appropriate training, and allocation of resources, but could otherwise force women into domestic roles[73].

There are many examples of post-conflict reconstruction according priority in employment, positions of authority and benefits to returning fighting men to facilitate their reintegration into civil society. In contrast, women have been denied paid employment[74]. High levels of unemployment, as exist in BiH, have the same consequence, which can be devastating for women-headed households. In addition, ethnic cleansing was targeted at people holding positions of authority and responsibility, leaving a void in experience and expertise at local and national levels. Those filling these vacancies will not necessarily be sensitive to women's rights. These conditions, coupled with the demands upon women in the rehabilitation of family life, are likely to reduce women's participation in public employment, minimising the relevance of workplace rights. It is essential for women that attention is paid to economic and social rights as well as to civil and political rights and that gendered analysis is obtained of the differential impact upon women and men of social reordering in both Entities.

B. Equality in Public and Private Domains

The international norm of non-discrimination entitles women to the same standard of legal treatment as similarly situated men. The starting point of equality in the public arena fails to address women's needs in a number of ways. In both western and communist political philosophy the standard of equality is measured in terms of men's lives and experiences. Thus, it fails women in situations where no similarly situated male exists. The liberal philosophy of equality of opportunity that assumes a world of autonomous individuals making free choices discounts the structural disempowerment of women and the fact that men and women are simply "running different

---

[71] Human Rights Abuses in the Former Yugoslavia, *supra*, at ¶¶ 4, 208. *Cf.*, Document of the Copenhagen Meeting of the Conference on the Human Dimension of the CSCE, 29 June 1990, ¶ 13.
[72] European Social Charter, *supra*, Art. 17.
[73] *Cf.*, D. Parker, *supra*, at 33.
[74] C. Enloe, *Does Kahki Become You? The Militarisation of Women's Lives* (1988).

races"[75]. Nor did socialist notions of equality entirely benefit women. Eisenstein has argued that they emphasised women's participation in the paid workforce and protective devices (child care, maternity leave) that were used "to assist women in their gender roles, rather than to reorganise gender responsibilities between men and women"[76]. Women are thus subjected to the double burden of workplace and inequality in the home where child rearing and other household responsibilities remain gendered. Women who fear (or face) unemployment at the time of reduced public commitment to these protective devices are understandably cautious about the changes.

The public/private construct that is critical to liberal theory has been attacked by western feminists as confining women to the private, unregulated arena. It carries less weight for women with a socialist heritage for whom the family could represent freedom from State control[77]. It can also hold little normative force where national imperatives include the rehabilitation of children and families, the reconstruction of vital services and employment policies.

International human rights law cannot adequately address these tensions, especially within its traditional parameters, wherein State responsibility is incurred only for abuses by public officials. The Women's Convention attempts to cut through the omission of accountablity for private actions. It makes a strong commitment to the role of women in public life, while controversially affirming equality in private life, most notably through Articles 5, 9 and 16[78]. Article 16 asserts equality between men and women before, during, and after the dissolution of marital relationships[79]. Nevertheless, it remains limited in that it envisages only marriage and does not take into account other forms of private ordering, or relationships between other family members. This omission is especially relevant in the context of BiH where family life has been shattered by the armed conflict and ethnic cleansing.

The standards articulated within the Women's Convention, including that of equality in private relationships, have been weakened by the entering of substantial reservations to key principles, such as those in Articles 2,

---

[75] N. Lacey, "Legislation against Sex Discrimination: Questions from a Feminist Perspective", 14 J. Law and Soc. 411, 415 (1987).

[76] Z. Eisenstein, "Eastern European Male Democracies: A Problem of Unequal Equality", *in* Funk and Mueller, *supra*, at 308.

[77] *Id.*, at 5.

[78] Women's Convention, in article 7, asserts women's right to equality in voting and eligibility for elected office, participation in government policy-making and implementation, participation in NGO activity.

[79] *Cf.*, ECHR, Protocol No. 7, ETS 117 (9184), 24 ILM 435 (1985), Art. 5 (1) ("Spouses shall enjoy equality of rights and responsibilities of a private law character between them, and in their relations with their children, as to marriage, during marriage and in the event of its dissolution.").

9 and 16[80]. Islamic states have prominently made such reservations, though they are not alone in doing so. The Convention prohibits reservations incompatible with its objects and purposes[81], but there have been few objections. During the war the Bosnian government sought support from Islamic governments such as Saudi Arabia, Iran and Pakistan that have either not ratified the Women's Convention or have ratified with reservations. BiH has made no reservations to the Women's Convention, but concern exists that the high number of reservations has weakened the Convention and given rise to an expectation of non-compliance. It is important that such concerns be minimised and that the BiH government adhere to its full commitment.

C. Violence against Women as a Human Rights Abuse

Feminists have argued that human rights law is formulated in terms of male experience within the public arena[82]. The paradigm of equality means that women's rights have been forced into this framework without accommodating their different life experiences. The Women's Convention takes on the standard of equality and, consequently, offers most to women who are operating in similar situations to men, such as in the paid workforce or elsewhere in the public arena. After the conclusion of the UN Decade for Women, issues that did not fit within this gendered perception were excluded from the discourse on human rights, in particular gender-specific violence and reproductive rights. This separation increasingly concerned women.

Violence against women during the armed conflict was accorded extensive international media coverage and unique legal response. The Statute of the War Crimes Tribunal for Former Yugoslavia includes rape as a crime against humanity and the Tribunal has issued indictments for forcible sexual penetration as an element of torture and enslavement and as a grave breach of international humanitarian law[83]. Co-operation with the War Crimes Tribunal is required by the GFA and must include admitting the severity of violent crimes against women, whoever the perpetrator. The impact of this international legal development will be minimised if rape and other forms of gendered violence (including exploitative and forced prostitution as an aspect of organised crime) are not taken seriously in domestic law. Tribunal judgments should be incorporated into domestic

---

[80] *See* L. Lijnzaad, *Reservations to UN – Human Rights Treaties Ratify and Ruin* (1995).

[81] Women's Convention, *supra*, Art. 28 (2).

[82] *E.g.*, C. Bunch, "Women's Rights as Human Rights: Towards a Revision of Human Rights", 12 Hum. Rts Q. 486 (1990); J. Kerr (ed.), *Ours by Right* (1993); K. Tomasevski, *Women and Human Rights* (1993); R. Cook, *Human Rights of Women, supra*.

[83] SC Res. 827 (25 May 1993); International Criminal Tribunal for the Former Yugoslavia, Indictment Gagovic & Others ('Foca'), *issued* 26 June 1996.

criminal law, including procedures for trying sexual assault cases that take account of the rights of victims[84].

Many reasons for the deliberate infliction of sexual violence against civilian women in armed conflict have been suggested[85]. Sexual abuse humiliates, terrifies and degrades women from the opposing side and, through them, the entire community. Use or threat of violence against women causes families to flee and, thus, is an element of ethnic cleansing. In armed conflict such offences are readily appropriated as propaganda, demonising the enemy and justifying continuing violence against them. What is easy to ignore is that violence against women does not cease with the end of the conflict, but is pervasive in many manifestations in peace-time societies. Women in BiH are living in an environment where gendered violence has been endemic, where military and para-military activities have engendered an expectation of violence, and where ethnic hatreds continue. But, violence is regularly committed against women in all societies by their own communities and by their own family members. Studies suggest that women's vulnerability to domestic violence is increased where men feel their masculinity to be undermined, where women suffer economic disempowerment (for example through unemployment, destruction of material assets), or where there is a pattern of using violence to resolve disputes and limitations upon the right to divorce[86].

Violence against life and bodily integrity is subsumed within mainstream human rights law under the rubric of the rights to life, to liberty and to be free from torture, cruel, inhuman and degrading treatment. These guarantees are drafted in gender-neutral terms, but, in conformity with traditional human rights discourse, their focus is upon public violence committed within state institutions and by state agents. Private acts of violence are not covered by these instruments, receive little condemnation and are too-often tolerated as acceptable or natural behaviour, or justified by reference to religious and cultural norms[87].

In 1992, CEDAW determined that gender-specific violence constituted discrimination against women in the terms of the Women's Convention. A year later the General Assembly adopted the Declaration on the Elimination of Violence against Women[88]. This Declaration (the wording of which was largely reiterated at Vienna and again at Beijing) represents a major advance in the recognition of obstacles to the enjoyment of women of their human rights. It asserts the structural roots of violence in the "historically

---

[84] *E.g.*, Prosecutor v. Tadic, Case IT/94/1/T, 10 August 1995.

[85] *E.g.*, C. Chinkin, "Rape And Sexual Abuse Of Women In International Law", 5 EJIL 326 (1994).

[86] *Strategies for Confronting Domestic Violence: A Resource Manual* (UN 1993).

[87] Preliminary Report Submitted by the Special Rapporteur on Violence against Women, its Causes and Consequences, UN Doc. E/CN.4/1995/42.

[88] CEDAW, General Recommendation No. 19, GAOR, 47th Session, Supp. No 38, UN Doc. A/47/38 (1992); GA Res. 48/103 (20 December 1993).

unequal power relations between men and women" and labels that inequality a social mechanism for forcing women into a "subordinate position compared with men"[89]. These international instruments condemn violence against women and require states 'to refrain from engaging in violence against women and to exercise due diligence to prevent, investigate and in accordance with national legislation punish acts of violence against women whether those acts are perpetrated by the state or by private persons.'[90] No defence, including customary or religious practices, can justify violence against women.

These international instruments asserting State responsibility for failure to exercise due diligence in preventing and punishing violence against women are not incorporated into the GFA and are not binding under international law. The BiH Constitution is silent on this aspect of personal security. Criminal law and process are reserved to the Entities and no assurance exists to promote, much less guarantee, uniformity throughout the country. It must be recognised that violence constitutes both a direct denial of women's rights and an impediment to the enjoyment of other civil and political and economic and social rights, for example the right to free movement[91], the right to highest attainable standard of physical and mental health[92], and the right to recognition as a person before the law[93]. Special attention must be given by those working on reform of criminal codes to ensuring adequate response to violence against women[94]. However criminal law and process, while important, cannot change a culture of violence alone and thus must be combined with other legal, social, educational and medical measures to protect women against violence and to eliminate the root causes of such violence. For example, a failure to implement the indictments issued by the International Tribunal against Radovan Karadzic and Ratko Mladic will undermine assertions of accountability for crimes of violence, including those committed against women.

D. Reproductive Rights

Another area in which human rights law is silent is women's reproductive rights. In the former socialist States of Eastern Europe, the question of state (male) control over women's bodies has assumed prominence that is especially significant in the nationalist conflicts of the former Yugoslavia. A four-fold interlocking categorisation has been made of the relationship between women and nationalism, which attempts to harness women's

---

[89] *C.f.*, Beijing Platform for Action, *supra*, ¶ 112.
[90] Beijing Platform for Action, *supra*, ¶ 124.
[91] ICCPR, *supra*, Art. 12.
[92] ICESCR, *supra*, Art. 12 (1).
[93] ICCPR, *supra*, Art. 16.
[94] *See e.g.*, Council of Europe Action in Bosnia and Herzegovina, Priority Areas, October 1996, SG/Inf (96)20.

bodies in the interests of the nation: women as responsible for the repopu-
lation of the nation; women as the symbols for the identification and de-
pository of the national character and culture; women as participants in the
national/political discourse and practice; and women as active participants
in the national/military conflict[95]. The first becomes imperative where
populations have been reduced by conflict and where national identity
defines political ordering. Elsewhere in the former Yugoslavia, population
policy has been undertaken through legislation[96]. In BiH, the sensitivity of
reproductive rights is further enhanced by the use of rape as an instrument
of war and of ethnic cleansing. Similarly, the "woman-mother is also ideal
for homogenizing the otherwise differentiated national being and produc-
ing a feeling of national communality, or national antagonism against the
other side"[97]. Determining national identity discounts the incidence of
inter-marriage and the devastating personal consequences where peoples
are forced to deny kinship. "Mixed marriages symbolize the possibility of
mutual assimilation and integration between different nations, the possibility of transcending the borders of national collectivity with no taboos
attached"[98].

The discourse of human rights offers little to women faced with these
demands. The Women's Convention accords women:

> The same rights to decide freely and responsibly on the number and
> spacing of their children and to have access to the information, educa-
> tion and means to enable them to exercise their rights[99].

Similarly, access to health care services, including those relating to family
planning, is on the basis of equality. These provisions make evident the
limitations of the standard of equality. Women's biological reproductive
role is given no priority through the bestowal of different rights, for example a commitment to the right to choose whether to continue a pregnancy to
term. States shall ensure appropriate services "in connection with pregnancy, confinement and the post-natal period" but this does not clarify
whether these services include termination[100].

The Convention on the Rights of the Child, which is not equality based,
is similarly ambiguous on the subject of abortion. The European Convention justifies intrusion into private and family life where necessary "in the
interests of national security, public safety or the economic well-being of
the country, ... for the protection of health or morals ... ", a claw-back
provision that is broad enough to accommodate the arguments for popula-

---

[95] A. Milic, "Women and Nationalism in the Former Yugoslavia", *in* Funk and Mueller,
supra, at 109, 112.
[96] *Id.*
[97] *Id.*, at 115.
[98] *Id.*, at 116.
[99] Women's Convention, *supra*, Art. 16 (d).
[100] *Id.*, Art. 12 (2).

tion policy described above[101]. The European Commission declined to interpret respect for privacy as including abortion rights, and elsewhere in Eastern Europe abortion has become an intensely fought political issue[102]. Only in the Cairo Declaration (another non-binding instrument) are women's reproductive rights recognised, but, again, this instrument is not included within the GFA[103].

Reproductive rights have the potential to conflict with other rights, for example freedom of religion[104]. The former Yugoslavia was a secular state, but religion has a high profile in divisions between Entities to some extent identified in religious terms. None of the relevant religions are hospitable to the observance of women's rights, including reproductive rights[105]. Pressures from religious groups within the other States of the former Yugoslavia, from external allies, and from the national imperatives described above might combine in ways detrimental to recognition of women's reproductive rights. Most importantly, violence and coercive reproductive policies must be perceived through a gendered, not ethnic, lens.

V. Strategies and Priorities

The primacy accorded by the GFA to non-discrimination on the basis of national identity and the protection of minorities is logical given the historic context of BiH. The Special Rapporteur has reported that the elimination of discrimination in access to services and necessities will be a 'key test' in seeking lasting peace. The Office of the Ombudsperson (established by the GFA) is documenting and responding to allegations of discrimination based upon national identity, although she comments that the relevant authorities have been slow to respond. However this emphasis can disguise the pervasiveness of other forms of discrimination, especially the vulnerability of women to multiple discriminations based on ethnicity, religion and gender[106]. The Ombudsperson must be equally sensitive to gender discrimination and take similar care in responding to it. It may seem perverse to emphasise the rights of women where the overall human rights problems are so daunting, but the guarantee of women's rights must be recognised as integral to the overall national imperatives. Women are an essential human resource in the redevelopment programme and in the

---

[101] ECHR, *supra*, Art. 8 (2).

[102] Funk and Mueller, *supra*.

[103] United Nations International Conference on Population and Development, September 1994, Chapter VII.

[104] ICCPR, *supra*, Art. 18; ECHR, *supra*, Art. 9.

[105] The alliance between the Vatican and certain Islamic states at the Conference on Population and Development, highlights this point.

[106] Human Rights Abuses in the Former Yugoslavia, *supra*, ¶¶ 40-43.

search for peace. Their leadership, political, organisational and management skills should be harnessed in the identification of priorities and strategies for their achievement.

The work of the Human Rights Commission in BiH is supplemented by European and international agencies that offer a wide range of services, including legal counselling and expertise, training, awareness-raising activities, translation of documents, offering support to NGOs, political and financial assistance and secondment of experts. A gendered perspective must be included in the human rights activities of these bodies, covering both the short and longer terms. In the short-term women's immediate needs must be identified and resources directed towards ensuring their access to means for realising rights to property, compensation and assistance. Women's legal resources centres should be funded and given other resources. In the longer term, a national action plan of action co-ordinating policies with respect to women should be drawn up in co-operation with the federal government and those of the Entities. It should set out goals, strategies and realistic targets that include defining responsibilities, costs analysis, indicators of progress and monitoring mechanisms. The Women's Convention and Beijing Platform for Action provide a blueprint that can be adapted and followed.

Specific attention should be given to collecting gender aggregated data, scrutinising proposed legislation and administrative practices from a gendered perspective (especially those appertaining to property, family, criminal and citizenship matters), providing gender awareness training for members of the legislature, judiciary, civil services and law enforcement agencies at local and national levels, and increasing women's participation in working groups, decision and policy making bodies. Special attention must also be directed towards the role of the media and their presentations of women[107]. A broad understanding of women's human rights that includes, but goes beyond, non-discrimination must be incorporated into such training. The demise of the federal commission in the former Yugoslavia that monitored implementation of international standards of women's rights left women without any protective mechanism. One solution would be a Ministry for Women but failing that a special unit/section on women within the Human Rights Commission would be valuable.

While there is perhaps a danger of too many agencies operating in Bosnia and Herzegovina that duplicate and complicate each others' work, there is no international or regional organisation specifically directed towards women. This fact accentuates the importance of working with local women's groups. World War II saw the development of women's

---

[107] The Special Rapporteur emphasises the need to constrain the media from advocating religious and national hatred and discrimination while promoting freedom of expression. *Id.*, ¶¶ 44-5. The need for restraint must be extended to gender discrimination, including pornography that humiliates and degrades women.

groups in the territory of the former Yugoslavia, notably the Antifascist Women's Front, that did much to liberate women both from legal oppression and from sexist stereotyping[108]. After the war, the communist party co-opted women's emancipation, thereby inhibiting independent women's organisations. In the 1970s new groups began to challenge the state's monopoly over women's issues. More recently, women's groups in BiH have mushroomed and are gaining confidence and skills, assisted by international women's NGOs.

The work described above for the protection of women's rights in BiH must include at all times the voices and input of local women. Such groups should be assisted in familiarising BiH women with the concept of women's rights and the terms of the instruments in local languages. Further tasks include training in legal literacy, in recognising discrimination and rights abuses and in accessing effectively local, regional, and international machinery. This undertaking will not be easy in face of the obstacles described above, but it is essential that women in BiH be seen by all concerned as active agents for change and not just as passive victims of the conflict, objects of sexual abuse and mothers. In the words of Slavenka Drakulic:

> Women must begin to see themselves as political actors. They need to define emancipation in their own terms, defend their already existing rights, prevent the manipulation of women's bodies. Otherwise democracy will retain its male face, and men will not be the only ones to blame[109].

---

[108] S. Drakulic, "Women and the New Democracy in the Former Yugoslavia", *in* Funk and Mueller, *supra*, at 123.

[109] *Id.*, at 130.

10. The Post-Dayton Role of the International Criminal Tribunal for the Former Yugoslavia

The tragic events in the former Yugoslavia have provided an opportunity for the post-Cold War international community to experiment with new types of action in local crisis. From the perspective of someone from that region and directly affected by the events there, the present author views the exercise as a general failure. Action has been inefficient, inadequate, often confused, and hypocritical. International efforts did not succeed in bringing the war to an end for more than five years. Concrete results finally were realized only after the General Framework Agreement for Peace in Bosnia and Herzegovina, which brought about the end of hostilities and provided some grounds for hope that the rest of disputed issues may be solved in a peaceful manner[1]. Even the success of that document comes more as a consequence of the authority of the United States than of the willingness of its signatories to honor their obligations arising from one of many agreements.

Within the scope of general efforts to re-establish peace in the region, the Security Council has created an international criminal tribunal to prosecute individuals who have committed war crimes[2] and crimes against humanity in the region of the former Yugoslavia. Although the Security Council's efforts affecting the region have been diverse, and innovative compared to its previous practice (the creation of security zones, for example), the establishment of an international criminal tribunal remains one of the most significant. Due to space limitations, in this chapter the present author attempts discuss only some of the issues relevant to the Tribunal's work in general and especially to its impact in the Post-Dayton era.

---

[1] General Framework Agreement for Peace in Bosnia and Herzegovina, *initialed* Dayton, Ohio, 21 November 1995, *signed* Paris, 14 December 1995, 35 ILM 75 (1996) [hereinafter "GFA"].

[2] This popular expression will be used to describe crimes covered by Articles 2 and 3 of the Tribunal's Statute. *See* Statute of the International Tribunal for the Prosecution of Persons Responsible for Serious Violations of International Humanitarian Law Committed in the Territory of the Former Yugoslavia since 1991, UN Docs. S/25704 (1993), at 36, and S/25704/Add.1 (1993) [hereinafter "Statute"].

M. O'Flaherty and G. Gisvold (eds.), Post-War Protection of Human Rights in Bosnia and Herzegovina, 195–214.
© 1998 *Kluwer Law International. Printed in Great Britain.*

I. Legal Basis for the Creation of the Tribunal

On 25 May 1993 the UN Security Council, acting on a Secretary General's report[3], unanimously adopted Resolution 827(1993), which established the Tribunal "for the sole purpose of prosecuting persons responsible for serious violations of international humanitarian law committed in the territory of the former Yugoslavia between 1 January 1991 and a date to be determined by the Security Council upon the restoration of peace." The Council creates the Tribunal

> Determined to put an end to such crimes and to take effective measures to bring to justice the persons who are responsible for them,

> Convinced that in the particular circumstances of the former Yugoslavia the establishment as an ad hoc measure by the Council of an international tribunal and the prosecution of persons responsible for serious violations of international humanitarian law would enable this aim to be achieved and would contribute to the restoration and maintenance of peace, and

> Believing that the establishment of an international tribunal and the prosecution of persons responsible for the above-mentioned violations of international humanitarian law will contribute to ensuring that such violations are halted and effectively redressed[4].

At the same time, it adopted the Statute of the Tribunal (annexed to the report). The creation of the Tribunal was the final step in a process that had begun with previous Security Council resolutions, including 764(1992), 771(1992), 780(1992), 780(1992) and 808(1993). These resolutions represent the Security Council's step-by-step approach, which as one author describes it, can be subdivided into four major steps in succession: condemnation, publication, investigation and punishment[5]．

The creation of the Tribunal is an important step from a international humanitarian legal perspective. It represents the reaffirmation of the obligations of that body of law, and specifically of those contained in the 1949 Geneva Conventions. The Tribunal is innovative inasmuch as it defines violations of humanitarian law as threats to international peace and creates an *ad hoc* body specifically to address them. Further, the Security Council distanced itself from existing fact-finding procedures. Rather than rely on those procedures established pursuant to Article 90 of Additional Protocol

---

[3] Report of the Secretary General on the Establishment of a International Criminal Tribunal for the Former Yugoslavia, UN Doc. S/25704, 3 May 1993 [hereinafter "Secretary General's report"].

[4] Security Council Resolution 827(1993), S/RES/827.

[5] James C. O'Brien, "The International Tribunal for Violations of International Humanitarian Law in the Former Yugoslavia", 87 Am. J. Intl.. L. 640 (1993).

I, it chose instead to create an entirely new international body. Lastly, the Tribunal created a new obligation, based on Chapter VII of the UN Charter, to cease the violations of international humanitarian law.

Throughout the process leading to the creation of the Tribunal, the Security Council reminded parties to the conflict in the former Yugoslavia of their obligations under international humanitarian law "in particular the Geneva Conventions of 12 August 1949"[6]. A Presidential Statement of the Council issued on 4 August 1992 noted "the imprisonment and abuse of civilians in camps, provisions and detention centers" and reaffirmed that "persons who commit or order the commission of grave breached of the Conventions are individually responsible in respect of such breaches", a clear reference to the Geneva Conventions of 1949[7]. The Security Council embraced humanitarian law, making it part of its jurisprudence of binding resolutions. In so doing, it not only reaffirmed the obligations inhering to humanitarian law, but also brought it within its own competence. For the first time in the context of Chapter VII of the UN Charter, the Security Council, in resolutions 770(1992) and 771(1992), demanded that "all parties and others concerned ... immediately cease and desist from all breaches of international humanitarian law ..."[8].

Although in the course the process resulting in the Tribunal, the Security Council reaffirmed the existing obligations of international humanitarian law, its efforts appear not to be limited to the mere confirmation of existing law. When it created an obligation pursuant to Chapter VII to respect the 1949 Geneva Conventions, it did not reference the nature of the conflict. Some provisions of the 1949 Geneva Conventions are inapplicable to, for example, an internal conflict[9]. Clearly, the Security Council did not foresee limiting its involvement in the former Yugoslavia to the application of existing mechanisms of international humanitarian law, but sought to use the existing law as a basis for its innovative action. The Security Council was establishing a new role for itself with respect to international humanitarian law, which would include the reallocation of resources. The Security Council did not make use of the existing fact-finding commission pursuant to Article 90 of the Protocol I, but created the Tribunal instead. The existing commission was not completely abandoned, however, as some of its members were appointed to the new commission. The Security Council

---

[6] Security Council Resolution 764, UN Doc. S/RES/764 (1992).

[7] Statement of the Security Council President, UN Doc. S/24378 (4 August 1992). *See also* Security Council Resolutions 771 and 780, UN Docs. S/RES/771 and S/RES/780 (1992).

[8] Security Council Resolution 771, UN Doc. S/RES/771 (1992), ¶ 3.

[9] The Secretary General's report notes that "since 1991" should "mean anytime on or after 1 January 1991. This is a neutral date which is not tied to any specific event and is clearly intended to convey the notion that no judgement as to the international or internal character of the conflict is being exercised." Secretary General's report, *supra*, ¶ 62.

even attempted to bring the International Committee of the Red Cross within the ambit of this new role[10].

In the post Cold War period, the Security Council has been generally keen to enlarge its practice and the media attention on the atrocities in the former Yugoslavia provided an adequate opportunity for innovative action. One can argue also that a motivating factor behind this need to evolve was that the Council was unable to fulfill its primary task: to re-establish peace and security in the region[11]. Regardless, the Security Council took an unprecedented step in the history of the United Nations when it created under Chapter VII a judicial organ to deal with international crimes. To justify this action, the Security Council had to determine that the situation in former Yugoslavia, or more specifically the violations of international humanitarian law occurring there, constituted "a threat to international peace and security"[12].

The Security Council's creation of the Tribunal was controversial[13]. Nevertheless, it was fully justified. In any analysis of the Tribunal's creation, two factors must be borne in mind. First, the Tribunal is an *ad hoc* body, created to deal with a very specific situation and limited both in time and territory[14]. The Security Council's concern obviously centered more on the political need to "do something" effective about the situation in the former Yugoslavia, especially Bosnia and Herzegovina, than on the development of international humanitarian law. The Tribunal was simply one step, albeit an important one, in the broader peace process[15]. Second,

---

[10] The Security Council impose obligations on some parties involving reporting to the ICRC. *See* Security Council Resolutions 770, UN Doc. S/RES/770 (1992) and 771, UN Doc. S/RES/771 (1992).

[11] "The Yugoslavia War Crimes Tribunal exists largely because of the rest of the world's sense of guilt." David A. Martin, "Reluctance to Prosecute War Crimes: Of Causes and Cures", 34 Va. J. Intl. L. 265 (1994).

[12] Security Council Resolution 827, UN Doc. S/RES/827 (1993).

[13] *See* 19 May 1993 Letter from the Chargé d'affaires(a.i.) of the Permanent Mission of Yugoslavia to the United Nations Secretary General, UN Doc. A/48/170, S/25801, 21 May 1993.

[14] The comments of some nations' representatives to the Security Council are illustrative: "My delegation recognizes that the Tribunal is intended to deal with a specific and limited crisis that the Council has been addressing under Chapter VII of the Charter." UN Doc. S/PV.3217, 25 May 1993, at 7 (comments of Mr. Arria, Representative of Venezuela); "The establishment of the Tribunal had been an exceptional step to deal with exceptional circumstances" *Id.,* at 18 (Sir Hunnay, Representative of the United Kingdom); "[T]he Chinese delegation emphasizes that the International Tribunal established in the current manner can only be an ad hoc arrangement suited only to the special circumstances of the former Yugoslavia and shall not constitute any precedent." *Id.,* at 33-34 (Mr. Zhaoxing, Representative of China).

[15] "My country hopes that this message will be understood by all and that it will help silence the guns on the territory of the former Yugoslavia." *Id.,* at 12 (Mr. Mérimée, Representative of France); "We are deeply convinced that it is impossible to envisage a lasting settlement of the conflict in the former Yugoslavia, including in the Republic of Bosnia and Herzegovina, without the prosecutions of those who massacre and burn children ...". *Id.,* at

"something" urgently needed to be done to address that situation, however that action might be limited. All other means aimed at convincing the parties to the conflict to stop massive violations of humanitarian law had failed[16]. It is likely that the Security Council's decision to utilitise its authority pursuant to Chapter VII was in part an attempt to avoid the application of the principle of non-interference in the internal affairs of the Member States embodied in Article 2(7) of the UN Charter. The immediate need prompted the Security Council not to broach complicated questions regarding the legitimacy and legality of its specific powers[17] and Chapter VII was the only means of imposing its will on all the relevant *de jure* and *de facto* authorities in the former Yugoslavia sufficiently quickly[18].

Not surprisingly, the legality of the Tribunal's creation became grounds for objections to its competence. At the first opportunity, defense lawyers for Mr. Dusko Tadic, the first individual to stand before the Tribunal, filed a motion questioning the legality of the Tribunal's creation. This motion provided the Tribunal an opportunity to analyse and pronounce upon its own existence. The Trial Chamber which considered the issue decided the Tribunal was not competent to elaborate on the legality of the Security Council's action[19]. In an important decision, the Appeals Chamber took a

---

21 (Mr. Erdös, Representative of Hungary); "[T]he establishment of the Tribunal and the prosecution of persons suspected of crimes against international humanitarian law is closely related to the wider efforts to restore peace and security to the former Yugoslavia ... The Co-Chairmen set it explicitly within the peace making process. Implementation of that process and the work of the Tribunal must mutually reinforce one another." *Id.,* at 22 (Mr. O'Brien, Representative of New Zealand); "The establishment of the International Tribunal, apart from the great juridical meaning of this step, is also an extremely important political act taken by the international community which at the same time fulfills a preventive function and also promotes the restoration of peace in the region." *Id.,* p. 46 (Mr. Vorontsov, Representative of the Russian Federation).

[16] One of the explanations for the Security Council's response "lies in the exhaustion of alternative remedies." O'Brien, *International Tribunal, supra,* at 640.

[17] *See* UN Doc. S/PV.3217, 25 May 1993, at 39-40 ("Finally, and most importantly, the goal of restoring peace in the territory of the former Yugoslavia requires prompt action ...") (Mr. Yanez-Barneuvo, Representative of Spain).

[18] Indeed, there was not even time for public or private discussion of the merits of the Tribunal. The Security Council's action was too fast for some Member States: "Given the legal difficulties involved, which in the normal course of events would have required much more extensive study and deliberation and could have prevented us from supporting the initiative ... [adoption of the resolution creating the Tribunal] should not be construed as an overall endorsement of legal formulas involved in the foundation or in the Statute of the International Tribunal. We would certainly have preferred that an initiative bearing such far-reaching political and legal implications had received a much deeper examination, in a context that allowed a broader participation by all State Member of the United Nations." UN Doc. S/PV.3217, *supra,* at 36 (Mr. Mota Sardenberg, Representative of Brazil).

[19] *See* Decision on the Defence Motion on Jurisdiction, Case No. IT-94-1-T, Trial Chamber of the International Tribunal, ¶¶ 4, 8, and 33 (10 August 1995).

different stand[20]. After hearing argument from all sides[21], the Appeals Chamber determined that, as a result of its "inherent jurisdiction", the Tribunal has "*compétence de la compétence*" to decide all questions relating to its jurisdiction, including those pertaining to the legality of its own creation[22].

Though the basis for the ruling is flawed, its result is sound. The Secretary General's report clearly stated that the competence of the Tribunal derived from the mandate set forth in a Security Council resolution[23]. The Tribunal is competent to decide upon the scope of its jurisdiction through the interpretation of its own Statute, its rules, even the text of Security Council resolutions relevant to its work. But any consideration of the legality of its creation was inappropriate. Had the Tribunal ruled its creation unlawful, it would have contravened the Security Council's resolutions and effectively dismantled itself, which only the Security Council had the authority to do. Judge Li's separate opinion that the Tribunal should have declared itself incompetent to rule on the issue of its own existence represents the more considered approach.

Similarly, another challenge to the Tribunal resulting from the method of its creation involved the question whether the Security Council could create an entirely independent judicial body. Here, the issue for the Tribunal should not be the independence of its existence, but of its ability to carry out its duties. The Secretary General's report makes it clear that

> the Security Council would be establishing as an enforcement measure under Chapter VII, a subsidiary organ within the terms of Article 29 of the Charter, but one of a judicial nature. This organ would, of course, have to perform its functions independently of political considerations; it would not be subject to the authority or control of the Security Council *with regard to the performance of its judicial functions.* As an enforcement measure under Chapter VII, however, *the life span of the international tribunal would be linked to the restoration and maintenance*

---

[20] *See* Decision on the Defence Motion for Interlocutory Appeal on Jurisdiction, Case No. IT-94-1-AR72, Appeals Chamber of the International Tribunal (2 October 1995) [hereinafter "Appeals Chamber Decision"]. The Appeals Chamber consisted of five judges: Cassese, Li, Dechênes, Abi-Saab and Sidhwa. The decision on two points were taken by unanimous vote and on two other by majority vote, with separate opinions of Judges Li and Sidhwa. Judges Abi-Saab and Dechênes filed also separate opinions.

[21] Indeed, the US, which was substantially involved in the creation of the Tribunal, filed an *amicus curiae* brief contending that the Tribunal did not have the authority to review the validity of Security Council decisions. On the other side of the issue, the NGO Juristes Sans Frontières submitted a brief arguing that the Tribunal has "la compétence de la compétence" to rule upon the lawfulness of its creation.

[22] The Appeals Chamber "finds that the International Tribunal has jurisdiction to examine the plea against its jurisdiction based on the invalidity of its establishment by the Security Council". Appeals Chamber Decision, *supra*, ¶ 22. *See also Id.* ¶¶ 14 – 21.

[23] *See* Secretary General's report, *supra*, ¶ 31.

*of international peace and security in the territory of the former Yugo-
slavia, and Security Council decisions related thereto*[24].

The report recommended that the Tribunal be able to "perform its functions independently of political considerations [and not] be subject to the
authority or control of the Security Council with regard to the performance
of its judicial functions". It was for the Security Council to set limits on the
duration of the Tribunal's existence. Resolution 827(1993) clearly sets
forth that the Tribunal may consider crimes committed between 1 January
1991 and "a date to be determined by the Security Council upon the restoration of peace". The Security Council's linking the Tribunal's life span to
the restoration of peace and security in the former Yugoslavia was proper
and has no bearing on the Tribunals consideration of those crimes.

The fact that the Tribunal is subsidiary to the Security Council does not
obviate its ability to act independently. The Security Council's consideration of Tribunal action is and should be limited. For example, when the
Tribunal requested amendment of its Statute to make more judges available[25], the Security Council refused[26]. Instead of acting in a global supervisory fashion, the Security Council decided to review problems on case-by-
case basis so as not to jeopardize the Tribunal's judicial independence.
Indeed, this dependent relationship is a direct result of the very structure of
the international community. In fact, any comparison between national
criminal courts and the Tribunal is inappropriate given the Tribunal's
specific powers and role. While national courts of law form part of a
complete global system of judicial protection including institutions charged
with implementing judicial decisions, the Tribunal is outside of the prevailing system of international public law. It depends on the States and
especially on the Security Council to ensure cooperation with its decisions
and requests. As Judge Cassese has remarked, "Our Tribunal is like a giant
who has no arms and no legs. To walk and work, he needs artificial limbs.
These artificial limbs are the State authorities, without their help the Tribunal cannot operate"[27].

---

[24] Security General's Report, *supra*, ¶ 28 (emphasis added).
[25] *See* 13 February 1996 letter from the Presidents of the International Criminal Tribunals
for the former Yugoslavia and Rwanda to the President of the Security Council, UN Doc.
S/1996/475, 27 June 1996.
[26] *See* 27 June 1996 letter from the President of the Security Council to the Presidents of
the International Criminal Tribunals for the former Yugoslavia and Rwanda, UN Doc.
S/1996/476, 27 June 1996.
[27] Judge Cassese, in a speech to the UN General Assembly, 7 November 1995.

II. Respect for the Tribunal

The Tribunal's jurisdiction includes not only violations of humanitarian law, but also arguably encompasses the protection of the fundamental values of civilized mankind. Despite the international community's express commitment not to allow repetition of the horrors of the Second World War, the parties to the war in the former Yugoslavia attempted to establish ethnically pure states. The Tribunal is the international community's answer to that attempt. Thus, respect for the Tribunal should derive from respect for the moral obligation to basic human values. If the Tribunal is truly to act "in the name of humanity," it should benefit from the support, political and otherwise, of all states. The choice is one between defence of basic notions of humanity or complicity in their violation[28].

Legally, the Tribunal's authority is grounded primarily in Chapter VII of the UN Charter. Resolution 827 establishes a general obligation, under Chapter VII, for all States to "cooperate fully with the International Tribunal and its organs", which would include the Security Council's specific requests regarding the work of the Tribunal. The Secretary General explains in his report:

> the establishment of the International Tribunal on the basis of a Chapter VII decision creates a binding obligation on all States to take whatever steps are required to implement the decision. In practical terms, this means that all States would be under an obligation to cooperate with the International Tribunal and to assist it in all stages of the proceedings to ensure compliance with requests for assistance in the gathering of evidence, hearing of witnesses, suspects and experts, identification and location of persons and the service of documents. Effect shall also be given to orders issued by the Trial Chambers, such as warrants of arrest, search warrants, warrants for surrender or transfer of persons, and any other orders necessary for the conduct of the trial.

> In this connection, an order by a Trial Chamber for the surrender or transfer of persons to the custody of the International Tribunal shall be considered to be the application of an enforcement measure under Chapter VII of the Charter of the United Nations[29].

The Tribunal Statute amplifies this obligation, noting that

> States shall comply without undue delay with any request for assistance or an order issued by a Trial Chamber, including, but not limited to: (a) the identification and location of persons; (b) the taking of testimony and the production of evidence; (c) the service of documents; (d) the ar-

---

[28] "Member States must now back the Tribunal that they have launched, both politically and financially." Ralph Zacklin, "Bosnia and Beyond", 34 Va. J. Intl. L. 281 (1994).

[29] Secretary General's Report, *supra*, ¶ 125.

rest or detention of persons; (e) the surrender or the transfer of the accused to the International Tribunal[30].

The Tribunal's Rules of Procedure and Evidence also clarify the obligations of States with respect to some aspects of the Tribunal's work. These obligations include, *inter alia*, the transmittal of all relevant information relative to investigations or criminal proceedings instituted in the national courts, upon request of the Prosecutor (Rule 8), the compliance with a request for deferral (Rules 10 and 11), the obligation not to institute any procedure at the national level (after the Tribunal) which would violate the principle *non-bis-in-idem* (Rule 13), the prompt action on the execution of a warrant or arrest including an information on the impossibility of its execution (Rules 56 and 59), the detention of the accused, notification of the fact to the Registrar (Rule 57), the obligation to permit the supervision of the Tribunal or a body designated by it to imprisonment (Rule 104), the notification of the State in which a convicted person is imprisoned about the eligibility for pardon or commutation of sentence (Rule 123)[31].

Resolution 827 also bases its requirement that "all States shall take any measures necessary under their domestic law to implement the provisions of the present resolution and the Statute, including the obligation of States to comply with requests for assistance or orders issued by a Trial Chamber under Article 29 of the Statute" on Chapter VII. However, the Rules of Procedure and Evidence state that "[t]he obligations laid down in Article 29 of the Statute shall prevail over any legal impediment to surrender or transfer of the accused to the Tribunal which may exist under the national law or extradition treaties of the State concerned"[32]. This provision may appear to contradict Article 29 of the Statute inasmuch as the Resolution requests States to adapt their national legislation to meet the requests of the Tribunal, the Rules indicate that even a failure to change legislation cannot create an excuse for non-compliance with the Tribunal's requests. Some States have changed their legal systems, and it seems that the Tribunal itself has accepted such a practice[33]. Although a change of legislation is a good evidence of the will of a State to cooperate with the Tribunal, the option provided by the Rules of Procedure is preferable. It is in conformity with increasing importance of norms in international law having direct effect, and its application in the field of war crimes punishment would be an important precedent in international law.

---

[30] Statute, *supra*, Art. 29.

[31] Rules of Procedure and Evidence for the International Tribunal for the Former Yugoslavia, UN Doc. IT/32/rev.7 (1996), *entered into force* 14 March 1994, *amended* 8 January 1996, at Rules 8, 10, 11, 13, 56, 59, 104,123 [hereinafter "Rules of Procedure and Evidence"].

[32] Rules of Procedure and Evidence, *supra*, at Rule 58.

[33] For example, Croatia has changed its domestic legislation in this sense, and the Tribunal has welcomed that step. *See* Press Release CC/PIO/067-E of 26 April 1996.

It is obvious that the Security Council's decision to include a cooperation requirement was directed primarily, though not exclusively, at the republics of the former Yugoslavia which have since the war become independent states[34]. Should one of these States, whose cooperation is crucial to the Tribunal's potential success, fail to comply with a Tribunal request, the Tribunal President would refer the matter to the Security Council for review[35]. Such noncompliance would violate a State's obligations under Chapter VII and allow the Security Council to take measures pursuant to Chapters VI and VII of the UN Charter. The GFA further strengthened the requirement of these particular States to cooperate with the Tribunal. It requires that "[t]he Parties shall cooperate fully with all entities involved in implementation of this peace settlement [including those] authorized by the United Nations Security Council, pursuant to the obligation of all Parties to cooperate in the investigation and prosecution of war crimes and other violations of international humanitarian law"[36].

The GFA also requires cooperation with the Tribunal[37]. Thus, this general obligation (pursuant to Security Council Resolution 827) has also become a treaty obligation for three States in the region. Croatia, Bosnia-Herzegovina and the rump Yugoslavia (Serbia and Montenegro) have thereby created a new contractual obligation to respect an international treaty according to the principle *pact sunt servanda*. They, as well as Slovenia and Macedonia, the two states from the territory of the former Yugoslavia with the jurisdiction of the Tribunal but not parties to the GFA, are legally bound by the Security Council's resolutions. While the Security Council has endorsed the GFA[38], the original obligation related to Security Council's decision on the cooperation with the Tribunal is undiminished[39]. In October 1996, the Security Council "reiterate[d] that all States and concerned parties have an obligation, in accordance with resolution 827 (1993) of 25 May 1993, other relevant resolutions, and the Peace Agreement, to cooperate fully with the International Tribunal and to comply without exception with requests for assistance or orders issued by a trial

---

[34] *See* Alain Pellet, "Le Tribunal criminel international pour l'ex-Yougoslavie: Poudre aux yeux ou avancée decisive?", 98 RGDIP 7, 22 (1994).

[35] A Trial Chamber may certify the non-cooperation of a State and, "[a]fter consulting the Presiding Judges of the Chambers, the President shall notify the Security Council thereof in such manner as he thinks fit." Rules of Procedure and Evidence, *supra*.

[36] GFA, *supra*, Art. IX.

[37] GFA, *supra* , Art. IX.

[38] The Security Council welcomed the GFA "and call[ed] upon the parties to fulfill in good faith the commitments entered into in that Agreement." Security Council Resolution 1031, UN Doc. S/RES/1031, (1995), ¶ 1.

[39] At the same time, the Security Council established a new obligation under Chapter VII when it called upon all States "to allow the establishment of offices of the Tribunal." *Id.*, ¶ 4.

chamber"[40]. States are "obliged to co-operate in accordance both with the binding decisions of the Security Council and [the GFA] signed in Paris on 14 December 1995 and reaffirmed in Rome on 18 February 1996"[41].

Practically, this could mean that if the GFA obligation is violated by one party, the other party(ies) could apply the principle of reciprocity and not comply with the GFA's provisions in accordance with Article 60 of the 1969 Vienna Convention on the Law of Treaties. But, with respect to the specific obligation related to the Tribunal, they would still be required to comply with the Security Council's decisions and, on that authority, with requests from the Tribunal and this obligation could be interpreted in accordance with Article 43 of the 1969 Vienna Convention. For this reason, the sole reference to the GFA with respect to the obligations related to the Tribunal is misleading. In any case, the Security Council has confirmed this obligation, stating that "compliance with the requests and orders of the International Tribunal for the former Yugoslavia constitutes an essential aspect of implementing the Peace Agreement"[42].

However, it has weakened this obligation by not taking serious action in light of repeated reports from the Tribunal that two States in the region do not cooperate in a satisfactory manner[43]. On lifting sanctions against Federal Republic of Yugoslavia[44], the Council made no reference to the obligation regarding the Tribunal, although it stated that the suspension of the trade embargo and other measures against FRY and "the Bosnian Serb authorities"[45] shall terminate automatically upon a report that those two entities "are failing significantly to meet their obligations under the Peace Agreement"[46]. In October 1996, the Council ended sanctions against the

---

[40] *See* Statements of the President of the Security Council, UN Docs. S/PRST/1996/34, 8 August 1996, and S/PRST/1996/23, 8 May 1996.

[41] Tribunal Press Release CC/PIO/038-E, 26 February 1996.

[42] Security Council Resolution 1022, UN Doc. S/RES/1022 (1995). *See also* Statement of the President of the Security Council, UN Doc. S/PRST/1996/23, 8 May 1996. John Shattuck, of the U.S. State Department, has noted the importance of that obligation and explained that "after all, one of the major reasons we are in Bosnia is to stop perhaps the worst crimes against humanity that have occurred in Europe since the Second World War and to hold accountable those who are responsible for those crimes." Briefing on War Crimes in Bosnia: U.S. Strongly Supports War Crimes Tribunal, 14 February 1996.

[43] The President of the Tribunal has reported the noncompliance of the Federal Republic of Yugoslavia, Croatia and Bosnia and Herzegovina. It is interesting to note that he chose to report the noncompliance of the entities of the Bosnian state, rather than the state itself. Though the Bosnian central authorities have cooperated with the Tribunal, those controlling the two entities have not and the President apparently wished to emphasize the distinction.

[44] Hereinafter FRY.

[45] The GFA has in fact recognized the existence of the "Republika Srpska". In the Statements of the President of the Council of 9 August and 10 October 1996, the Council clearly refers to "Republika Srpska", by hoping that the recent visit by the delegation from Republika Srpska to the Tribunal "marks a turning point in relations between Republika Srpska and the International Tribunal ... "(Statement of 10 October 1996).

[46] Security Council Resolution 1022 (1995), ¶ 3.

FRY notwithstanding the fact that the cooperation of this country with the Tribunal was, by all evidence, poor[47]. Reference to the Tribunal is made only in the preamble of the Resolution, while the dispositive contains only general calls "upon all parties to comply strictly with all their commitments under the Peace Agreement", which, as noted above, is not the same as the obligation of all States based on Chapter VII. Although the Council "[f]urther decides to consider the imposition of measures if any party fails significantly to meet specific obligations under the Peace Agreement", the respect for the obligation regarding the Tribunal has already been significantly weakened[48].

For the time being, even after repeated reports of the President of the Tribunal that two States in the region do not cooperate in a satisfactory manner[49], the Security Council does not seem to be ready to take any serious actions. Rather than adopt formal resolutions, the Security Council decided to address the issue only in the form of President's statements[50]. The only indication the Council has given that it might opt for more serious measures came in its statement of 8 August 1996, wherein it "condemn[ed] any attempt to challenge the authority of the International Tribunal" and stressed that it is "ready to consider the application of economic enforcement measures to ensure compliance by all parties with their obligations under the Peace Agreement"[51].

While the obligations imposed on the authorities in the region by the GFA to respect the Tribunal seems very clear, it is important to note that this agreement reduced the sovereign power of all the authorities within Bosnia and Herzegovina. In many respects, the exercise of their constitutional authority has been transferred to the representatives of the international community[52]. The territory has become a *de facto* military and political protectorate of the international community; thus, the responsibility to respect obligations created by the Security Council cannot lie only

---

[47] Security Council Resolution 1074 (1996).

[48] *Id.*

[49] *See*, for example, letters of the President of the Tribunal to the Security Council of 24 April 1996, 22 May 1996 and 11 July 1996, reporting on non-compliance of FRY and of 16 September 1996 reporting non-compliance of Croatia. It is interesting to note that, in the some occasions, the President of the Tribunal reported non-compliance of "Republika Srpska" and "The Federation". As the State Bosnia and Herzegovina consists of those two entities, it would imply non-compliance of Bosnia and Herzegovina, although the central authorities in Sarajevo have cooperated fully with the Tribunal.

[50] *See, e.g.,* Statements of the President of the Security Council, UN Docs. S/PRST/1996/23, 8 May 1996; S/PRST/1996/34, 8 August 1996; and S/PRST/1996/39, 20 September 1996.

[51] At the meeting in Florence, Tribunal President Judge Cassese proposed considering selected economic sanctions and a sports boycott against the States that do not execute arrest warrants of the Tribunal. The Security Council had no reaction. *See* Press Release CC/PIO/088-E, 13 June 1996.

[52] *See* GFA, *supra*, Annex 4.

with the "entities", but also with the international representatives and organizations involved with the enforcement of the GFA. With reference to the obligation to cooperate with the Tribunal, the responsibility for which in theory lies primarily with the local authorities, it would be illusory to expect them to fulfill an obligation that runs contrary to their respective policies during the war[53]. Even if these authorities attempted to fulfill these obligations, they may lack the ability to do so due to their limited control of their territory[54]. For this reason, the international community cannot simply continue to remind the parties of their obligations, but must take part of the responsibility and cooperate with the Tribunal directly.

There are a number of means for the international community to support the Tribunal directly. First, the Tribunal should receive the full support of the entire UN system. Differences in mandate should not deter such cooperation; respect for the Tribunal should be larger than any specific mandate. Thus, statements such as the following cannot contribute to the credibility of the Tribunal:

> The mandate of the International Criminal Tribunal is quite different from the UNPROFOR mandate, so the decisions are within the competence and concern of Tribunal while we have to continue our mission ... . Thus, [indictments against Kordic and Blaskic should] not affect their cooperation with the UN officials [in Bosnia and Herzegovina] as it is vital for the peace keeping forces mission. We do not hold that our co-operation with Blaskic, Kordic and others charged with war crimes could threaten the credibility of the Hague Tribunal[55].

Respect for the Tribunal should be much larger than a specific mandate. Second, the legally binding character of decisions taken by the Security Council is the same for all States, whether acting individually or as part of an intergovernmental body or multi-national effort. Therefore, a legal obligation to impliment Security Council resolutions exists upon all international bodies in a position to do so[56]. For example, OSCE member states

---

[53] Those authorities have applied a policy of so-called "ethnic cleansing." *See* Drazen Petrovic, "Ethnic Cleansing – An Attempt at Methodology", 5 EJIL 342, 342-359 (1994) and "Beyond Xenophobia: Ethnic Cleansing", *in* Bernd Baumgartl and Adrian Favell (eds.), *New Xenophobia in Europe*, (1995), at 46-54.

[54] Judge Cassese has noted that "the government authorities in Sarajevo do not yet have the means to impose their will in the areas under the control of Bosnian Croats or Bosnian Serbs" and that "according to reliable reports, Croatian authorities exercise control on at least part of [of the Federation]." "Dayton Four Months On: The Parties' Co-operation with the International Criminal Tribunal for the Former Yugoslavia," Statement of Tribunal President Cassese to the Parliamentary Assembly of the Council of Europe, 25 April 1996.

[55] A. Ivanko, UNPROFOR spokesman in Sarajevo, 14 November 1995 (the day following the indictments).

[56] The Security Council President has "call[ed] upon all States *and others concerned* to comply fully with their obligations with respect to cooperation with the Tribunal, and in particular their obligation to execute arrest warrants transmitted to them by the Tribunal".

should have directed their representatives to inform IFOR where Mr. Radovan Karadzic intended to vote and not treat that information as confidential[57]. Mr. Karadzic's rights under the International Covenant on Civil and Political Rights have already been seriously restricted by the GFA and OSCE's position reflects more an unwillingness to contribute to the arrest of a person indicted by the Tribunal than a desire to protect Mr. Karadzic's rights.

Securing the cooperation of IFOR, the international actor most able to help the Tribunal, is more complicated. According to IFOR officials, the mandate of IFOR includes assistance to the Tribunal on a limited basis inasmuch as it

> [a]uthorizes the Member States acting through or in cooperation with the organization referred to in Annex 1-A of the Peace Agreement to establish a multinational implementation force (IFOR) under unified command and control in order to fulfil the role specified in Annex 1-A and Annex 2 of the Peace Agreement[58].

In addition, IFOR has an enforcement role, which

> [a]uthorizes the Member States acting under paragraph 14 above *to take all necessary measures* to effect the implementation of and to ensure compliance with Annex 1-A of the Peace Agreement, stresses that the parties shall be held equally responsible for compliance with that Annex, and shall be equally subject to such enforcement action by IFOR as may be necessary to ensure implementation of that Annex and the protection of IFOR, and takes note that the parties have consented to IFOR's taking such measures[59];

From this, it is clear that the Security Council created IFOR to ensure compliance with Annex 1-A of the GFA, which specifies

> The Parties shall cooperate fully with all entities involved in implementation of this peace settlement, as described in the General Framework Agreement, or which are otherwise authorized by the United Nations Security Council, including the International Tribunal for the Former Yugoslavia[60].

Statement of the Security Council President, UN Doc. S/PRST/1996/23, 8 May 1996 (emphasis added). Judge Cassese has also noted his understanding that Security Council Resolution 827 created an obligation for all States "and other international legal subjects." "Dayton Four Months On," Statement of Judge Cassese to the Parliamentary Assembly of the Council of Europe, 25 April 1996.

[57] Press Briefing by Mr. Thomas Leary, deputy spokesperson, OSCE, held 13 September 1996 (available at http://www.nato.int/ifor/ afsouth/t960913a.htm).

[58] *See* Memorandum of Understanding between NATO and the Tribunal, 9 May 1996.

[59] *Id.*, ¶ 15.

[60] GFA, *supra*, Annex 1-A, Art. X.

Regarding this obligation and with specific reference to the Tribunal, the Security Council

> [r]ecognizes that the parties shall cooperate fully with all entities involved in implementation of the peace settlement, as described in the Peace Agreement, or which are otherwise authorized by the Security Council, including the International Tribunal for the Former Yugoslavia, and that the parties have in particular authorized the multinational force referred to in paragraph 14 below to take such actions as required, including the use of necessary force, to ensure compliance with Annex 1-A of the Peace Agreement[61];

IFOR has rendered assistance to the Tribunal: for example, it has assisted with the transfer of persons from Sarajevo to the Hague[62]. But, it maintains that, with respect to the arrest of the indicted persons – which is IFOR's potentially most important contribution to the Tribunal's work – that it "will detain and transfer to [the Tribunal] persons indicted for war crimes ... when it comes into contact with such persons in carrying out [its] duties"[63]. The Tribunal has expressed its frustration with this position on several occasions[64]. Its concern is whether IFOR's specific mandate should not relieve (wholly or on a limited basis) it of the obligation to cooperate with the Tribunal; the obligation to cooperate with the Tribunal, after all, has been imposed on those States participating in IFOR. In addition, the obligation may independently apply to IFOR itself. Though the IFOR's mandate is based on the GFA, the force itself was established by the Security Council[65]. While it did not *expressly* authorize IFOR to arrest indicted persons, it did not prevent it either. IFOR's restriction of its own mandate represents its failure to ensure compliance with Annex 1-A of the GFA, which obliges cooperation with the Tribunal, and thus, a violation of its obligation pursuant to Resolution 1031. It seems that the IFOR is deliberately avoiding assisting the Tribunal in that respect[66].

---

[61]   Security Council Resolution 1931(1995), ¶ 5.

[62]   *See* UN Doc. S/1996/131, February 1996. NATO provided ground security and transportation for the transfer of prisoners from detention in Sarajevo to The Hague. NATO Press Release (96)93 (13 June 1996) (available on the NATO website, http://www.nato.int/docu/pr/1996/).

[63]   NATO Press Release (96)26 (14 February 1996) (available on the NATO website, http://www.nato.int/docu/pr/1996/).

[64]   Judge Cassese has stated that "[i]f the major powers of the world are not consistent and don't make arrests in the next 10 months, we are prepared to pack up and go home. We think our job is to try leaders, not small fry." Title, in *The Christian Science Monitor*, 21 October 1996. *See also* Interview with Mr. Richard Goldstone, in *The Times*, 21 September 1996.

[65]   Security Council Resolution 1031, UN Doc. S/RES/1031, 15 December 1995, ¶ 14.

[66]   *See* Anthony Lewis, "Winking at Karadzic", *The New York Times*, October 28, 1996 (noting that IFOR soldiers see Mr. Karadzic almost every day).

III. POSSIBLE ROLES OF THE TRIBUNAL

To date, the Tribunal has accomplished remarkable work. It is well-organized, has issued numerous indictments (17 indictments and 74 indictees) and promulgated legal reasoning that will influence the development of international law in this matter. But one question remains: what is the real impact of the Tribunal? To answer this question, it is necessary to identify the purposes for the Tribunal. The present author agrees with Professor Pellet's three possible roles of the Tribunal: preventive, repressive and symbolic[67]. The present author agrees with his conclusions, but nevertheless believes the Tribunal can fulfill other roles as well.

A. *The Tribunal should Contribute to the Peace Efforts*

The Tribunal's task should be seen as part of the broad scheme for establishing peace in the region. A narrow interpretation of this task would put the Tribunal in an uncomfortable situation. It would tie the Tribunal's efforts to political initiatives, which are often confused, contradictory, and/or transitory. The Vance-Owen plan, for example, was under consideration at the time of the Tribunal's creation, but was later abandoned. If a particular political figure was considered indispensable to the sucessful conclusion of an agreement, a narrow interpretation of the Tribunal's ability to contribute to peace efforts might shield that figure from prosecution and thereby compromise the Tribunal's independence. It will be impossible to establish a viable peace through negotiation with alleged war criminals unless one wishes to accept the proposition that there can be peace without justice, in which case the Tribunal should have a different role.

The war crimes tribunals consituted in the wake of the Second World War contributed to the restoration of peace by establishing the responsibility of individuals so that a populace might not be held accountable[68]. It is essential therefore that the Tribunal's work be free from political considerations and have the full support of the international community at all levels. Thus, the recent statements of the new Tribunal Prosecutor, Ms. Louise Arbour, that "those members States refusing to comply with the Dayton accords by turning over suspects might be given 'rewards' for compliance, such as membership in international organizations" are far from helpful[69].

---

[67] Pellet, "Poudre aux yeux", *supra*, at 60.

[68] Consequently, the reference to the "Bosnian Serbs" and the "Bosnian Croats" in the official documents of the Tribunal are contra-productive. The clear distance to those terms made, for example, by Mr. Tadeusz Mazowiecki, Special Rapporteur to the Commission on Human Rights on the Former Yugoslavia, is preferable. *See* his report of 5 July 1995, UN Doc. E/CN.4/1996/6.

[69] *The Washington Post*, 1 October 1996.

Also, the Tribunal should not be pressured by the current events. The Tribunal should not allow frustration over noncooperation to cause it to alter its methods of conducting its business. Frustration is understandable given that those who truly had decisive influence on the massive level of the crimes committed remain beyond the Tribunal's reach due, in part, to noncooperation. In this context, it is doubtful whether a systematic application of procedure "Rule 61" would contribute to or weaken the Tribunal's credibility. Rule 61 is intended to prevent a clogging of the Tribunal's work due to the fact that some indicted persons have not been arrested and thus have not appeared before the Tribunal. This *exceptional* procedure is an incomplete replacement of trial *in absentia* which was not permitted under the Statute and could result in the issuance of an international arrest warrant and a certification on the failure of a given State to comply with the Tribunal's orders. It is designed for use only in very exceptional circumstances. It was astonishing, therefore, to see, on the eve of the first trial (22-23 April 1996), Rule 61 hearings placed on the forefront of scheduled judicial activity for the following months, rather than new trials or new indictments[70]. Even the Security Council does not appear to share the Tribunal's enthusiasm for the application of Rule 61: its response (to the Presidents of both Tribunals) suggests "cautious use of the provisions of Rule 61"[71]. Despite understanding for the potential need for this procedure, its application should be considered an indication of the Tribunal's weakness resulting from a lack of support, namely the apparent impossibility to arrest and transfer to the Tribunal accused persons and thereby enable proper trial procedures to start.

B. The Tribunal's Role is an Exemplary One

The Tribunal is the central organ for the international community to express its unwillingness to tolerate war crimes. This role can only be achieved by bringing to justice major war criminals, whose responsibility for war crimes and crimes against humanity is not that of simply carrying out orders, but of conceiving and giving them[72]. The responsibility for this function falls most heavily on the Prosecutor, who has the ability to choose whom to indict and when[73]. The Tribunal cannot physically bring to justice all persons who have committed war crimes in the territory of the former Yugoslavia. The rest of that difficult task should be undertaken by national

---

[70] *See*, Press Release, CC/PIO/067-E, 26 April 1996.

[71] UN Doc. S/1996/476, 27 June 1996.

[72] *See* Herman von Habel, "An International Tribunal for the Former Yugoslavia: An Act of Powerlessness or a New Challenge for the International Community?", 11 Neth. Q. Hum. Rts. 450, 450-51 (1993).

[73] On 30 January 1995, the Judges of the Tribunal expressed "their concern about the urgency with which appropriate indictments should be issued." Tribunal Press Release CC/PIO/003-E, 1 February 1995.

courts. The Tribunal was not intended "to preclude or prevent the exercise of jurisdiction by national courts with respect to [war crimes]. Indeed national courts should be encouraged to exercise their jurisdiction in accordance with their relevant national laws and procedures"[74]. Unfortunately, the "Rules of the Road" negotiated in Rome do not promote use of national courts[75]. These rules are counterproductive, but have unfortunately been confirmed by the Security Council[76].

Implementation of the GFA is not an easy task. Genuine concerns exist over how the entities will use their national courts. Persons might be arrested arbitrarily and tried for war crimes. Prisoner transfers might be delayed or refused in the name of possible national war crimes trials. Still, despite these concerns, obliging national courts to turn first to the Tribunal before proceeding is a complete denial of the competence of such national courts. It is also an unnecessary burden on the Tribunal, which does not need further administrative responsibilities. Creation of this obligation may also represent a revision of the Tribunal's Statute, which established a level of concurrent jurisdiction between the Tribunal and national courts.

C. The Tribunal's Role is Preventive

The Tribunal cannot accomplish this task alone. Despite the stated intention of the Security Council, the Tribunal's creation could not have halted war crimes in the territory of the former Yugoslavia[77]. The Tribunal bears no responsibility for this fact: its creation followed series of measures

---

[74] Secretary General's report, *supra*, ¶ 64.

[75] The Rules were negotiated in Rome on 18 February 1996. They note that "[p]ersons, other than those already indicted by the International Tribunal, may be arrested and detained for serious violations of international humanitarian law only pursuant to a previously issued order, warrant, or indictment that has been reviewed and deemed consistent with international legal standards by the International Tribunal. Procedures will be developed for expeditious decision by the Tribunal and will be effective immediately upon such action." *See* Agreed Measures, 18 February 1996 (available on the OHR website, http://www.ohr.int/docu/d960218a.htm). They oblige parties, *inter alia*, to submit immediately to ICTY for review lists of people suspected of having committed violations of international humanitarian law with the supporting evidence and to release persons arrested on suspicion of war crimes for whom files have not been sent to the Tribunal or for whom the Tribunal has determined the evidence does not warrant further detention. *See* Conclusions of the Peace Implementation Council Meeting in Florence, 13-14 June 1996, UN Doc. S/1996/542, 10 July 1996 (available on NATO's website, http://www.nato.int/ifor/un/).

[76] The Council observed "that no individual should be arrested and detained on the territory of the former Yugoslavia for serious violations of international humanitarian law until and unless the International Tribunal has reviewed the case and agreed that the warrant, order, or indictment meets international legal standards." Statement of the Security Council President, UN Doc. S/PRST/1996/39, 20 September 1996.

[77] Security Council Resolution 827, UN Doc. S/RES/827 (1993), preamble.

adopted by the Security Council but never properly implemented[78]. To accomplish prevention, the Tribunal requires the firm determination of the international community, especially from those bodies operating on the ground in the former Yugoslavia.

D. The Tribunal's Role is to Render Justice

The Tribunal's efforts are limited to the specific situation of the former Yugoslavia and it should adapt its methods of work to the specific purpose for which it was created. For example, the Rules of Procedure bear many of the characteristics of the judicial procedure of common law legal systems. However, the former Yugoslavia and its successor States employ a civil law legal system. Lawyers from the region will not necessarily be familiar with common law principles and procedures. The Tribunal Prosecutor will therefore have a professional advantage over those defence lawyers likely to be chosen by those indicted to mount their defence.

The Rules of Procedure also establish English and French as the working languages of the Tribunal. Correspondence, motions, written arguments and other documents must be filed in one or the other of these languages. In the *Celebici* case, the Trial Chamber ordered that all motions, written arguments and other documents as well as all correspondence to and from an organ of the Tribunal shall be filed in one of the working languages of the Tribunal[79]. No one would expect the judges to learn one of the official languages of the region, but the defence lawyers are still thereby put in an inferior situation compared to the Prosecutor. Every lawyer will agree that in criminal cases especially, clear and precise legal terminology is extremely important and that mere command of a language may not suffice. Such disadvantages might compromise the justice the Tribunal is charged to dispense[80].

E. The Tribunal is a Step towards the Creation of a
Permanent International Tribunal

This fact is important but not primary. If it succeeds, the Tribunal will make an important contribution to the development of international humanitarian law. Its decisions concerning its jurisdiction and how to accomplish its work will have far-reaching consequences and will no doubt spark important discussions both at the International Law Commission and

---

[78] *See* Drazen Petrovic and Luigi Condorelli, "L'ONU et la crise yougoslave", 38 AFDI at 58-59 (1992).

[79] Decision on Defence Application for Forwarding the Documents in the Language of the Accused, Case IT-96-21-T, Trial Chamber of the International Tribunal (25 September 1996).

[80] Rules of Procedure and Evidence, *supra*, at Rule 21.

among scholars. If the Tribunal fails in its mission, the establishment on the permanent tribunal would be in danger[81]. Thus, this role of the Tribunal provides an additional reason to undertake all measures to ensure the Tribunal's succcess.

IV. SOME FINAL REMARKS

The Tribunal's role after the GFA is indeed an essential part of the process to restore peace in the former Yugoslavia. It is not simply a constituent part of the GFA, but a part of the international community's overall efforts to bring peace and stability in the region. Thus, the obligation to cooperate with the Tribunal does not originate solely in the GFA. All States and the organizations in which they participate, military and political, are bound by the decisions of the Security Council and therefore to support the Tribunal. The Tribunal is part of the system newly created to safeguard human rights in the former Yugoslavia. If States in the region are allowed to flout the Tribunal and representatives of the international community involved in the implementation of the GFA fail to give its decisions full effect, the Tribunal's credibility will be fatally undermined and the protection of human rights compromised. The Tribunal's jurisdiction encompasses thousands of victims seeking justice. Moreover, beyond these many, the Tribunal was created to punish individuals for the worst types of crimes that mankind has defined. Thus, it is not just the question of human rights in the former Yugoslavia that is at stake, but the general system protecting human rights created in the fifty or so years since the creation of the United Nations. The Tribunal should not be sacrificed for short-term political gain. The need to enable the Tribunal to successfully begin its mission is plain. The only remaining question is: When will we begin?

---

[81] *See* Christian Tomuschat, "International Criminal Prosecution: The Precedent of Nuremberg Confirmed", in 5 Criminal Law Forum, 237, 247 (1994); Ralph Zacklin, "Bosnia and Beyond", *supra.*

MICHAEL O'FLAHERTY

11. The United Nations Treaty Bodies and Bosnia and Herzegovina

I. INTRODUCTION

In all the panoply of international human rights interventions in Bosnia and Herzegovina little attention is paid to the roles of six United Nations Committees which have an ongoing monitoring role. These bodies, each of which is charged with international supervision of implementation of a specific human rights instrument, derive their competencies primarily from Bosnia and Herzegovina's ratification of the respective instruments. The Treaty Bodies are also invited to be involved in Bosnia and Herzegovina[1] by virtue of provisions of the Constitution of the Federation and the General Framework Agreement (GFA).

The Treaty Bodies carry out their activities primarily through the examination of reports submitted by State parties and the issuing of comments and recommendations. They have also developed procedures to deal with emergency situations and may undertake missions to the territory. Certain of the Treaty Bodies may examine and deliberate on individual petitions. To varying extents the Treaty Bodies have already taken action with regard to BiH. Before dissolution of Yugoslavia they dealt with that State through the reporting procedures. Since accession to the instruments by Bosnia and Herzegovina, certain of the Treaty Bodies have applied their mechanisms to address emergency situations. Now, in the context of a fragile peace they are presented with opportunities to help shape the future through judicious application of their various procedures.

This chapter examines the roles in Bosnia and Herzegovina of the six Treaty Bodies. It evaluates the effectiveness of their interventions and identifies conditions which must be met in the future if they are to be able to make a real contribution to the consolidation of peace and re-

---

[1] Bosnia and Herzegovina [hereinafter "BiH"] is one of the states formerly a part of the Socialist Federal Republic of Yugoslavia (SFRY), which existed until 1992. Post-1992, other former constituents of the SFRY, Serbia and Montenegro now comprise the state known as the Federal Republic of Yugoslavia [hereinafter "FRY" or "Serbia"].

M. O'Flaherty and G. Gisvold (eds.), Post-War Protection of Human Rights in Bosnia and Herzegovina, 215–239.
© 1998 Kluwer Law International. Printed in Great Britain.

establishment of civil society. The chapter begins with a general introduction to the Treaty Body system.

II. THE UNITED NATIONS TREATY BODY SYSTEM

Under the auspices of the United Nations, the world community has elaborated a range of internationally binding legal instruments in the field of human rights. The principal of these are the:

International Covenant on Civil and Political Rights (ICCPR)
International Covenant on Economic, Social and Cultural Rights (ICESCR)
International Convention on the Elimination of All Forms of Racial Discrimination (ICERD)
Convention on the Elimination of Discrimination Against Women (CEDAW)
Convention Against Torture and Other Cruel, Inhuman or Degrading Treatment (CAT)
Convention on the Rights of the Child (CRC)

Together, these instruments constitute a formidable armoury in the fight against violation of the various categories of human rights, including certain group rights and against invidious discrimination in their enjoyment. The instruments have a complementary relationship to regional instruments such as the European Convention on Human Rights and Fundamental Freedoms and the European Social Charter. In many instances better protection is afforded under either the regional or UN (universal) instrument. For instance, ICCPR generally affords the State less discretion in implementing rights than does the European Convention[2]. Specialised instruments, such as CRC and CAT, also articulate rights to a far higher degree of detail than the instruments in the European system.

International supervision of the implementation by States parties of the rights in the instruments is undertaken primarily by independent bodies (the Committees/Treaty Bodies)[3] which, in all but one case, the Committee on Economic, Social and Cultural Rights, are established pursuant to the provisions of the various instruments. These are the:

---

[2] *Id.*, L. Heffernan, "A Comparative View of Individual Petition Procedures under the European Convention on Human Rights and the International Covenant on Civil and Political Rights", in 19 Hum. Rts Q. 78 (1997) and M. Schmidt, "The Complementarity of the Covenant and the European Convention on Human Rights-Recent Developments," *in* D. Harris and S. Joseph (eds.), *The International Covenant on Civil and Political Rights and United Kingdom Law* (1995).

[3] For a recent overview of the activities of the Committees see, O'Flaherty, *Human Rights and the UN: Practice Before the Treaty Bodies* (1996).

Human Rights Committee (for ICCPR)
Committee on Economic Social and Cultural Rights
Committee on the Elimination of Racial Discrimination
Committee on the Elimination of Discrimination Against Women
Committee Against Torture
Committee on the Rights of the Child

The Committees are comprised of small groups of experts, elected by the States parties, to serve in their personal capacities. Each Committee meets for a number of weeks in each year in either Geneva or New York.

By far the most significant activity of the Treaty Bodies is the examination of reports submitted by the States parties on implementation of the human rights provisions in the respective instruments[4]. Depending on the instrument, the periodicity can range from every two to every five years. Reports are considered in public session by the relevant Treaty Body which then issues a set of observations on the State's compliance with the international obligations. Normally, representatives of the State attend the examination and engage in dialogue with the members of the Treaty Body. NGOs and others are also welcome to attend and they can usually make informal submissions (in most cases written rather than oral)[5].

It is difficult to evaluate the effectiveness of the reporting procedures in promoting State party compliance with treaty obligations. Surveys[6] have however indicated that the procedure can stimulate significant legislative review and reform. It can also help develop sensitivity to human rights issues within a State. For the reporting procedures to work well it is necessary for governments, Treaty Bodies, non-governmental organisations and the media to be appropriately engaged in the process. Recent years have seen a much improved participation by each of these actors. Thus, for instance, State reports are increasingly being drawn up in compliance with the stipulated formats[7], the Committees are, to the extent which their resources allow (see below), performing their function in a more penetrating and incisive manner[8] and NGOs are devoting increased attention to the

---

[4] For a somewhat dated overview of the reporting procedures of five of the six Treaty Bodies, see United Nations, *Manual on Human on Rights Reporting* (1991). The procedures are explained in O'Flaherty, *Human Rights, supra.*

[5] O'Flaherty, *supra.*

[6] *Id., e.g.,* C. Cohn, "The Early Harvest: Domestic Legal Changes Related to the Human Rights Committee and the Covenant on Civil and Political Rights", 13 Hum. Rts Q. (1991), and M. Banton, *International Action Against Racial Discrimination* (1996), at chapters 8 – 12.

[7] *Id., e.g.,* M. O'Flaherty, "The Committee on the Elimination of Racial Discrimination as an Implementation Agency", *in* M. MacEwen (ed.), *Anti Discrimination Law Enforcement – A Comparative Perspective*, (1997).

[8] *Id.*

process[9]. A *sine qua non* for effective operation of the procedures is, however, a relatively stable society with an effective central government.

The Human Rights Committee and the Committee Against Torture, seemingly[10], have competency to receive and consider communications from individuals in Bosnia and Herzegovina who claim that the State has violated their rights under the respective instrument[11]. The Committees may subsequently issue non-binding opinions on whether the State has violated its obligations and make appropriate recommendations. At the present time this is the only form of international redress procedure available to residents of this State. If and when Bosnia and Herzegovina becomes party to the European Convention and its individual petition system, the UN procedures will remain in force. There will be many instances where issues of substance or procedure will dictate that they rather than the European procedures be pursued[12].

The individual petition procedures have had some success in obtaining redress for individual victims of human rights violations[13]. One of the Committees, the Human Rights Committee, has also become vigorous in recent years in pursing States with regard to implementation of the Committee's opinions[14]. As with the reporting procedure, the petition mechanism is most likely to be effective in a stable society, with respect for the rule of law and the independence of the judicial process.

To respond to emergency situations or the collapse of civil society, most of the Treaty Bodies are developing or have already put in place special procedures. These may include demands for submission of special reports, examination of a situation in the absence of a report, the issuing of recommendations to States, warring parties and the international community, the

---

[9] *Id.*

[10] Yugoslavia submitted itself to the procedure on 10 September 1991. Bosnia and Herzegovina succeeded to the obligations of Yugoslavia under the Convention Against Torture on 6 March 1992. *Id.*, Convention against Torture and Other Cruel, Inhuman or Degrading Treatment or Punishment, 23 ILM 1027 (1984), *as modified* 24 ILM 535 (1985). A new declaration concerning the procedures was not submitted. However, Treaty Bodies have made it clear that the successor States of former Yugoslavia have succeeded to all the obligations undertaken regarding the human rights instruments. *See, e.g.*, Report of the Human Rights Committee, UN Doc. A/48/40, ¶ 311.

[11] Procedures of both Committees are described in O'Flaherty, *Human Rights, supra*, at Chapters 2 and 6. For examination in detail see M. Nowak, *CCPR Commentary*, (1995), at 647 *et seq.*, and A. Byrnes, "The Committee Against Torture", *in* P. Alston (ed.), *The United Nations and Human Rights*, (1992).

[12] For an evaluation of the relationship between the procedures under the European Convention on Human Rights and ICCPR see, L. Heffernan, "A Comparative View", *supra*.

[13] *See, e.g.*, the report on cooperation of States with the procedure of the Human Rights Committee, Annual Report of the Human Rights Committee to the General Assembly, UN Doc. A/51/40, at Chapter 8.

[14] *Id.*,

undertaking of missions, etc[15].. The procedures have developed to a large extent in response to the conflicts in the former Yugoslavia.

The Committee Against Torture operates one further mechanism which has no equivalent for the other treaty bodies concerning the investigation of egregious allegations of perpetration of torture by a State party. The Committee has only publicly reported on two applications of the procedure, concerning Turkey and Egypt[16].

Application of the procedure requires that States have indicated their acceptance of the applicable provisions of the Convention Against Torture as contained in article 20. Yugoslavia submitted itself to the procedure on 10 September 1991. Bosnia and Herzegovina succeeded to the obligations of Yugoslavia under the Convention on 6 March 1992. A new declaration concerning the procedures was not submitted. However, Treaty Bodies have made it clear that the successor States of former Yugoslavia have succeeded to all the obligations undertaken regarding the human rights instruments[17]. The procedure will not receive further examination in this paper.

No examination of the activities of Treaty Bodies is complete without acknowledgement of the somewhat accidental results which can follow on application of any of the mechanisms or the undertaking of *ad-hoc* action. These can include:

i.   conveying of a sense of solidarity with or otherwise empowering victims of human rights abuse simply through the process of their situation being sympathetically examined in an international forum[18];

ii.   obtaining the benefit of the accumulated wisdom of the Treaty Bodies regarding issues of domestic application of international human rights law in general as well as of the specific instruments in particular[19];

---

[15]   Each of the procedures is described in the periodic reports drawn up by the Treaty Bodies on their activities during the reporting period. A brief overview of the procedures can be found in, in O'Flaherty, *Human Rights, supra*. The procedures of the Human Rights Committee are analyzed in S. Joseph, "New Procedures Concerning the Human Rights Committee's Examination of State Reports", in 13 Netherlands Quarterly of Human Rights 5 (1995), and I. Boerfijn, "Towards a Strong System of Supervision: The Human Rights Committee's Role in Reforming the Reporting Procedure under Article 40 of the Covenant on Civil and Political Rights", 17 Hum. Rts Q. 766 (1995).

[16]   *Id.*, O'Flaherty, *Human Rights, supra*, at 154-158.

[17]   *See, e.g.*, Annual Report of the Human Rights Committee, UN Doc. A/48/40, *supra*.

[18]   Direct experience of the present writer both in his experience as an NGO representative and as a member of the UN's Treaty Body secretariat.

[19]   The accumulated body of work of the Treaty Bodies constitutes a formidable treasury of insight on these issues. Inevitably, also, the deliberations in common of groups of experts significantly propel thought and ideas on the substance and application of the instruments.

iii.   entering into the public record of these UN bodies of information made available by a disparate range of sources on patterns of abuse and attributions of responsibility[20].

One must acknowledge two serious constraints on treaty body capacity to be effective:

i.   The Committees, each of which only meets for a number of weeks in each year, are absurdly over-loaded with work and have great difficulties in affording adequate time to their primary tasks such as consideration of reports. It is into this context that they are attempting to innovate and refine their procedures. Inevitabley all aspects of their work suffer,

ii.   At its present staffing and resource levels the UN secretariat servicing the Treaty Bodies is barely able to carry out its tasks with regard to their regular activities. It is thus not in a position to adequately provide useful services such as the gathering of all pertinent documentation, liaising with non-conventional mechanisms, providing political advice, assisting in a professional manner in the drafting of appropriate decisions and concluding observations and ensuring their wide and speedy distribution.

III. The Treaty Bodies and Bosnia and Herzegovina

For the formerly constituted Yugoslavia and for Bosnia and Herzegovina the various instruments came into effect as follows:

ICCPR: 23 March 1976 for Yugoslavia. 6 March 1992 for Bosnia and Herzegovina

For the individual petition procedure (ratification of the First Optional Protocol): 1 June 1995

ICESCR: 3 January 1976 for Yugoslavia. 6 March 1992 for Bosnia and Herzegovina

ICERD: 4 January 1969 for Yugoslavia. 16 July 1993 for Bosnia and Herzegovina

CEDAW: 28 March 1982 for Yugoslavia. 1 October 1993 for Bosnia and Herzegovina

CAT: 10 October 1991 for Yugoslavia. 6 March 1992 for Bosnia and Herzegovina

---

[20] Information from any source can be adopted by members of a Treaty Body in order for it to be inserted into the proceedings and recorded in the summary record. Such information may also, directly or indirectly be included in the reports prepared by the Treaty Bodies on their activities.

CAT petition procedure (article 22) and the article 20 procedure were accepted by Yugoslavia on 10 September 1991.

CRC: 2 February 1991 for Yugoslavia. 6 March 1992 for Bosnia and Herzegovina.

An examination of the relationship between the Treaty Bodies and Bosnia and Herzegovina can be divided in five parts:

i.   The Treaty Bodies and former Yugoslavia in the period until 1990. The relationship in this period was dominated by application of the reporting procedures. It can be characterised as non-confrontational and quietist: a typical example of the ineffectual Treaty Body practice of the time.

ii.   The Treaty Bodies and former Yugoslavia after 1990. This period provided clear indications of the major weakness of the regular reporting procedures in addressing crises such as the dissolution of a federal State. It was also marked by the first manifestations of the emergency or urgent procedures.

iii. The Treaty Bodies and Bosnia and Herzegovina before the GFA. This period confirmed the limitations of reporting procedures in war time. Also, notwithstanding some modest successes, it demonstrated the extreme difficulty in developing procedural models to enable the Treaty Bodies to play a useful role in such situations.

iv.   The GFA and Treaty Bodies. GFA provided the Treaty Bodies with a rich range of opportunities for participation in the process of peace-building in Bosnia and Herzegovina. The Agreement itself might also have benefited from critical or interpretative comment. Treaty Bodies have yet to take appropriate advantage of the range of options open to them.

v.   Treaty Bodies and the future. In the long term it is to be hoped that Bosnia and Herzegovina will take its place among the stable nations of Europe. In that context the regular procedures of the Treaty Bodies should have a useful role to play. That role can be optimised through extensive programmes of training and information for Government, NGOs, the legal community and the general public.

A. The Treaty Bodies and the former Yugoslavia

Yugoslavia was consistently among the first of States to ratify human rights instruments and it was accordingly scrutinised by Treaty Bodies on a number of occasions.

Until the 1990s Yugoslavia exhibited extreme self-confidence regarding its compliance with international human rights standards. Thus, for instance, in 1977 it reported that, "The ratification of the International Covenant (ICCPR) does not call for the adoption of new measures which give effect to the rights recognised in this Covenant since all these rights are already guaranteed by the Yugoslav legislation"[21]. Similar assertions were made with regard to other human rights instruments. The various reports also described a high level of enjoyment of each of the specific human rights contained in the instruments. Occasionally such assertions were rendered especially incongruous by their juxtaposition with lengthy explanations of the idiosyncratic Yugoslav interpretation of such rights as freedom of association or religion[22].

Looking back now at the early reports of Yugoslavia it is not difficult to detect problems and a failure of the State to submit accurate reports which focus on the actual situation of respect for human rights rather than exclusively on the legal regime. It is no less easy to spot the inconsistencies between the Yugoslav socialist interpretation of various rights and the international standards. Yugoslavia itself, in a 1992 report to the Human Rights Committee admitted that its earlier practice in meeting international human rights obligations had been based on the conviction that, "there was no need for harmonisation with international standards". It also described the extent to which issues of ideology influenced its practice: "a characteristic of that period was the strong influence of ideological prejudices, particularly in facing criticism in connection with human rights coming from the west, from countries of opposite ideological convictions, which was reflected in communications with members of the international community regarding issues concerning the protection and control of recognised rights"[23].

The Treaty Bodies made little of the inadequacies in the Yugoslav reports and, indeed, occasionally afforded great praise to that State. One member of CERD, for example, stated that, "it was quite remarkable that a country like Yugoslavia could exist", and that its viability could be attributed to its "concerted policy of mutual respect for the various groups, languages, customs and religions present in the country". Another CERD member declared that, "racial discrimination did not exist in Yugoslavia"[24].

The manner in which Yugoslavia undertook its reporting obligations and was dealt with by Treaty Bodies was largely reflective of the general practice in the fist years of Treaty Body activity and illustrates a quietism in international supervision of implementation of the instruments.

---

[21] International Covenant on Civil and Political Rights, 999 UNTS 171, *adopted* 16 December 1966, at Add. 23 at the introductory (unnumbered) paragraph [hereinafter "ICCPR"].

[22] *See, e.g., Id.,* ¶¶ 20, 25.

[23] UN Doc. CCPR/C/52/Add. 9, ¶ 79.

[24] The present writer is grateful to Michael Banton, current Chairman of CERD for these citations which can be found, with others of the ilk in M. Banton, *International Action, supra,* at 187.

B. The Treaty Bodies and former Yugoslavia after 1990

Already, at the beginning of this decade, the Treaty Bodies addressed with a new incisiveness the situation of Yugoslavia. In August 1990, CERD undertook a vigorous examination and its members made consistently critical comments. On that occasion they emphasised that issues of ethnic discrimination must be faced in addressing the problems of Kosovo and Vojvodina. Concerning Kosovo they drew attention to allegations of displacement of persons and observed that, "any attempt to modify the demographic composition of a country or a region on the basis of ethnic criteria would be in violation of the Convention (ICERD)"[25]. Questions were also asked about the "decline in relations between Croats and Serbs"[26]. It is noteworthy in terms of Committee practice that the report of the examination of the report of Yugoslavia makes reference to the importance as an information source of a submission by an NGO, Amnesty International[27].

The Yugoslav delegation which met with the Committee attempted to answer a number of the questions and took the opportunity to make a number of commitments for the promotion and protection of human rights. The delegation undertook to answer all remaining questions in its next periodic report[28]. This commitment, of a type frequently entered into by States dealing with Treaty Bodies, proved to be inadequate to the rapidly changing circumstances of Yugoslavia: by the time the next report (a special one in 1993) came to be submitted, all that was left of the State was a rump comprising Serbia and Montenegro.

An account of CERD's consideration of the Yugoslav report appeared in its annual report for 1990[29], which was considered by the General Assembly at the end of that year. It would not appear to have elicited any attention and there is no indication that the Committee's findings were addressed in any other international forum. Failures such as this were to eventually be understood by CERD and other Treaty Bodies as necessitating development of new procedures for the effective engagement of appropriate international attention.

In 1991, Yugoslavia provided one of the contexts for the elaboration by the Human Rights Committee of a new procedure to address emergency situations. In April 1991, the Committee had requested submission by Iraq

---

[25] UN Doc. A/45/18, ¶ 194

[26] *Id.,* ¶ 195.

[27] *Id.,* ¶ 196. NGOs have no formal part in the proceedings of CERD and their essential role has still to be appropriately acknowledged in the Committee's working methods. It was not until a year later that the Committee issues a Decision stating that, " members of the Committee must have access, as independent experts, to all (other) available sources of information, governmental and non-governmental". UN Doc. A/46/18, at Annex VII.

[28] UN Doc. A/45/18, *supra,* ¶¶ 193, 201-205. *See also* UN Docs CERD/C/SR, ¶¶ 874, 875.

[29] UN Doc. A/45/18, *supra.*

of an urgent report[30]. At its 43rd session, on 4 November 1991, it decided that the procedure, though exceptional, could be applied to other States as necessary, and it invited Yugoslavia to submit a special report no later than 31 January 1992[31]. This was subsequently reported to be a request for submission, within the same time-frame, of the State's already overdue third periodic report[32]. The Government delivered the report to the Committee on 10 March 1992.

The report[33] is noteworthy as a commentary by the Belgrade Government on the ongoing dissolution of the State and contains a lengthy argument as to the illegality under article 1, ICERD, of the declarations of independence by Slovenia, Croatia and Macedonia. The report acknowledges a severe deterioration in the situation of human rights and respect for humanitarian law and blame is placed primarily on "the behaviour of republics based on an unclear concept of the set-up of the country; disregard and bypassing of the legal order and legal institutions of the system and the adoption of unilateral and secessionist acts, thereby completely disregarding the international obligations of the Socialist Federal Republic of Yugoslavia"[34]. The collapse of the federal system is also blamed for the failure to maintain a programme of constitutional and legislative reform in the field of human rights.

In the context of a highly unusual paean of praise for international human rights supervision procedures, the report states that the Federal Government had unsuccessfully attempted to obtain the necessary parliamentary consent for ratification of the First Optional Protocol to ICCPR, thus permitting individuals to petition the Human Rights Committee[35].

The Committee considered the report on 8 and 9 April 1992. Normal report-consideration procedures were followed and a set of agreed "Comments" were adopted. The official summary report[36] of the dialogue between Committee members and the delegation of the Federal Government suggests that the discussion had to it an unreal quality as by then the Federation only had full control over two republics and yet was expected to speak for all of Yugoslavia. The rapidly deteriorating conditions in the region also seem to have escaped appropriate consideration in that disproportionate attention was paid to circumstances in Kosovo whereas Bosnia and Herzegovina did not even merit one mention[37].

---

[30] *Id.*, UN Doc. CCPR/C/SR.1062/Add.1

[31] *Id.*, UN Doc. CCPR/C/SR. 1112.

[32] UN Doc. A/47/40 at Annex VII.

[33] UN Doc. CCPR/C/52/Add. 9, *supra*

[34] *Id.*, ¶ 82.

[35] *Id.*, at Part III.

[36] UN Doc. A/47/40, *supra*, ¶¶ 431-469.

[37] It will be recalled that on the days in early April when CERD was considering the report, Bosnia and Herzegovina was hurtling towards war.

The Committee's "Comments"[38] suffer similarly and conclude with a set of suggestions and recommendations directed exclusively to the Federal Government: "In view of the serious situation prevailing in the State party, the Committee recommends that the Government take all necessary measures to stop violations of human rights, particularly those relating to the right to life and the prohibition of torture. These measures should include re-establishment of control over the army, dissolution of paramilitary militias and groups, punishment of those guilty of violations and adoption of measures to prevent a recurrence of such abuses. The Committee also recommends full application of article 27 of the Covenant, which recognises the rights of persons belonging to ethnic, religious or linguistic minorities to enjoy their own culture, to profess and practice their own religion and to use their own language"[39].

The proceedings attracted little publicity internationally or in the region and had no discernible impact on behaviour of the Federal Government or of authorities or parties in the various republics. They were however brought to the attention of the special session of the Human Rights Commission which met in August of that year and were submitted to the General Assembly in October of that year as part of the Committee's annual report.

C. The Treaty Bodies and the war in Bosnia and Herzegovina

Four of the Treaty Bodies have taken action concerning Bosnia and Herzegovina in the 1992 – 1995 period, the Human Rights Committee, the Committee on the Elimination of Racial Discrimination, the Committee on the Elimination of Discrimination Against Women and the Committee on the Rights of the Child.

(a) The Human Rights Committee

On 7 October, 1992, the Committee, in an innovative development of its procedure for the requesting of urgent reports[40], through its Chairman, requested Bosnia and Herzegovina, the Federal Republic of Yugoslavia and Croatia to submit, before the end of that month, urgent reports on the human rights situation in each of the States. The reports were to deal in particular with issues of respect for articles 6, 7, 9, 10,12 and 20 of ICCPR. At the time of this request, Bosnia and Herzegovina had not yet stated its intention to accede to the Covenant. However, the Committee was of the view that all people of the former Yugoslavia were entitled to the guaran-

---

[38] *Id.,* ¶¶ 463-469.

[39] *Id.,* ¶ 469.

[40] Subsequently incorporated into the Committee's Rules of Procedure. *See generally*, S. Joseph, "New Procedures", *supra*.

tees provided by the Covenant and that the Committee had jurisdiction to request submission of the reports pursuant to article 40 ICCPR[41].

All three States did submit reports in time for them to be considered early in the month of November[42]. The report of Bosnia and Herzegovina did not comply in form with the request of the Committee and notably contained no references whatsoever to the responsibilities of the Government for compliance with international human rights standards. It instead comprised an extensive list of allegations of war crimes and human rights violations perpetrated by Bosnian Serb forces and individuals.

The Committee met with the delegation of Bosnia and Herzegovina on 3 November and 3 days later adopted its Concluding Comments. The discussion[43] afforded opportunities for Committee members to focus on the behaviour of the Government and to query its compliance with the Covenant and with overlapping provisions of the Geneva Conventions. Positions taken by members were considerable influenced by the reports of the Special Rapporteur of the Commission on Human Rights, Mr. Mazowiecki. In reply, the Government delegation acknowledged both that the State considered itself bound by the Covenant and that it did have *de-jure* responsibility regarding protection of the human rights of persons in regions outside its *de-facto* control. The delegation also acknowledged that Government forces had been responsible for a limited number of human rights violations in the context of the war and that perpetrators had been removed from their posts.

From the perspective of Committee procedures, the consideration of the 1992 special reports from Bosnia and Herzegovina and other States of former Yugoslavia was especially significant. It demonstrated the capacity of the Committee to act speedily in an emergency situation as well as reaffirming the applicability of international human rights law to situations of armed conflict. It also, in a context of very limited capacity for fact-finding by Treaty Bodies, established the valuable practice of relying heavily on findings of other UN mechanisms: in this case the Special Rapporteur. From the immediate point of view of Bosnia and Herzegovina the proceedings were also of value. Above all, they provided a context for the State's acknowledgement of its responsibilities under the Covenant. They also served to both elucidate certain facts and attribute responsibility. These achievements were however greatly diminished by the lack of timely publicity given to the proceedings before the Committee.

A significant weakness of the proceedings was that the only dialogue partner was the Government. The Committee exacerbated the effects of this circumstance by directing their comments and recommendations only

---

[41] UN Doc. A/48/40, *supra*, ¶ 311.

[42] Bosnia and Herzegovina, UN Doc. CCPR/C/89; Croatia, UN Doc. CCPR/C/87; Federal Republic of Yugoslavia, UN Doc. CCPR/C/88

[43] *Id.*, UN Doc. A/48/40, *supra*, ¶¶ 311 -332.

to the State authorities. Thus an opportunity was missed to evaluate such matters as the behaviour of the various warring parties[44] and the international community, including the peace negotiators, the United Nations Protection Force (UNPROFOR) and the Special Rapporteur. While it is acknowledged that the Committee may have felt constrained in this regard in terms of its mandate, it does appear that an opportunity was lost to draw attention to the imperatives and non-negotiability of human rights obligations.

The Committee's Concluding Comments were, on the request of the Committee Chairman, brought to the attention of the Third Committee of the General Assembly, on 20 November[45]. The interim report of the Committee of Experts established pursuant to Security Council Resolution 780 (1992)[46] indicates that these Concluding Comments were among its sources of information. (Interestingly, the final report contains no reference to any use being made by the Commission of the findings of the treaty bodies).

Surprisingly, given the subsequent events in former Yugoslavia and increasing self-confidence in administration of the emergency procedure, there has been no Committee follow-up to the 1992 consideration of Bosnia and Herzegovina.

(b) The Committee on the Elimination of Racial Discrimination

In March 1993, the Committee requested Bosnia and Herzegovina to confirm its adherence to ICERD and to submit information, no later than 31 July 1993, on implementation of the Convention[47]. A report was submitted on 29 July[48]. In it the Government confirmed its adherence and presented an analysis of what it described as the "war of aggression" currently being waged on its territory. The report also acknowledged "individual" violations of human rights perpetrated in areas under Government control.

---

[44] Effects of exclusion from the dialogue of all but the Government were somewhat mitigated by the manner in which the Committee addressed the delegation which presented the report of the Federal Republic of Yugoslavia, on 4 November. On that occasion, the Committee, with reference to military attacks on, inter-alia, Dubrovnik, Vukovar and Sarajevo stated that, " the (military) means deployed and the matters at issue indicate links between nationalists and Serbia which render unacceptable the Federal Government's protestations of innocence". *Id.*, ¶ 386.

[45] UN Doc. A/C.3/47/CRP.1.

[46] UN Doc. S/25274 of 10 February 1993. The final report, UN Doc. S/1994/674, of 27 May 1996, contains no reference to the Human Rights Committee or any other human rights treaty body.

[47] The request is contained in Decision 1 (42). *Id.*, UN Doc. A/48/18 at Annex VIII.

[48] UN Doc. CERD/C/247.

The report was examined by the Committee on 12 August 1993[49], in the absence of a Government delegation. The debate was noteworthy in a number of respects:

i.   The Committee member charged to lead the examination, Mrs. Sadiq Ali, read into the record a comprehensive analysis of the human rights situation, which critically addressed the roles of the warring parties as well as the international community.

ii. There was a tension in the Committee regarding its competence. While a number of members were anxious to make recommendations concerning such matters as an appropriate form of political settlement in Bosnia and Herzegovina, others felt, in the words of one member, that, "it was not the Committee's role to make proposals about the internal ordering of Bosnia and Herzegovina: that was a political issue, which was now being discussed in another forum"[50]. A preponderance of members supported the former position on the basis that issues of ethnicity suffused the conflict and that therefore models for its resolution were clearly within the Committee's competence.

One member expressed the view that, issues of competence aside, the Committee should consider where it might be most useful. In this regard he noted that whereas many international bodies were engaged with Bosnia and Herzegovina, very few were addressing the situation in Kosovo[51].

The Committee's Concluding Observations[52] reflect the tensions in the discussion in that, while addressing broader issues of the conflict, they do not include a number of recommendations which Committee members had proposed: there is thus, for instance, no support for the "safe areas" proposal which had been recently made by the Special Rapporteur. There is however support for the International Criminal Tribunal established pursuant to Security Council Resolution 808 (1993).

The Concluding Observations are notable in addressing all the belligerent parties. They also forcefully affirm that the creation of "ethnically pure" States is, "totally contrary to the spirit and principles of the Convention"[53]. The Concluding Observations contain one eccentric element: the offer to Bosnia and Herzegovina of a technical co-operation mission of the Committee to "promote the elimination of all forms of racial discrimination and to assist the State in elaborating its next report"[54]. Given the

---

[49]   *Id.*, UN Doc. CERD/C/SR.1001. For references to the manner in which the Committee considered the three reports from former Yugoslavia dealt with at that session, see M. Banton, *International Action*, *supra*, at 187, *et seq.*

[50]   *Id.*, ¶ 32.

[51]   *Id.*, ¶ 52.

[52]   *Id.*, UN Doc. A/48/18, *supra*, ¶¶ 464-473.

[53]   *Id.*, ¶ 468.

[54]   *Id.*, ¶ 472.

circumstances in the country at that time there can only rarely have ever been made a more redundant offer to any State!

The CERD proceedings[55] were primarily of value as a context for the State to affirm its commitment to its obligations under the Convention and because of the reading into the record of Mrs. Sadiq Ali's' analysis. Furthermore, they drew attention to the normative limits which the Convention placed on political solutions to the conflict. The impact of these achievements was of course limited by the problem of the lack of publicity already noted as endemic to the proceedings of all Treaty Body activities.

CERD began its first session of 1995 with a meeting with the Special Rapporteur, Mr. Mazowiecki[56]. This encounter, innovative in terms of Committee practice, had a subversive element in that the Special Rapporteur queried whether the conflict in former Yugoslavia was primarily political rather than racial or ethnic. The Committee members, their competency to comment on the situation under threat, were stung into vehemently contesting this point of view. Members also expressed unease that their analysis seemed to attract so little attention and have such marginal influence by contrast with positions taken by the Special Rapporteur who "had the ear of the highest policy-making bodies in the United Nations"[57].

A few days later, the Committee considered an urgent updating report by Bosnia and Herzegovina, requested during the 1993 proceedings, and which was finally submitted on 20 January 1995[58]. The report constitutes a list of allegations of atrocities by forces in conflict with the Government and it was entirely ignored in the Committee discussions[59]. Instead, the discussions afforded an opportunity for another valuable review of the circumstances in Bosnia and Herzegovina by Mrs. Sadiq Ali. They also elicited similar uncertainties as those expressed in 1993 regarding the Committee's competence. Thus, on the one hand, one member suggested that CERD call for a lifting of the arms embargo on Bosnia and Herzegovina and a withdrawal of UNPROFOR, while others mused on whether the Committee could do anything at all that might be useful.

The Committee's Concluding Observations[60], though brief, vigorously condemn all attacks on the Government and against the integrity of the State. In what is presumably an oblique reference to the effects of the

---

[55] In the same Session, CERD also considered reports submitted by Croatia and the Federal Republic of Yugoslavia. It took the opportunity to draw attention to links between Croatian groups and the warring parties in Bosnia and Herzegovina – *Id.*, ¶ 502. In the Concluding Observations regarding the Federal Republic, the Committee indicated its preoccupation that, " the Serbs of Bosnia and Herzegovina frustrate the efforts of the Government of that State to implement the Convention". *Id.*, ¶ 541.

[56] *Id.*, UN Doc. CERD/C/SR. 1071

[57] *Id.*, ¶ 46.

[58] UN Doc. CERD/C/247/Add. 1.

[59] UN Doc. CERD/C/SR. 1082.

[60] UN Doc. A/50/18, ¶¶ 217 – 225.

international arms embargo, "(T)he Committee, being aware of the inherent right to self-defence of all States, as recognised in article 51 of the Charter of the United Nations, notes that the Government has been prevented from protecting human rights throughout its territory"[61]. One of the Committee's recommendations, on the basis, inter-alia, of persistent violations of ICERD, is, "the application of enforcement measures by the Security Council in connection with the situation in Bosnia and Herzegovina"[62]. This recommendation is noteworthy in terms of substance and procedure. Substantively it associates CERD with the view in international law that enforcement actions under chapter 7 of the UN Charter can be taken in response to situations of massive violations of human rights[63]. Procedurally the recommendation is significant in term of Treaty Body practice in that it is addressed not to the State but to the United Nations. Any possible impact of this innovatory recommendation or of the forthright terms of the Concluding Observations was negated by the failure to either ensure publicity for the proceedings or to have them drawn to the attention of the Security Council and other relevant actors.

In August of 1995, the Committee again addressed the situation in Bosnia and Herzegovina, this time under its "urgent procedure", whereby it does not need to base its discussion on a report submitted by the Government. The discussion took place against the background of such events as the fall of Srebrenica and Zepa, as well as the displacement of Serbs from the Krajina region of Croatia. The Decision adopted by the Committee[64] is noteworthy in both its forcefulness and lack of reference to the provisions of the Convention. Among the key elements are the following:

i.   A statement that, "any attempt to change or to uphold a changed demographic composition of an area against the will of the original inhabitants, by whatever means, is a violation of international law".

ii.   A call to the international community to both assist refugees and co-operate fully with the International Tribunal

iii. An urgent call, "for the provision to Bosnia and Herzegovina of all means to protect itself in accordance with article 51 of the Charter of the United Nations and to live within safe and secure borders"[65]

The Committee, in an attempt to overcome past problems of poor distribution of its proceedings, instructed that the Decision be transmitted immedi-

---

[61] *Id.,* ¶ 221.

[62] *Id.,* ¶ 224.

[63] For a review of the literature, see P.R. Baehr, "The Security Council and Human Rights", *in* R. Lawson and M. de Blois, (eds.), *The Dynamics of the Protection of Human Rights in Europe, Essays in Honour of Henry G. Schermers,* Volume III, (1994).

[64] Decision 2 (47), reported in UN Doc. A/50/18, ¶ 26.

[65] Inclusion of this paragraph necessitated adoption of the decision by vote. In explanations after the vote a number of members indicated their unease with the paragraph: *See Id.,* at Note 3.

ately to the Secretary-General of the United Nations for his attention and, through him, to the General Assembly and the Security Council.

This Decision, while raising legitimate concerns of Committee competence and mandate, constitutes one of the most forceful attempts of any Treaty Body to engage and influence international efforts to resolve the conflict in Bosnia and Herzegovina. It is not clear, however, whether it exercised any influence. In this regard it may be noted that none of the UN addressees even acknowledged its receipt[66].

(c) The Committee on the Elimination of Discrimination Against Women
In January 1993, CEDAW requested States of the former Yugoslavia, including Bosnia and Herzegovina to submit reports on an exceptional basis to be considered at the next session of the Committee in January 1994[67]. Bosnia and Herzegovina failed to submit a report and instead, a representative of the Government gave an oral presentation at a meeting of the Committee in February 1994[68]. Following a wide-ranging discussion on conditions for woman and their place in Bosnian society the Committee issued very brief Concluding Comments. These, addressed only to the Government, condemned violence against women and expressed solidarity with all women of Bosnia and Herzegovina. Women were also called on to become activist in order that they might generate the political will requisite for change and an urgent end to "fratricidal"[69] war.

It would be easy to dismiss the CEDAW proceedings as entirely inappropriate, given, not least, the one year-delay in implementing this "exceptional" procedure, the naïve level of questioning by members, the assumption that the war was being waged among men only, the lack of any attempt to mould the proceedings to an outcome that might impact on the situation, etc. However, despite these limitations, the consideration by CEDAW gave considerable encouragement to at least one women's group in central Bosnia, stimulating it to engage actively in politics within the Federation area[70].

(d) The Committee on the Rights of the Child
The Committee neither sought nor received a report of Bosnia and Herzegovina during the war period. However, at its third session, in January 1993, it adopted Recommendation 3 (Third Session) in which it, *inter alia*, "requests the Special Rapporteur of the Commission on Human Rights on the situation of human rights in the territory of the former Yugoslavia to

---

[66] Personal knowledge of the present writer in his capacity as Secretary of the Committee during the period until early 1996.

[67] *Id.*, UN Doc. A/49/38, ¶ 730.

[68] *Id.*, UN Doc. CEDAW/C/SR.253 and ¶¶ 732 – 757 of UN Doc. A/49/38.

[69] UN Doc. A/49/38, *supra*, ¶ 757.

[70] Stated to the present writer during 1996 by members of women's groups in central Bosnia.

take the Convention on the Rights of the Child into full consideration in the fulfilment of his mandate and in his future reports"[71].

In direct response to the request of the Committee, the Special Rapporteur included a lengthy examination of the situation of children in his sixth periodic report[72]. This analysis provided not only an important document of record but also a significant contribution to an overall understanding of the impact on children of armed conflict.

IV. THE TREATY BODIES AND THE GENERAL FRAMEWORK AGREEMENT FOR PEACE

The signing of GFA[73] might reasonably be assumed to have afforded significant opportunities to the Treaty Bodies for useful intervention in Bosnia and Herzegovina:

i. GFA refers to the various international human rights instruments and the parties undertake extensive obligations with regard thereto[74]. The manner in which the obligations and interrelationship of instruments is set out in the various annexes is, however, confusing and creates significant interpretative uncertainty. Of particular concern is the need for clarification of the status of the UN instruments with regard to the European Convention on Human Rights. The instruments have a potentially important role in clarifying those issues not least in the present context of Bosnia and Herzegovina where there is a strong tendency to assume a supremacy to the European Convention even in situations where a UN instrument affords greater protection[75].

ii. No less useful would be provision by Treaty Bodies of technical co-operation regarding practical implementation of the obligations through law reform, administrative action, effective functioning of the human rights mechanisms of GFA and the Federation of Bosnia and Herzegovina, etc. Such technical co-operation might take the form of expert advise from the Committees, provision of training, the undertaking of missions to the territory, etc.[76], and directed, as appropriate, to all levels of government officials, judiciary, lawyers,

---

[71] Reported in UN Doc. A/49/41 at Section 1 (E).

[72] UN Doc. E/CN.4/1994/110 at Section VII.

[73] 14 December 1995. Reproduced in Office of the High Representative, *Bosnia and Herzegovina, Essential Texts*, (1996).

[74] *Id.*, especially, the terms of Annexes 4 and 6, GFA, *supra*.

[75] For instance the UN instruments against torture racial discrimination and discrimination against women, as well as the Convention on the Rights of the Child. Note also that the Second Optional Protocol to ICCPR contains an absolute prohibition on the death penalty whereas the European instruments only provide for a partial abolition.

[76] In a manner analogous to that in which the Council of Europe has been active in Bosnia and Herzegovina since early 1996.

NGOs and members of the various human rights mechanisms and institutions. It is to be assumed of course that such projects of technical co-operation would be accompanied by initiatives of the High Commissioner for Human Rights to promote general knowledge of the human rights instruments, reporting and individual petition procedures etc.

A willingness by the Treaty Bodies to address such matters as these would benefit Bosnia and Herzegovina by strengthening those human rights commitments which are at the heart of the peace agreement. That State and the Treaty Bodies might also benefit from the manner in which active involvement would draw attention to the role of the Treaty Bodies as long term monitors in a context where the various international operations will have quit the region in a few years time. Involvement now would also advance general understanding of the relationship and mutuality of human rights instruments belonging to the regional and universal regimes.

The Treaty Bodies might also have turned their attention directly to an analysis of the terms of GFA itself. At the first instance such an examination might consider compatibility of the agreement with the international standards, particularly with regard to the creation of two (effectively ethnic) Entities and the reserving of certain high offices of State for members of designated ethnic groups. In this regard it may be recalled that CERD had some time before forcefully stated that an ethnisisation of society would be unacceptable in terms of the provisions of ICERD[77]. At another level of examination, the Treaty Bodies might legitimately have queried the capacity of the new constitutional arrangement to permit the State to ensure that its international human rights obligations be honoured. A particular concern in this regard might be the very weak form of central Government established by GFA[78] in a context where the implementation of international obligations require the capacity of central government to ensure ongoing compliance by the regions.

Attention to issues such as these, especially outside the context of submission of a State report, would pose problems of mandate for certain Committees. The Treaty Bodies have however, especially with regard to the emergency procedures, shown a capacity and willingness to widen the scope of their activities. Addressing the issues of Bosnia and Herzegovina could, in any case, be presented as a continuation of earlier initiatives.

The General Framework Agreement itself contains a form of invitation to the Treaty Bodies: annex 6, article XIII, paragraph 4, states that, "all competent authorities in Bosnia and Herzegovina shall co-operate with and provide unrestricted access to (inter-alia)...the supervisory bodies established by any of the international agreements listed in the appendix to the

---

[77] *Id.*, note 48 *supra.*

[78] *Id.*, relevant provisions of the Constitution of Bosnia and Herzegovina, GFA, Article III, Annex 4, [hereinafter "Constitution"].

Annex". The six UN human rights instruments are to be found in the Appendix. The Annex is signed for Bosnia and Herzegovina, the Federation of Bosnia and Herzegovina and the Republika Srpska. It entered into force upon signature. This provision is reinforced within the Federation area by virtue of the Constitution of the Federation, article 7, "All competent authorities in the Federation shall co-operate with (inter-alia)…the supervisory bodies established by any of the instruments listed in the Annex". The six UN instruments are so listed.

The invitations contained in GFA and the Federation Constitution are highly innovative devices to introduce directly into the domestic order the expertise of Treaty Bodies. Among their principal characteristics are the following:

i.   An "open-ended" nature whereby the Treaty Bodies may become involved whenever they wish

ii. The granting of a consent such that the Treaty Bodies may involve themselves without waiting for any form of invitation by the Government

iii. The absence of a specificity of the types of action which might be undertaken by Treaty Bodies , thus allowing for the possibility of such activities as the conducting of missions, provision of technical co-operation, etc.

iv. An instruction to all levels of government, "all competent authorities", to co-operate with the Treaty Bodies. In the case of the provision of the GFA it is also significant that the parties include not only the State itself but also, severally, the Republika Srpska and Federation of Bosnia and Herzegovina.

Notwithstanding the range of issues to be addressed and the unprecedented open invitation for participation, the Treaty Bodies have shown little enthusiasm in addressing the immediate issues of post-Dayton Bosnia and Herzegovina.

No Treaty Body reacted in any way to the invitation contained in the Federation Constitution. Since GFA, two have considered Bosnia and Herzegovina, only one of which, CERD, has taken any form of action.

A. The Committee on the Elimination of Racial Discrimination.

CERD marked the signing of GFA by deciding at its session in March 1996[79] to authorise its Chairman to consult as appropriate in order to make recommendations for action. It also decided to consult with the Government , etc., on how the Committee's good-offices might be put to best use. The Government was also invited to arrange a meeting between it and the

---

[79]   Decision 1 (48) reported in UN Doc. A/51/18, at Chapter II.

Commission on Human Rights of Bosnia and Herzegovina. It is somewhat surprising that the Decision includes no analytical references to GFA given that CERD had, in earlier Decisions, expressed itself forthrightly on the necessity of compliance of political solutions with international standards[80].

The Decision neither refers to nor takes advantage of Annex 6, article XIII. Thus it is expressed in traditionalist terms and couches its range of options in forms which both focus on and depend upon the further consent and co-operation of the "State party". The Decision also lacks a sense of urgency in that it would appear to have precluded any further action until the next Committee session in August of 1996[81].

Prior to the August session, the present writer, in his capacity as a human rights advisor to the High Representative, made an informal submission to the Committee members inviting them to take appropriate advantage of the opportunities of the moment and focus their contribution on matters of immediate concern within the perspective of ICERD. Thus it was suggested that they direct their comments not just to the State party but to all parties to GFA, as well as to international actors such as OSCE and the Special Rapporteur. It was also suggested, inter-alia, that the Committee offer technical co-operation assistance regarding implementation of the provisions of the Convention regarding expressions of racial and ethnic hatred (article 4) and education against racism (article 7).

On 22 August, CERD adopted Decision 1 (49)[82]. This refers to but does not build upon the March Decision. It does, however contain some elements of the informal submission. Thus it is addressed to all parties to GFA, expresses its concern regarding the appropriateness of the holding of the then forthcoming national elections, reiterates a willingness to assist in implementation of GFA from a perspective of ICERD and offers assistance regarding implementation of articles 4 and 7. The Decision concludes with an invitation to the Security Council, through the Secretary-General to decide on establishment of a successor force to IFOR.

The Decision was widely distributed within Bosnia and Herzegovina and received some local press coverage. It was also made available to the quasi-judicial body[83] adjudicating on alleged violations of the electoral

---

[80] *Id.*

[81] The Committee "entrusts its Chairman, in close communication with its officers, to consult, in close co-ordination with the United Nations High Commissioner for Human Rights and other United Nations bodies, notably the Special Rapporteur on the situation of human rights in the former Yugoslavia, as well as competent regional bodies, with a view to making recommendations for follow-up action by the Committee on the Elimination of Racial Discrimination".

[82] Reported in A/51/18, *supra*, at Chapter II.

[83] The Election Appeals Sub-commission, established pursuant to the provisions of Annex III of GFA, *supra*.

rules and was consulted by them in their adjudication of matters which appeared to raise issues under the Convention[84].

B. The Committee on the Rights of the Child

On 25 September 1996, the Special Rapporteur, Mrs. Rehn[85], wrote to the Committee requesting it to immediately address the situation in Bosnia and Herzegovina on an exceptional basis[86]. She based her request on the acute problems facing the hundreds of thousands of displaced and marginalised children and on her view that, "the Committee's capacity to influence the State's development of policy is greatly increased at the present time by virtue of the fundamental review and reform of institutions which is already underway". With her letter she submitted a brief report on the situation of children, prepared by UNHCHR, OSCE, WHO, UNHCR and the Office of the High Representative.

The reaction of the Committee was extremely muted. No action was taken at the next session of the Committee and, instead, Mrs. Rehn was invited to meet informally with the members during the session in January 1997[87]. At that session the Committee declined to take any particular action. It did, however, invite Mrs. Rehn to compile a special report on the situation of children in former Yugoslavia[88].

V. THE TREATY BODIES AND THE FUTURE

Apart from the exceptional opportunities afforded by GFA, the Treaty Bodies will continue to deal with Bosnia and Herzegovina in the context of existing procedures, particularly the reporting and individual communications mechanisms. The potential of these procedures can only, however, be properly exploited in the context of a relatively stable peace and a functioning central Government. As has already been noted, it will be essential that central Government be in a position to ensure that the Entities respect the terms of the instruments, provide necessary information for the compiling of reports and other communications to Treaty Bodies and implement whatever recommendations might be made. The present Constitu-

---

[84] Discussion held by the present writer with members of the Election Appeals Subcommission legal team.

[85] Appointed in 1995 to replace Mr. Mazowiecki.

[86] Letter and attached report on file with the present writer.

[87] Letter to Mrs. Rehn from the Chairperson of the Committee on file with the present writer.

[88] There are no official records of Mrs. Rehn's informal meeting with the Committee, on 20 January 1997, though it is referred to in the Committee's Session Report. UN Doc. CRC/C/62, ¶ 6. There is no reference to the request made of Mrs. Rehn to compile the special report.

tional provisions and the experience to date in Bosnia and Herzegovina do not bode well in this regard.

Even if the fundamental difficulty of an enfeebled central Government can be overcome there will remain a number of areas in which Bosnia and Herzegovina will require assistance:

i.   The Government will require technical assistance in deepening its understanding of its implementation obligations and complying with its reporting obligations. The reporting obligation is an onerous one and each Treaty Body stipulates that highly detailed information be presented in conformity with established reporting guidelines[89]. The reporting task is further complicated by the complexity of addressing multiple reporting obligations often at the same time. The task of gathering and condensing the necessary information will be especially complex in a State based on two entities, one of which is subdivided in cantons. No less difficult will be the process of publicising the findings of Treaty Bodies and implementing their recommendations.

ii. The Government will probably also require assistance in creating or adapting already existing national human rights institutions or mechanisms to play their role in promoting implementation of the instruments, including through participation in the process of report preparation.

iii. There are various valid models for participation by NGOs and independent human rights institutions in the report-drafting process[90]. It will be necessary to train the Government in the value of some role for these bodies and the range of valid options and to elicit public debate on the matter.

iv. NGOs themselves will require assistance in coming to understand their vital role in, (i) promoting implementation of the instruments and, (ii) in the reporting process as "independent voices" and counter-weights to the Government point of view. As a first step efforts will be required to broaden the geographical distribution of NGOs capable of undertaking human rights monitoring, reporting and training activities. At present NGOs in only a handful of population centres have this capacity[91]. Such organisations will then require training on the preparation and submission of independent submissions, the dissemination of the conclusions reached by Treaty Bodies

---

[89] For an overview of the reporting requirements of the six Treaty Bodies see, O'Flaherty, *Human Rights, supra.*

[90] *Id.,* at chapter 1.

[91] At the time of writing, perhaps only in Sarajevo and Tuzla, though certain Sarajevo groups may be able to provide the necessary technical assistance to groups in Bijeljina and Mostar.

and on appropriate models for relationship with each other and the State.

v. The State, judges and lawyers will require training on the individual petition procedures. This must be predicated on a deepening of understanding of the provisions of the instruments and must also focus on issues such as interpretation for Bosnia and Herzegovina of rules concerning exhaustion of local remedies, etc. The mutuality and relationship of the various mechanisms will also require examination.

vi. Publicity is central to effective use of the international procedures and the media will have a crucial role to play in publicising the various processes, including submissions, findings, follow-up, etc. In large part, the process of educating the media in these matters will fall largely to the NGO community.

The primary initiative for implementation of training programmes should come from the United Nations High Commissioner for Human Rights, whose office has amassed considerable experience in the field at least regarding the training of government officials[92]. Any initiatives of the High Commissioner will require to be supported and paralleled by projects for the NGO community and these can probably best be implemented by those international NGOs which work closely with the Treaty Bodies[93].

VI. CONCLUSION

In just a few years time the array of *ad-hoc* international human rights operations in Bosnia and Herzegovina will have disappeared. Perhaps the only international protection procedures still having jurisdiction and competence will be the human rights Treaty Bodies. This prospect may not fill all with confidence given the flawed pedigrees of the Committees with regard to the former Yugoslavia.

Certainly those who only recall the empty proceedings of the 1970s and 1980s will have little hope. However, the record since then, as described in this chapter, is not all bad. As certain of the Committees (Human Rights Committee, CERD, Committee on the Rights of the Child) struggled to be both apposite and engaged, they developed and improvised procedures which occasionally achieved modest successes: the creation of documents of record, the drawing of attention to the immutability of the international

---

[92] Each year, his Office, together with the UN Staff Training College in Turin, runs a successful training programme for Government officials on reporting procedures. Training on reporting is also frequently included in technical co-operation programmes offered by his Office to requesting States.

[93] Such as Amnesty International, SOS Torture, Anti Racism Information Service, International Service for Human Rights, International Women's Rights Action Watch and the NGO Group for the Convention on the Rights of the Child.

standards, influencing the work programme of the Special Rapporteur, giving encouragement to victims of war[94], etc. Significantly, in the fashioning of the various emergency procedures, certain of the committees demonstrated a flexibility and capacity to adapt to circumstances in a manner which bodes well for their future responses to situations as complex as that of Bosnia and Herzegovina. It must, however, be recalled that all activities of the treaty bodies occur in the context of severely straitened circumstances of overwork and inadequate secretariat servicing and that there is little hope of any immediate improvements in that regard.

In the immediate future it is to be hoped that all the Treaty Bodies will make whatever adjustments to practice and procedure as are needed to enable them to seize opportunities for participation in the process of civil society building in BiH, through, above all, ensuring that central attention is paid to the universal human rights standards contained in the UN instruments. In the longer term the Treaty Bodies and their partners, the State, the international and NGO communities, must create conditions in Bosnia and Herzegovina for effective implementation of those tasks which Treaty Bodies do best and for which they are primarily intended: supervision of the reporting and individual petition mechanisms.

---

[94] In which regard even the inappropriate procedures of the Committee on the Elimination of Discrimination Against Women registered some success.

12. A Truth Commission for Bosnia and Herzegovina?
Anticipating the Debate

The notion that reconciliation between the once warring, still antagonistic parties to the conflict in Bosnia and Herzegovina[1] may be realized in the near future seems illusory[2]. Any recent description of the Bosnian conflict will likely speak of simmering ethnic hatred, ancient feuds, the indulgent violence of this war which seemingly preclude *ab initio* the possibility of forgiveness, accountablility, reconciliation, and peace[3]. Such an intimation is quite legitimate: the nation fragmented on many levels. Retribution is carried out in diverse contexts, such as arbitrary arrests and beatings in response to other, equally arbitrary detentions or attacks. Property is being redistributed, further solidifying ethnic divisions as some are disenfranchised to the benefit of others. Reconciliation is clearly not a universally agreed upon goal for either the government of post-war BiH, nor for some portions of its citizenry.

Similar observations were recently applied to the nation of South Africa as well; yet, today that nation is working steadily towards building a sustainable democracy and promoting reconciliation among its once-divided populace. Certainly, problems and obstacles continue to exist in South Africa, but its transition from *de facto* and *de jure* racial segregation to a society making steady progress towards democracy and reconciliation can serve as an example to BiH that reconciliation is plausible from even the worst of wars.

Though the two States took different routes to the milestone of holding reasonably democratic elections, the problems – such as financial solvency, ethnic conflict, providing basic services to citizens – faced by the two newly elected governments are similiar. Discussions of reconciliation in

---

[1] Bosnia and Herzegovina refers to the state, which is comprised of two Entities, the Republika Srpska and the Federation of Bosnia and Herzegovina. Hereinafter, Bosnia and Herzegovina the state will be referred to as "BiH."

[2] *See, e.g.*, Human Rights Reports, Human Rights Coordination Centre, Office of the High Representative, January 27 – 31, 1997.

[3] *See* Bosnian Serbs drop secession demands, but new splits emerge, CNN, September 19, 1996 (available on the CNN website, http://www.cnn.com/world/9609/19/bosnia.elex).

M. O'Flaherty and G. Gisvold (eds.), Post-War Protection of Human Rights in Bosnia and Herzegovina, 241–261.
© 1998 *Kluwer Law International. Printed in Great Britain.*

BiH could benefit from careful analysis and comparison to efforts underway in South Africa. A central component of South Africa's transition to a multicultural society has been the establishment and work of its Truth and Reconciliation Commission (TRC). The TRC has been conducting hearings throughout the country, taking testimony regarding activities and events of the *apartheid* era. When the parties to the Bosnian conflict initialed the General Framework Agreement for Peace in Bosnia and Herzegovina at Dayton, Ohio[4], they committed themselves to a similar body. The parties agreed to "actively support the establishment and activities" of an international commission of inquiry[5]. The mandate of this commission was envisioned thus: "to conduct fact-finding and other necessary studies into the causes, conduct, and consequences of the recent conflict on as broad and objective a basis as possible, and to issue a report thereon, to be made available to all interested countries and organizations"[6].

At this point in the reconstruction and peace-making efforts in BiH an accurate forecast regarding the success or failure of reconciliation cannot even be guessed at, but the fact remains that work is underway now to address the problems noted above and hopefully to encourage reconciliation. Some NGOs, international, or intergovernmental agencies have begun or plan to begin a variety of multilateral reconciliation projects[7]. In addition to addressing the problems now facing BiH (many of which are explored in other chapters of the present volume), a possible means of fostering reconciliation is the formation of a truth commission. Such an organ would investigate and report on human rights violations that occurred during the Bosnian conflict. Separately, at least two NGOs have begun to explore the possibility of a truth commission for BiH[8].

---

[4] General Framework Agreement for Peace in Bosnia and Herzegovina, *initialed* Dayton, Ohio, 21 November 1995, *signed* Paris, 14 December 1995, 35 ILM 75 (1996) [hereinafter "GFA"].

[5] Side letters to the GFA, reprinted 35 ILM 75, 160-162 (1996).

[6] *Id.*

[7] To name just a few: the Office of the High Representative, the Organization for Cooperation and Security in Europe, the International Crisis Group, the Foundation for A Civil Society, and the United States Institute For Peace.

[8] The Foundation for a Civil Society (a U.S.-based NGO) and the United States Institute for Peace anticipate separate independent conferences soon to discuss and develop strategies for reconciliation in BiH and Herzegovina. The Justice in Times of Transition Project of the Foundation for a Civil Society conference hopes to hold an event co-sponsored by the British Association for Central and Eastern Europe. At the latter event, representatives from the Bosnian Muslim, Croat and Serb government, religious, civic, journalistic and intellectual communities will meet with counterparts from Palestine, Israel, Northern Ireland, South Africa, and El Salvador. The USIP conference, organized by Neil Kritz, editor of a recently published three-volume work on transitional democracies, was co-sponsored by OSCE's Office for Democratic Institutions and Human Rights and the Council of Europe. It was held the 2nd through the 4th of July 1997 in Strasbourg and involved meetings between all sides of the Bosnian conflict and key personnel and experts from other transitional democratic states.

Truth commissions have been widely utilized by States making the difficult transition to democracy. As institutions constituted after a national conflict, they are unusual, focused as they are simultaneously on the collective and individual. For a State attempting such a transition, a truth commission can be an opportunity to acknowledge past human rights violations, lay them to rest, and begin to move forward. For particular individuals, a truth commission may be the only accessible forum in which to tell their story and/or seek justice for such violations, either in the form of compensation or the prosecution of those responsible. Both of these aspects of a truth commission's mission can contribute towards addressing the recent conflict and begin the process of healing. A truth commission may yield a reconciliatory effect that no branch of government or journalistic media can produce. However, none of these positive results are guaranteed. A truth commission's success depends on many factors. To function properly a truth commission requires a difficult blend of popular and governmental cooperation, adequate resources, sufficient time, and circumstances. Not every truth commission constituted by States emerging from a period marked by human rights violations has been successful[9]. To minimize the possibility of a truth commission failing to fulfill its potential, it is important that the possibilities, drawbacks, attributes, powers, and functions of a commission be thoroughly debated. Preferably this debate should occur on a national scale, so that each citizen feels informed and part of the decision to hold a truth commission.

Given the track record of other nations' use of truth commissions to address the aftermath of devisive internal conflicts and the currently succesful use of such a commission in South Africa, it is likely that efforts in BiH to recover from the war will eventually include a discussion of the efficacy and plausibility of such a body. This paper attempts to anticipate, and perhaps contribute to, this discussion. The present chapter of course cannot encompass the breadth of issues and information that must be part of this debate. Instead, it focuses on four central questions – the nature of the commission's composition, the existence of sufficient popular support for its efforts, the nature of its mandate, and its relationship with the justice system of BiH – that will be part of this debate and applies some of the lessons of other States' reconciliatory efforts.

---

[9] For three excellent reviews of particular truth commissions, the legal, political, and social conditions in which they operated, their successes and failures, please consult Naomi Roht-Arriaza, ed., Impunity and Human Rights in International Law and Practice (Oxford Univ. Press 1995), Neil J. Kritz, ed., Transitional Justice: How Emerging Democracies Reckon with Former Regimes, Vols. I and II (United States Institutes of Peace, 1995), and Priscilla B. Hayner, "Fifteen Truth Commissions – 1974 to 1994: A Comparative Study", 16 Hum. Rts Q. 597 (1994).

I. PROMOTING RECONCILIATION: ADVANTAGES AND DISADVANTAGES OF A BiH TRUTH COMMISSION

The first miscalculation that might be made in any discussion of a truth commission for BiH would be to lose sight of the ultimate goal, to simply presuppose that a truth commission would be beneficial and move directly to discussions of its nature. With reconciliation as the goal, any discussion of achievement of that goal must encompass the possibility that a truth commission might do nothing to advance it, or, worse still, become an obstacle. Another misstep would be to move too quickly to comparisons between the severity of the Bosnian conflict and the atrocities of World War II. Such a contrast has validity and usefulness, as the creation by the international community, for the first time since World War II, of an international war crimes tribunal demonstrates. However, the similiarities should not be extrapolated to such a degree as to cast the Bosnian conflict as so singular, so unique that it cannot benefit from the experiences of other nations recovering from conflict. Parallels and comparisons validly drawn between the conflict in the former Yugoslavia and other conflicts that did not result in similiarly extraordinary international action can yet be instructive.

A. General Considerations

A truth commission for BiH may be a some ways off. As noted above, despite the recent elections and the on-going reconstruction of the State, BiH remains a country internally at odds. The establishment of a truth commission is not a *panacea* for such problems. Moreover, it can only contribute towards solving them if appropriately structured, timed, supported, and implemented. In addition, significant obstacles beyond the current climate of political trust exist. Before it is even established the debate over whether to form a commission could collapse and leave in its wake only increased animosity and blame. Once formed, a truth commission might be coopted by one side or another, or beset by internal defects, such as members or staff with separate agendas. Once begun, despite all best efforts, a truth commission may fail. Its success cannot be guaranteed. Political and social realities may render its efforts void: if a society is not prepared to hear the truth, it is likely not to listen. Public revelation of the commission of acts of violence and those who committed such acts may, in fact, not bring about the anticipated deterrent and reconciliatory effect.

In spite of the conceivable pitfalls, benefits are possible. BiH is emerging from a period of tragedy and war and every possible means of making that emergence successful ought to be employed. Revelation of the truth about the human rights violations of the Bosnian conflict may help put the conflict to rest. Also, the cooperative effort of addressing the past may help solidify the current peace and avoid a recurrence of war when the NATO troop presence is reduced or eliminated. A truth commission could also significantly supplement the operation of the International War Crimes Tribunal. Lastly, truth commissions are hardly new innovations. The historical record of, and significant scholarship about, prior truth commissions and other States' efforts to address their pasts offers a blueprint, a means of avoiding the difficulties. Since World War II, numerous States, starting down the difficult path to democracy from a violent past, have through some organized and official means sought to confront and deal with that past[10]. Building on the successes and failures of those other States, a Bosnian truth commission might be an opportunity to plan for and work towards what now seems unlikely: reconciliation.

By their very nature as a means of discovering, verifying, and proclaiming the truth about prior human rights violations, truth commissions can perform a valuable service and assist a government and a populace to make significant progress towards successfully putting a violent past behind. A truth commission's ability to render such assistance lies in its ability to fulfill a well-conceived mandate. Such commissions function positively when a focus is maintained on the discovery and revelation of the truth about the events in question[11]. A clear picture of the past, including the nature and abuses of the prior regime, gives a moral, and often political, legitimacy to the new regime. In addition to a revealing the truth, commissions can also promote reconciliation by holding perpetrators of human rights violations responsible and compensating their victims. The prosecution of perpetrators of human rights abuses will bring a State which formerly violated the human rights of its citizens into the community of those which do not[12]. It symbolically puts the past behind[13]. In addition, providing a forum for victims and either prosecuting the perpetrators or publishing accounts of human rights violations may lessen a victim's need to redress the violation and, thus, stop violence from becoming cyclical.

---

[10] Kritz's work discusses the transitions to democracy in Germany (after Nazism and after Communism), France, Denmark, Belgium, Italy, South Korea, Greece, Portugal, Spain, Argentina, Uruguay, Brazil, Chile, Uganda, Czechoslovakia, Hungary, Bulgaria, Russia, and Lithuania. Kritz, Transitional Justice, Vol. II, *supra* note 5. Hayner examines some of these as well as Bolivia, Zimbabwe, the Philippines, Chad, South Africa, Rwanda, and Ethiopia. Hayner, Fifteen Truth Commissions, *supra* note 5. In addition to some of these, Roht-Arriaza's volume contains analyses of Romania, Cambodia, and Haiti. Roht-Arriaza, Impunity and Human Rights, *supra*.

[11] *See* José Zalaquett, "Confronting Human Rights Violations Committed By Former Governments: Principles Applicable and Political Constraints", in Kritz, *Transitional Justice*, Vol. I, *supra* note 5, at 6-8.

[12] *See* Roht-Arriaza, Impunity and Human Rights, *supra*, at 293-99.

[13] Jaime Malamud-Goti, "Transitional Governments in the Breach: Why Punish State Criminals?", in Kritz, Transitional Justice, Vol. I., *supra*, at 193-95, 199.

Compensating victims of human rights abuses can also have a powerful ameliorative effect[14].

B. Considerations Specific to Bosnia and Herzegovina

The situation in BiH is distinguishable from other States' effort to confront the human rights violations of their pasts for several reasons. Unlike other States that have employed truth commissions, BiH has not made a clean break with its past. Ethnic divisions continue to divide the population and factions still struggle for control of every level of government. The cessation of a state of war has of course not generated a unity of viewpoint regarding the recent past. Cooperative popular support of a new and fragile government is necessary to that government's long term survival. Whether a truth commission can of its own accord and by its cooperative nature and difficult task generate some such support remains to be seen.

Another consideration regarding a truth commission in the context of BiH is the damage done by the war. The nation exists in a state of effectively permanent population displacement. Such realignment of the populace may be an inherent flaw in any plan for reconciliation. After all, regardless of its origin, nationalism was an important encouraging factor of the war. The population displacement serves as both a reminder and a reason for that nationalism. It may be too much to expect to overcome such feelings. The GFA calls for the return of refugees as a necessary step towards resolving the difficulties remaining after the war. Work towards such a goal might either involve or prohibit the possibility of a truth commission.

Many of the states that have dealt with a prior regime's human rights abuses did so after a period of war. However, these conflicts usually were resolved without outside military intervention. Not since World War II has a state been the subject of the sort large scale military and humanitarian intervention now underway in BiH. War here was halted by outside forces rather than by those engaged in the conflict. Popular wisdom holds that when the NATO IFOR/SFOR troops withdraw, little exists to prevent the former combatants from renewing their hostilities. A central challenge to the creation of national institutions, as a truth commission would have to be despite probable limitations on its existence, will be ensuring their survival upon the transfer of jurisdiction from NATO to national authorities[15].

A truth commission should be a national institution. In BiH such a body would require the cooperation of both Entities. Its successful operation

---

[14] *See* Ellen L. Lutz, "After the Elections: Compensating Victims of Human Rights Abuses", in Kritz, Transitional Justice, Vol. I, *supra*, at 575-81.

[15] *See* Kritz, Transitional Justice, Vol. II, *supra*, at 4-8, 19-27 (assessment of Germany after Nazism).

would be proof that the new Bosnian national authorities can function and not break down when confronted with difficult issues. As a State rebuilding its internal structure, it is important for BiH to develop respect for the laws of the new State. By operating according to and within parameters of that law, a truth commission could set an important example. As a democratic style of government is implemented, the examination of the human rights abuses of the past provides an important test of the universality and predictability of the rule of law. A truth commission able to strike the correct balance "between a whitewash on the one hand and a witch-hunt on the other"[16] will solidify the new regime's civilian authority. However, BiH is also a constituent part of a state with a significant history of communism. Communist regimes generally were highly effective in the destruction of national historical memory. Citizens of communist countries are unused to hearing the truth from their governments[17]. BiH's populace may not believe the truth if it comes from a source that is perceived to be biased. A truth commission that operates as a cooperative effort involving each Entity may successfully "teach" the populace to believe its new government.

In addition to these considerations, it is possible that the nature and interrelationship of the problems confronting postwar Bosnia may be too complex for a truth commission. Generally speaking, other nations have used truth commissions to address civil and political rights such as arbitrary executions, disappearances, assaults, torture, and the like. However, BiH has been victimized by massive destruction and appropriation of property. Political rights are now subject to routine denial. It is an open question beyond the scope of this chapter whether and how a body conceived in response to violations of civil and political rights can begin to address deprivations on a massive scale of economic, social and political rights.

C. Supplementing the International Tribunal

The International Criminal Tribunal for the former Yugoslavia further complicates the Bosnian situation. Unlike any other State save one which has attempted to emerge from war and move towards democracy, BiH is the subject of an international war crimes tribunal inquiry[18]. It was after the successful military conclusion of World War II that the concept of war crimes and a special tribunal to prosecute those alleged to have committed

---

[16] Neil J. Kritz, "The Dilemmas of Transitional Justice", *in* Kritz, Transitional Justice, Vol. I, *supra*, at ix, xx.

[17] *See* Kathleen E. Smith, "Destalinization in the Former Soviet Union", *in* Roht-Arriaza, Impunity and Human Rights, *supra*, at 118-21.

[18] For a more comprehensive discussion of the role of the Tribunal, see Chapter 10 of this volume.

them was developed. Thus, only post-World War II Germany has had to cope simultaneously with international prosecution of its some of its citizenry, recovery from war, and a transition to democracy. The Tribunal fulfills some of the many requirements which inhere to a state's transition from a human rights abusing regime to a democratic human rights protecting one. The Tribunal's work, which will no doubt continue for some years, addresses the need to deter future abuses and ameliorate past violations. Prosecution has been a constituent part of several states' transitional efforts. Bringing human rights violators to public justice can demonstrate, on a national basis, a break with the past and the atrocities associated with it. It also may create – or at least assist in the creation of – new behavioral norms that might prevent a recurrence of similar events.

Yet, despite its efforts, the Tribunal alone is insufficient to meet the entirety of this task. Its scope is not sufficiently broad, its efforts not suitably accessible to the public, and the closure it may bring will not arrive soon enough to meet BiH's needs as it moves from war to democracy. According to its statute, the Tribunal will redress violations of international humanitarian law – that is, those committed during times of armed conflict[19]. Other violations of human rights will require another avenue of recourse, such as national courts. It is likely therefore that non-prosecutorial efforts to redress the past will also be necessary. Richard Goldstone, the former Chief Prosecutor for the Tribunal, made this point in a recent speech:

> Many lessons can be learned from [the] experiences of national commissions in Europe, Latin America, and Africa. The first and most important is the deep need of victims for acknowledgment. They cannot forget what has happened to them and cannot get on with building the future until their calls for justice have been answered. The worse the violations and the longer the time during which they were committed, the louder are their calls. Forgiveness cannot be granted without knowledge; and without forgiveness, there cannot be any meaningful reconciliation[20].

There has been much discussion in the media and among commentators about the lack of political will on the part of the international community, the political powers in BiH, and the other Balkan states to fully respect and support the Tribunal[21]. Progress has been slow and will, without significant

---

[19] Statute of the International Tribunal for the Prosecution of Persons Responsible for Serious Violations of International Humanitarian Law Committed in the Territory of the Former Yugoslavia since 1991, U.N. Doc. S/25704 at 36, annex (1993) and S/25704/Add.1 (1993), *adopted by* Security Council, U.N. Doc. S/RES/827 (25 May 1993).

[20] Richard Goldstone, "The Matthew O. Tobriner Memorial Lecture: 'Exposing Human Rights Abuses – A Help or Hindrance to Reconciliation?' ", 22 Hastings Const. L. Q. 607, 615 (1995).

[21] *See, e.g.,* Paul D. Marquardt, "Law Without Borders: The Constitutionality of An International Criminal Court", 33 Colum. J. Transnat'l L. 73, 95 (1995); Stephen Engelberg,

change in the *status quo*, continue as such. Indictments have been released and the trial of some relatively minor offenders have begun, but the arrests of the likes of Mladic or Karadic cannot be forecast in the near future.

In addition, the activity of the Tribunal is carried on in The Hague, far removed from the Bosnian countryside. It is natural to expect that reports of events there will sound quite different when filtered through partisan media or political rhetoric. There is no significant opportunity for average BiH citizens, whatever their ethnicity, to get a true picture of the Tribunal's efforts. The Tribunal's real success will be in the measure of satisfaction that it gives the international community that something is being done to redress the atrocities of the Bosnian conflict.

Lastly, the Tribunal functions as a criminal court. It will not bring every human rights violator to justice and perhaps not even every war criminal[22]. The Tribunal focuses on victimization on a large scale. The smaller incidents of the Bosnian conflict, which may range from destruction of property to murder, may not rise to the level of war crimes. In addition, such incidents may not be susceptible to proof in a courtroom. The Tribunal cannot address these smaller crimes, nor would it be a wise use of prosecutorial effort or the Tribunal's scarce funds to do so. What would be the sanction? The Tribunal is not a civil court; it cannot grant the sort of relief, monetary or equitable, that some victims may need or seek.

II. Aspects of a Possible Truth Commission for Bosnia and Herzegovina

Assuming it is agreed that a truth commission would be useful, the exact nature of such a body must be explored. The debate over whether or not to have a truth commission will necessarily include such discussions. Several questions must be answered: Is this country ready for reconciliation? Is political, military, and police co-operation ensured? Will an effort to focus on the past and the truth deter future violations? Is there a need in the populace to tell their stories, to testify about what occurred, and to do so truthfully? If so, has there been a sufficient break with that past such that this sort of effort with its necessary but upsetting focus on past human rights violations can proceed statewide? A truth commission must be at least condoned, if not supported, by the populace for it to succeed. How fragile is the democracy – will it withstand the revelation and/or publication of the truth?

The specific nature and powers of a truth commission will also require careful consideration. Should any such commission have the power to

---

"Bosnian Croat Sought by Tribunal Is Freed Despite Pledge", *N.Y. Times*, Dec. 8, 1995, A18.

[22] Petrovic, Post-Dayton Tribunal, *supra*.

punish, or institute reparative, or compensative measures? How should such powers be limited? Should this body be able to grant clemency and/or immunity? What sort of investigatory mandate should it have (e.g., human rights abuses generally, or specific violations, such as murder, disappearances, genocide, torture, arbitrary detention, denials of freedom of speech, seizure of property, etc.) How long should that mandate last? The membership of a truth commission can be of extreme importance, as it may lend a mantle of trust and/or impartiality. Who should be a part of such a body? Should the truth commission be undertaken under the aegis of a specific national or international entity, such as the executive, the judiciary, the international community, a coalition of nongovernmental organizations?

Contemplating a truth commission as a possible mechanism of addressing the problems of post-war BiH means presaging a difficult debate. This debate, like the one which took place during 1994-95 in South Africa, will be at times acrimonious and exciting, plodding or rapid[23]. To be constructive, however, it must be national and comprehensive. It must range from the objectives and functions of a possible truth commission to the possibilities of amnesties and the plausibility of reparations. Below, four key questions that will be part of this debate are discussed in light of certain lessons drawn from previous states' truth commissions.

A. A Commitment to Reconciliation and to a Truth Commission

For a truth commission to function efficiently it should have the support of both the new government and the populace. Generally speaking, measures designed to address a previous government's human rights abuses ought to be put into place following the change in government from human rights violating to human rights observing. The pace of establishment and of the work of a truth commission must be gauged carefully against the available political capital for its support.

This calculus presupposes a "clean break" between the two regimes. However, as previously noted, BiH's conflict did not end as such – rather, the combatants were forced apart by the international community and by NATO forces. Thus, the timing of holding a truth commission for BiH will involves a complicated analysis which will encompass the political will for such a body at many levels, international, national, and local, as well as a realistic assessment whether a truth commission will under then existing circumstances accomplish its task and contribute to the peace. Convincing the tripartite Bosnian government to support a truth commission will not be an easy task. Each side will likely see such a body either as a weapon, or a

---

[23] "Alternatives and Adjuncts to Criminal Prosecutions," speech by Dr. Alexander Boraine, Vice Chairperson of the South African Truth and Reconciliation Commission, given in Brussels, Belgium, 20-21 July 1996 (available on the TRC website, http://www.truth.org.za/speech01.htm).

threat, or both. Of course, it is possible for a truth commission to function much as the Tribunal is now operating: with the support of the Bosnian Entities in word only. To do so, however, might result in a less efficacious truth commission, such as that held in Chile in the early 1990s.

Fifteen years after staging the bloody 1973 military coup in Chile, Augusto Pinochet allowed a general plebiscite on whether his military rule should continue. He lost, and peaceful general elections were held in 1989. Though Pinochet negotiated retaining his post as chief of the military until 1997, a new civilian president, Patricio Aylwin, took office in 1990. Following the example of Argentina, Aylwin appointed a National Commission on Truth and Reconciliation, giving it nine months to investigate and report on human rights violations of the 1973-1989 period and make recommendations to prevent future abuses. Aylwin accepted the report and offered a nationally-televised apology on behalf of the government. However, Pinochet subsequently made clear that he would cause the events of 1973 to be repeated if any soldiers were prosecuted. As of 1994, only twenty convictions for human rights abuses had been obtained.

The current divisiveness of the Bosnian political climate does not necessarily doom a truth commission's effectiveness. Ethnic control over Bosnian local and national politics is not absolute: despite human rights abuses by the majority parties, opposition parities garnered significant public support during the campaigning leading up to the 1996 elections. With a earnest media campaign, a truth commission constituted by the national authorities with international assistance might generate its own popular support.

In Argentina, for example, a truth commission's efforts managed to garner the country's new president sufficient political capital to repeal a law put in place by the former military regime. The Argentinean military lost its hold on power after Britain defeated it in the Falklands war. Elections were held in 1982 and the following year Raul Alfonsin took office as the new civilian leader. He immediately instituted measures to deal with the abuses committed by the military-run government during the previous decade, forming the National Commission on Disappeared Persons (CONADEP). In 1984, CONADEP began hearing testimony from relatives of persons who had disappeared under the military regime. Testimony was taken by CONADEP staff at branches established around the country and at Argentinean embassies abroad. In less than a year, a long report, containing more than 50,000 pages of documentation and an annex listing the names of 8,961 disappeared persons, was submitted to the president. A two hour television program was also prepared and broadcast nationally. The report was widely distributed in Argentina and abroad. Capitalizing on the enthusiasm over the report, Alfonsin was able to orchestrate the repeal of an amnesty law passed by the military. Alfonsin's government was then able to prosecute several officers of the former military regime[24].

A Bosnian truth commission could not only generate its own support, but also contribute towards encouraging a civil society in the new State. During the 1996 elections in BiH, free speech for political candidates was a difficult problem[25]. By taking testimony from average BiH citizens about their suffering during the war and publicizing those stories, a truth commission would demonstrate that political participation and free speech are possible in the new Bosnian political system.

B. The Question of A Truth Commission's Membership

The *status quo* in BiH is not unlike that of other nations prior to their use of truth commissions. A high level of mistrust infuses the interaction of the Bosnian Entities, which indicates that neither Entity would trust the other's participation in a truth commission. Instead, if one Entity were to support the creation of such a body, it is likely that the other would oppose it, fearing that it will be used against it. These fears will have to be allayed if a truth commission is ever to come about. One possible solution would be a commission comprised of international figures or a commission constituted under the sponsorship of a particular international agency. International membership can be a useful addition to a truth commission. However, international sponsorship also has drawbacks – it does little to advance the new government's interest in repudiating the human rights abuses of the past or in demonstrating its commitment to democracy.

On the question of sponsorship or membership of a possible truth commission, the uniqueness of the Bosnian situation is an important consideration. Unlike other nations that have employed truth commissions, BiH has been the subject of an unprecedented international intervention. Pursuant to a unusual international effort, a large multinational NATO force (originally named IFOR and now renamed SFOR) separates the former warring factions. In addition, unique international positions or organs have been active in the affairs of the recovering nation, e.g, the High Representative, the Peace Implementation Council, the Contact Group, the Human Rights

---

[24] The support, however, was not sufficient ultimately to counterbalance the military's threat of a return to military rule. Alfonsin was eventually pressured to stop the prosecutions. The government passed the "Full Stop Law" in December 1986, setting a two month deadline for the filing of criminal complaints against military officers. And, after a small 1987 rebellion on the part of some officers still facing prosecution, the Congress, with Alfonsin's support, passed the "Due Obedience Law," which exonerated lower ranking officers with a superior orders defense. Carlos Menem, who succeeded Alfonsin as president, eventually pardoned many of those convicted. *See generally* Kritz, Transitional Justice, Vol. II, *supra*, at 323-83.

[25] *See* Human Rights Reports, published daily by the Human Rights Coordination Centre, Office of the High Representative.

Chamber. A commission with international membership and/or sponsorship has both risks and benefits and the international community's involvement in BiH could both complicate and support the use of international membership on a truth commission. A United Nations-sponsored commission, for example, can bring the benefits of neutrality, legitimacy, access to funds, information, and an ability to deal directly with prominent officials[26]. Indeed, a truth commission can only make effective progress towards reconciliation if its progress is public. The BiH media is currently in shambles and hardly independent. International membership on a truth commission could partially address the problem of dissemination of accurate information. Moreover, membership is also a means of involving other avenues of possible progress towards reconciliation, such as NGOs, intergovernmental organizations, and religious institutions. All of these could provide resources and experience for a truth commission and all could be involved, tied to a possible truth commission through membership. It is, for example, unlikely that Archbishop Desmond Tutu became chair of the South African Truth and Reconciliation Commission without an analysis of this possibility.

The truth commission in El Salvador, which was comprised of international figures, is often cited as one of the more successful such commissions[27]. In that conflict, both government and the rebel insurgency it fought committed serious atrocities and neither side was able to achieve a clear victory. Instead, a negotiated peace agreement concluded the war. The peace settlement was helped along by international diplomats at the United Nations and from the so-called "friends of the peace process", the governments of Colombia, Mexico, Spain, and Venezuela. The negotiators recognized quickly that El Salvador needed to guarantee human rights protections[28]. The peace agreement included the establishment of a significant international presence in the country, including a United Nations mission (ONUSAL) with military, civil police, and civilian personnel. ONUSAL set up offices around the country; its presence had the effect of pacifying the country and separating the combatants. In addition, ONUSAL was able to provide important logistical support to the truth commission suggested by the UN[29].

The El Salvadoran Truth Commission consisted of three persons appointed by the U.N. Secretary General in consultation with the parties to the conflict[30]. It investigated the "serious acts of violence" perpetrated in

---

[26] Hayner, Fifteen Truth Commissions, *supra*, at 642-44.

[27] Margaret Popkin, "El Salvador: A Negotiated End to Impunity?", *in* Roht-Arriaza, Impunity and Human Rights, *supra*, at 211.

[28] *Id.* at 202-07.

[29] *See id.* at 204-07; Hayner, Fifteen Truth Commissions, *supra*, at 627-29.

[30] The Secretary General's initial choices met with no opposition from the parties and so former President of Colombia Belisario Bentacur, former Venezuelan Foreign Minister

El Salvador during the 1980-91 period "whose impact on society urgently requires that the public should know the truth". The Commission did not examine every act of violence, but focused on those having unique or broad impact on society in general as part of an effort to foster reconciliation. Professor Buergenthal has since written that the Commission's eight months of work and three volume report had a cathartic impact on the state inasmuch as the Commission's search for the truth in the stories of acts of violence meant that stories had to be told from all sides, pent-up anger and frustration released, and a record made[31].

Because El Salvadoran society was so polarized by the military conflict and because at least one portion of society deeply distrusted the then-functioning judicial system, there was no possibility that this investigation could have been carried out by any group of El Salvadorans no matter how prestigious. As foreigners well-known in the region but with no overt ties to the country, the Commissioners acquired instant legitimacy and credibility and, thus, people who testified to the Commission were willing not only to testify, but to do so at length despite knowing that a report would be produced. The Commission membership was seen as a sign that information given would be kept confidential, something that was not true of virtually any other El Salvadoran institution.

The Bosnian situation bears some similarity to El Salvador. There is significant international presence in the country. The current peace is governed by a negotiated settlement which is enshrined in the Dayton Accords. In addition, Bosnian society is plagued by political polarization similar to that experienced by El Salvador. Given these circumstances, any Bosnian truth commission will require some degree of international participation. Already, many of the new national institutions created by the Bosnian Constitution have international members, including the Constitutional Court, the Central Bank, and the Human Rights Commission[32]. Along these same lines, an additional national institution charged with investigating and revealing past human rights violations is possible. Now that the NATO forces appear to be remaining in the country, international membership will help ensure that such a truth commission would have the resources and access to the country to function properly. Also, the international members will be in a position not only to prevent such a commission from becoming partisan, but also from bogging down in internal conflict.

Reinaldo Figueredo, and former President of the Inter-American Court of Human Rights and U.S. law professor Thomas Buergenthal were named to the Commission.

[31] *See* Thomas Buergenthal, "The United Nations Truth Commission for El Salvador", 27 Vand. J. Transnat'l. L. 498, 540 (1994).

[32] *See* Constitution of Bosnia and Herzegovina, GFA, *supra*, Annex 4; *see also* Fred L. Morrison, "The Constitution of Bosnia-Herzegovina", 13 Const. Comment. 145 (1996).

C. The Scope of a Truth Commission's Mandate

The scope and duration of a truth commission's mandate can have significant implications for its effectiveness. The existence of the Tribunal is apt testimony to the horrible breadth of atrocities that might be the subject of investigation by a Bosnian truth commission. However, that same sheer volume may be too much for a truth commission. If such a commission is to work in conjunction and in supplement to the Tribunal, its mandate should be carefully plotted as to maximize its effectiveness.

One possible means of defining a commission's scope is to limit the subject of its investigation. A commission in the Philippines was granted the power to conduct only a limited investigation, focusing on just one event that was well-known internationally. In 1986, after grassroots efforts toppled the martial law rule of President Ferdinand Marcos, the "people power revolution" installed Corazon Aquino, widow of assassinated Marcos political opponent Benigno Aquino, as President of the Philippines. Initially, the new government sought to establish rule of law and the protection of human rights: President Aquino announced the formation of the Presidential Commission on Human Rights (later reformed as the Commission on Human Rights). The Commission re-opened the investigation into the assassination of Benigno Aquino, which had been closed after a Marcos-controlled investigatory board established the guilt of a lone gunman in a trial internationally regarded as a sham. Subsequently, after three years of investigation and trial, the Philippine Supreme Court found sixteen military personnel guilty in connection with the assassination and sentenced them all to life imprisonment[33].

Still, despite the new government's pledged support for human rights, political struggles at the highest level stalled its effectiveness. The political will necessary for forceful investigation was absent. The military had played a central role in ousting Marcos. Thus, Aquino's transitional government continued to keep key military personnel in the same positions they held during the Marcos regime. Military support was crucial to her government's political power base. To remain in power, Aquino was forced to compromise and her government's commitment to human rights protection was undermined. By the beginning of 1988, all of the former human rights activists who had gained key positions in the new government in 1986 were gone from government[34].

It is unlikely that such a signal event in the course of the Bosnian conflict could be agreed upon. Even if it were, given the nature of the war, any event of sufficient magnitude is likely to be the subject of investigation by the Tribunal. While the Tribunal and a truth commission would often work

---

[33] Belinda A. Aquino, "The Human Rights Debacle in the Philippines", *in* Roht-Arriaza, Impunity and Human Rights, *supra*, at 234-36.

[34] *Id.* at 236-38.

in parallel, limiting the mandate of a truth commission to a single or series of events is impracticable. Rather, the creators of a Bosnian truth commission will likely find a more useful example in the origins and workings of the Truth and Reconciliation Commission, which is currently hearing testimony and issuing reports in South Africa.

The South African commission has its origins in the passage of a new constitution for South Africa in 1993, the peaceful nationwide elections for all of South Africa's citizenry in 1994, and the passage in 1995 of a parliamentary act aimed towards national reconciliation through the investigation and disclosure of gross human rights violations of the past[35]. The 1993 Constitution provided that "in order to advance reconciliation and reconstruction, amnesty shall be granted in respect of acts, omissions and offences associated with political objectives and committed in the course of the conflicts of the past. To this end, Parliament under the Constitution shall adopt a law providing the mechanisms, criteria and procedures, including tribunals, if any, through which such amnesty shall be dealt with at any time after the law has been passed"[36]. The 1995 Act provided for the establishment of the Commission and assigned it the task of

> establishing as complete a picture as possible of the causes, nature and extent of the gross violations of human rights which were committed during the period 1 March 1960 to the cut-off date [5 December 1993] ... by conducting investigations and holding hearings; facilitating the granting of amnesty to persons who make full disclosure of all the relevant facts ... and comply with the requirements of this Act; establishing and making known the fate or whereabouts of victims and restoring the human and civil dignity of such victims by granting them an opportunity to relate their own accounts of the violations of which they are the victims, and by recommending reparation measures in respect of them; compiling a report providing as comprehensive an account as possible of the activities and findings of the Commission, and containing recommendations of measures to prevent the future violations of human rights[37].

The Commission began its work on 16 December 1996; it will work for 18 months and has an option for a six month extension. It has a wide-ranging subject mandate, but is limited in terms of the dates of its charge and the duration of its ability to complete it. It can investigate, inspect, hold hearings, subpoena witnesses, compel testimony (though testimony or documents provided may not be used against the provider in court), grant

---

[35] *See* Explanatory Memorandum to the Promotion of National Unity and Reconciliation Bill, No. 34, 1995 (available at the Truth and Reconciliation Commission's website, http://www.truth.org.za/back/bill.htm) [hereinafter "Explanitory Memorandum"].

[36] *Id. See also* Interim Report of the Truth and Reconciliation Commission (June 1996) (also available on the TRC's website) [hereinafter "Interim Report"].

[37] Interim Report, *supra.*

amnesty and recommend reparations for victims[38]. Its proceedings are open to the media and the general public and are conducted at regional sites around the country.

A long national debate preceded the formation of the South African Commission. Two major conferences were held in South Africa as the views of international scholars and human rights practitioners were solicited. During the debate, the idea of a truth commission gained credence as a tool for reconciliation as well as a mechanism for healing. However, it was not seen as a substitute for criminal prosecution. The debate was, therefore, not "won" by one side or another; instead, it produced a compromise and made the Commission a reality[39].

South Africa provides a better example for BiH. Though no such comparison can ever be exact, the schism between the entities in BiH is similar to that between the peoples of South Africa. Both states suffered a prolonged and violent conflict; both states were the subject of intense media scrutiny; and in both South Africa and BiH there is a perceived need for criminal prosecution of those responsible for human rights violations. To fully confront the problems created by these similar circumstances, the mandate of a Bosnian truth commission will need to be similarly wideranging as that of South Africa's Truth and Reconciliation Commission. In BiH's tripartite conflict, only a "complete picture" will do.

D. Relations Between the Judicial System and a Truth Commission

An enduring question with regard to truth commissions mandates is the possession of the ability to punish violations of human rights. A related question is whether the commission should be able to encourage truthful testimony with the power to grant amnesties from prosecution. Each question is difficult. On the one hand, a prosecutorial commission with the capacity to impose punishment represents a significant danger if it is coopted by one side or another. Also, prosecutorial ability might conflict with or be seen as usurping the role of either the national courts or the Tribunal, or both. On the other, the mistrust between Entities could result in competing, "tit for tat" prosecutions in national courts. Further, as noted previously, the Tribunal will overlook many who merit punishment. Amnesties raise thorny punishment and responsibility issues. Is the truth worth allowing the perpetrator to go free? South Africa is currently confronting this issue as the security officers who may have murdered black activist Steve Biko in 1977 have sought amnesty from the Truth and Reconciliation

---

[38] Explanatory Memorandum, *supra*, at 4-5.
[39] Boraine, " 'Alternatives and Adjuncts' to Criminal Prosecutions", *supra*.

Commission as a prerequisite of their testimony[40]. This question of the relationship of a possible amnesty power and the role of the Tribunal is utterly unique inasmuch as it has not been faced by any other truth commission. BiH, for example, has no power to alter the mandate of the Tribunal. It can only request the Security Council to act. In contrast, the Security Council has obligated States, including those not parties to the Bosnian conflict, to turn over suspects to Tribunal authorities. None of these possibly competing considerations exist in South Africa, or in any other truth commission.

It should be a prerequisite for any truth commission, and especially any commission involving in some manner the international community, to abide by international legal and human rights norms. These norms, embodied in international treaties and non-treaty-based law, impose obligations relating to investigation, prosecution, and redress for victims of human rights violations[41]. The GFA reaffirms the BiH commitment to abide by two comprehensive treaties securing substantive protection for human rights, the International Covenant on Civil and Political Rights and the European Convention[42]. Both treaties have clauses requiring States parties to "respect and ensure to all individuals within its territory and subject to its jurisdiction the rights recognized" enumerated therein[43]. This general commitment amounts to an affirmative obligation to take action to investigate violations, to prosecute or otherwise bring to justice perpetrators of such violations, and to prevent future violations of the rights to life, to freedom from torture, and to freedom from arbitrary detention. Indeed, the Human Rights Committee, which is charged with the interpretation of the Covenant, as well as the European Commission on Human Rights have expressly decided that this obligation is imposed upon the parties to these agreements[44].

---

[40] Associated Press, South African Ex-Cops Admit Killings, Washington Post, January 28, 1997 (also available on the Washington Post website at http://www.washingtonpost.com/wp-srv/WAPO/19970128/
V000404-012897-idx.html).

[41] This discussion of international law and truth commissions is, by necessity, heavily abbreviated. For a more detailed treatment of international legal obligations relating to the human rights abuses of former regimes, please consult Professor Naomi Roht-Arriaza's fine survey. Naomi Roht-Arriaza, Impunity and Human Rights, *supra*, at 24-70.

[42] GFA, *supra*, Annex 6 (Agreement on Human Rights).

[43] International Covenant on Civil and Political Rights, 999 UNTS 171, *adopted* 16 December 1966 [hereinafter "ICCPR"], Art. 2(1); [European] Convention for the Protection of Human Rights and Fundamental Freedoms, 213 U.N.T.S. 221, 1 E.T.S. 5, *signed* 4 November 1950 [hereinafter "ECHR"], Art. 1.

[44] For example, commenting on article 7, which prohibits torture, the HRC stated that violations must be investigated, those responsible held accountable, and victims provided with access to appropriate remedies, including possible compensation. *See* General Comments under Article 40, *Report of the Human Rights Committee*, 37 U.N. GAOR Supp. (No. 40) Annex V, General Comment 7 (16), at 94 (1982) and General Comment No. 20(44), art. 7, General Comments Adopted by the Human Rights Committee under Article 40, U.N.

In addition, both treaties also contain specific provisions regarding the right to a remedy and/or the right to a judicial remedy[45]. The general provision, specifying a right to "an effective remedy", may and has been read to require States parties to take affirmative action beyond merely providing access to a tribunal. The European Court of Human Rights has interpreted ECHR Article 13 as requiring investigation and prosecution of human rights violators[46]. In addition, specific requirements in these treaties to provide victims of violations of these rights access to a court or similar tribunal[47] supplement the more general "right to a remedy" provisions, providing another source for the obligation to investigate and prosecute. In a corollary to the opportunity actually to seek redress, the ICCPR (as well as other treaties) have provisions relating to the right to compensation for violations of rights specified therein[48].

Other treaty obligations applicable to BiH also impose obligations regarding the duty to prosecute human rights violators. The Genocide Convention defines genocide to include the deliberate attacks on any religious, racial or national group and specifies that it is a crime under international law which parties to the Convention undertake to prevent and punish. The "constitutionally responsible rulers, public officials or private individuals," of states parties to the Convention are to provide for effective penalties and a competent tribunal[49]. Similarly, the Convention on Torture contains provisions for the investigation of allegations of torture and

---

Doc. No. CCPR/C/21/Rev.1/Add.3 (7 April 1992). The European Commission has held that article 2, which protects the right to life, imposes an obligation to prosecute criminally those that violate the right. *Mrs. W.* v. *United Kingdom*, 32 Collection of Decisions of the European Commission on Human Rights 190, 200 (28 February 1983).

[45] *See* ICCPR, Art. 2(3), ECHR, Art. 13; *see also* Universal Declaration of Human Rights, *adopted by* General Assembly, GA Res. 217 A (III), 10 December 1948 [hereinafter UDHR], Art. 8.

[46] *Klass et al.* v. *Federal Republic of Germany*, 28 Eur. Ct. H.R. (ser. A) (1978).

[47] UDHR, *supra*, Art. 10; ICCPR, *supra*, Art. 14; ECHR, *supra*, Art. 6.

[48] *See* ICCPR, *supra*, Arts. 9(5) and 14(6); *see also* Study Concerning the Right to Restitution, Compensation and Rehabilitation for Victims of Gross Violations of Human Rights and Fundamental Freedoms, U.N. Sub-Commission on Prevention of Discrimination and Protection of Minorities, U.N. Doc. E/CN.4/Sub.2/1993/8 (2 July 1993) (Mr. Theo Van Boven, Special Rapporteur). Of course the question of a truth commission's power to award compensation is a difficult one: the state is bankrupt. Discussions on this "power" of the truth commission will be significantly informed by the developments regarding the Property Commission created to address issues involving distribution of property, abandoned and otherwise. The Property Commission has no significant reserve of funds to offer compensation for the the property taken from many in both Entities. In addition, the war involve massive destruction as well as appropriation of property. It is entirely possible that the scale of the compensation may be so vast as to negate the possibility of vindicating this right. Lastly, as noted earlier, truth commissions have generally been conceived to address questions of civil and political rights, a fact which prompts the question can a such a body adequately address economic, social and political rights?

[49] Convention on the Prevention and Punishment of the Crime of Genocide, 78 UNTS 277, *adopted* 9 December 1948, at Arts. I-VI.

prosecution of alleged torturers, regardless of their political status. While this Convention rests the responsibility for such prosecutions with domestic courts, it also establishes a firm State obligation to extradite or prosecute alleged torturers[50]. In addition, the humanitarian law norms in the 1949 Geneva Conventions insist that the High Contracting Parties "search for persons alleged to have committed, or to have ordered to be committed," grave breaches of international law, including willful killing, torture or inhuman treatment, willfully causing great suffering, and unlawful deportation or confinement[51]. It is safe to state that international law imposes an obligation on states to address past human rights violations with an eye towards providing victims of those violations with some form of remedy[52].

However, whether that remedy takes the form of a prosecution of an alleged violator or the opportunity for the victim to tell his or her story, and perhaps seek reparations, is a decision for the national government. Unlike the previous questions, here no example of a prior truth commission's success or failure in either the choice or the effort to prosecute perpetrators of human rights violations is necessary or possible. Every State that has employed a truth commission has confronted, in one fashion or another, this choice and its inherent political and social questions. Trying to draw a

---

[50] Convention against Torture and Other Cruel, Inhuman or Degrading Treatment or Punishment, 23 ILM 1027 (1984) as modified 24 ILM 535 (1985) (revised), Arts. 1, 2, 4-8, 12. Other human rights treaties address one or another of the prohibit-prosecute-prevent trilogy of possible state action relating to human rights abuses, but not all three. The Racial Discrimination Convention, for example, while requiring states to outlaw some acts of racial hatred, does not require prosecution of such acts. It does, however, provide for redress and the right to a remedy. States must assure that persons within their jurisdiction have "effective protection and remedies through the competent national tribunals ... against acts of racial discrimination ... as well as the right to seek ... just and adequate reparation ... ." Convention on the Elimination of All Forms of Racial Discrimination, 660 UNTS 195, *adopted* 21 December 1965, Arts. 1, 2, 4-7.

[51] *See* Geneva Convention for the Amelioration of the Condition of the Wounded and Sick in Armed Forces in the Field, *entered into force* 21 October 1950, Arts. 49 and 50; Geneva Convention for the Amelioration of the Condition of the Wounded, Sick and Shipwrecked Member of the Armed Forces at Sea, *entered into force* 21 October 1950, arts. 50 and 51; Geneva Convention Relative to the Protection of Civilians in Time of War, *entered into force* 21 October 1950, Arts 146 and 147.

[52] The foregoing discussion of treaty provisions applicable to a duty to prosecute alleged perpetrators of human rights violations is by no means complete. Reference should also be made to customary international law, which comprises the general and consistent practice of states and which supplements the obligations imposed by treaties by imposing the same obligations on states not party to the treaty. In the case of "widespread and representative participation" by states in the a treaty, it may come to embody general norms of state practice, to which nonparty states should adhere. *See North Sea Cases*, 1969 I.C.J. 3, 41-42 (20 February 1969). It is arguable that the abovementioned treaty provisions, the work of United Nations organs, treaty bodies, and conferences, as well as the general practice of states together form an obligation to prohibit, prosecute, and prevent human rights violations. *See* Roht-Arriaza, Impunity and Human Rights, *supra*, at 39-56.

lesson from another State's struggle with the punishment/amnesty choice is to beg the question. By virtue of the GFA, BiH agreed to secure for its citizenry the rights and protections represented by the treaties mentioned above[53]. To abide by this commitment, a Bosnian truth commission must attempt to bring human rights violators to justice and to make reparations of some manner to their victims. Inasmuch as cross-allegations of and conflict over blame and responsibility for wartime human rights violations continue to be central to the ongoing animosity between the Entities, a truth commission that failed to address issues of retribution, prosecution, and reparations would be an ineffective mechanism for reconciliation. The exact resolution of these issues must be decided by the people of BiH after a deliberate weighing of the obligations of the State as a member of the international community and the realities of being a fledgling democracy recently emerged from war.

III. CONCLUSION

As Carl Bildt, formerly the international community's representative in BiH has noted, the path to reconciliation and reconstruction in BiH will be lengthy. Traversing it will require the sustained commitment of the international community. Economic, political, military aid is only the beginning, as the new State will benefit as well from the significant coordination and encouragement of its progress[54]. A truth commission can assist in this effort, or not, depending on its formation, resources, support, and mandate.

Despite the complexities involved in deciding to have and then in actually establishing such a commission, the benefits outweigh the drawbacks. As mentioned earlier, every means of encouraging reconciliation that has a chance of succeeding should at least be discussed, if not seriously employed. However, many of the factors that will figure into the decision to constitute a truth commission have yet to be settled or developed. Time will tell. Should conditions be available for a possible truth commission, this decision should be made deliberately, after careful consultation with representatives of governments, international NGOs and intergovernmental agencies and complete internal debate involving every segment of Bosnian society. Building on the other efforts, domestic and international, to rebuild BiH, a truth commission can help make reconciliation seem no longer an illusion, but just a distant and distinct possibility.

---

[53] GFA, *supra*, Annex 6.
[54] Carl Bildt, "Bosnia can't do it alone", *The Financial Times*, October 4, 1996.

Afterword:
Human Rights, Identity and Bosnia and Herzegovina

I write these lines in Sarajevo. This city has become a symbol, and indeed has had such a status given to it several times in this century. Many of the internationals presently working in this town have been shown, when they arrived here at the beginning of their mission, the corner where Prince Ferdinand of Austria was killed in 1914, the starting point of World War One. But I would like to talk much more of recent times, when Sarajevo has become a symbol once again.

Many of us other Europeans, especially those of my and of younger generations, were for a long time not aware of the fact that Sarajevo was a city with a long tradition of different peoples with different ethnic backgrounds living together. It was the war in this country that brought to our consciousness this tradition of living together in all of Bosnia and in particular in Sarajevo. This town became a symbol again, a symbol of this fact. I am obviously aware that things have changed and that there are many problems today. But I know, as well, that many people in this town were always convinced about living together with everyone else and throughout the terrible years of war they wanted, and still want to continue the tradition of living together. It is still the symbolism of Sarajevo.

Sarajevo, then has much to tell us about the requirements for and possibilities of mutual respect for human rights and about the relationship between human rights and identity.

Sometimes people tell me, that their Human Rights as Croatians have been violated, or their Human Rights as Serbs, or their Human Rights as Bosniaks. This is to my mind impossible, because Human Rights can never belong to one group or another. Everyone has Human Rights, by virtue of the simple fact of being born as a Human Being. This is even the genuine definition of Human Rights. They belong to everybody without discrimination.

It seems that a point can be reached in the development of a society, where the notion of dignity is no longer attached to individuals but to groups. If really the notion of dignity changes to groups, those groups have

M. O'Flaherty and G. Gisvold (eds.), Post-War Protection of Human Rights in Bosnia and Herzegovina, 263–266.
© 1998 *Kluwer Law International. Printed in Great Britain.*

an identity of origin, be it ethnic or religous, origin of a village or a region, origin of a family or of clans. In any case this kind of identity is based on elements that are supposed to be in the nature of a person and not in the free choice of this person. I will come back to these differences in identities later.

When a society develops identities based on the background of origin and when those identities start to become political identities, then in every case politics become dangerous, sometimes extremely dangerous. And let it not be said that there is a big difference between Western and Central and Eastern Europe. There are differences, but the root phenomenon of political danger is the same all over Europe. Let me first talk about the differences between Central and Eastern and Western Europe and come to the common elements later.

The European States were built as nation-states. The concept of the nation-state is not very old. The first ones were built around the time of the French Revolution, and one should be aware that the history in this field is slightly different in Western and Central and Eastern Europe. When the idea of national identity first arose in Western Europe the possibility was there of constructing nation-states more or less out of existing States, or of building new nation-states out of smaller entities existing previously, like for example in Italy or Germany. In Central and Eastern Europe, on the other hand, the big empires of the same period were existing much longer, so that the idea of national identity possibly took the form of romantic dreams without the conditions for implementation. Many people think that the reason for the fact that nationalism on ethnic grounds is more frequent in Central and Eastern than in Western Europe was to do only with the totalitarian regimes in those countries in this century. This is not completely true: historically the starting point for the differences is located in the last century as well.

So much for the differences. But let me come now to what is common to Central and Eastern and Western Europe. And let me ask you: what is the difference between what happened in the Balkans and the growing phenomena of xenophobia and racism in Western European countries? If in certain regions in Western Europe there is a growing movement towards separatism, what is the difference? If in many Western European States there are parties pronouncing anti-European slogans in a very nationalistic way, what is the difference?

The difference is only a gradual one, and one of intensity. But the quality of the phenomena is absolutely the same: it is a return to identities of origin.

What is the relationship between identities of origin and Human Rights? It is a very fundamental one: when the identity of origin becomes a political identity, then Human Rights are in danger. The point where political activity starts to be attached to an identity based on elements that are not a free choice of the individual but that relate to the unchangeable nature of the individual, is necessarily and automatically the beginning of the end of Human Rights. This crucial point is in any case the starting point of eth-nonationalistic feelings, whether this happens in racist or xenophobically oriented circles in Western European countries, or, in the same countries, in parties that are in a nationalist way anti-European, or if it features in nationalist-oriented slogans in Southeast European countries.

When identity of origin becames a political identity, this phenomenon is always combined with populism. Populism is a political method that wants to make people believe in so-called <natural> differences between persons belonging to different groups, thus leading people automatically to believe in the inferiority of other groupes. And this is totally incompatible with the concept of all Human Rights.

Let me at this point go back very shortly in history: When the idea of the nation-state came up in the French Revolution, it was opposite to the older concept of states belonging to principalities and kingdoms. But the new concept of states was linked with another idea born during the French Revolution, the idea of the free and independent citizen who participates democratically in the building of the state and of its institutions.

The citizen, according to the idea emerging from the French Revolution is not defined at all by any identity of origin or elements of so-called <nature> that he could not decide upon. This citizen has his fundamental rights, and is completely free to choose his political identity, and to belong to the political party of his choice or the religion of his choice (or even to no religion). He is even free to change State, to move from one country to another and to participate democratically in this new country of his choice, in the framework, of course, of the law of this country. It is obvious that today there are other limits to the free choice of the country in which one wants to live. But this does not change the concept, now two hundred years old, that the nation-state is based on citizens who are defined by an identity of their free choice, and not by an identity of whatever so-called <natural> background of origin.

We do not know how Europe will look in fifty years, but for the time being the basic structure of Europe is the states. Having built nation-states in the last century, Europe has today to make the next step from the nation-state to the state based clearly on the identity of the individual citizen in the tradition of Human Rights, democracy and the rule of law. This is a step that the whole of Europe has to take, both Central and Eastern and Western Europe, perhaps at slightly different speeds.

Political identity must be based on Human Rights, Democracy and the rule of law. And this political identity of every citizen, as well as the clear will of every citizen, to contribute democratically to the building of the community is today the only solid foundation for States. It is obvious, that origin can be a very important identity for people, along with cultural heritage. I would even like to say that the diversity and the very rich plu-ralism of cultural identities is very characteristic of Europe. But, and this is very important: those kinds of identities must be cultural ones and must not be political ones.

I met a Bosnian man who today lives abroad, and I asked him why he would not come back to Bosnia. His answer was very simple. He said if he would come back to Bosnia, everybody would ask him if he was a Bosnian Croat, a Bosnian Serb or a Bosniak, and he had no wish to be asked such questions, because he had no identity in any ethnic background. I hope very much that at some stage this man will come back to Bosnia.

An important condition for this is that everybody has multiple identities, cultural ones, and even possibly different cultural ones, political ones, different ones as well on different levels, the community level, state level and even the European level, perhaps religous ones, as well as identities in all kinds of groups or friends. A person with multiple identities is a balanced person able to contribute to building democratic societies. A person with only one identity easily becomes an extremist in the field of this identity. Multiple identities are the precondition for democratic societies and for Human Rights.

Let me come to a conclusion that is again linked to Sarajevo. When I was working in Strasbourg I sometimes had the feeling that Strasbourg was still a symbol for what must never again happen between European States after the Second World War. Being now here in Sarajevo I sometimes have the feeling that this town becomes a symbol a third time this century. A symbol for the next step that Europe has to take: to overcome the context of the nation-state and to follow the path , in a very consequent way, to a clear new concept of the state, based on the freely chosen identity of its citizens, participating democratically in the building of the common institutions, and this on different levels, the community, perhaps the region, the state itself and Europe as a whole.

DR. GRET HALLER
Ambassador
Human Rights Ombudsperson for Bosnia and Herzegovina

Notes on Contributors

Christine Chinkin is Professor of International Law at the London School of Economics. Previously, she studied and taught at law schools in Oxford, New York, Singapore, Sydney, and Southampton. She has published widely in international law journals, primarily on women and international law, dispute resolution, and treaty law.

Gret Haller holds a doctorate in Law from the University of Zurich and has served as the Swiss representative to the Council of Europe. She has been a private lawyer and a municipal councillor. From 1990 through 1994, she was a member of the Swiss Parliamentary Delegation to the Council of Europe and, in 1994, she was President of the Swiss National Council. In 1995, OSCE's Chairman-in-Office appointed her as the Human Rights Ombudsperson for Bosnia and Herzegovina.

Gregory Dean Gisvold holds degrees from Amherst College and the University of Minnesota Law School. He has been active in several human rights non-governmental organisations, including the University of Minnesota Human Rights Center, and in 1994 served as Legal Fellow for Minnesota Advocates for Human Rights. After serving as a judicial law clerk for the Minnesota Supreme Court, he assumed his current post as an Assistant Attorney General in Minnesota. In 1996, he was a Human Rights Officer for the Office of the High Representative in Sarajevo and in 1997 served as Rapporteur for the Roundtable on Justice and Reconciliation in Bosnia and Herzegovina, held in Strasbourg, France in 1997.

Susanne Malmstrom previously served as a Senior Researcher at the Raul Wallenberg Institute for Human Rights and Humanitarian Law in Lund, Sweden. She has contributed to numerous journals, conferences, and publications. Currently, she serves as a Human Rights Officer for the Organisation for Security and Cooperation in Europe Mission in Croatia.

Nedo Milicevic currently lives and works in Sarajevo, Bosnia and Herzegovina. Born in 1938, he received his doctorate in law from the University of Ljubljana, Republic of Slovenia, where he is also a Professor in the Faculty of Law. Previously, he has been a judge of the Constitutional Court of Bosnia and Herzegovina and President of the Association of Lawyers of Bosnia and Herzegovina. Presently, Milicevic serves as a member of the Administrative Board of the Helsinki Committee for the Protection of Human Rights for Bosnia and Herzegovina, as Vice President of "Circle 99", an independent association of intellectuals in Sarajevo, and as the Manager for the Legal Bureau of Non-governmental organisations in Bosnia and Herzegovina.

Nico Mol was born in the Netherlands in 1958 and graduated from the Faculty of Law, University of Amsterdam in 1985. Subsequently, he completed post-graduate diploma programme in International Law at the Institute of Social Studies in The Hague. From 1990 to the present, he has served as a case lawyer at the Secretariat of the European Commission of Human Rights in Strasbourg, France. During 1996, Mol served as Deputy Ombudsperson for Bosnia and Herzegovina in Sarajevo.

Manfred Nowak received a juris doctor from the University of Vienna in 1973, an LLM from Columbia University, New York, USA in 1975, and a doctorate of constitutional law from the University of Vienna in 1986. He has been a Professor of Law at several universities and served as the Director of the Netherlands Institute of Human Rights (SIM) at the University of Utrecht. Since 1992, he has directed the Ludwig-Boltzmann Institute for Human Rights in Vienna. From 1986 – 1993, Nowak served as a member of the Austrian delegation to the UN Commission on Human Rights and since 1993, he has also served as an expert member of the UN Working Group on Involuntary and Enforced Disappearances. He is active with numerous non-governmental organisations, has participated in many fact-finding missions, and published over 250 works. From 1994 – 1997, he was the UN Expert in charge of the Special Process on missing persons in the former Yugoslavia.

Michael O'Flaherty holds degrees from the National University of Ireland, Pontifical Gregorian University, Rome and the University of Amsterdam, and is a Solicitor of the Irish Courts. He established the field presence of the United Nations Centre for Human Rights in Bosnia and Herzegovina in 1994. Subsequently he became Secretary of the United Nations Committee on the Elimination of Racial Discrimination. In 1996 he was appointed by the UN High Commissioner for Human Rights to be Human Rights Advisor at the Human Rights Coordination Centre in Bosnia and Herzegovina and also took up the position of Focal Point for the UN Commission on Human Rights Special Rapporteur for former Yugoslavia. Currently he is Chief of the Human Rights Unit in the UN Observer Mission in Sierra Leone. He has published widely on human rights and, among other honorary positions, is a member of the Legal Advisory Board of the European Roma Rights Centre and Consultant in Human Rights Practice to the Law Society of Ireland

Zoran Pajic spent 20 years of his academic career at the University of Sarajevo, in the Faculty of Law, becoming ultimately a Professor of Public International Law. He served the United Nations Commission on Human Rights from 1989 to 1995 as a UN human rights expert in the Group of Experts on Southern Africa. Dr. Pajic has been the President of the Yugoslav Association of International Law (1989 – 1992) and a member of the Commission for Constitutional Affairs of the Parliament of Bosnia and Herzegovina (1991 – 1992). Pajic has also served as a Visiting Professor at the University of Essex Human Rights Centre (1992 – 1994) and now holds a Senior Research Fellowship at King's College, University of London.

Drazen Petrovic was born in Dubrovnik in 1963 and lived in Sarajevo until 1992. He graduated from the University of Sarajevo, Faculty of Law, in 1985; subsequently, he received a Master of Science in Law from the University of Belgrade School of Law in 1990 and a LLM in Comparative European and International Law from the European University Institute in Florence in 1995. Currently, Petrovic is completing his doctoral studies in law at the Université de Genève. He served as a senior teaching and research assistant for Public International Law at the University of Sarajevo. He is also a former leader of the environmental organisation "Greens of Bosnia and Herzegovina" and stood as a candidate for the Parliament of the Republic of Bosnia and Herzegovina and the Sarajevo City Parliament in the 1990 elections. He has contributed to several conferences and published on the subject of ethnic cleansing in Yugoslavia.

Elena Popovic graduated from the University of Belgrade School of Law in 1991. Subsequently, she served as Secretary-General of the Council for Human Rights of the Centre for Anti-War Action. Until 1995, she also worked as Secretary-General of the Helsinki Committee for Human Rights in Serbia. In 1995, she completed the Human Rights Advocates Training Program at the Center for the Study of Human Rights at Columbia University, New York, USA. Currently, she works with the Open Society Institute in New York.

Maria Stavropoulou holds degrees in law from the Universities of Athens and London as well as Harvard University and is currently pursuing doctoral studies in Germany. For many years she has worked on human rights and displacement issues, beginning as a legal advisor for refugees in her native Greece. Later, she served as a staff member of the United Nations Centre for Human Rights, where she worked as the professional assistant to the Special Representative of the Secretary-General on internally dis-placed persons. During 1997 she served as a consultant to several non-governmental organisations and is now engaged in the Protection Division of UNHCR.

Appendix

The General Framework Agreement for Peace in Bosnia and Herzegovina

Initialled in Dayton on 21 November 1995 and signed in Paris on 14 December 1995

The Republic of Bosnia and Herzegovina, the Republic of Croatia and the Federal Republic of Yugoslavia (the "Parties"),

Recognizing the need for a comprehensive settlement to bring an end to the tragic conflict in the region,

Desiring to contribute toward that end and to promote an enduring peace and stability,

Affirming their commitment to the Agreed Basic Principles issued on September 8, 1995, the Further Agreed Basic Principles issued on September 26, 1995, and the cease-fire agreements of September 14 and October 5, 1995,

Noting the agreement of August 29, 1995, which authorized the delegation of the Federal Republic of Yugoslavia to sign, on behalf of the Republika Srpska, the parts of the peace plan concerning it, with the obligation to implement the agreement that is reached strictly and consequently,

Have agreed as follows:

Article I

The Parties shall conduct their relations in accordance with the principles set forth in the United Nations Charter, as well as the Helsinki Final Act and other documents of the Organization for Security and Cooperation in Europe. In particular, the Parties shall fully respect the sovereign equality of one another, shall settle disputes by peaceful means, and shall refrain from any action, by threat or use of force or otherwise, against the territorial integrity or political independence of Bosnia and Herzegovina or any other State.

Article II

The Parties welcome and endorse the arrangements that have been made concerning the military aspects of the peace settlement and aspects of regional stabilization, as set forth in the Agreements at Annex 1-A and Annex 1-B. The Parties shall fully respect and promote fulfillment of the commitments made in Annex 1-A, and shall comply fully with their commitments as set forth in Annex 1-B.

Article III

The Parties welcome and endorse the arrangements that have been made concerning the boundary demarcation between the two Entities, the Federation of Bosnia and Herzegovina and Republika Srpska, as set forth in the Agreement at Annex 2. The Parties shall fully respect and promote fulfillment of the commitments made therein.

Article IV

The Parties welcome and endorse the elections program for Bosnia and Herzegovina as set forth in Annex 3. The Parties shall fully respect and promote fulfillment of that program.

Article V

The Parties welcome and endorse the arrangements that have been made concerning the Constitution of Bosnia and Herzegovina, as set forth in Annex 4. The Parties shall fully respect and promote fulfillment of the commitments made therein.

Article VI

The Parties welcome and endorse the arrangements that have been made concerning the establishment of an arbitration tribunal, a Commission on Human Rights, a Commission on Refugees and Displaced Persons, a Commission to Preserve National Monuments, and Bosnia and Herzegovina Public Corporations, as set forth in the Agreements at Annexes 5-9. The Parties shall fully respect and promote fulfillment of the commitments made therein.

Article VII

Recognizing that the observance of human rights and the protection of refugees and displaced persons are of vital importance in achieving a lasting peace, the Parties agree to and shall comply fully with the provisions concerning human rights set forth in Chapter One of the Agreement at Annex 6, as well as the provisions concerning refugees and displaced persons set forth in Chapter One of the Agreement at Annex 7.

Article VIII

The Parties welcome and endorse the arrangements that have been made concerning the implementation of this peace settlement, including in particular those pertaining to the civilian (non-military) implementation, as set forth in the Agreement at Annex 10, and the international police task force, as set forth in the Agreement at Annex 11. The Parties shall fully respect and promote fulfillment of the commitments made therein.

Article IX

The Parties shall cooperate fully with all entities involved in implementation of this peace settlement, as described in the Annexes to this Agreement, or which are otherwise authorized by the United Nations Security Council, pursuant to the obligation of all Parties to cooperate in the investigation and prosecution of war crimes and other violations of international humanitarian law.

Article X

The Federal Republic of Yugoslavia and the Republic of Bosnia and Herzegovina recognize each other as sovereign independent States within their international borders. Further aspects of their mutual recognition will be subject to subsequent discussions.

Article XI

This Agreement shall enter into force upon signature.

DONE at Paris, this [14th] day of December, 1995, in the Bosnian, Croatian, English and Serbian languages, each text being equally authentic.

For the Republic of Bosnia and Herzegovina

For the Republic of Croatia

For the Federal Republic of Yugoslavia

Witnessed by:

European Union Special Negotiator

For the French Republic

For the Federal Republic of Germany

For the Russian Federation

For the United Kingdom of Great Britain and Northern Ireland

For the United States of America

Annexes

Annex 1-A: Agreement on Military Aspects of the Peace Settlement

Annex 1-B: Agreement on Regional Stabilization

Annex 2:   Agreement on Inter-Entity Boundary Line and Related Issues

Annex 3:   Agreement on Elections

Annex 4:   Constitution

Annex 5:   Agreement on Arbitration

Annex 6:   Agreement on Human Rights

Annex 7:   Agreement on Refugees and Displaced Persons

Annex 8:   Agreement on the Commission to Preserve National Monuments

Annex 9:   Agreement on Bosnia and Herzegovina Public Corporations

Annex 10:   Agreement on Civilian Implementation

Annex 11:   Agreement on International Police Task Force

ANNEX 1A

Agreement on the Military Aspects of the Peace Settlement

The Republic of Bosnia and Herzegovina, the Federation of Bosnia and Herzegovina, and the Republika Srpska (hereinafter the "Parties") have agreed as follows:

Article I: General Obligations

1.   The Parties undertake to recreate as quickly as possible normal conditions of life in Bosnia and Herzegovina. They understand that this requires a major contribution on their part in which they will make strenuous efforts to cooperate with each other and with the international organizations and agencies which are assisting them on the ground. They welcome the willingness of the international community to send to the region, for a period of approximately one year, a force to assist in implementation of the territorial and other militarily related provisions of the agreement as described herein.

(a)   The United Nations Security Council is invited to adopt a resolution by which it will authorize Member States or regional organizations and arrangements to establish a multinational military Implementation Force (hereinafter "IFOR"). The Parties understand and agree that this Implementation Force may be composed of ground, air and maritime units from NATO and non-NATO nations, deployed to Bosnia and Herzegovina to help ensure compliance with the provisions of this Agreement (hereinafter "Annex"). The Parties understand and agree that the IFOR will begin the implementation of the military aspects of this Annex upon the transfer of authority from the UNPROFOR Commander to the IFOR Commander (hereinafter "Transfer of Authority"), and that until the Transfer of Authority, UNPROFOR will continue to exercise its mandate.

(b)   It is understood and agreed that NATO may establish such a force, which will operate under the authority and subject to the direction and political control of the North Atlantic Council ("NAC") through the NATO chain of command. They undertake to facilitate its operations. The Parties, therefore, hereby agree and freely undertake to fully comply with all obligations set forth in this Annex.

(c)   It is understood and agreed that other States may assist in implementing the military aspects of this Annex. The Parties understand and agree that the modalities of those States' participation will be the subject of agreement between such participating States and NATO.

2.   The purposes of these obligations are as follows:

(a)   to establish a durable cessation of hostilities. Neither Entity shall threaten or use force against the other Entity, and under no circumstances shall any armed forces of either Entity enter into or stay within the territory of the other Entity without the consent of the government of the latter and of the Presidency of Bosnia and Herzegovina. All armed forces in Bosnia and Herzegovina shall operate consistently with the sovereignty and territorial integrity of Bosnia and Herzegovina;

(b)   to provide for the support and authorization of the IFOR and in particular to authorize the IFOR to take such actions as required, including the use of necessary force, to ensure compliance with this Annex, and to ensure its own protection; and

(c)   to establish lasting security and arms control measures as outlined in Annex 1-B to the General Framework Agreement, which aim to promote a permanent reconciliation between all Parties and to facilitate the achievement of all political arrangements agreed to in the General Framework Agreement.

3.   The Parties understand and agree that within Bosnia and Herzegovina the obligations undertaken in this Annex shall be applied equally within both Entities. Both Entities shall be held equally responsible for compliance herewith, and both shall be equally subject to such enforcement action by the IFOR as may be necessary to ensure implementation of this Annex and the protection of the IFOR.

Article II: Cessation of Hostilities

1.   The Parties shall comply with the cessation of hostilities begun with the agreement of October 5, 1995 and shall continue to refrain from all offensive operations of any type against each other. An offensive operation in this case is an action that includes projecting forces or fire forward of a Party's own lines. Each Party shall ensure that all personnel and organizations with military capability under its control or within territory under its control, including armed civilian groups, national guards, army reserves, military police, and the Ministry of Internal Affairs Special Police (MUP) (hereinafter "Forces") comply with this Annex. The term "Forces" does not include UNPROFOR, the International Police Task Force referred to in the General Framework Agreement, the IFOR or other elements referred to in Article I, paragraph 1 (c).

2.   In carrying out the obligations set forth in paragraph 1, the Parties undertake, in particular, to cease the firing of all weapons and explosive devices except as authorized by this Annex. The Parties shall not place any additional minefields, barriers, or protective obstacles. They shall not engage in patrolling, ground or air reconnaissance forward of their own force positions, or into the Zones of Separation as provided for in Article IV below, without IFOR approval.

3.   The Parties shall provide a safe and secure environment for all persons in their respective jurisdictions, by maintaining civilian law enforcement agencies operating in accordance with internationally recognized standards and with respect for internationally recognized human rights and fundamental freedoms, and by taking such other measures as appropriate. The Parties also commit themselves to disarm and disband all armed civilian groups, except for authorized police forces, within 30 days after the Transfer of Authority.

4.   The Parties shall cooperate fully with any international personnel including investigators, advisors, monitors, observers, or other personnel in Bosnia and Herzegovina pursuant to the General Framework Agreement, including facilitating free and unimpeded access and movement and by providing such status as is necessary for the effective conduct of their tasks.

5.   The Parties shall strictly avoid committing any reprisals, counter-attacks, or any unilateral actions in response to violations of this Annex by another Party. The Parties shall respond to alleged violations of the provisions of this Annex through the procedures provided in Article VIII

Article III: Withdrawal of Foreign Forces

1.   All Forces in Bosnia and Herzegovina as of the date this Annex enters into force which are not of local origin, whether or not they are legally and militarily subordinated to the Republic of Bosnia and Herzegovina, the Federation of Bosnia and Herzegovina, or Republika Srpska, shall be withdrawn together with their equipment from the territory of Bosnia and Herzegovina within thirty (30) days. Furthermore, all Forces that remain on the territory of Bosnia and Herzegovina must act consistently with the territorial integrity, sovereignty, and political independence of Bosnia and Herzegovina. In accordance with Article II, paragraph 1, this paragraph does not apply to UNPROFOR, the International Police Task Force referred to in the General Framework Agreement, the IFOR or other elements referred to in Article I, paragraph 1 (c).

2.   In particular, all foreign Forces, including individual advisors, freedom fighters, trainers, volunteers, and personnel from neighboring and other States, shall be withdrawn from the territory of Bosnia and Herzegovina in accordance with Article III, paragraph 1.

Article IV: Redeployment of Forces

1.   The Republic of Bosnia and Herzegovina and the Entities shall redeploy their Forces in three phases:

2.   PHASE I

(a)   The Parties immediately after this Annex enters into force shall begin promptly and proceed steadily to withdraw all Forces behind a Zone of Separation which shall be established on either side of the Agreed Cease-Fire Line that represents a clear and distinct demarcation between any and all opposing Forces. This withdrawal shall be completed within thirty (30) days after the Transfer of Authority. The precise Agreed Cease-Fire Line and Agreed Cease-Fire Zone of Separation are indicated on the maps at Appendix A of this Annex.

(b)   The Agreed Cease-Fire Zone of Separation shall extend for a distance of approximately two (2) kilometers on either side of the Agreed Cease-Fire Line. No weapons other than those of the IFOR are permitted in this Agreed Cease-Fire Zone of Separation except as provided herein. No individual may retain or possess any military weapons or explosives within this four kilometer Zone without specific approval of the IFOR. Violators of this provision shall be subject to military action by the IFOR, including the use of necessary force to ensure compliance.

(c)   In addition to the other provisions of this Annex, the following specific provisions shall also apply to Sarajevo and Gorazde:

Sarajevo

(1)   Within seven (7) days after the Transfer of Authority, the Parties shall transfer and vacate selected positions along the Agreed Cease-Fire Line according to instructions to be issued by the IFOR Commander.

(2)   The Parties shall complete withdrawal from the Agreed Cease-Fire Zone of Separation in Sarajevo within thirty (30) days after the Transfer of Authority, in accordance with Article IV, paragraph 2 The width of this Zone of Separation will be approximately one (I) kilometer on either side of the Agreed Cease-Fire Line. However, this Zone of Separation may be adjusted by the IFOR Commander either to narrow the Zone of Separation to take account of the urban area of Sarajevo or to widen the Zone of Separation up to two (2) kilometers on either side of the Agreed Cease-Fire Line to take account of more open terrain.

(3)   Within the Agreed Cease-Fire Zone of Separation, no individual may retain or possess any weapons or explosives, other than a member of the IFOR or the local police exercising official duties as authorized by the IFOR in accordance with Article IV, paragraph 2(b).

(4)   The Parties understand and agree that violators of subparagraphs (1), (2) and (3) above shall be subject to military action by the IFOR, including the use of necessary force to ensure compliance.

Gorazde

(1)   The Parties understand and agree that a two lane all-weather road will be constructed in the Gorazde Corridor. Until such road construction is complete, the two interim routes will be used by both Entities. The Grid coordinates for these alternate routes are (Map References: Defense Mapping Agency 1:50,000 Topographic Line Maps, Series M709, Sheets 2782-1, 2782-2, 2782-3, 2782-4, 2881-4, 2882-1, 2882-2, 2882-3, and 2882-4; Military Grid Reference System grid coordinates referenced to World Geodetic System 84 (Horizontal Datum)):

Interim Route 1 From Gorazde (34TCP361365), proceed northeast following Highway 5 along the Drina River to the Ustipraca area (34TCP456395). At that point, proceed north on Highway 19-3 through Rogatica (34TCP393515) continuing northwest past Stienice (34TCP294565) to the road intersection at Podromanija (34TCP208652). From this point, proceed west following Highway 19 to where it enters the outskirts of Sarajevo (34TBP950601).

Interim Route 2: From Gorazde (34TCP361365), proceed south following Highway 20. Follow Highway 20 through Ustinkolina (34TCP218281). Continue south following Highway 20 passing Foca along the west bank of the Drina River (34TCP203195) to a point (34TCP175178) where the route turns west following Highway 18. From this point, follow Highway 18 south of Miljevina (34TCP097204) continuing through Trnovo (34TBP942380) north to the outskirts of Sarajevo where it enters the town at Vaskovici (34TBP868533).

There shall be complete freedom of movement along these routes for civilian traffic. The Parties shall only utilize these interim routes for military forces and equipment as authorized by and under the control and direction of the IFOR. In this regard, and in order to reduce the risk to civilian traffic, the IFOR shall have the right to manage movement of military and civilian traffic from both Entities along these routes.

(2)   The Parties understand and agree that violators of subparagraph (1) shall be subject to military action by the IFOR, including the use of necessary force to ensure compliance.

(3)   The Parties pledge as a confidence building measure that they shall not locate any Forces or heavy weapons as defined in paragraph 5 of this Article within two (2) kilometers of the designated interim routes. Where those routes run in or through the designated Zones of Separation, the provisions relating to Zones of Separation in this Annex shall also apply.

(d)   The Parties immediately after this Annex enters into force shall begin promptly and proceed steadily to complete the following activities within thirty (30) days after the Transfer of Authority or as determined by the IFOR Commander: (1) remove, dismantle or destroy all mines, unexploded ordnance, explosive devices, demolitions, and barbed or razor wire from the Agreed Cease-Fire Zone of Separation or other areas from which their Forces are withdrawn; (2) mark all known mine emplacements, unexploded ordnance, explosive devices and demolitions within Bosnia and Herzegovina; and (3) remove, dismantle or destroy all mines, unexploded ordnance, explosive devices and demolitions as required by the IFOR Commander.

(e)   The IFOR is authorized to direct that any military personnel, active or reserve, who reside within the Agreed Cease-Fire Zone of Separation register with the appropriate IFOR Command Post referred to in Article VI which is closest to their residence.

3.   PHASE II (AS REQUIRED IN SPECIFIC LOCATIONS)

This phase applies to those locations where the Inter-Entity Boundary Line does not follow the Agreed Cease-Fire Line.

(a)   In those locations in which, pursuant to the General Framework Agreement, areas occupied by one Entity are to be transferred to another Entity, all Forces of the withdrawing Entity shall have forty-five (45) days after the Transfer of Authority to completely vacate and clear this area. This shall include the removal of all Forces as well as the removal, dismantling or destruction of equipment, mines, obstacles, unexploded ordnance, explosive devices, demolitions, and weapons. In those areas being transferred to a different Entity, in order to provide an orderly period of transition, the Entity to which an area is transferred shall not put Forces in this area for ninety (90) days after the Transfer of Authority or as determined by the IFOR Commander. The Parties understand and agree that the IFOR shall have the right to provide the military security for these transferred areas from thirty (30) days after the Transfer of Authority until ninety-one (91) days after the Transfer of Authority, or as soon as possible as determined by the

IFOR Commander, when these areas may be occupied by the Forces of the Entity to which they are transferred. Upon occupation by the Entity to which the area is transferred, a new Zone of Separation along the Inter-Entity Boundary Line as indicated on the map at Appendix A shall be established by the IFOR, and the Parties shall observe the same limitations on the presence of Forces and weapons in this Zone as apply to the Agreed Cease-Fire Zone of Separation.

(b)   The IFOR is authorized to direct that any military personnel, active or reserve, who reside within the Inter-Entity Zone of Separation register with the appropriate IFOR Command Post referred to in Article VI which is closest to their residence.

4.   GENERAL. *The following provisions apply to Phases I and II:*

(a)   In order to provide visible indication, the IFOR shall supervise the selective marking of the Agreed Cease-Fire Line and its Zone of Separation, and the Inter-Entity Boundary Line and its Zone of Separation. Final authority for placement of such markers shall rest with the IFOR. All Parties understand and agree that the Agreed Cease-Fire Line and its Zone of Separation and the Inter-Entity Boundary Line and its Zone of Separation are defined by the maps and documents agreed to as part of the General Framework Agreement and not the physical location of markers.

(b)   All Parties understand and agree that they shall be subject to military action by the IFOR, including the use of necessary force to ensure compliance, for:

(1)   failure to remove all their Forces and unauthorized weapons from the four (4) kilometer Agreed Cease-Fire Zone of Separation within thirty (30) days after the Transfer of Authority, as provided in Article IV, paragraph 2(a) and (b) above;

(2)   failure to vacate and clear areas being transferred to another Entity within forty-five (45) days after the Transfer of Authority, as provided in Article IV, paragraph 3(a) above;

(3)   deploying Forces within areas transferred from another Entity earlier than ninety (90) days after the Transfer of Authority or as determined by the IFOR Commander, as provided in Article IV, paragraph 3(a) above;

(4)   failure to keep all Forces and unauthorized weapons outside the Inter-Entity Zone of Separation after this Zone is declared in effect by the IFOR, as provided in Article IV, paragraph 3(a) above; or

(5)   violation of the cessation of hostilities as agreed to by the Parties in Article II

5.   PHASE III

The Parties pledge as confidence building measures that they shall:

(a)   within 120 days after the Transfer of Authority withdraw all heavy weapons and Forces to cantonment/barracks areas or other locations as designated by the IFOR Commander. "Heavy weapons" refers to all tanks and armored vehicles, all artillery 75 mm and above, all mortars 81 mm and above, and all anti-aircraft weapons 20 mm and above. This movement of these Forces to cantonment/barracks areas is intended to enhance mutual confidence by the Parties in the success of this Annex and help the overall cause of peace in Bosnia and Herzegovina.

(b)   within 120 days after the Transfer of Authority demobilize Forces which cannot be accommodated in cantonment/barracks areas as provided in subparagraph (a) above. Demobilization shall consist of removing from the possession of these personnel all weapons, including individual weapons, explosive devices, communications equipment, vehicles, and all other military equipment. All personnel belonging to these Forces shall be released from service and shall

not engage in any further training or other military activities.

6.   Notwithstanding any other provision of this Annex, the Parties understand and agree that the IFOR has the right and is authorized to compel the removal, withdrawal, or relocation of specific Forces and weapons from, and to order the cessation of any activities in, any location in Bosnia and Herzegovina whenever the IFOR determines such Forces, weapons or activities to constitute a threat or potential threat to either the IFOR or its mission, or to another Party. Forces failing to redeploy, withdraw, relocate, or to cease threatening or potentially threatening activities following such a demand by the IFOR shall be subject to military action by the IFOR, including the use of necessary force to ensure compliance, consistent with the terms set forth in Article I, paragraph 3

Article V: Notifications

1.   Immediately upon establishment of the Joint Military Commission provided for in Article VIII, each Party shall furnish to the Joint Military Commission information regarding the positions and descriptions of all known unexploded ordnance, explosive devices, demolitions, minefields, booby traps, wire entanglements, and all other physical or military hazards to the safe movement of any personnel within Bosnia and Herzegovina, as well as the location of lanes through the Agreed Cease-Fire Zone of Separation which are free of all such hazards. The Parties shall keep the Joint Military Commission updated on changes in this information.

2.   Within thirty (30) days after the Transfer of Authority, each Party shall furnish to the Joint Military Commission the following specific information regarding the status of its Forces within Bosnia and Herzegovina and shall keep the Joint Military Commission updated on changes in this information:

(a)   location, type, strengths of personnel and weaponry of all Forces within ten (10) kilometers of the Agreed Cease-Fire Line and Inter-Entity Boundary Line.

(b)   maps depicting the forward line of troops and front lines;

(c)   positions and descriptions of fortifications, minefields, unexploded ordnance, explosive devices, demolitions, barriers, and other man-made obstacles, ammunition dumps, command headquarters, and communications networks within ten (10) kilometers of the Agreed Cease-Fire Line or Inter-Entity Boundary Line;

(d)   positions and descriptions of all surface to air missiles/launchers, including mobile systems, anti-aircraft artillery, supporting radars and associated command and control systems;

(e)   positions and descriptions of all mines, unexploded ordnance, explosive devices, demolitions, obstacles, weapons systems, vehicles, or any other military equipment which cannot be removed, dismantled or destroyed under the provisions of Article IV, paragraphs 2(d) and 3(a); and

(f)   any further information of a military nature as requested by the IFOR.

3.   Within 120 days after the Transfer of Authority, the Parties shall furnish to the Joint Military Commission the following specific information regarding the status of their Forces in Bosnia and Herzegovina and shall keep the Joint Military Commission updated on changes in this information:

(a)   location, type, strengths of personnel and weaponry of all Forces;

(b)   maps depicting the information in sub-paragraph (a) above;

(c)   positions and descriptions of fortifications, minefields, unexploded ordnance, explosive devices, demolitions, barriers, and other man-made obstacles, ammunition dumps, command headquarters, and communications networks; and

(d) any further information of a military nature as requested by the IFOR.

Article VI: Deployment of the Implementation Force

1. Recognizing the need to provide for the effective implementation of the provisions of this Annex, and to ensure compliance, the United Nations Security Council is invited to authorize Member States or regional organizations and arrangements to establish the IFOR acting under Chapter VII of the United Nations Charter. The Parties understand and agree that this Implementation Force may be composed of ground, air and maritime units from NATO and non-NATO nations, deployed to Bosnia and Herzegovina to help ensure compliance with the provisions of this Annex. The Parties understand and agree that the IFOR shall have the right to deploy on either side of the Inter-Entity Boundary Line and throughout Bosnia and Herzegovina.

2. The Parties understand and agree that the IFOR shall have the right:

(a) to monitor and help ensure compliance by all Parties with this Annex (including, in particular, withdrawal and redeployment of Forces within agreed periods, and the establishment of Zones of Separation);

(b) to authorize and supervise the selective marking of the Agreed Cease-Fire Line and its Zone of Separation and the Inter-Entity Boundary Line and its Zone of Separation as established by the General Framework Agreement;

(c) to establish liaison arrangements with local civilian and military authorities and other international organizations as necessary for the accomplishment of its mission; and

(d) to assist in the withdrawal of UN Peace Forces not transferred to the IFOR, including, if necessary, the emergency withdrawal of UNCRO Forces.

3. The Parties understand and agree that the IFOR shall have the right to fulfill its supporting tasks, within the limits of its assigned principal tasks and available resources, and on request, which include the following:

(a) to help create secure conditions for the conduct by others of other tasks associated with the peace settlement, including free and fair elections;

(b) to assist the movement of organizations in the accomplishment of humanitarian missions;

(c) to assist the UNHCR and other international organizations in their humanitarian missions;

(d) to observe and prevent interference with the movement of civilian populations, refugees, and displaced persons, and to respond appropriately to deliberate violence to life and person; and,

(e) to monitor the clearing of minefields and obstacles.

4. The Parties understand and agree that further directives from the NAC may establish additional duties and responsibilities for the IFOR in implementing this Annex.

5. The Parties understand and agree that the IFOR Commander shall have the authority, without interference or permission of any Party, to do all that the Commander judges necessary and proper, including the use of military force, to protect the IFOR and to carry out the responsibilities listed above in paragraphs 2, 3 and 4, and they shall comply in all respects with the IFOR requirements.

6. The Parties understand and agree that in carrying out its responsibilities, the IFOR shall have the unimpeded right to observe, monitor, and inspect any Forces, facility or activity in Bosnia and Herzegovina that the IFOR believes may have military capability. The refusal, interference, or denial by any Party of this right to observe, monitor, and inspect by the IFOR shall constitute a breach of this Annex and the violating Party shall be subject to military action by the IFOR, including the use of necessary force to ensure compliance with this Annex.

7. The Army of the Republic of Bosnia and Herzegovina, the Croat Defense Council Forces, and the Army of Republika Srpska shall establish Command Posts at IFOR brigade, battalion, or other levels which shall be co-located with specific IFOR command Vocations, as determined by the IFOR Commander. These Command Posts shall exercise command and control over all Forces of their respective sides which are located within ten (10) kilometers of the Agreed Cease-Fire Line or Inter-Entity Boundary Line, as specified by the IFOR. The Command Posts shall provide, at the request of the IFOR, timely status reports on organizations and troop levels in their areas.

8. In addition to co-located Command Posts, the Army of the Republic of Bosnia and Herzegovina, the Croat Defense Council Forces, and the Army of Republika Srpska shall maintain liaison teams to be co-located with the IFOR Command, as determined by the IFOR Commander, for the purpose of fostering communication, and preserving the overall cessation of hostilities.

9. Air and surface movements in Bosnia and Herzegovina shall be governed by the following provisions:

(a) The IFOR shall have complete and unimpeded freedom of movement by ground, air, and water throughout Bosnia and Herzegovina. It shall have the right to bivouac, maneuver, billet, and utilize any areas or facilities to carry out its responsibilities as required for its support, training, and operations, with such advance notice as may be practicable. The IFOR and its personnel shall not be liable for any damages to civilian or government property caused by combat or combat related activities. Roadblocks, checkpoints or other impediments to IFOR freedom of movement shall constitute a breach of this Annex and the violating Party shall be subject to military action by the IFOR, including the use of necessary force to ensure compliance with this Annex.

(b) The IFOR Commander shall have sole authority to establish rules and procedures governing command and control of airspace over Bosnia and Herzegovina to enable civilian air traffic and non-combat air activities by the military or civilian authorities in Bosnia and Herzegovina, or if necessary to terminate civilian air traffic and non-combat air activities.

(1) The Parties understand and agree there shall be no military air traffic, or non-military aircraft performing military missions, including reconnaissance or logistics, without the express permission of the IFOR Commander. The only military aircraft that may be authorized to fly in Bosnia and Herzegovina are those being flown in support of the IFOR, except with the express permission of the IFOR. Any flight activities by military fixed-wing or helicopter aircraft within Bosnia and Herzegovina without the express permission of the IFOR Commander are subject to military action by the IFOR, including the use of necessary force to ensure compliance.

(2) All air early warning, air defense, or fire control radars shall be shut down within 72 hours after this Annex enters into force, and shall remain inactive unless authorized by the IFOR Commander. Any use of air traffic, air early warning, air defense or fire control radars not authorized by the IFOR Commander shall constitute a breach of this Annex and the violating Party shall be subject to military action by the IFOR, including the use of necessary force to ensure compliance.

(3) The Parties understand and agree that the IFOR Commander will implement the transfer to civilian control of air space over Bosnia and Herzegovina to the appropriate institutions of Bosnia and Herzegovina in a gradual fashion consistent with the objective of the IFOR to ensure smooth and safe operation of an air traffic system upon IFOR departure.

(c) The IFOR Commander is authorized to promulgate appropriate rules for the control and regulation of surface military traffic throughout Bosnia and Herzegovina, including the movement of the Forces of the Parties. The Joint Military Commission referred to in

Article VIII may assist in the development and promulgation of rules related to military movement.

10. The IFOR shall have the right to utilize such means and services as required to ensure its full ability to communicate and shall have the right to the unrestricted use of all of the electromagnetic spectrum for this purpose. In implementing this right, the IFOR shall make every reasonable effort to coordinate with and take into account the needs and requirements of the appropriate authorities.

11. All Parties shall accord the IFOR and its personnel the assistance, privileges, and immunities set forth at Appendix B of this Annex, including the unimpeded transit through, to, over and on the territory of all Parties.

12. All Parties shall accord any military elements as referred to in Article I, paragraph I(c) and their personnel the assistance, privileges and immunities referred to in Article VI, paragraph 11.

Article VII: Withdrawal of UNPROFOR

It is noted that as a consequence of the forthcoming introduction of the IFOR into the Republic of Bosnia and Herzegovina, the conditions for the withdrawal of the UNPROFOR established by United Nations Security Council Resolution 743 have been met. It is requested that the United Nations, in consultation with NATO, take all necessary steps to withdraw the UNPROFOR from Bosnia and Herzegovina, except those parts incorporated into the IFOR.

Article VIII: Establishment of a Joint Military Commission

1. A Joint Military Commission (the "Commission") shall be established with the deployment of the IFOR to Bosnia and Herzegovina.

2. The Commission shall:

(a) Serve as the central body for all Parties to this Annex to bring any military complaints, questions, or problems that require resolution by the IFOR Commander, such as allegations of cease-fire violations or other noncompliance with this Annex.

(b) Receive reports and agree on specific actions to ensure compliance with the provisions of this Annex by the Parties.

(c) Assist the IFOR Commander in determining and implementing a series of local transparency measures between the Parties.

3. The Commission shall be chaired by the IFOR Commander or his or her representative and consist of the following members:

(a) the senior military commander of the forces of each Party within Bosnia and Herzegovina;

(b) other persons as the Chairman may determine;

(c) each Party to this Annex may also select two civilians who shall advise the Commission in carrying out its duties;

(d) the High Representative referred to in the General Framework Agreement or his or her nominated representative shall attend Commission meetings, and offer advice particularly on matters of a political-military nature.

4. The Commission shall not include any persons who are now or who come under indictment by the International Tribunal for the Former Yugoslavia.

5. The Commission shall function as a consultative body for the IFOR Commander. To the extent possible, problems shall be solved promptly by mutual agreement. However, all final decisions concerning its military matters shall be made by the IFOR Commander.

6. The Commission shall meet at the call of the IFOR Commander. The High Representative may when necessary request a meeting of the Commission. The Parties may also request a meeting of the Commission.

7. The IFOR Commander shall have the right to decide on military matters, in a timely fashion, when there are overriding considerations relating to the safety of the IFOR or the Parties' compliance with the provisions of this Annex.

8. The Commission shall establish subordinate military commissions for the purpose of providing assistance in carrying out the functions described above. Such commissions shall be at the brigade and battalion level or at other echelons as the local IFOR Commander shall direct and be composed of commanders from each of the Parties and the IFOR. The representative of the High Representative shall attend and offer advice particularly on matters of a political-military nature. The local IFOR Commander shall invite local civilian authorities when appropriate.

9. Appropriate liaison arrangements will be established between the IFOR Commander and the High Representative to facilitate the discharge of their respective responsibilities.

Article IX: Prisoner Exchanges

1. The Parties shall release and transfer without delay all combatants and civilians held in relation to the conflict (hereinafter "prisoners"), in conformity with international humanitarian law and the provisions of this Article.

(a) The Parties shall be bound by and implement such plan for release and transfer of all prisoners as may be developed by the ICRC, after consultation with the Parties.

(b) The Parties shall cooperate fully with the ICRC and facilitate its work in implementing and monitoring the plan for release and transfer of prisoners.

(c) No later than thirty (30) days after the Transfer of Authority, the Parties shall release and transfer all prisoners held by them.

(d) In order to expedite this process, no later than twenty-one (21) days after this Annex enters into force, the Parties shall draw up comprehensive lists of prisoners and shall provide such lists to the ICRC, to the other Parties, and to the Joint Military Commission and the High Representative. These lists shall identify prisoners by nationality, name, rank (if any) and any internment or military serial number, to the extent applicable.

(e) The Parties shall ensure that the ICRC enjoys full and unimpeded access to all places where prisoners are kept and to all prisoners. The Parties shall permit the ICRC to privately interview each prisoner at least forty-eight (48) hours prior to his or her release for the purpose of implementing and monitoring the plan, including determination of the onward destination of each prisoner.

(f) The Parties shall take no reprisals against any prisoner or his/her family in the event that a prisoner refuses to be transferred.

(g) Notwithstanding the above provisions, each Party shall comply with any order or request of the International Tribunal for the Former Yugoslavia for the arrest, detention, surrender of or access to persons who would otherwise be released and transferred under this Article, but who are accused of violations within the jurisdiction of the Tribunal. Each Party must detain persons reasonably suspected of such violations for a period of time sufficient to permit appropriate consultation with Tribunal authorities.

2. In those cases where places of burial, whether individual or mass, are known as a matter of record, and graves are actually found to exist, each Party shall permit graves registration personnel of the other Parties to enter, within a mutually agreed period of time, for the limited purpose of proceeding to such graves, to recover and evacuate the bodies of deceased military and civilian personnel of that side, including deceased prisoners.

Article X: Cooperation

The Parties shall cooperate fully with all entities involved in implementation of this peace settlement, as described in the General Framework Agreement, or which are otherwise authorized by the United Nations Security Council, including the International Tribunal for the Former Yugoslavia.

Article XI: Notification to Military Commands

Each Party shall ensure that the terms of this Annex, and written orders requiring compliance, are immediately communicated to all of its Forces.

Article XII: Final Authority to Interpret

In accordance with Article I, the IFOR Commander is the final authority in theatre regarding interpretation of this agreement on the military aspects of the peace settlement, of which the Appendices constitute an integral part.

Article XIII: Entry into Force

This Annex shall enter into force upon signature.

For the Republic of Bosnia and Herzegovina
For the Federation of Bosnia and Herzegovina
For the Republika Srpska

Endorsed:
For the Republic of Croatia

Endorsed:
For the Federal Republic of Yugoslavia

Appendices to Annex 1A Agreement on the Military Aspects of the Peace Settlement

Appendix A to Annex 1-A

Appendix A to Annex 1-A consists of this document together with (a) a 1:600,000 scale UNPROFOR road map consisting of one map sheet, attached hereto; and (b) a 1:50,000 scale Topographic Line Map, to be provided as described below.

On the basis of the attached 1:600,000 scale map, the Parties request that the United States Department of Defense provide a 1:50,000 scale Topographic Line Map, consisting of as many map sheets as necessary, in order to provide a more precise delineation of the lines and zones indicated. Such map shall be incorporated as an integral part of this Appendix, and the Parties agree to accept such map as controlling and definitive for all purposes.

For the Republic of Bosnia and Herzegovina

For the Federation of Bosnia and Herzegovina

For the Republika Srpska

Endorsed:

For the Republic of Croatia

Endorsed:

For the Federal Republic of Yugoslavia

[MAP COPY NOT AVAILABLE]

Appendix B to Annex 1A

Agreement Between the Republic of Bosnia and Herzegovina and the North Atlantic Treaty Organisation (NATO) Concerning the Status of NATO and its Personnel

The Republic of Bosnia and Herzegovina and the North Atlantic Treaty Organisation have agreed as follows:

1. For the purposes of the present agreement, the following expressions shall have the meanings hereunder assigned to them:

- "the Operation" means the support, implementation, preparation and participation by NATO and NATO personnel in a peace plan in Bosnia and Herzegovina or a possible withdrawal of U.N. Forces from former Yugoslavia;

- "NATO personnel" means the civilian and military personnel of the North Atlantic Treaty Organisation with the exception of personnel locally hired;

- "NATO" means the North Atlantic Treaty Organisation, its subsidiary bodies, its military Headquarters and all its constituent national elements/units acting in support of, preparing and participating in the Operation;

- "Facilities" mean all premises and land required for conducting the operational, training and administrative activities by NATO for the Operation as well as for accommodations of NATO personnel.

2. The provisions of the Convention on the Privileges and Immunities of the United Nations of 13 February 1946 concerning experts on mission shall apply mutatis mutandis to NATO personnel involved in the Operation, except as otherwise provided for in the present agreement. Moreover NATO, its property and assets shall enjoy the privileges and immunities specified in that convention and as stated in the present agreement.

3. All personnel enjoying privileges and immunities under this Agreement shall respect the laws of the Republic of Bosnia and Herzegovina insofar as it is compatible with the entrusted tasks/mandate and shall refrain from activities not compatible with the nature of the Operation.

4. The Government of the Republic of Bosnia and Herzegovina recognizes the need for expeditious departure and entry procedures for NATO personnel. They shall be exempt from passport and visa regulations and the registration requirements applicable to aliens. NATO personnel shall carry identification which they may be requested to produce for the authorities of the Republic of Bosnia and Herzegovina but operations, training and movement shall not be allowed to be impeded or delayed by such requests.

5. NATO military personnel shall normally wear uniforms, and NATO personnel may possess and carry arms if authorized to do so by their orders. The authorities of the Republic of Bosnia and Herzegovina shall accept as valid, without tax or fee, drivers' licenses and permits issued to NATO personnel by their respective national authorities.

6. NATO shall be permitted to display the NATO flag and/or national flags of its constituent national elements/units on any NATO uniform, means of transport or facility.

7. NATO military personnel under all circumstances and at all times shall be subject to the exclusive jurisdiction of their respective national elements in respect of any criminal or disciplinary offenses which may be committed by them in the Republic of Bosnia and Herzegovina. NATO and the authorities of the Republic of Bosnia and Herzegovina shall assist each other in the exercise of their respective jurisdictions.

8. As experts on mission, NATO personnel shall be immune from personal arrest or detention. NATO personnel mistakenly arrested or detained shall immediately be turned over to NATO authorities.

9. NATO personnel shall enjoy, together with their vehicles, vessels, aircraft and equipment, free and unrestricted passage and unimpeded access throughout the Republic of Bosnia and Herzegovina including airspace and territorial waters of the Republic of Bosnia and Herzegovina. This shall include, but not be limited to, the right of bivouac, maneuver, billet, and utilization of any areas or facilities as required for support, training, and operations. NATO shall be exempt from providing inventories or other routine customs documentation on personnel, vehicles, vessels, aircraft, equipment, supplies, and provisions entering, exiting, or transiting the territory of the Republic of Bosnia and Herzegovina in support of the Operation. The authorities of the Republic of Bosnia and Herzegovina shall facilitate with all appropriate means all movements of personnel, vehicles, vessels, aircraft, equipment or supplies, through ports, airports or roads used. Vehicles, vessels and aircraft used in support of the Operation shall not be subject to licensing or registration requirements, nor commercial insurance. NATO will use airports, roads and ports without payment of duties, dues, tolls or charges. However, NATO shall not claim exemption from reasonable charges for services requested and received, but operations/movement and access shall not be allowed to be impeded pending payment for such services.

10. NATO personnel shall be exempt from taxation by the Republic of Bosnia and Herzegovina on the salaries and emoluments received from NATO and on any income received from outside the Republic of Bosnia and Herzegovina.

11. NATO personnel and their tangible movable property imported into or acquired in the Republic of Bosnia and Herzegovina shall also be- exempt from all identifiable taxes by the Republic of Bosnia and Herzegovina, except municipal rates for services enjoyed, and from all registration fees and related charges.

12. NATO shall be allowed to import and to export free of duty or other restriction equipment, provisions, and supplies, necessary for the Operation, provided such goods are for the official use of NATO or for sale via commissaries or canteens provided for NATO personnel. Goods sold shall be solely for the use of NATO personnel and not transferable to other parties.

13. It is recognized by the Government of the Republic of Bosnia and Herzegovina that the use of communications channels shall be necessary for the Operation. NATO shall be allowed to operate its own internal mail and telecommunications services, including broadcast services. This shall include the right to utilize such means and services as required to assure full ability to communicate, and the right to use all of the electro-magnetic spectrum for this purpose, free of cost. In implementing this right, NATO shall make every reasonable effort to coordinate with and take into account the needs and requirements of appropriate authorities of the Republic of Bosnia and Herzegovina.

14. The Government of the Republic of Bosnia and Herzegovina shall provide, free of cost, such facilities NATO needs for the preparation for and execution of the Operation. The Government of the Republic of Bosnia and Herzegovina shall assist NATO in obtaining, at the lowest rate, the necessary utilities such as electricity, water and other resources necessary for the Operation.

15. Claims for damage or injury to Government personnel or property, or to private personnel or property of the Republic of Bosnia and Herzegovina shall be submitted through governmental authorities of the Republic of Bosnia and Herzegovina to the designated NATO Representatives.

16. NATO shall be allowed to contract direct with suppliers for services and supplies in the Republic of Bosnia and Herzegovina without payment of tax or duties. Such services and supplies shall not be subject to sales and other taxes. NATO may hire local personnel who shall remain subject to local laws and regulations. However, local personnel hired by NATO shall:

(a) be immune from legal process in respect of words spoken or written and all acts performed by them in their official capacity;

(b) be immune from national services and/or national military service obligations;

(c) be exempt from taxation on the salaries and emoluments paid to them by NATO.

17. NATO may in the conduct of the Operation, have need to make improvements or modifications to certain infrastructure of the Republic of Bosnia and Herzegovina such as roads, utility systems, bridges, tunnels, buildings, etc. Any such improvements or modifications of a non-temporary nature shall become part of and in the same ownership as that infrastructure. Temporary improvements or modifications may be removed at the discretion of the NATO Commander, and the facility returned to as near its original condition as possible.

18. Failing any prior settlement, disputes with regard to the interpretation or application of the present agreement shall be settled between the Republic of Bosnia and Herzegovina and NATO Representatives by diplomatic means.

19. The provisions of this agreement shall also apply to the civilian and military personnel, property and assets of national elements/units of NATO states, acting in connection to the Operation or the relief for the civilian population which however remain under national command and control.

20. Supplemental arrangements may be concluded to work out details for the Operation also taking into account its further development.

21. The Government of the Republic of Bosnia and Herzegovina shall accord non-NATO states and their personnel participating in the Operation the same privileges and immunities as those accorded under this agreement to NATO states and personnel.

22. The provisions of this agreement shall remain in force until completion of the Operation or as the Parties otherwise agree.

23. This Agreement shall enter into force upon signature.

Done at Wright-Patterson Air Force Base, Ohio on November 21, 1995 and in Paris on December 14, 1995.

For the Republic of Bosnia and Herzegovina:

For the North Atlantic Treaty Organisation:

Agreement Between the Republic of Croatia and the North Atlantic Treaty Organisation (NATO) Concerning the Status of NATO and its Personnel

The Republic of Croatia and the North Atlantic Treaty Organisation have agreed as follows:

1. For the purposes of the present agreement, the following expressions shall have the meanings hereunder assigned to them:

- "the Operation" means the support, implementation, preparation and participation by NATO and NATO personnel in a peace plan in Bosnia and Herzegovina or a possible withdrawal of U.N. Forces from former Yugoslavia;

- "NATO personnel" means the civilian and military personnel of the North Atlantic Treaty Organisation with the exception of personnel locally hired;

- "NATO" means the North Atlantic Treaty Organisation, its subsidiary bodies, its military Headquarters and all its constituent national elements/units acting in support of, preparing and participating in the Operation;

- "Facilities" mean all premises and land required for conducting the operational, training and administrative activities by NATO for the Operation as well as for accommodations of NATO personnel.

2. The provisions of the Convention on the Privileges and Immunities of the United Nations of 13 February 1946 concerning experts on mission shall apply mutatis mutandis to NATO personnel involved in the Operation, except as otherwise provided for in the present agreement. Moreover NATO, its property and assets shall enjoy the privileges and immunities specified in that convention and as stated in the present agreement.

3. All personnel enjoying privileges and immunities under this Agreement shall respect the laws of the Republic of Croatia insofar as it is compatible with the entrusted tasks/mandate and shall refrain from activities not compatible with the nature of the Operation.

4. The Government of Croatia recognizes the need for expeditious departure and entry procedures for NATO personnel. They shall be exempt from passport and visa regulations and the registration requirements applicable to aliens. NATO personnel shall carry identification which they may be requested to produce for the authorities of the Republic of Bosnia and Herzegovina but operations, training and movement shall not be allowed to be impeded or delayed by such requests.

5. NATO military personnel shall normally wear uniforms, and NATO personnel may possess and carry arms if authorized to do so by their orders. Croatian authorities shall accept as valid, without tax or fee, drivers' licenses and permits issued to NATO personnel by their respective national authorities.

6. NATO shall be permitted to display the NATO flag and/or national flags of its constituent national elements/units on any NATO uniform, means of transport or facility.

7. NATO military personnel under all circumstances and at all times shall be subject to the exclusive jurisdiction of their respective national elements in respect of any criminal or disciplinary offenses which may be committed by them in the

Republic of Croatia. NATO and Croatian authorities shall assist each other in the exercise of their respective jurisdictions.

8.   As experts on mission, NATO personnel shall be immune from personal arrest or detention. NATO personnel mistakenly arrested or detained shall immediately be turned over to NATO authorities.

9.   NATO personnel shall enjoy, together with their vehicles, vessels, aircraft and equipment, free and unrestricted passage and unimpeded access throughout Croatia including Croatian airspace and territorial waters. This shall include, but not be limited to, the right of bivouac, maneuver, billet, and utilization of any areas or facilities as required for support, training, and operations. NATO shall be exempt from providing inventories or other routine customs documentation on personnel, vehicles, vessels, aircraft, equipment, supplies, and provisions entering, exiting, or transiting Croatian territory in support of the Operation. The Croatian authorities shall facilitate with all appropriate means all movements of personnel, vehicles, vessels, aircraft, equipment or supplies, through ports, airports or roads used. Vehicles, vessels and aircraft used in support of the Operation shall not be subject to licensing or registration requirements, nor commercial insurance. NATO will use airports, roads and ports without payment of duties, dues, tolls or charges. However, NATO shall not claim exemption from reasonable charges for services requested and received, but operations/movement and access shall not be allowed to be impeded pending payment for such services.

10.   NATO personnel shall be exempt from taxation by the Republic of Croatia on the salaries and emoluments received from NATO and on any income received from outside the Republic of Croatia.

11.   NATO personnel and their tangible movable property imported into or acquired in Croatia shall also be- exempt from all identifiable taxes by the Republic of Croatia, except municipal rates for services enjoyed, and from all registration fees and related charges.

12.   NATO shall be allowed to import and to export free of duty or other restriction equipment, provisions, and supplies, necessary for the Operation, provided such goods are for the official use of NATO or for sale via commissaries or canteens provided for NATO personnel. Goods sold shall be solely for the use of NATO personnel and not transferable to other parties.

13.   NATO shall be allowed to operate its own internal mail and telecommunications services, including broadcast services. Telecommunications channels and other communications needs which may interfere with Croatian telecommunication services shall be coordinated with appropriate Croatian authorities free of cost. It is recognized by the Government of Croatia that the use of communications channels shall be necessary for the Operation.

14.   The Government of Croatia shall provide, free of cost, such facilities NATO needs for the preparation for and execution of the Operation. The Government of Croatia shall assist NATO in obtaining, at the lowest rate, the necessary utilities such as electricity, water and other resources necessary for the Operation.

15.   Claims for damage or injury to Croatian Government personnel or property, or to private personnel or property shall be submitted through governmental authorities of the Republic of Bosnia and Herzegovina to the designated NATO Representatives.

16.   NATO shall be allowed to contract direct with suppliers for services and supplies in the Republic of Croatia without payment of tax or duties. Such services and supplies shall not be subject to sales and other taxes. NATO may hire local personnel who shall remain subject to local laws and regulations. However, local personnel hired by NATO shall:

(a)   be immune from legal process in respect of words spoken or written and all acts performed by them in their official capacity;

(b)   be immune from national services and/or national military service obligations;

(c)   be exempt from taxation on the salaries and emoluments paid to them by NATO.

17.   NATO may in the conduct of the Operation, have need to make improvements or modifications to certain Croatian infrastructure such as roads, utility systems, bridges, tunnels, buildings, etc. Any such improvements or modifications of a non-temporary nature shall become part of and in the same ownership as that infrastructure. Temporary improvements or modifications may be removed at the discretion of the NATO Commander, and the facility returned to as near its original condition as possible.

18.   Failing any prior settlement, disputes with regard to the interpretation or application of the present agreement shall be settled between Croatia and NATO Representatives by diplomatic means.

19.   The provisions of this agreement shall also apply to the civilian and military personnel, property and assets of national elements/units of NATO states, acting in connection to the Operation or the relief for the civilian population which however remain under national command and control.

20.   Supplemental arrangements may be concluded to work out details for the Operation also taking into account its further development.

21.   The Government of Croatia shall accord non-NATO states and their personnel participating in the Operation the same privileges and immunities as those accorded under this agreement to NATO states and personnel.

22.   The provisions of this agreement shall remain in force until completion of the Operation or as the Parties otherwise agree.

23.   This Agreement shall enter into force upon signature.

Done at Wright-Patterson Air Force Base, Ohio on November 21, 1995 and in Paris on December 14, 1995.

For the Republic of Croatia:

For the North Atlantic Treaty Organisation:

Agreement Between the Federal Republic of Yugoslavia and the North Atlantic Treaty Organisation (NATO) Concerning the Status of NATO and its Personnel

Considering that the North Atlantic Treaty Organization is conducting contingency planning in coordination with the United Nations to support the implementation of a peace plan in Bosnia and Herzegovina or a possible withdrawal of U.N. Forces from former Yugoslavia, and may be requested by the United Nations to execute either such operation;

Considering the necessity to establish adequate transit arrangements for the execution/implementation of this Operation;

It is agreed that:

1.   For the purposes of the present agreement, the following expressions shall have the meanings hereunder assigned to them:

-         "the Operation" means the support, implementation, preparation and participation by NATO and NATO personnel in a peace plan in Bosnia and Herzegovina or a possible withdrawal of U.N. Forces from former Yugoslavia;

-         "NATO personnel" means the civilian and military personnel of the North Atlantic Treaty Organisation with the exception of personnel locally hired;

-         "NATO" means the North Atlantic Treaty Organisation, its subsidiary bodies, its military Headquarters and all its constituent national elements/units acting in support of, preparing and participating in the Operation;

2.   The Government of the Federal Republic of Yugoslavia shall allow the free transit over land, rail, road, water or through air of all personnel and cargo, equipment, goods and material of whatever kind, including ammunition required by NATO for the execution of the Operation, through the territory of the Federal Republic of Yugoslavia including the Federal Republic of Yugoslavia airspace and territorial waters.

3.   The Government of the Federal Republic of Yugoslavia shall provide or assist to provide, at the lower cost, such facilities or services as determined by NATO as are necessary for the transit.

4.   NATO shall be exempt from providing inventories or other routine customs documentation on personnel, equipment, supplies and provisions entering, exiting or transiting the Federal Republic of Yugoslavia territory in support of the Operation. The Federal Republic of Yugoslavia authorities shall facilitate with all appropriate means all movements of personnel, vehicles and/or supplies through ports, airports or roads used. Vehicles, vessels and aircraft in transit shall not be subject to licensing or registration requirements, nor commercial insurance. NATO shall be permitted to use airports, roads and ports without payment of duties, dues, tolls or charges. NATO shall not claim exemption for reasonable charges for services requested and received, but transit shall not be allowed to be impeded pending negotiations on payment for such services. The modes of transport will be communicated by NATO to the Government of the Federal Republic of Yugoslavia in advance. The routes to be followed will be commonly agreed upon.

5.   The provisions of the Convention on the Privileges and Immunities of the United Nations of 13 February 1946 concerning experts on mission shall apply mutatis mutandis to NATO personnel involved in the transit, except as otherwise provided for in the present agreement. Moreover NATO, its property and assets shall enjoy the privileges and immunities specified in that convention and as stated in the present agreement.

6.   All personnel enjoying privileges and immunities under this Agreement shall respect the laws of the Federal Republic of Yugoslavia insofar as respect for said laws is compatible with the entrusted tasks/mandate and shall refrain from activities not compatible with the nature of the Operation.

7.   The Government of the Federal Republic of Yugoslavia recognizes the need for expeditious departure and entry procedures for NATO personnel. They shall be exempt from passport and visa regulations and the registration requirements applicable to aliens. NATO personnel shall carry identification which they may be requested to produce for Federal Republic of Yugoslavia authorities but transit shall not be allowed to be impeded or delayed by such requests.

8.   NATO military personnel shall normally wear uniforms, and NATO personnel may possess and carry arms if authorized to do so by their orders. The Federal Republic of Yugoslavia authorities shall accept as valid, without tax or fee, drivers' licenses and permits issued to NATO personnel by their respective national authorities.

9.   NATO shall be permitted to display the NATO flag and/or national flags of its constituent national elements/units on any NATO uniform, means of transport or facility.

10.   NATO military personnel under all circumstances and at all times shall be subject to the exclusive jurisdiction of their respective national elements in respect of any criminal or disciplinary offenses which may be committed by them in the Federal Republic of Yugoslavia. NATO and the Federal Republic of Yugoslavia authorities shall assist each other in the exercise of their respective jurisdictions.

11.   As experts on mission, NATO personnel shall be immune from personal arrest or detention. NATO personnel mistakenly arrested or detained shall immediately be turned over to NATO authorities.

12.   NATO personnel and their tangible movable property in transit through the Federal Republic of Yugoslavia shall also be- exempt from all identifiable taxes by the Government of the Federal Republic of Yugoslavia.

13.   NATO shall be allowed to operate its own telecommunications services. This shall include the right to utilize such means and services as required to assure full ability to communicate, and the right to use all of the electro-magnetic spectrum for this purpose, free of cost. In implementing this right, NATO shall make every reasonable effort to coordinate with and take into account the needs and requirements of appropriate Federal Republic of Yugoslavia authorities.

14.   Claims for damage or injury to Federal Republic of Yugoslavia Government personnel or property, or to private persons or property shall be submitted through the Federal Republic of Yugoslavia governmental authorities to the designated NATO Representatives.

15.   Failing any prior settlement, disputes with regard to the interpretation or application of the present agreement shall be settled between the Federal Republic of Yugoslavia and NATO Representatives by diplomatic means.

16.   The provisions of this agreement shall also apply to the civilian and military personnel, property and assets of national elements/units of NATO states, acting in connection to the Operation of the relief for the civilian population which however remain under national command and control.

17.   Supplemental arrangements may be concluded to work out details for the transit also taking into account its further development.

18.   The Government of the Federal Republic of Yugoslavia shall accord for the transit of non-NATO states and their personnel participating in the Operation the same privileges and immunities as those accorded under this agreement to NATO states and personnel.

19.   The provisions of this agreement shall remain in force until completion of the Operation or as the Parties otherwise agree.

20.   This Agreement shall enter into force upon signature.

Done at Wright-Patterson Air Force Base, Ohio on November 21, 1995 and in Paris on December 14, 1995.

For the Republic of Bosnia and Herzegovina:

For the North Atlantic Treaty Organisation:

ANNEX 1B

Agreement on Regional Stabilization

The Republic of Bosnia and Herzegovina, the Republic of Croatia, the Federal Republic of Yugoslavia, the Federation of Bosnia and Herzegovina, and the Republika Srpska (hereinafter the "Parties") have agreed as follows:

Article I: General Obligations

The Parties agree that establishment of progressive measures for regional stability and arms control is essential to creating a stable peace in the region. To this end, they agree on the importance of devising new forms of cooperation in the field of security aimed at building transparency and confidence and achieving balanced and stable defense force levels at the lowest numbers consistent with the Parties' respective security and the need to avoid an arms race in the region. They have approved the following elements for a regional structure for stability.

Article II: Confidence- and Security-Building Measures in Bosnia and Herzegovina

Within seven days after this Agreement (hereinafter "Annex") enters into force, the Republic of Bosnia and Herzegovina, the Federation of Bosnia and Herzegovina, and the Republika Srpska shall at an appropriately high political level commence negotiations under the auspices of the Organization for Security and Cooperation in Europe (hereinafter "OSCE") to agree upon a series of measures to enhance mutual confidence and reduce the risk of conflict, drawing fully upon the 1994 Vienna Document of the Negotiations on Confidence- and Security-Building Measures of the OSCE. The objective of these negotiations is to agree upon an initial set of measures within forty-five (45) days after this Annex enters into force including, but not necessarily limited to, the following:

(a)   restrictions on military deployments and exercises in certain geographical areas;

(b)   restraints on the reintroduction of foreign Forces in light of Article III of Annex 1-A to the General Framework Agreement;

(c)   restrictions on locations of heavy weapons;

(d)   withdrawal of Forces and heavy weapons to cantonment/barracks areas or other designated locations as provided in Article IV of Annex 1-A;

(e)   notification of disbandment of special operations and armed civilian groups;

(f)   notification of certain planned military activities, including international military assistance and training programs;

(g)   identification of and monitoring of weapons manufacturing capabilities;

(h)   immediate exchange of data on the holdings of the five Treaty on Conventional Armed Forces in Europe (hereinafter "CFE") weapons categories as defined in the CFE Treaty, with the additional understanding that artillery pieces will be defined as those of 75mm calibre and above; and

(i)   immediate establishment of military liaison missions between the Chiefs of the Armed Forces of the Federation of Bosnia and Herzegovina and the Republika Srpska;

Article III: Regional Confidence- and Security-Building Measures

To supplement the measures in Article II above on a wider basis, the Parties agree to initiate steps toward a regional agreement on confidence- and security-building measures. The Parties agree:

(a)   not to import any arms for ninety (90) days after this Annex enters into force;

(b)   not to import for 180 days after this Annex enters into force or until the arms control agreement referred to in Article IV below takes effect, whichever is the earlier, heavy weapons or heavy weapons ammunition, mines, military aircraft, and helicopters. Heavy weapons refers to all tanks and armored vehicles, all artillery 75 mm and above, all mortars 81 mm and above, and all anti-aircraft weapons 20 mm and above.

Article IV: Measures for Sub-Regional Arms Control

1.   Recognizing the importance of achieving balanced and stable defense force levels at the lowest numbers consistent with their respective security, and understanding that the establishment of a stable military balance based on the lowest level of armaments will be an essential element in preventing the recurrence of conflict, the Parties within thirty (30) days after this Annex enters into force shall commence negotiations under the auspices of the OSCE to reach early agreement on levels of armaments consistent with this goal. Within thirty (30) days after this Annex enters into force, the Parties shall also commence negotiations on an agreement establishing voluntary limits on military manpower.

2.   The Parties agree that the armaments agreement should be based at a minimum on the following criteria: population size, current military armament holdings, defense needs, and relative force levels in the region.

(a)   The agreement shall establish numerical limits on holdings of tanks, artillery, armored combat vehicles, combat aircraft, and attack helicopters, as defined in the relevant sections of the CFE Treaty, with the additional understanding that artillery pieces will be defined as those of 75 mm calibre and above.

(b)   In order to establish a baseline, the Parties agree to report within thirty (30) days after this Annex enters into force their holdings as defined in sub-paragraph (a) above, according to the format prescribed in the 1992 Vienna Document of the OSCE.

(c)   This notification format shall be supplemented to take into account the special considerations of the region.

3.   The Parties agree to complete within 180 days after this Annex enters into force the negotiations above on agreed numerical limits on the categories referred to in paragraph 2(a) of this Article. If the Parties fail to agree to such limits within 180 days after this Annex enters into force, the following limits shall apply, according to a ratio of 5:2:2 based on the approximate ratio of populations of the Parties:

(a)   the baseline shall be the determined holdings of the Federal Republic of Yugoslavia (hereinafter the "baseline");

(b)   the limits for the Federal Republic of Yugoslavia shall be seventy-five (75) percent of the baseline;

(c)   the limits for the Republic of Croatia shall be thirty (30) percent of the baseline;

(d)   the limits for Bosnia and Herzegovina shall be thirty (30) percent of the baseline; and

(e)   the allocations for Bosnia and Herzegovina will be divided between the Entities on the basis of a ratio of

two (2) for the Federation of Bosnia and Herzegovina
and one (1) for the Republika Srpska.

4.   The OSCE will assist the Parties in their negotiations
under Articles II and IV of this Annex and in the
implementation and verification (including verification of
holdings declarations) of resulting agreements.

Article V: Regional Arms Control Agreement

The OSCE will assist the Parties by designating a special
representative to help organize and conduct negotiations
under the auspices of the OSCE Forum on Security
Cooperation ("FSC") with the goal of establishing a regional
balance in and around the former Yugoslavia. The Parties
undertake to cooperate fully with the OSCE to that end and to
facilitate regular inspections by other parties. Further, the
Parties agree to establish a commission together with
representatives of the OSCE for the purpose of facilitating the
resolution of any disputes that might arise.

Article VI: Entry into Force

This Annex shall enter into force upon signature.

For the Republic of Bosnia and Herzegovina

For the Republic of Croatia

For the Federal Republic of Yugoslavia

For the Federation of Bosnia and Herzegovina

For the Republika Srpska

ANNEX 2

Agreement on Inter-Entity Boundary Line and Related Issues
(With Appendix)

The Republic of Bosnia and Herzegovina, the Federation of Bosnia and Herzegovina and the Republika Srpska (the "Parties") have agreed as follows:

Article I: Inter-Entity Boundary Line

The boundary between the Federation of Bosnia and Herzegovina and the Republika Srpska (the "Inter-Entity Boundary Line") shall be as delineated on the map at the Appendix.

Article II: Adjustment by the Parties

The Parties may adjust the Inter-Entity Boundary Line only by mutual consent. During the period in which the multinational military Implementation Force ("IFOR") is deployed pursuant to Annex 1-A to the General Framework Agreement, the Parties shall consult with the IFOR Commander prior to making any agreed adjustment and shall provide notification of such adjustment to the IFOR Commander.

Article III: Rivers

1.   Where the Inter-Entity Boundary Line follows a river, the line shall follow natural changes (accretion or erosion) in the course of the river unless otherwise agreed.   Artificial changes in the course of the river shall not affect the location of the Inter-Entity Boundary Line unless otherwise agreed. No artificial changes may be made except by agreement among the Parties.

2.   In the event of sudden natural changes in the course of the river (avulsion or cutting of new bed), the line shall be determined by mutual agreement of the Parties. If such event occurs during the period in which the IFOR is deployed, any such determination shall be subject to the approval of the IFOR Commander.

Article IV: Delineation and Marking

1.   The line on the 1:50,000 scale map to be provided for the Appendix delineating the Inter-Entity Boundary Line, and the lines on the 1:50,000 scale map to be provided for Appendix A to Annex 1-A delineating the Inter-Entity Zone of Separation and the Agreed Cease-Fire Line and its Zone of Separation, which are accepted by the Parties as controlling and definitive, are accurate to within approximately 50 meters. During the period in which the IFOR is deployed, the IFOR Commander shall have the right to determine, after consultation with the Parties, the exact delineation of such Lines and Zones, provided that with respect to Sarajevo the IFOR Commander shall have the right to adjust the Zone of Separation as necessary.

2.   The Lines and Zones described above may be marked by representatives of the Parties in coordination with and under the supervision of the IFOR.   Final authority for placement of such markers shall rest with the IFOR. These Lines and Zones are defined by the maps and documents agreed to by the Parties and not by the physical location of markers.

3.   Following entry into force of this Agreement, the Parties shall form a joint commission, comprised of an equal number of representatives from each Party, to prepare an agreed technical document containing a precise description of the Inter-Entity Boundary Line.   Any such document prepared during the period in which the IFOR is deployed shall be subject to the approval of the IFOR Commander.

Article V: Arbitration for the Brcko Area

1.   The Parties agree to binding arbitration of the disputed portion of the Inter-Entity Boundary Line in the Brcko area indicated on the map attached at the Appendix.

2.   No later than six months after the entry into force of this Agreement, the Federation shall appoint one arbitrator, and the Republika Srpska shall appoint one arbitrator.   A third arbitrator shall be selected by agreement of the Parties' appointees within thirty days thereafter.   If they do not agree, the third arbitrator shall be appointed by the President of the International Court of Justice.   The third arbitrator shall serve as presiding officer of the arbitral tribunal.

3.   Unless otherwise agreed by the Parties, the proceedings shall be conducted in accordance with the UNCITRAL rules. The arbitrators shall apply relevant legal and equitable principles.

4.   Unless otherwise agreed, the area indicated in paragraph 1 above shall continue to be administered as currently.

5.   The arbitrators shall issue their decision no later than one year from the entry into force of this Agreement.   The decision shall be final and binding, and the Parties shall implement it without delay.

Article VI: Transition

In those areas transferring from one Entity to the other in accordance with the demarcation described herein, there shall be a transitional period to provide for the orderly transfer of authority.   The transition shall be completed forty-five (45) days after the Transfer of Authority from the UNPROFOR Commander to the IFOR Commander, as described in Annex 1-A.

Article VII: Status of Appendix

The Appendix shall constitute an integral part of this Agreement.

Article VIII: Entry into Force

This Agreement shall enter into force upon signature.

For the Republic of Bosnia and Herzegovina

For the Federation of Bosnia and Herzegovina

For the Republika Srpska

Endorsed:
For the Republic of Croatia

Endorsed:
For the Federal Republic of Yugoslavia

Appendix to Annex 2

The Appendix to Annex 2 consists of this document together with (a) a 1:600,000 scale UNPROFOR road map consisting of one map sheet, attached hereto; and (b) 1:50,000 scale Topographic Line Map, to be provided as described below.

On the basis of the attached 1:600,000 scale map, the Parties request that the United States Department of Defense provide a 1:50,000 scale Topographic Line Map, consisting of as many map sheets as necessary, in order to provide a more precise delineation of the Inter-Entity Boundary Line. Such map shall be incorporated as an integral part of this Appendix, and the Parties agree to accept such map as controlling and definitive for all purposes.

For the Republic of Bosnia and Herzegovina

For the Federation of Bosnia and Herzegovina

For the Republika Srpska

Endorsed:
For the Republic of Croatia

Endorsed:
For the Federal Republic of Yugoslavia

[MAP NOT AVAILABLE]

ANNEX 3

Agreement on Elections

In order to promote free, fair, and democratic elections and to lay the foundation for representative government and ensure the progressive achievement of democratic goals throughout Bosnia and Herzegovina, in accordance with relevant documents of the Organization for Security and Cooperation in Europe (OSCE), the Republic of Bosnia and Herzegovina, the Federation of Bosnia and Herzegovina and the Republika Srpska ("the Parties") have agreed as follows:

Article I: Conditions for Democratic Elections

1.   The Parties shall ensure that conditions exist for the organization of free and fair elections, in particular a politically neutral environment; shall protect and enforce the right to vote in secret without fear or intimidation; shall ensure freedom of expression and of the press; shall allow and encourage freedom of association (including of political parties); and shall ensure freedom of movement.

2.   The Parties request the OSCE to certify whether elections can be effective under current social conditions in both Entities and, if necessary, to provide assistance to the Parties in creating these conditions.

3.   The Parties shall comply fully with paragraphs 7 and 8 of the OSCE Copenhagen Document, which are attached to this Agreement.

Article II: The OSCE Role

1.   OSCE. The Parties request the OSCE to adopt and put in place an elections program for Bosnia and Herzegovina as set forth in this Agreement.

2.   Elections. The Parties request the OSCE to supervise, in a manner to be determined by the OSCE and in cooperation with other international organizations the OSCE deems necessary, the preparation and conduct of elections for the House of Representatives of Bosnia and Herzegovina; for the Presidency of Bosnia and Herzegovina; for the House of Representatives of the Federation of Bosnia and Herzegovina; for the National Assembly of the Republika Srpska; for the Presidency of the Republika Srpska; and, if feasible, for cantonal legislatures and municipal governing authorities.

3.   The Commission. To this end, the Parties request the OSCE to establish a Provisional Election Commission ("the Commission").

4.   Timing. Elections shall take place on a date ("Election Day") six months after entry into force of this Agreement or, if the OSCE determines a delay necessary, no later than nine months after entry into force.

Article III: The Provisional Election Commission

1.   Rules and Regulations. The Commission shall adopt electoral rules and regulations regarding: the registration of political parties and independent candidates; the eligibility of candidates and voters; the role of domestic and international election observers; the ensuring of an open and fair electoral campaign; and the establishment, publication, and certification of definitive election results. The Parties shall comply fully with the electoral rules and regulations, any internal laws and regulations notwithstanding.

2.   Mandate of the Commission. The responsibilities of the Commission, as provided in the electoral rules and regulations, shall include:

(a)   supervising all aspects of the electoral process to ensure that the structures and institutional framework for free and fair elections are in place;

(b)   determining voter registration provisions;

(c)   ensuring compliance with the electoral rules and regulation established pursuant to this Agreement;

(d)   ensuring that action is taken to remedy any violation of any provision of this Agreement or of the electoral rules and regulations established pursuant to this Agreement, including imposing penalties against any person or body that violates such provisions; and

(e)   accrediting observers, including personnel from international organizations and foreign and domestic non-governmental organizations, and ensuring that the Parties grant accredited observers unimpeded access and movement.

3.   Composition and Functioning of the Commission. The Commission shall consist of the Head of the OSCE Mission, the High Representative or his or her designee, representatives of the Parties, and such other persons as the Head of the OSCE Mission, in consultation with the Parties, may decide. The Head of the OSCE Mission shall act as Chairman of the Commission. In the event of disputes within the Commission, the decision of the Chairman shall be final.

4.   Privileges and Immunities. The Chairman and Commission shall enjoy the right to establish communications facilities and to engage local and administrative staff, and the status, privileges and immunities accorded to a diplomatic agent and mission under the Vienna Convention on Diplomatic Relations.

Article IV: Eligibility

1.   Voters. Any citizen of Bosnia and Herzegovina aged 18 or older whose name appears on the 1991 census for Bosnia and Herzegovina shall be eligible, in accordance with electoral rules and regulations, to vote. A citizen who no longer lives in the municipality in which he or she resided in 1991 shall, as a general rule, be expected to vote, in person or by absentee ballot, in that municipality, provided that the person is determined to have been registered in that municipality as confirmed by the local election commission and the Provisional Election Commission.

Such a citizen may, however, apply to the Commission to cast his or her ballot elsewhere. The exercise of a refugee's right to vote shall be interpreted as confirmation of his or her intention to return to Bosnia and Herzegovina. By Election Day, the return of refugees should already be underway, thus allowing many to participate in person in elections in Bosnia and Herzegovina. The Commission may provide in the electoral rules and regulations for citizens not listed in the 1991 census to vote.

Article V: Permanent Election Commission

The Parties agree to create a permanent Election Commission with responsibilities to conduct future elections in Bosnia and Herzegovina.

Article VI: Entry into Force

This Agreement shall enter into force upon signature.

For the Republic of Bosnia and Herzegovina

For the Federation of Bosnia and Herzegovina

For the Republika Srpska

Attachment to Annex 3 on Elections

Document of the Second Meeting of the Conference on the Human Dimension of the Conference on Security and Cooperation in Europe, Copenhagen, 1990.

Paragraphs 7 and 8:

(7) To ensure that the will of the people serves as the basis of the authority of government, the participating States will:

(7.1) - hold free elections at reasonable intervals, as established by law;

(7.2) - permit all seats in at least one chamber of the national legislature to be freely contested in a popular vote;

(7.3) - guarantee universal and equal suffrage to adult citizens;

(7.4) - ensure that votes are cast by secret ballot or by equivalent free voting procedure, and that they are counted and reported honestly with the official results made public;

(7.5) - respect the right of citizens to seek political or public office, individually or as representatives of political parties or organizations, without discrimination;

(7.6) - respect the right of individuals and groups to establish, in full freedom, their own political parties or other political organizations and provide such political parties and organizations with the necessary legal guarantees to enable them to compete with each other on a basis of equal treatment before the law and by the authorities;

(7.7) - ensure that law and public policy work to permit political campaigning to be conducted in a fair and free atmosphere in which neither administrative action, violence nor intimidation bars the parties and the candidates from freely presenting their views and qualifications, or prevents the voters from learning and discussing them or from casting their vote free of fear of retribution;

(7.8) - provide that no legal or administrative obstacle stands in the way of unimpeded access to the media on a non-discriminatory basis for all political groupings and individuals wishing to participate in the electoral process;

(7.9) - ensure that candidates who obtain the necessary number of votes required by law are duly installed in office and are permitted to remain in office until their term expires or is otherwise brought to an end in a manner that is regulated by law in conformity with democratic parliamentary and constitutional procedures.

(8) - The participating States consider that the presence of observers, both foreign and domestic, can enhance the electoral process for States in which elections are taking place. They therefore invite observers from any other CSCE participating States and any appropriate private institutions and organizations who may wish to do so to observe the course of their national election proceedings, to the extent permitted by law. They will also endeavour to facilitate similar access for election proceedings held below the national level. Such observers will undertake not to interfere in the electoral proceedings.

ANNEX 4

Constitution of Bosnia and Herzegovina

Preamble

Based on respect for human dignity, liberty, and equality,

Dedicated to peace, justice, tolerance, and reconciliation,

Convinced that democratic governmental institutions and fair procedures best produce peaceful relations within a pluralist society,

Desiring to promote the general welfare and economic growth through the protection of private property and the promotion of a market economy,

Guided by the Purposes and Principles of the Charter of the United Nations,

Committed to the sovereignty, territorial integrity, and political independence of Bosnia and Herzegovina in accordance with international law,

Determined to ensure full respect for international humanitarian law,

Inspired by the Universal Declaration of Human Rights, the International Covenants on Civil and Political Rights and on Economic, Social and Cultural Rights, and the Declaration on the Rights of Persons Belonging to National or Ethnic, Religious and Linguistic Minorities, as well as other human rights instruments,

Recalling the Basic Principles agreed in Geneva on September 8, 1995, and in New York on September 26, 1995,

Bosniacs, Croats, and Serbs, as constituent peoples (along with Others), and citizens of Bosnia and Herzegovina hereby determine that the Constitution of Bosnia and Herzegovina is as follows:

Article I:
Bosnia and Herzegovina

1.   Continuation

The Republic of Bosnia and Herzegovina, the official name of which shall henceforth be "Bosnia and Herzegovina," shall continue its legal existence under international law as a state, with its internal structure modified as provided herein and with its present internationally recognized borders. It shall remain a Member State of the United Nations and may as Bosnia and Herzegovina maintain or apply for membership in organizations within the United Nations system and other international organizations.

2.   Democratic Principles

Bosnia and Herzegovina shall be a democratic state, which shall operate under the rule of law and with free and democratic elections.

3.   Composition

Bosnia and Herzegovina shall consist of the two Entities, the Federation of Bosnia and Herzegovina and the Republika Srpska (hereinafter "the Entities").

4.   Movement of Goods, Services, Capital, and Persons

There shall be freedom of movement throughout Bosnia and Herzegovina. Bosnia and Herzegovina and the Entities shall not impede full freedom of movement of persons, goods, services, and capital throughout Bosnia and Herzegovina. Neither Entity shall establish controls at the boundary between the Entities.

5.   Capital

The capital of Bosnia and Herzegovina shall be Sarajevo.

6.   Symbols

Bosnia and Herzegovina shall have such symbols as are decided by its Parliamentary Assembly and approved by the Presidency.

7.   Citizenship

There shall be a citizenship of Bosnia and Herzegovina, to be regulated by the Parliamentary Assembly, and a citizenship of each Entity, to be regulated by each Entity, provided that:

(a)   All citizens of either Entity are thereby citizens of Bosnia and Herzegovina.

(b)   No person shall be deprived of Bosnia and Herzegovina or Entity citizenship arbitrarily or so as to leave him or her stateless. No person shall be deprived of Bosnia and Herzegovina or Entity citizenship on any ground such as sex, race, color, language, religion, political or other opinion, national or social origin, association with a national minority, property, birth or other status.

(c)   All persons who were citizens of the Republic of Bosnia and Herzegovina immediately prior to the entry into force of this Constitution are citizens of Bosnia and Herzegovina. The citizenship of persons who were naturalized after April 6, 1992 and before the entry into force of this Constitution will be regulated by the Parliamentary Assembly.

(d)   Citizens of Bosnia and Herzegovina may hold the citizenship of another state, provided that there is a bilateral agreement, approved by the Parliamentary Assembly in accordance with Article IV(4)(d), between Bosnia and Herzegovina and that state governing this matter. Persons with dual citizenship may vote in Bosnia and Herzegovina and the Entities only if Bosnia and Herzegovina is their country of residence.

(e)   A citizen of Bosnia and Herzegovina abroad shall enjoy the protection of Bosnia and Herzegovina. Each Entity may issue passports of Bosnia and Herzegovina to its citizens as regulated by the Parliamentary Assembly. Bosnia and Herzegovina may issue passports to citizens not issued a passport by an Entity. There shall be a central register of all passports issued by the Entities and by Bosnia and Herzegovina.

Article II:
Human Rights and Fundamental Freedoms

1.   Human Rights

Bosnia and Herzegovina and both Entities shall ensure the highest level of internationally recognized human rights and fundamental freedoms. To that end, there shall be a Human Rights Commission for Bosnia and Herzegovina as provided for in Annex 6 to the General Framework Agreement.

2.   International Standards

The rights and freedoms set forth in the European Convention for the Protection of Human Rights and Fundamental Freedoms and its Protocols shall apply directly in Bosnia and Herzegovina. These shall have priority over all other law.

3.   Enumeration of Rights

All persons within the territory of Bosnia and Herzegovina shall enjoy the human rights and fundamental freedoms referred to in paragraph 2 above; these include:

(a) The right to life.

(b) The right not to be subjected to torture or to inhuman or degrading treatment or punishment.

(c) The right not to be held in slavery or servitude or to perform forced or compulsory labor.

(d) The rights to liberty and security of person.

(e) The right to a fair hearing in civil and criminal matters, and other rights relating to criminal proceedings.

(f) The right to private and family life, home, and correspondence.

(g) Freedom of thought, conscience, and religion.

(h) Freedom of expression.

(i) Freedom of peaceful assembly and freedom of association with others.

(j) The right to marry and to found a family.

(k) The right to property.

(l) The right to education.

(m) The right to liberty of movement and residence.

4. Non-Discrimination

The enjoyment of the rights and freedoms provided for in this Article or in the international agreements listed in Annex I to this Constitution shall be secured to all persons in Bosnia and Herzegovina without discrimination on any ground such as sex, race, color, language, religion, political or other opinion, national or social origin, association with a national minority, property, birth or other status.

5. Refugees and Displaced Persons

All refugees and displaced persons have the right freely to return to their homes of origin. They have the right, in accordance with Annex 7 to the General Framework Agreement, to have restored to them property of which they were deprived in the course of hostilities since 1991 and to be compensated for any such property that cannot be restored to them. Any commitments or statements relating to such property made under duress are null and void.

6. Implementation

Bosnia and Herzegovina, and all courts, agencies, governmental organs, and instrumentalities operated by or within the Entities, shall apply and conform to the human rights and fundamental freedoms referred to in paragraph 2 above.

7. International Agreements

Bosnia and Herzegovina shall remain or become party to the international agreements listed in Annex I to this Constitution.

8. Cooperation

All competent authorities in Bosnia and Herzegovina shall cooperate with and provide unrestricted access to: any international human rights monitoring mechanisms established for Bosnia and Herzegovina; the supervisory bodies established by any of the international agreements listed in Annex I to this Constitution; the International Tribunal for the Former Yugoslavia (and in particular shall comply with orders issued pursuant to Article 29 of the Statute of the Tribunal); and any other organization authorized by the United Nations Security Council with a mandate concerning human rights or humanitarian law.

Article III:
Responsibilities of and Relations Between the Institutions of Bosnia and Herzegovina and the Entities

1. Responsibilities of the Institutions of Bosnia and Herzegovina.

The following matters are the responsibility of the institutions of Bosnia and Herzegovina:

(a) Foreign policy.

(b) Foreign trade policy.

(c) Customs policy.

(d) Monetary policy as provided in Article VII.

(e) Finances of the institutions and for the international obligations of Bosnia and Herzegovina.

(f) Immigration, refugee, and asylum policy and regulation.

(g) International and inter-Entity criminal law enforcement, including relations with Interpol.

(h) Establishment and operation of common and international communications facilities.

(i) Regulation of inter-Entity transportation.

(j) Air traffic control.

2. Responsibilities of the Entities

(a) The Entities shall have the right to establish special parallel relationships with neighboring states consistent with the sovereignty and territorial integrity of Bosnia and Herzegovina.

(b) Each Entity shall provide all necessary assistance to the government of Bosnia and Herzegovina in order to enable it to honor the international obligations of Bosnia and Herzegovina, provided that financial obligations incurred by one Entity without the consent of the other prior to the election of the Parliamentary Assembly and Presidency of Bosnia and Herzegovina shall be the responsibility of that Entity, except insofar as the obligation is necessary for continuing the membership of Bosnia and Herzegovina in an international organization.

(c) The Entities shall provide a safe and secure environment for all persons in their respective jurisdictions, by maintaining civilian law enforcement agencies operating in accordance with internationally recognized standards and with respect for the internationally recognized human rights and fundamental freedoms referred to in Article II above, and by taking such other measures as appropriate.

(d) Each Entity may also enter into agreements with states and international organizations with the consent of the Parliamentary Assembly. The Parliamentary Assembly may provide by law that certain types of agreements do not require such consent.

3. Law and Responsibilities of the Entities and the Institutions

(a) All governmental functions and powers not expressly assigned in this Constitution to the institutions of Bosnia and Herzegovina shall be those of the Entities.

(b) The Entities and any subdivisions thereof shall comply fully with this Constitution, which supersedes inconsistent provisions of the law of Bosnia and Herzegovina and of the constitutions and law of the Entities, and with the decisions of the institutions of Bosnia and Herzegovina. The general principles of international law shall be an integral part of the law of Bosnia and Herzegovina and the Entities.

4.   Coordination

The Presidency may decide to facilitate inter-Entity coordination on matters not within the responsibilities of Bosnia and Herzegovina as provided in this Constitution, unless an Entity objects in any particular case.

5.   Additional Responsibilities

(a)   Bosnia and Herzegovina shall assume responsibility for such other matters as are agreed by the Entities; are provided for in Annexes 5 through 8 to the General Framework Agreement; or are necessary to preserve the sovereignty, territorial integrity, political independence, and international personality of Bosnia and Herzegovina, in accordance with the division of responsibilities between the institutions of Bosnia and Herzegovina. Additional institutions may be established as necessary to carry out such responsibilities.

(b)   Within six months of the entry into force of this Constitution, the Entities shall begin negotiations with a view to including in the responsibilities of the institutions of Bosnia and Herzegovina other matters, including utilization of energy resources and cooperative economic projects.

Article IV:
Parliamentary Assembly

The Parliamentary Assembly shall have two chambers: the House of Peoples and the House of Representatives.

1.   House of Peoples

The House of Peoples shall comprise 15 Delegates, two-thirds from the Federation (including five Croats and five Bosniacs) and one-third from the Republika Srpska (five Serbs).

(a)   The designated Croat and Bosniac Delegates from the Federation shall be selected, respectively, by the Croat and Bosniac Delegates to the House of Peoples of the Federation. Delegates from the Republika Srpska shall be selected by the National Assembly of the Republika Srpska.

(b)   Nine members of the House of Peoples shall comprise a quorum, provided that at least three Bosniac, three Croat, and three Serb Delegates are present.

2.   House of Representatives

The House of Representatives shall comprise 42 Members, two-thirds elected from the territory of the Federation, one-third from the territory of the Republika Srpska.

(a)   Members of the House of Representatives shall be directly elected from their Entity in accordance with an election law to be adopted by the Parliamentary Assembly. The first election, however, shall take place in accordance with Annex 3 to the General Framework Agreement.

(b)   A majority of all members elected to the House of Representatives shall comprise a quorum.

3.   Procedures

(a)   Each chamber shall be convened in Sarajevo not more than 30 days after its selection or election.

(b)   Each chamber shall by majority vote adopt its internal rules and select from its members one Serb, one Bosniac, and one Croat to serve as its Chair and Deputy Chairs, with the position of Chair rotating among the three persons selected.

(c)   All legislation shall require the approval of both chambers.

(d)   All decisions in both chambers shall be by majority of those present and voting. The Delegates and Members shall make their best efforts to see that the majority includes at least one-third of the votes of Delegates or Members from the territory of each Entity. If a majority vote does not include one-third of the votes of Delegates or Members from the territory of each Entity, the Chair and Deputy Chairs shall meet as a commission and attempt to obtain approval within three days of the vote. If those efforts fail, decisions shall be taken by a majority of those present and voting, provided that the dissenting votes do not include two-thirds or more of the Delegates or Members elected from either Entity.

(e)   A proposed decision of the Parliamentary Assembly may be declared to be destructive of a vital interest of the Bosniac, Croat, or Serb people by a majority of, as appropriate, the Bosniac, Croat, or Serb Delegates selected in accordance with paragraph l(a) above. Such a proposed decision shall require for approval in the House of Peoples a majority of the Bosniac, of the Croat, and of the Serb Delegates present and voting.

(f)   When a majority of the Bosniac, of the Croat, or of the Serb Delegates objects to the invocation of paragraph (e), the Chair of the House of Peoples shall immediately convene a Joint Commission comprising three Delegates, one each selected by the Bosniac, by the Croat, and by the Serb Delegates, to resolve the issue. If the Commission fails to do so within five days, the matter will be referred to the Constitutional Court, which shall in an expedited process review it for procedural regularity.

(g)   The House of Peoples may be dissolved by the Presidency or by the House itself, provided that the House's decision to dissolve is approved by a majority that includes the majority of Delegates from at least two of the Bosniac, Croat, or Serb peoples. The House of Peoples elected in the first elections after the entry into force of this Constitution may not, however, be dissolved.

(h)   Decisions of the Parliamentary Assembly shall not take effect before publication.

(i)   Both chambers shall publish a complete record of their deliberations and shall, save in exceptional circumstances in accordance with their rules, deliberate publicly.

(j)   Delegates and Members shall not be held criminally or civilly liable for any acts carried out within the scope of their duties in the Parliamentary Assembly.

4.   Powers

The Parliamentary Assembly shall have responsibility for:

(a)   Enacting legislation as necessary to implement decisions of the Presidency or to carry out the responsibilities of the Assembly under this Constitution.

(b)   Deciding upon the sources and amounts of revenues for the operations of the institutions of Bosnia and Herzegovina and international obligations of Bosnia and Herzegovina.

(c)   Approving a budget for the institutions of Bosnia and Herzegovina.

(d)   Deciding whether to consent to the ratification of treaties.

(e)   Such other matters as are necessary to carry out its duties or as are assigned to it by mutual agreement of the Entities.

Article V:
Presidency

The Presidency of Bosnia and Herzegovina shall consist of three Members: one Bosniac and one Croat, each directly elected from the territory of the Federation, and one Serb directly elected from the territory of the Republika Srpska.

1. Election and Term

(a) Members of the Presidency shall be directly elected in each Entity (with each voter voting to fill one seat on the Presidency) in accordance with an election law adopted by the Parliamentary Assembly. The first election, however, shall take place in accordance with Annex 3 to the General Framework Agreement. Any vacancy in the Presidency shall be filled from the relevant Entity in accordance with a law to be adopted by the Parliamentary Assembly.

(b) The term of the Members of the Presidency elected in the first election shall be two years; the term of Members subsequently elected shall be four years. Members shall be eligible to succeed themselves once and shall thereafter be ineligible for four years.

2. Procedures

(a) The Presidency shall determine its own rules of procedure, which shall provide for adequate notice of all meetings of the Presidency.

(b) The Members of the Presidency shall appoint from their Members a Chair. For the first term of the Presidency, the Chair shall be the Member who received the highest number of votes. Thereafter, the method of selecting the Chair, by rotation or otherwise, shall be determined by the Parliamentary Assembly, subject to Article IV(3).

(c) The Presidency shall endeavor to adopt all Presidency Decisions (i.e., those concerning matters arising under Article V(3) (a)-(e)) by consensus. Such decisions may, subject to paragraph (d) below, nevertheless be adopted by two Members when all efforts to reach consensus have failed.

(d) A dissenting Member of the Presidency may declare a Presidency Decision to be destructive of a vital interest of the Entity from the territory from which he was elected, provided that he does so within three days of its adoption. Such a Decision shall be referred immediately to the National Assembly of the Republika Srpska, if the declaration was made by the Member from that territory; to the Bosniac Delegates of the House of Peoples of the Federation, if the declaration was made by the Bosniac Member; or to the Croat Delegates of that body, if the declaration was made by the Croat Member. If the declaration is confirmed by a two-thirds vote of those persons within ten days of the referral, the challenged Presidency Decision shall not take effect.

3. Powers

The Presidency shall have responsibility for:

(a) Conducting the foreign policy of Bosnia and Herzegovina.

(b) Appointing ambassadors and other international representatives of Bosnia and Herzegovina, no more than two-thirds of whom may be selected from the territory of the Federation.

(c) Representing Bosnia and Herzegovina in international and European organizations and institutions and seeking membership in such organizations and institutions of which Bosnia and Herzegovina is not a member.

(d) Negotiating, denouncing, and, with the consent of the Parliamentary Assembly, ratifying treaties of Bosnia and Herzegovina.

(e) Executing decisions of the Parliamentary Assembly.

(f) Proposing, upon the recommendation of the Council of Ministers, an annual budget to the Parliamentary Assembly.

(g) Reporting as requested, but not less than annually, to the Parliamentary Assembly on expenditures by the Presidency.

(h) Coordinating as necessary with international and nongovernmental organizations in Bosnia and Herzegovina.

(i) Performing such other functions as may be necessary to carry out its duties, as may be assigned to it by the Parliamentary Assembly, or as may be agreed by the Entities.

4. Council of Ministers

The Presidency shall nominate the Chair of the Council of Ministers, who shall take office upon the approval of the House of Representatives. The Chair shall nominate a Foreign Minister, a Minister for Foreign Trade, and other Ministers as may be appropriate, who shall take office upon the approval of the House of Representatives.

(a) Together the Chair and the Ministers shall constitute the Council of Ministers, with responsibility for carrying out the policies and decisions of Bosnia and Herzegovina in the fields referred to in Article III(1), (4), and (5) and reporting to the Parliamentary Assembly (including, at least annually, on expenditures by Bosnia and Herzegovina).

(b) No more than two-thirds of all Ministers may be appointed from the territory of the Federation. The Chair shall also nominate Deputy Ministers (who shall not be of the same constituent people as their Ministers), who shall take office upon the approval of the House of Representatives.

(c) The Council of Ministers shall resign if at any time there is a vote of no-confidence by the Parliamentary Assembly.

5. Standing Committee

(a) Each member of the Presidency shall, by virtue of the office, have civilian command authority over armed forces. Neither Entity shall threaten or use force against the other Entity, and under no circumstances shall any armed forces of either Entity enter into or stay within the territory of the other Entity without the consent of the government of the latter and of the Presidency of Bosnia and Herzegovina. All armed forces in Bosnia and Herzegovina shall operate consistently with the sovereignty and territorial integrity of Bosnia and Herzegovina.

(b) The members of the Presidency shall select a Standing Committee on Military Matters to coordinate the activities of armed forces in Bosnia and Herzegovina. The Members of the Presidency shall be members of the Standing Committee.

Article VI:
Constitutional Court

1. Composition

The Constitutional Court of Bosnia and Herzegovina shall have nine members.

(a) Four members shall be selected by the House of Representatives of the Federation, and two members by the Assembly of the Republika Srpska. The remaining three members shall be selected by the President of the European Court of Human Rights after consultation with the Presidency.

(b) Judges shall be distinguished jurists of high moral standing. Any eligible voter so qualified may serve as a judge of the Constitutional Court. The judges selected by the President of the European Court of Human Rights shall not be citizens of Bosnia and Herzegovina or of any neighboring state.

(c) The term of judges initially appointed shall be five years, unless they resign or are removed for cause by consensus of the other judges. Judges initially appointed shall not be eligible for reappointment. Judges subsequently appointed shall serve until age 70, unless they resign or are removed for cause by consensus of the other judges.

(d) For appointments made more than five years after the initial appointment of judges, the Parliamentary Assembly may provide by law for a different method of selection of the three judges selected by the President of the European Court of Human Rights.

2. Procedures

(a) A majority of all members of the Court shall constitute a quorum.

(b) The Court shall adopt its own rules of court by a majority of all members. It shall hold public proceedings and shall issue reasons for its decisions, which shall be published.

3. Jurisdiction

The Constitutional Court shall uphold this Constitution.

(a) The Constitutional Court shall have exclusive jurisdiction to decide any dispute that arises under this Constitution between the Entities or between Bosnia and Herzegovina and an Entity or Entities, or between institutions of Bosnia and Herzegovina, including but not limited to:

• Whether an Entity's decision to establish a special parallel relationship with a neighboring state is consistent with this Constitution, including provisions concerning the sovereignty and territorial integrity of Bosnia and Herzegovina.

• Whether any provision of an Entity's constitution or law is consistent with this Constitution.

Disputes may be referred only by a member of the Presidency, by the Chair of the Council of Ministers, by the Chair or a Deputy Chair of either chamber of the Parliamentary Assembly, by one-fourth of the members of either chamber of the Parliamentary Assembly, or by one-fourth of either chamber of a legislature of an Entity.

(b) The Constitutional Court shall also have appellate jurisdiction over issues under this Constitution arising out of a judgment of any other court in Bosnia and Herzegovina.

(c) The Constitutional Court shall have jurisdiction over issues referred by any court in Bosnia and Herzegovina concerning whether a law, on whose validity its decision depends, is compatible with this Constitution, with the European Convention for Human Rights and Fundamental Freedoms and its Protocols, or with the laws of Bosnia and Herzegovina; or concerning the existence of or the scope of a general rule of public international law pertinent to the court's decision.

4. Decisions

Decisions of the Constitutional Court shall be final and binding.

Article VII: Central Bank

There shall be a Central Bank of Bosnia and Herzegovina, which shall be the sole authority for issuing currency and for monetary policy throughout Bosnia and Herzegovina.

1. The Central Bank's responsibilities will be determined by the Parliamentary Assembly. For the first six years after the entry into force of this Constitution, however, it may not extend credit by creating money, operating in this respect as a currency board; thereafter, the Parliamentary Assembly may give it that authority.

2. The first Governing Board of the Central Bank shall consist of a Governor appointed by the International Monetary Fund, after consultation with the Presidency, and three members appointed by the Presidency, two from the Federation (one Bosniac, one Croat, who shall share one vote) and one from the Republika Srpska, all of whom shall serve a six-year term. The Governor, who shall not be a citizen of Bosnia and Herzegovina or any neighboring state, may cast tie-breaking votes on the Governing Board.

3. Thereafter, the Governing Board of the Central Bank of Bosnia and Herzegovina shall consist of five persons appointed by the Presidency for a term of six years. The Board shall appoint, from among its members, a Governor for a term of six years.

Article VIII: Finances

1. The Parliamentary Assembly shall each year, on the proposal of the Presidency, adopt a budget covering the expenditures required to carry out the responsibilities of institutions of Bosnia and Herzegovina and the international obligations of Bosnia and Herzegovina.

2. If no such budget is adopted in due time, the budget for the previous year shall be used on a provisional basis.

3. The Federation shall provide two-thirds, and the Republika Srpska one-third, of the revenues required by the budget, except insofar as revenues are raised as specified by the Parliamentary Assembly.

Article IX: General Provisions

1. No person who is serving a sentence imposed by the International Tribunal for the Former Yugoslavia, and no person who is under indictment by the Tribunal and who has failed to comply with an order to appear before the Tribunal, may stand as a candidate or hold any appointive, elective, or other public office in the territory of Bosnia and Herzegovina.

2. Compensation for persons holding office in the institutions of Bosnia and Herzegovina may not be diminished during an officeholder's tenure.

3. Officials appointed to positions in the institutions of Bosnia and Herzegovina shall be generally representative of the peoples of Bosnia and Herzegovina.

Article X: Amendment

1. Amendment Procedure

This Constitution may be amended by a decision of the Parliamentary Assembly, including a two-thirds majority of those present and voting in the House of Representatives.

2. Human Rights and Fundamental Freedoms

No amendment to this Constitution may eliminate or diminish any of the rights and freedoms referred to in Article II of this Constitution or alter the present paragraph.

Article XI:
Transitional Arrangements

Transitional arrangements concerning public offices, law, and other matters are set forth in Annex II to this Constitution.

Article XII:
Entry Into Force

1. This Constitution shall enter into force upon signature of the General Framework Agreement as a constitutional act amending and superseding the Constitution of the Republic of Bosnia and Herzegovina.

2. Within three months from the entry into force of this Constitution, the Entities shall amend their respective constitutions to ensure their conformity with this Constitution in accordance with Article III(3)(b).

Annex I:
Additional Human Rights Agreements to be Applied in Bosnia and Herzegovina

1. Convention on the Prevention and Punishment of the Crime of Genocide

2. 1949 Geneva Conventions I-IV on the Protection of the Victims of War, and the 1977 Geneva Protocols I-II thereto

3. 1951 Convention relating to the Status of Refugees and the 1966 Protocol thereto

4. 1957 Convention on the Nationality of Married Women

5. 1961 Convention on the Reduction of Statelessness

6. 1965 International Convention on the Elimination of All Forms of Racial Discrimination

7. 1966 International Covenant on Civil and Political Rights and the 1966 and 1989 Optional Protocols thereto

8. 1966 Covenant on Economic, Social and Cultural Rights

9. 1979 Convention on the Elimination of All Forms of Discrimination against Women

10. 1984 Convention against Torture and Other Cruel, Inhuman or Degrading Treatment or Punishment

11. 1987 European Convention on the Prevention of Torture and Inhuman or Degrading Treatment or Punishment

12. 1989 Convention on the Rights of the Child

13. 1990 International Convention on the Protection of the Rights of All Migrant Workers and Members of Their Families

14. 1992 European Charter for Regional or Minority Languages

15. Framework Convention for the Protection of National Minorities

Annex II:
Transitional Arrangements

1. Joint Interim Commission

(a) The Parties hereby establish a Joint Interim Commission with a mandate to discuss practical questions related to the implementation of the Constitution of Bosnia and Herzegovina and of the General Framework Agreement and its Annexes, and to make recommendations and proposals.

(b) The Joint Interim Commission shall be composed of four persons from the Federation, three persons from the Republika Srpska, and one representative of Bosnia and Herzegovina.

(c) Meetings of the Commission shall be chaired by the High Representative or his or designee.

2. Continuation of Laws

All laws, regulations, and judicial rules of procedure in effect within the territory of Bosnia and Herzegovina when the Constitution enters into force shall remain in effect to the extent not inconsistent with the Constitution, until otherwise determined by a competent governmental body of Bosnia and Herzegovina .

3. Judicial and Administrative Proceedings

All proceedings in courts or administrative agencies functioning within the territory of Bosnia and Herzegovina when the Constitution enters into force shall continue in or be transferred to other courts or agencies in Bosnia and Herzegovina in accordance with any legislation governing the competence of such courts or agencies.

4. Offices

Until superseded by applicable agreement or law, governmental offices, institutions, and other bodies of Bosnia and Herzegovina will operate in accordance with applicable law.

5. Treaties

Any treaty ratified by the Republic of Bosnia and Herzegovina between January 1, 1992 and the entry into force of this Constitution shall be disclosed to Members of the Presidency within 15 days of their assuming office; any such treaty not disclosed shall be denounced. Within six months after the Parliamentary Assembly is first convened, at the request of any member of the Presidency, the Parliamentary Assembly shall consider whether to denounce any other such treaty.

Declaration On Behalf Of The Republic Of Bosnia And Herzegovina

The Republic of Bosnia and Herzegovina approves the Constitution of Bosnia and Herzegovina at Annex 4 to the General Framework Agreement.

Muhamed Sacirbegovic

For the Republic
of Bosnia and Herzegovina

Declaration On Behalf Of The Federation Of Bosnia And Herzegovina

The Federation of Bosnia and Herzegovina, on behalf of its constituent peoples and citizens, approves the Constitution of Bosnia and Herzegovina at Annex 4 to the General Framework Agreement.

Kresimir Zubak

For the Federation
of Bosnia and Herzegovina

Declaration On Behalf Of The Republika Srpska

The Republika Srpska approves the Constitution of Bosnia and Herzegovina at Annex 4 to the General Framework Agreement.

Nikola Koljevic

For the Republika Srpska

ANNEX 5

Agreement on Arbitration

The Federation of Bosnia and Herzegovina and the Republika Srpska agree to honor the following obligations as set forth in the Agreed Basic Principles adopted at Geneva on September 8, 1995, by the Republic of Bosnia and Herzegovina, the Republic of Croatia, and the Federal Republic of Yugoslavia, the latter representing also the Republika Srpska:

Paragraph 2.4. "The two entities will enter into reciprocal commitments. . .(c) to engage in binding arbitration to resolve disputes between them."

Paragraph 3. "The entities have agreed in principle to the following:...3.5 The design and implementation of a system of arbitration for the solution of disputes between the two entities."

For the Federation of Bosnia and Herzegovina

For the Republika Srpska

ANNEX 6

Agreement on Human Rights

The Republic of Bosnia and Herzegovina, the Federation of Bosnia and Herzegovina and the Republika Srpska (the "Parties") have agreed as follows:

Chapter One: Respect for Human Rights

Article I: Fundamental Rights and Freedoms

The Parties shall secure to all persons within their jurisdiction the highest level of internationally recognized human rights and fundamental freedoms, including the rights and freedoms provided in the European Convention for the Protection of Human Rights and Fundamental Freedoms and its Protocols and the other international agreements listed in the Appendix to this Annex. These include:

(1) The right to life.

(2) The right not to be subjected to torture or to inhuman or degrading treatment or punishment.

(3) The right not to be held in slavery or servitude or to perform forced or compulsory labor.

(4) The rights to liberty and security of person.

(5) The right to a fair hearing in civil and criminal matters, and other rights relating to criminal proceedings.

(6) The right to private and family life, home, and correspondence.

(7) Freedom of thought, conscience and religion.

(8) Freedom of expression.

(9) Freedom of peaceful assembly and freedom of association with others.

(10) The right to marry and to found a family.

(11) The right to property.

(12) The right to education.

(13) The right to liberty of movement and residence.

(14) The enjoyment of the rights and freedoms provided for in this Article or in the international agreements listed in the Annex to this Constitution secured without discrimination on any ground such as sex, race, color, language, religion, political or other opinion, national or social origin, association with a national minority, property, birth or other status.

Chapter Two: The Commission on Human Rights

Part A: General

Article II: Establishment of the Commission

1. To assist in honoring their obligations under this Agreement, the Parties hereby establish a Commission on Human Rights (the "Commission"). The Commission shall consist of two parts: the Office of the Ombudsman and the Human Rights Chamber.

2. The Office of the Ombudsman and the Human Rights Chamber shall consider, as subsequently described:

(a) alleged or apparent violations of human rights as provided in the European Convention for the Protection of Human Rights and Fundamental Freedoms and the Protocols thereto, or

(b) alleged or apparent discrimination on any ground such as sex, race, color, language, religion, political or other opinion, national or social origin, association with a national minority, property, birth or other status arising in the enjoyment of any of the rights and freedoms provided for in the international agreements listed in the Appendix to this Annex, where such violation is alleged or appears to have been committed by the Parties, including by any official or organ of the Parties, Cantons, Municipalities, or any individual acting under the authority of such official or organ.

3. The Parties recognize the right of all persons to submit to the Commission and to other human rights bodies applications concerning alleged violations of human rights, in accordance with the procedures of this Annex and such bodies. The Parties shall not undertake any punitive action directed against persons who intend to submit, or have submitted, such allegations.

Article III: Facilities, Staff and Expenses

1. The Commission shall have appropriate facilities and a professionally competent staff. There shall be an Executive Officer, appointed jointly by the Ombudsman and the President of the Chamber, who shall be responsible for all necessary administrative arrangements with respect to facilities and staff. The Executive Officer shall be subject to the direction of the Ombudsman and the President of the Chamber insofar as concerns their respective administrative and professional office staff.

2. The salaries and expenses of the Commission and its staff shall be determined jointly by the Parties and shall be borne by Bosnia and Herzegovina. The salaries and expenses shall be fully adequate to implement the Commission's mandate.

3. The Commission shall have its headquarters in Sarajevo, including both the headquarters Office of the Ombudsman and the facilities for the Chamber. The Ombudsman shall have 'at least one additional office in the

territory of the Federation and the Republika Srpska and at other locations as it deems appropriate. The Chamber may meet in other locations where it determines that the needs of a particular case so require, and may meet at any place it deems appropriate for the inspection of property, documents or other items.

4. The Ombudsman and all members of the Chamber shall not be held criminally or civilly liable for any acts carried out within the scope of their duties. When the Ombudsman and members of the Chamber are not citizens of Bosnia and Herzegovina, they and their families shall be accorded the same privileges and immunities as are enjoyed by diplomatic agents and their families under the Vienna Convention on Diplomatic Relations.

5. With full regard for the need to maintain impartiality, the Commission may receive assistance as it deems appropriate from any governmental, international, or non-governmental organization.

Part B: Human Rights Ombudsman

Article IV: Human Rights Ombudsman

1. The Parties hereby establish the Office of the Human Rights Ombudsman (the "Ombudsman").

2. The Ombudsman shall be appointed for a non-renewable term of five years by the Chairman- in-Office of the Organization for Security and Cooperation in Europe (OSCE), after consultation with the Parties. He or she shall be independently responsible for choosing his or her own staff. Until the transfer described in Article XIV below, the Ombudsman may not be a citizen of Bosnia and Herzegovina or of any neighboring state. The Ombudsman appointed after that transfer shall be appointed by the Presidency of Bosnia and Herzegovina.

3. Members of the Office of the Ombudsman must be of recognized high moral standing and have competence in the field of international human rights.

4. The Office of the Ombudsman shall be an independent agency. In carrying out its mandate, no person or organ of the Parties may interfere with its functions.

Article V: Jurisdiction of the Ombudsman

1. Allegations of violations of human rights received by the Commission shall generally be directed to the Office of the Ombudsman, except where an applicant specifies the Chamber.

2. The Ombudsman may investigate, either on his or her own initiative or in response to an allegation by any Party or person, non-governmental organization, or group of individuals claiming to be the victim of a violation by any Party or acting on behalf of alleged victims who are deceased or missing, alleged or apparent violations of human rights within the scope of paragraph 2 of Article II. The Parties undertake not to hinder in any way the effective exercise of this right.

3. The Ombudsman shall determine which allegations warrant investigation and in what priority, giving particular priority to allegations of especially severe or systematic violations and those founded on alleged discrimination on prohibited grounds.

4. The Ombudsman shall issue findings and conclusions promptly after concluding an investigation. A Party identified as violating human rights shall, within a specified period, explain in writing how it will comply with the conclusions.

5. Where an allegation is received which is within the jurisdiction of the Human Rights Chamber, the Ombudsman may refer the allegation to the Chamber at any stage.

6. The Ombudsman may also present special reports at any time to any competent government organ or official. Those receiving such reports shall reply within a time limit specified by the Ombudsman, including specific responses to any conclusions offered by the Ombudsman.

7. The Ombudsman shall publish a report, which, in the event that a person or entity does not comply with his or her conclusions and recommendations, will be forwarded to the High Representative described in Annex 10 to the General Framework Agreement while such office exists, as well as referred for further action to the Presidency of the appropriate Party. The Ombudsman may also initiate proceedings before the Human Rights Chamber based on such Report. The Ombudsman may also intervene in any proceedings before the Chamber.

Article VI: Powers

1. The Ombudsman shall have access to and may examine all official documents, including classified ones, as well as judicial and administrative files, and can require any person, including a government official, to cooperate by providing relevant information, documents and files. The Ombudsman may attend administrative hearings and meetings of other organs and may enter and inspect any place where persons deprived of their liberty are confined or work.

2. The Ombudsman and staff are required to maintain the confidentiality of all confidential information obtained, except where required by order of the Chamber, and shall treat all documents and files in accordance with applicable rules.

Part C: Human Rights Chamber

Article VII: Human Rights Chamber

1. The Human Rights Chamber shall be composed of fourteen members.

2. Within 90 days after this Agreement enters into force, the Federation of Bosnia and Herzegovina shall appoint four members and the Republika Srpska shall appoint two members. The Committee of Ministers of the Council of Europe, pursuant to its resolution (93)6, after consultation with the Parties, shall appoint the remaining members, who shall not be citizens of Bosnia and Herzegovina or any neighboring state, and shall designate one such member as the President of the Chamber.

3. All members of the Chamber shall possess the qualifications required for appointment to high judicial office or be jurists of recognized competence. The members of the Chamber shall be appointed for a term of five years and may be reappointed.

4. Members appointed after the transfer described in Article XIV below shall be appointed by the Presidency of Bosnia and Herzegovina.

Article VIII: Jurisdiction of the Chamber

1. The Chamber shall receive by referral from the Ombudsman on behalf of an applicant, or directly from any Party or person, non-governmental organization, or group of individuals claiming to be the victim of a violation by any Party or acting on behalf of alleged victims who are deceased or missing, for resolution or decision applications concerning alleged or apparent violations of human rights within the scope of paragraph 2 of Article II.

2. The Chamber shall decide which applications to accept and in what priority to address them. In so doing, the Chamber shall take into account the following criteria:

(a) Whether effective remedies exist, and the applicant has demonstrated that they have been exhausted and that the application has been filed with the Commission within six months from such date on which the final decision was taken.

(b) The Chamber shall not address any application which is substantially the same as a matter which has already been examined by the Chamber or has already been submitted to another procedure or international investigation or settlement.

(c) The Chamber shall also dismiss any application which it considers incompatible with this Agreement, manifestly ill-founded, or an abuse of the right of petition.

(d) The Chamber may reject or defer further consideration if the application concerns a matter currently pending before any other international human rights body responsible for the adjudication of applications or the decision of cases, or any other Commission established by the Annexes to the General Framework Agreement.

(e) In principle, the Chamber shall endeavor to accept and to give particular priority to allegations of especially severe or systematic violations and those founded on alleged discrimination on prohibited grounds.

(f) Applications which entail requests for provisional measures shall be reviewed as a matter of priority in order to determine (1) whether they should be accepted and, if so (2) whether high priority for the scheduling of proceedings on the provisional measures request is warranted.

3. The Chamber may decide at any point in its proceedings to suspend consideration of, reject or strike out, an application on the ground that (a) the applicant does not intend to pursue his application; (b) the matter has been resolved; or (c) for any other reason established by the Chamber, it is no longer justified to continue the examination of the application; provided that such result is consistent with the objective of respect for human rights.

Article IX: Friendly Settlement

1. At the outset of a case or at any stage during the proceedings, the Chamber may attempt to facilitate an amicable resolution of the matter on the basis of respect for the rights and freedoms referred to in this Agreement.

2. If the Chamber succeeds in effecting such a resolution it shall publish a Report and forward it to the High Representative described in Annex 10 to the General Framework Agreement while such office exists, the OSCE and the Secretary General of the Council of Europe. Such a Report shall include a brief statement of the facts and the resolution reached. The report of a resolution in a given case may, however, be confidential in whole or in part where necessary for the protection of human rights or with the agreement of the Chamber and the parties concerned.

Article X: Proceedings before the Chamber

1. The Chamber shall develop fair and effective procedures for the adjudication of applications. Such procedures shall provide for appropriate written pleadings and, on the decision of the Chamber, a hearing for oral argument or the presentation of evidence. The Chamber shall have the power to order provisional measures, to appoint experts, and to compel the production of witnesses and evidence.

2. The Chamber shall normally sit in panels of seven, composed of two members from the Federation, one from the Republika Srpska, and four who are not citizens of Bosnia and Herzegovina or any neighboring state. When an application is decided by a panel, the full Chamber may decide, upon motion of a party to the case or the Ombudsman, to review the decision; such review may include the taking of additional evidence where the Chamber so decides. References in this Annex to the Chamber shall include, as appropriate, the Panel, except that the power to develop general rules, regulations and procedures is vested in the Chamber as a whole.

3. Except in exceptional circumstances in accordance with rules, hearings of the Chamber shall be held in public.

4. Applicants may be represented in proceedings by attorneys or other representatives of their choice, but shall also be personally present unless excused by the Chamber on account of hardship, impossibility, or other good cause.

5. The Parties undertake to provide all relevant information to, and to cooperate fully with, the Chamber.

Article XI: Decisions

1. Following the conclusion of the proceedings, the chamber shall promptly issue a decision, which shall address:

(a) whether the facts found indicate a breach by the Party concerned of its obligations under this Agreement; and if so

(b) what steps shall be taken by the Party to remedy such breach, including orders to cease and desist, monetary relief (including pecuniary and non-pecuniary injuries), and provisional measures.

2. The Chamber shall make its decision by a majority of members. In the event a decision by the full Chamber results in a tie, the President of the Chamber shall cast the deciding vote.

3. Subject to review as provided in paragraph 2 of Article X, the decisions of the Chamber shall be final and binding.

4. Any member shall be entitled to issue a separate opinion on any case.

5. The Chamber shall issue reasons for its decisions. Its decisions shall be published and forwarded to the parties concerned, the High Representative described in Annex 10 to the General Framework Agreement while such office exists, the Secretary General of the Council of Europe and the OSCE.

6. The Parties shall implement fully decisions of the Chamber.

Article XII: Rules and Regulations

The Chamber shall promulgate such rules and regulations, consistent with this Agreement, as may be necessary to carry out its functions, including provisions for preliminary hearings, expedited decisions on provisional measures, decisions by panels of the Chamber, and review of decisions made by any such panels.

Chapter Three: General Provisions

Article XIII: Organizations Concerned with Human Rights

1. The Parties shall promote and encourage the activities of non-governmental and international organizations for the protection and promotion of human rights.

2. The Parties join in inviting the United Nations Commission on Human Rights, the OSCE, the United Nations High Commissioner for Human Rights, and other intergovernmental or regional human rights missions or organizations to monitor closely the human rights situation in Bosnia and Herzegovina, including through the establishment of local offices and the assignment of observers, rapporteurs, or other relevant persons on a permanent or mission-by-mission basis and to provide them with full and effective facilitation, assistance and access.

3. The Parties shall allow full and effective access to non-governmental organizations for purposes of investigating and monitoring human rights conditions in Bosnia and Herzegovina and shall refrain from hindering or impeding them in the exercise of these functions.

4. All competent authorities in Bosnia and Herzegovina shall cooperate with and provide unrestricted access to the organizations established in this Agreement; any international human rights monitoring mechanisms established for Bosnia and Herzegovina; the supervisory bodies established by any of the international agreements listed in the Appendix to this Annex; the International Tribunal for the Former Yugoslavia; and any other organization authorized by the U.N. Security Council with a mandate concerning human rights or humanitarian law.

Article XIV: Transfer

Five years after this Agreement enters into force, the responsibility for the continued operation of the Commission shall transfer from the Parties to the institutions of Bosnia and Herzegovina, unless the Parties otherwise agree. In the latter case, the Commission shall continue to operate as provided above.

Article XV: Notice

The Parties shall give effective notice of the terms of this Agreement throughout Bosnia and Herzegovina.

Article XVI: Entry into Force

This Agreement shall enter into force upon signature.

For the Republic of Bosnia and Herzegovina

For the Federation of Bosnia and Herzegovina

For the Republika Srpska

Appendix: Human Rights Agreements

1. Convention on the Prevention and Punishment of the Crime of Genocide

2. 1949 Geneva Conventions I-IV on the Protection of the Victims of War, and the 1977 Geneva Protocols I-II thereto

3. 1950 European Convention for the Protection of Human Rights and Fundamental Freedoms, and the Protocols thereto

4. 1951 Convention relating to the Status of Refugees and the 1966 Protocol thereto

5. 1957 Convention on the Nationality of Married Women

6. 1961 Convention on the Reduction of Statelessness

7. 1965 International Convention on the Elimination of All Forms of Racial Discrimination

8. 1966 International Covenant on Civil and Political Rights and the 1966 and 1989 Optional Protocols thereto

9. 1966 Covenant on Economic, Social and Cultural Rights

10. 1979 Convention on the Elimination of All Forms of Discrimination against Women

11. 1984 Convention against Torture and Other Cruel, Inhuman or Degrading Treatment or Punishment

12. 1987 European Convention on the Prevention of Torture and Inhuman or Degrading Treatment or Punishment

13. 1989 Convention on the Rights of the Child

14. 1990 Convention on the Protection of the Rights of All Migrant Workers and Members of Their Families

15. 1992 European Charter for Regional or Minority Languages

16. 1994 Framework Convention for the Protection of National Minorities

ANNEX 7

Agreement on Refugees and Displaced Persons

The Republic of Bosnia and Herzegovina, the Federation of Bosnia and Herzegovina, and the Republika Srpska (the "Parties") have agreed as follows:

Chapter One: Protection

Article I: Rights of Refugees and Displaced Persons

1.   All refugees and displaced persons have the right freely to return to their homes of origin. They shall have the right to have restored to them property of which they were deprived in the course of hostilities since 1991 and to be compensated for any property that cannot be restored to them. The early return of refugees and displaced persons is an important objective of the settlement of the conflict in Bosnia and Herzegovina. The Parties confirm that they will accept the return of such persons who have left their territory, including those who have been accorded temporary protection by third countries.

2.   The Parties shall ensure that refugees and displaced persons are permitted to return in safety, without risk of harassment, intimidation, persecution, or discrimination, particularly on account of their ethnic origin, religious belief, or political opinion.

3.   The Parties shall take all necessary steps to prevent activities within their territories which would hinder or impede the safe and voluntary return of refugees and displaced persons. To demonstrate their commitment to securing full respect for the human rights and fundamental freedoms of all persons within their jurisdiction and creating without delay conditions suitable for return of refugees and displaced persons, the Parties shall take immediately the following confidence building measures:

(a)   the repeal of domestic legislation and administrative practices with discriminatory intent or effect;

(b)   the prevention and prompt suppression of any written or verbal incitement, through media or otherwise, of ethnic or religious hostility or hatred;

(c)   the dissemination, through the media, of warnings against, and the prompt suppression of, acts of retribution by military, paramilitary, and police services, and by other public officials or private individuals;

(d)   the protection of ethnic and/or minority populations wherever they are found and the provision of immediate access to these populations by international humanitarian organizations and monitors;

(e)   the prosecution, dismissal or transfer, as appropriate, of persons in military, paramilitary, and police forces, and other public servants, responsible for serious violations of the basic rights of persons belonging to ethnic or minority groups.

4.   Choice of destination shall be up to the individual or family, and the principle of the unity of the family shall be preserved. The Parties shall not interfere with the returnees' choice of destination, nor shall they compel them to remain in or move to situations of serious danger or insecurity, or to areas lacking in the basic infrastructure necessary to resume a normal life. The Parties shall facilitate the flow of information necessary for refugees and displaced persons to make informed judgements about local conditions for return.

5.   The Parties call upon the United Nations High Commissioner for Refugees ("UNHCR") to develop in close consultation with asylum countries and the Parties a repatriation plan that will allow for an early, peaceful, orderly and phased return of refugees and displaced persons, which may include priorities for certain areas and certain categories

of returnees. The Parties agree to implement such a plan and to conform their international agreements and internal laws to it. They accordingly call upon States that have accepted refugees to promote the early return of refugees consistent with international law.

Article II: Creation of Suitable Conditions for Return

1.   The Parties undertake to create in their territories the political, economic, and social conditions conducive to the voluntary return and harmonious reintegration of refugees and displaced persons, without preference for any particular group. The Parties shall provide all possible assistance to refugees and displaced persons and work to facilitate their voluntary return in a peaceful, orderly and phased manner, in accordance with the UNHCR repatriation plan.

2.   The Parties shall not discriminate against returning refugees and displaced persons with respect to conscription into military service, and shall give positive consideration to requests for exemption from military or other obligatory service based on individual circumstances, so as to enable returnees to rebuild their lives.

Article III: Cooperation with International Organizations and International Monitoring

1.   The Parties note with satisfaction the leading humanitarian role of UNHCR, which has been entrusted by the Secretary-General of the United Nations with the role of coordinating among all agencies assisting with the repatriation and relief of refugees and displaced persons.

2.   The Parties shall give full and unrestricted access by UNHCR, the International Committee of the Red Cross ("ICRC"), the United Nations Development Programme ("UNDP"), and other relevant international, domestic and nongovernmental organizations to all refugees and displaced persons, with a view to facilitating the work of those organizations in tracing persons, the provision of medical assistance, food distribution, reintegration assistance, the provision of temporary and permanent housing, and other activities vital to the discharge of their mandates and operational responsibilities without administrative impediments. These activities shall include traditional protection functions and the monitoring of basic human rights and humanitarian conditions, as well as the implementation of the provisions of this Chapter.

3.   The Parties shall provide for the security of all personnel of such organizations.

Article IV: Repatriation Assistance

The Parties shall facilitate the provision of adequately monitored, short-term repatriation assistance on a nondiscriminatory basis to all returning refugees and displaced persons who are in need, in accordance with a plan developed by UNHCR and other relevant organizations, to enable the families and individuals returning to reestablish their lives and livelihoods in local communities.

Article V: Persons Unaccounted For

The Parties shall provide information through the tracing mechanisms of the ICRC on all persons unaccounted for. The Parties shall also cooperate fully with the ICRC in its efforts to determine the identities, whereabouts and fate of the unaccounted for.

Article VI: Amnesty

Any returning refugee or displaced person charged with a crime, other than a serious violation of international humanitarian law as defined in the Statute of the International Tribunal for the Former Yugoslavia since January 1, 1991 or a common crime unrelated to the conflict, shall upon return enjoy an amnesty. In no case shall charges for crimes be imposed for political or other inappropriate reasons or to circumvent the application of the amnesty.

Chapter Two: Commission for Displaced Persons and Refugees

Article VII: Establishment of the Commission

The Parties hereby establish an independent Commission for Displaced Persons and Refugees (the "Commission"). The Commission shall have its headquarters in Sarajevo and may have offices at other locations as it deems appropriate.

Article VIII: Cooperation

The Parties shall cooperate with the work of the Commission, and shall respect and implement its decisions expeditiously and in good faith, in cooperation with relevant international and nongovernmental organizations having responsibility for the return and reintegration of refugees and displaced persons.

Article IX: Composition

1. The Commission shall be composed of nine members. Within 90 days after this Agreement enters into force, the Federation of Bosnia and Herzegovina shall appoint four members, two for a term of three years and the others for a term of four years, and the Republika Srpska shall appoint two members, one for a term of three years and the other for a term of four years. The President of the European Court of Human Rights shall appoint the remaining members, each for a term of five years, and shall designate one such member as the Chairman. The members of the Commission may be reappointed.

2. Members of the Commission must be of recognized high moral standing.

3. The Commission may sit in panels, as provided in its rules and regulations. References in this Annex to the Commission shall include, as appropriate, such panels, except that the power to promulgate rules and regulations is vested only in the Commission as a whole.

4. Members appointed after the transfer described in Article XVI below shall be appointed by the Presidency of Bosnia and Herzegovina.

Article X: Facilities, Staff and Expenses

1. The Commission shall have appropriate facilities and a professionally competent staff, experienced in administrative, financial, banking and legal matters, to assist it in carrying out its functions. The staff shall be headed by an Executive Officer, who shall be appointed by the Commission.

2. The salaries and expenses of the Commission and its staff shall be determined jointly by the Parties and shall be borne equally by the Parties.

3. Members of the Commission shall not be held criminally or civilly liable for any acts carried out within the scope of their duties. Members of the Commission, and their families, who are not citizens of Bosnia and Herzegovina shall be accorded the same privileges and immunities as are enjoyed by diplomatic agents and their families under the Vienna Convention on Diplomatic Relations.

4. The Commission may receive assistance from international and nongovernmental organizations, in their areas of special expertise falling within the mandate of the Commission, on terms to be agreed.

5. The Commission shall cooperate with other entities established by the General Framework Agreement, agreed by the Parties, or authorized by the United Nations Security Council.

Article XI: Mandate

The Commission shall receive and decide any claims for real property in Bosnia and Herzegovina, where the property has not voluntarily been sold or otherwise transferred since April 1, 1992, and where the claimant does not now enjoy possession of that property. Claims may be for return of the property or for just compensation in lieu of return.

Article XII: Proceedings before the Commission

1. Upon receipt of a claim, the Commission shall determine the lawful owner of the property with respect to which the claim is made and the value of that property. The Commission, through its staff or a duly designated international or nongovernmental organization, shall be entitled to have access to any and all property records in Bosnia and Herzegovina, and to any and all real property located in Bosnia and Herzegovina for purposes of inspection, evaluation and assessment related to consideration of a claim.

2. Any person requesting the return of property who is found by the Commission to be the lawful owner of that property shall be awarded its return. Any person requesting compensation in lieu of return who is found by the Commission to be the lawful owner of that property shall be awarded just compensation as determined by the Commission. The Commission shall make decisions by a majority of its members.

3. In determining the lawful owner of any property, the Commission shall not recognize as valid any illegal property transaction, including any transfer that was made under duress, in exchange for exit permission or documents, or that was otherwise in connection with ethnic cleansing. Any person who is awarded return of property may accept a satisfactory lease arrangement rather than retake possession.

4. The Commission shall establish fixed rates that may be applied to determine the value of all real property in Bosnia and Herzegovina that is the subject of a claim before the Commission. The rates shall be based on an assessment or survey of properties in the territory of Bosnia and Herzegovina undertaken prior to April 1, 1992, if available, or may be based on other reasonable criteria as determined by the Commission.

5. The Commission shall have the power to effect any transactions necessary to transfer or assign title, mortgage, lease, or otherwise dispose of property with respect to which a claim is made, or which is determined to be abandoned. In particular, the Commission may lawfully sell, mortgage, or lease real property to any resident or citizen of Bosnia and Herzegovina, or to either Party, where the lawful owner has sought and received compensation in lieu of return, or where the property is determined to be abandoned in accordance with local law. The Commission may also lease property pending consideration and final determination of ownership.

6. In cases in which the claimant is awarded compensation in lieu of return of the property, the Commission may award a monetary grant or a compensation bond for the future purchase of real property. The Parties welcome the willingness of the international community assisting in the construction and financing of housing in Bosnia and Herzegovina to accept compensation bonds awarded by the Commission as payment, and to award persons holding such compensation bonds priority in obtaining that housing.

7. Commission decisions shall be final, and any title, deed, mortgage, or other legal instrument created or awarded by the Commission shall be recognized as lawful throughout Bosnia and Herzegovina.

8. Failure of any Party or individual to cooperate with the Commission shall not prevent the Commission from making its decision.

Article XIII: Use of Vacant Property

The Parties, after notification to the Commission and in coordination with UNHCR and other international and nongovernmental organizations contributing to relief and reconstruction, may temporarily house refugees and displaced persons in vacant property, subject to final determination of ownership by the Commission and to such temporary lease provisions as it may require.

Article XIV: Refugees and Displaced Persons Property Fund

1.   A Refugees and Displaced Persons Property Fund (the "Fund") shall be established in the Central Bank of Bosnia and Herzegovina to be administered by the Commission. The Fund shall be replenished through the purchase, sale, lease and mortgage of real property which is the subject of claims before the Commission. It may also be replenished by direct payments from the Parties, or from contributions by States or international or nongovernmental organizations.

2.   Compensation bonds issued pursuant to Article XII(6) shall create future liabilities on the Fund under terms and conditions to be defined by the Commission.

Article XV: Rules and Regulations

The Commission shall promulgate such rules and regulations, consistent with this Agreement, as may be necessary to carry out its functions. In developing these rules and regulations, the Commission shall consider domestic laws on property rights.

Article XVI: Transfer

Five years after this Agreement takes effect, responsibility for the financing and operation of the Commission shall transfer from the Parties to the Government of Bosnia and Herzegovina, unless the Parties otherwise agree. In the latter case, the Commission shall continue to operate as provided above.

Article XVII: Notice

The Parties shall give effective notice of the terms of this Agreement throughout Bosnia and Herzegovina, and in all countries known to have persons who were citizens or residents of Bosnia and Herzegovina.

Article XVIII: Entry into Force

This Agreement shall enter into force upon signature.

For the Republic of Bosnia and Herzegovina

For the Federation of Bosnia and Herzegovina

For the Republika Srpska

ANNEX 8

Agreement on Commission to Preserve National Monuments

The Republic of Bosnia and Herzegovina, the Federation of Bosnia and Herzegovina and the Republika Srpska (the "Parties") have agreed as follows:

Article I: Establishment of the Commission

The Parties hereby establish an independent Commission to Preserve National Monuments (the "Commission"). The Commission shall have its headquarters in Sarajevo and may have offices at other locations as it deems appropriate.

Article II: Composition

1. The Commission shall be composed of five members. Within 90 days after this Agreement enters into force, the Federation of Bosnia and Herzegovina shall appoint two members, and the Republika Srpska one member, each serving a term of three years. The Director-General of the United Nations Educational, Scientific and Cultural Organization shall appoint the remaining members, each for a term of five years, and shall designate one such member as the Chairman. The members of the Commission may be reappointed. No person who is serving a sentence imposed by the International Tribunal for the Former Yugoslavia, and no person who is under indictment by the Tribunal and who has failed to comply with an order to appear before the Tribunal, may serve on the Commission.

2. Members appointed after the transfer described in Article IX below shall be appointed by the Presidency of Bosnia and Herzegovina.

Article III: Facilities, Staff and Expenses

1. The Commission shall have appropriate facilities and a professionally competent staff, generally representative of the ethnic groups comprising Bosnia and Herzegovina, to assist it in carrying out its functions. The staff shall be headed by an executive officer, who shall be appointed by the Commission.

2. The salaries and expenses of the Commission and its staff shall be determined jointly by the Entities and shall be borne equally by them.

3. Members of the Commission shall not be held criminally or civilly liable for any acts carried out within the scope of their duties. Members of the Commission, and their families, who are not citizens of Bosnia and Herzegovina shall be accorded the same privileges and immunities as are enjoyed by diplomatic agents and their families under the Vienna Convention on Diplomatic Relations.

Article IV: Mandate

The Commission shall receive and decide on petitions for the designation of property having cultural, historic, religious or ethnic importance as National Monuments.

Article V: Proceedings before the Commission

1. Any Party, or any concerned person in Bosnia and Herzegovina, may submit to the Commission a petition for the designation of property as a National Monument. Each such petition shall set forth all relevant information concerning the property, including:

(a) the specific location of the property;

(b) its current owner and condition;

(c) the cost and source of funds for any necessary repairs to the property;

(d) any known proposed use; and

(e) the basis for designation as a National Monument.

2. In deciding upon the petition, the Commission shall afford an opportunity for the owners of the proposed National Monument, as well as other interested persons or entities, to present their views.

3. For a period of one year after such a petition has been submitted to the Commission, or until a decision is rendered in accordance with this Annex, whichever occurs first, all Parties shall refrain from taking any deliberate measures that might damage the property.

4. The Commission shall issue, in each case, a written decision containing any findings of fact it deems appropriate and a detailed explanation of the basis for its decision. The Commission shall make decisions by a majority of its members. Decisions of the Commission shall be final and enforceable in accordance with domestic law.

5. In any case in which the Commission issues a decision designating property as a National Monument, the Entity in whose territory the property is situated (a) shall make every effort to take appropriate legal, scientific, technical, administrative and financial measures necessary for the protection, conservation, presentation and rehabilitation of the property, and (b) shall refrain from taking any deliberate measures that might damage the property.

Article VI: Eligibility

The following shall be eligible for designation as National Monuments: movable or immovable property of great importance to a group of people with common cultural, historic, religious or ethnic heritage, such as monuments of architecture, art or history; archaeological sites; groups of buildings; as well as cemeteries.

Article VII: Rules and Regulations

The Commission shall promulgate such rules and regulations, consistent with this Agreement, as may be necessary to carry out its functions.

Article VIII: Cooperation

Officials and organs of the Parties and their Cantons and Municipalities, and any individual acting under the authority of such official or organ, shall fully cooperate with the Commission, including by providing requested information and other assistance.

Article IX: Transfer

Five years after this Agreement enters into force, the responsibility for the continued operation of the Commission shall transfer from the Parties to the Government of Bosnia and Herzegovina, unless the Parties otherwise agree. In the latter case, the Commission shall continue to operate as provided above.

Article X: Notice

The Parties shall give effective notice of the terms of this Agreement throughout Bosnia and Herzegovina.

Article XI: Entry Into Force

This Agreement shall enter into force upon signature.

For the Republic of Bosnia and Herzegovina

For the Federation of Bosnia and Herzegovina

For the Republika Srpska

ANNEX 9

Agreement on Establishment of Bosnia and Herzegovina Public Corporations

Bearing in mind that reconstruction of the infrastructure and the functioning of transportation and other facilities are important for the economic resurgence of Bosnia and Herzegovina, and for the smooth functioning of its institutions and the organizations involved in implementation of the peace settlement, the Federation of Bosnia and Herzegovina and the Republika Srpska (the "Parties") have agreed as follows:

Article I: Commission on Public Corporations

1.   The Parties hereby establish a Commission on Public Corporations (the "Commission") to examine establishing Bosnia and Herzegovina Public Corporations to operate joint public facilities, such as for the operation of utility, energy, postal and communication facilities, for the benefit of both Entities.

2.   The Commission shall have five Members. Within fifteen days after this Agreement enters into force, the Federation of Bosnia and Herzegovina shall appoint two Members, and the Republika Srpska one Member. Persons appointed must be familiar with the specific economic, political and legal characteristics Bosnia and Herzegovina and be of high recognized moral standing. Recognizing that the Commission will benefit from international expertise, the Parties request the President of the European Bank for Reconstruction and Development to appoint the remaining two Members and to designate one as the Chairman.

3.   The Commission shall in particular examine the appropriate internal structure for such Corporations, the conditions necessary to ensure their successful, permanent operation, and the best means of procuring long-term investment capital.

Article II: Establishment of a Transportation Corporation

1.   The Parties, recognizing an immediate need to establish a Public Corporation to organize and operate transportation facilities, such as roads, railways and ports, for their mutual benefit, hereby establish a Bosnia and Herzegovina Transportation Corporation (the "Transportation Corporation") for such purpose.

2.   The Transportation Corporation shall have its headquarters in Sarajevo and may have offices at other locations as it deems appropriate. It shall have appropriate facilities and choose a professionally competent Board of Directors, Officers and Staff, generally representative of the ethnic groups comprising Bosnia and Herzegovina, to carry out its functions. The Commission shall choose the Board of Directors, which shall in turn appoint the Officers and select the Staff.

3.   The Transportation Corporation is authorized to construct, acquire, hold, maintain and operate and dispose of real and personal property in accordance with specific plans that it develops. It is also authorized to fix and collect rates, fees, rentals and other charges for the use of facilities it operates; enter into all contracts and agreements necessary for the performance of its functions; and take other actions necessary to carry out these functions.

4.   The Transportation Corporation shall operate transportation facilities as agreed by the Parties. The Parties shall, as part of their agreement, provide the Corporation with necessary legal authority. The Parties shall meet within fifteen days after this Agreement enters into force to consider which facilities the Corporation will operate.

5.   Within thirty days after this Agreement enters into force, the Parties shall agree on sums of money to be contributed to the Transportation Corporation for its initial operating budget. The Parties may at any time transfer to the Transportation Corporation additional funds or facilities that belong to them and the rights thereto. The Parties shall decide the means by which the Transportation Corporation will be authorized to raise additional capital.

Article III: Other Public Corporations

The Parties may decide, upon recommendation of the Commission, to use establishment of the Transportation Corporation as a model for the establishment of other joint public corporations, such as for the operation of utility, energy, postal and communication facilities.

Article IV: Cooperation

The Commission, the Transportation Corporation and other Public Corporations shall cooperate fully with all organizations involved in implementation of the peace settlement, or which are otherwise authorized by the United Nations Security Council, including the International Tribunal for the Former Yugoslavia.

Article V: Ethics

Members of the Commission and Directors of the Transportation Corporation may not have an employment or financial relationship with any enterprise that has, or is seeking, a contract or agreement with the Commission or the Corporation, respectively, or otherwise has interests that can be directly affected by its actions or inactions.

Article VI: Entry into Force

This Agreement shall enter into force upon signature.

For the Federation of Bosnia and Herzegovina

For the Republika Srpska

ANNEX 10

Agreement on Civilian Implementation of the Peace Settlement

The Republic of Bosnia and Herzegovina, the Republic of Croatia, the Federal Republic of Yugoslavia, the Federation of Bosnia and Herzegovina, and the Republika Srpska (the "Parties") have agreed as follows:

Article I: High Representative

1. The Parties agree that the implementation of the civilian aspects of the peace settlement will entail a wide range of activities including continuation of the humanitarian aid effort for as long as necessary; rehabilitation of infrastructure and economic reconstruction; the establishment of political and constitutional institutions in Bosnia and Herzegovina; promotion of respect for human rights and the return of displaced persons and refugees; and the holding of free and fair elections according to the timetable in Annex 3 to the General Framework Agreement. A considerable number of international organizations and agencies will be called upon to assist.

2. In view of the complexities facing them, the Parties request the designation of a High Representative, to be appointed consistent with relevant United Nations Security Council resolutions, to facilitate the Parties' own efforts and to mobilize and, as appropriate, coordinate the activities of the organizations and agencies involved in the civilian aspects of the peace settlement by carrying out, as entrusted by a U.N. Security Council resolution, the tasks set out below.

Article II: Mandate and Methods of Coordination and Liaison

1. The High Representative shall:

(a) Monitor the implementation of the peace settlement;

(b) Maintain close contact with the Parties to promote their full compliance with all civilian aspects of the peace settlement and a high level of cooperation between them and the organizations and agencies participating in those aspects.

(c) Coordinate the activities of the civilian organizations and agencies in Bosnia and Herzegovina to ensure the efficient implementation of the civilian aspects of the peace settlement. The High Representative shall respect their autonomy within their spheres of operation while as necessary giving general guidance to them about the impact of their activities on the implementation of the peace settlement. The civilian organizations and agencies are requested to assist the High Representative in the execution of his or her responsibilities by providing all information relevant to their operations in Bosnia-Herzegovina.

(d) Facilitate, as the High Representative judges necessary, the resolution of any difficulties arising in connection with civilian implementation.

(e) Participate in meetings of donor organizations, particularly on issues of rehabilitation and reconstruction.

(f) Report periodically on progress in implementation of the peace agreement concerning the tasks set forth in this Agreement to the United Nations, European Union, United States, Russian Federation, and other interested governments, parties, and organizations.

(g) Provide guidance to, and receive reports from, the Commissioner of the International Police Task Force established inAnnex11to the General Framework Agreement.

2. In pursuit of his or her mandate, the High Representative shall convene and chair a commission (the "Joint Civilian Commission") in Bosnia and Herzegovina. It will comprise senior political representatives of the Parties, the IFOR Commander or his representative, and representatives of those civilian organizations and agencies the High Representative deems necessary.

3. The High Representative shall, as necessary, establish subordinate Joint Civilian Commissions at local levels in Bosnia and Herzegovina.

4. A Joint Consultative Committee will meet from time to time or as agreed between the High Representative and the IFOR Commander.

5. The High Representative or his designated representative shall remain in close contact with the IFOR Commander or his designated representatives and establish appropriate liaison arrangements with the IFOR Commander to facilitate the discharge of their respective responsibilities.

6. The High Representative shall exchange information and maintain liaison on a regular basis with IFOR, as agreed with the IFOR Commander, and through the commissions described in this Article.

7. The High Representative shall attend or be represented at meetings of the Joint Military Commission and offer advice particularly on matters of a political-military nature. Representatives of the High Representative will also attend subordinate commissions of the Joint Military Commission as set out Article VIII(8) of Annex 1A to the General Framework Agreement.

8. The High Representative may also establish other civilian commissions within or outside Bosnia and Herzegovina to facilitate the execution of his or her mandate.

9. The High Representative shall have no authority over the IFOR and shall not in any way interfere in the conduct of military operations or the IFOR chain of command.

Article III: Staffing

1. The High Representative shall appoint staff, as he or she deems necessary, to provide assistance in carrying out the tasks herein.

2. The Parties shall facilitate the operations of the High Representative in Bosnia and Herzegovina, including by the provision of appropriate assistance as requested with regard to transportation, subsistence, accommodations, communications, and other facilities at rates equivalent to those provided for the IFOR under applicable agreements.

3. The High Representative shall enjoy, under the laws of Bosnia and Herzegovina, such legal capacity as may be necessary for the exercise of his or her functions, including the capacity to contract and to acquire and dispose of real and personal property.

4. Privileges and immunities shall be accorded as follows:

(a) The Parties shall accord the office of the High Representative and its premises, archives, and other property the same privileges and immunities as are enjoyed by a diplomatic mission and its premises, archives, and other property under the Vienna Convention on Diplomatic Relations.

(b) The Parties shall accord the High Representative and professional members of his or her staff and their families the same privileges and immunities as are enjoyed by diplomatic agents and their families under the Vienna Convention on Diplomatic Relations.

(c)   The Parties shall accord other members of the High Representative staff and their families the same privileges and immunities as are enjoyed by members of the administrative and technical staff and their families under the Vienna Convention on Diplomatic Relations.

Article IV: Cooperation

The Parties shall fully cooperate with the High Representative and his or her staff, as well as with the international organizations and agencies as provided for in Article IX of the General Framework Agreement.

Article V: Final Authority to Interpret

The High Representative is the final authority in theater regarding interpretation of this Agreement on the civilian implementation of the peace settlement.

Article VI: Entry into Force

This Agreement shall enter into force upon signature.

For the Republic of Bosnia and Herzegovina

signed: Muhamed Sacirbey
          Minister of Foreign Affairs for the Republic of Bosnia and Herzegovina

For the Republic of Croatia

signed: Mate Granic
          Minister of Foreign Affairs for the Republic of Croatia

For the Federal Republic of Yugoslavia

signed: Milan Milutinovic
          Minister of Foreign Affairs for the Federal Republic of Yugoslavia

For the Federation of Bosnia and Herzegovina

signed: Kresimir Zubak
          President of the Federation of Bosnia and Herzegovina

For the Republika Srpska

signed: Nikola Koljevic
          Vice President of the Republika Srpska

ANNEX 11

Agreement on International Police Force

The Republic of Bosnia and Herzegovina, the Federation of Bosnia and Herzegovina, and the Republika Srpska (the "Parties") have agreed as follows:

Article I: Civilian Law Enforcement

1.   As provided in Article III(2)(c) of the Constitution agreed as Annex 4 to the General Framework Agreement, the Parties shall provide a safe and secure environment for all persons in their respective jurisdictions, by maintaining civilian law enforcement agencies operating in accordance with internationally recognized standards and with respect for internationally recognized human rights and fundamental freedoms, and by taking such other measures as appropriate.

2.   To assist them in meeting their obligations, the Parties request that the United Nations establish by a decision of the Security Council, as a UNCIVPOL operation, a U.N. International Police Task Force (IPTF) to carry out, throughout Bosnia and Herzegovina, the program of assistance the elements of which are described in Article III below.

Article II: Establishment of the IPTF

1.   The IPTF shall be autonomous with regard to the execution of its functions under this Agreement. Its activities will be coordinated through the High Representative described in Annex 10 to the General Framework Agreement.

2.   The IPTF will be headed by a Commissioner, who will be appointed by the Secretary General of the United Nations in consultation with the Security Council. It shall consist of persons of high moral standing who have experience in law enforcement. The IPTF Commissioner may request and accept personnel, resources, and assistance from states and international and nongovernmental organizations.

3.   The IPTF Commissioner shall receive guidance from the High Representative.

4.   The IPTF Commissioner shall periodically report on matters within his or her responsibility to the High Representative, the Secretary General of the United Nations, and shall provide information to the IFOR Commander and, as he or she deems appropriate, other institutions and agencies.

5.   The IPTF shall at all times act in accordance with internationally recognized standards and with respect for internationally recognized human rights and fundamental freedoms, and shall respect, consistent with the IPTF's responsibilities, the laws and customs of the host country.

6.   The Parties shall accord the IPTF Commissioner, IPTF personnel, and their families the privileges and immunities described in Sections 18 and 19 of the 1946 Convention on the Privileges and Immunities of the United Nations. In particular, they shall enjoy inviolability, shall not be subject to any form of arrest or detention, and shall have absolute immunity from criminal jurisdiction. IPTF personnel shall remain subject to penalties and sanctions under applicable laws and regulations of the United Nations and other states.

7.   The IPTF and its premises, archives, and other property shall be accorded the same privileges and immunities, including inviolability, as are described in Articles II and III of the 1946 Convention on the Privileges and Immunities of the United Nations.

8.   In order to promote the coordination by the High Representative of IPTF activities with those of other civilian organizations and agencies and of the (IFOR), the IPTF Commissioner or his or her representatives may attend meetings of the Joint Civilian Commission established in Annex 10 to the General Framework Agreement and of the Joint Military Commission established in Annex 1, as well as meetings of their subordinate commissions. The IPTF Commissioner may request that meetings of appropriate commissions be convened to discuss issues within his or her area of responsibility.

Article III: IPTF Assistance Program

1.   IPTF assistance includes the following elements, to be provided in a program designed and implemented by the IPTF Commissioner in accordance with the Security Council decision described in Article I(2):

(a)   monitoring, observing, and inspecting law enforcement activities and facilities, including associated judicial organizations, structures, and proceedings;

(b)   advising law enforcement personnel and forces;

(c)   training law enforcement personnel;

(d)   facilitating, within the IPTF's mission of assistance, the Parties' law enforcement activities;

(e)   assessing threats to public order and advising on the capability of law enforcement agencies to deal with such threats;

(f)   advising governmental authorities in Bosnia and Herzegovina on the organization of effective civilian law enforcement agencies; and

(g)   assisting by accompanying the Parties' law enforcement personnel as they carry out their responsibilities, as the IPTF deems appropriate.

2.   In addition to the elements of the assistance program set forth in paragraph 1, the IPTF will consider, consistent with its responsibilities and resources, requests from the Parties or law enforcement agencies in Bosnia and Herzegovina for assistance described in paragraph 1.

3.   The Parties confirm their particular responsibility to ensure the existence of social conditions for free and fair elections, including the protection of international personnel in Bosnia and Herzegovina in connection with the elections provided for in Annex 3 to the General Framework Agreement. They request the IPTF to give priority to assisting the Parties in carrying out this responsibility.

Article IV: Specific Responsibilities of the Parties

1.   The Parties shall cooperate fully with the IPTF and shall so instruct all their law enforcement agencies.

2.   Within 30 days after this Agreement enters into force, the Parties shall provide the IPTF Commissioner or his or her designee with information on their law enforcement agencies, including their size, location, and force structure. Upon request of the IPTF Commissioner, they shall provide additional information, including any training, operational, or employment and service records of law enforcement agencies and personnel.

3.   The Parties shall not impede the movement of IPTF personnel or in any way hinder, obstruct, or delay them in the performance of their responsibilities. They shall allow IPTF personnel immediate and complete access to any site, person, activity, proceeding, record, or other item or event in Bosnia and Herzegovina as requested by the IPTF in carrying out its responsibilities under this Agreement. This shall include the right to monitor, observe, and inspect any site or facility at which it believes that police, law enforcement, detention, or judicial activities are taking place.

4.   Upon request by the IPTF, the Parties shall make available for training qualified personnel, who are expected to take up law enforcement duties immediately following such training.

5.   The Parties shall facilitate the operations of the IPTF in Bosnia and Herzegovina, including by the provision of appropriate assistance as requested with regard to transportation, subsistence, accommodations, communications, and other facilities at rates equivalent to those provided for the IFOR under applicable agreements.

Article V: Failure to Cooperate

1.   Any obstruction of or interference with IPTF activities, failure or refusal to comply with an IPTF request, or other failure to meet the Parties' responsibilities or other obligations in this Agreement, shall constitute a failure to cooperate with the IPTF.

2.   The IPTF Commissioner will notify the High Representative and inform the IFOR Commander of failures to cooperate with the IPTF. The IPTF Commissioner may request that the High Representative take appropriate steps upon receiving such notifications, including calling such failures to the attention of the Parties, convening the Joint Civilian Commission, and consulting with the United Nations, relevant states, and international organizations on further responses.

Article VI: Human Rights

1.   When IPTF personnel learn of credible information concerning violations of internationally recognized human rights or fundamental freedoms or of the role of law enforcement officials or forces in such violations, they shall provide such information to the Human Rights Commission established in Annex 6 to the General Framework Agreement, the International Tribunal for the Former Yugoslavia, or to other appropriate organizations.

2.   The Parties shall cooperate with investigations of law enforcement forces and officials by the organizations described in paragraph 1.

Article VII: Application

This Agreement applies throughout Bosnia and Herzegovina to law enforcement agencies and personnel of Bosnia and Herzegovina, the Entities, and any agency, subdivision, or instrumentality thereof. Law enforcement agencies are those with a mandate including law enforcement, criminal investigations, public and state security, or detention or judicial activities.

Article VIII: Entry into Force

This Agreement shall enter into force upon signature.

For the Republic of Bosnia and Herzegovina

For the Federation of Bosnia and Herzegovina

For the Republika Srpska

Index

International Studies in Human Rights

International Studies in Human Rights

International Studies in Human Rights

International Studies in Human Rights

56.   M. Jones and L.A. Basser Marks (eds.): *Disability, Divers-ability and Legal Change.*
     1998   ISBN 90-411-1086-0

This series is designed to shed light on current legal and political aspects of process and organization in the field of human rights.

MARTINUS NIJHOFF PUBLISHERS – THE HAGUE / BOSTON / LONDON